Microsoft® Outlook® 2013

Step by Step

Joan Lambert
Joyce Cox

PUBLISHED BY
Microsoft Press
A Division of Microsoft Corporation
One Microsoft Way
Redmond, Washington 98052-6399

Library of Congress Control Number: 2013931602
ISBN: 978-0-7356-6909-3

Printed and bound in the United States of America.

First Printing

Microsoft Press books are available through booksellers and distributors worldwide. If you need support related to this book, email Microsoft Press Book Support at mspinput@microsoft.com. Please tell us what you think of this book at http://www.microsoft.com/learning/booksurvey.

Microsoft and the trademarks listed at http://www.microsoft.com/about/legal/en/us/IntellectualProperty/Trademarks/EN-US.aspx are trademarks of the Microsoft group of companies. All other marks are property of their respective owners.

The example companies, organizations, products, domain names, email addresses, logos, people, places, and events depicted herein are fictitious. No association with any real company, organization, product, domain name, email address, logo, person, place, or event is intended or should be inferred.

This book expresses the author's views and opinions. The information contained in this book is provided without any express, statutory, or implied warranties. Neither the authors, Microsoft Corporation, nor its resellers, or distributors will be held liable for any damages caused or alleged to be caused either directly or indirectly by this book.

Acquisitions Editor: Rosemary Caperton
Editorial Production: Online Training Solutions, Inc.
Technical Reviewer: Rob Carr
Copyeditor: Jaime Odell
Indexer: Jan Bednarczuk
Cover: Microsoft Press Brand Team

Contents

Introduction xi
    Who this book is for. xi
    How this book is organized xi
    Download the practice files xii
    Your companion ebook. xiv
    Get support and give feedback. xiv
        Errata xiv
        We want to hear from you xv
        Stay in touch. xv

PART 1

Basic skills

1   Get started with Outlook 2013   3

        Sidebar: Outlook Web App. 5
    Identifying new features of Outlook 2013. 6
    Connecting to email accounts 8
        Sidebar: Adapting exercise steps. 11
    Troubleshooting connection problems 20
        Connecting to Exchange accounts 20
        Connecting to Internet email accounts 21
    Working in the Outlook 2013 user interface. 24
        Working with the ribbon 27
        Working in the Backstage view 32
    Getting help with Outlook 2013 33
    Key points 37

2 Explore Outlook 2013 — 39

Working in the Outlook program window. 40
    Program window elements 40
    Navigation Bar 42
Working in the Mail module 45
    Folder Pane content 46
    Content area views 48
    The ribbon. 49
    Message windows 50
Working in the Calendar module 65
    Calendar module content. 65
    Calendar item windows. 68
Working in the People module 73
    People module content 73
    Contact record windows. 75
Working in the Tasks module. 81
    Tasks module content 81
    Task windows 83
Key points 85

3 Send and receive email messages — 87

Creating and sending messages 88
    Addressing messages 88
    Troubleshooting message addressing 91
    Entering content. 93
    Saving and sending messages. 94
Attaching external content to messages 103
    Sidebar: Managing multiple accounts 104
    Sidebar: Working with new mail notifications. 106
    Sidebar: Troubleshooting file types and extensions. 107
Viewing messages and message attachments 108
    Viewing conversations 112
    Viewing content in the Reading Pane 112

Viewing message participant information. 119

    Presence icons 119

    Contact cards 119

    The People Pane. 121

    Sidebar: Troubleshooting the People Pane 123

Responding to messages 123

    Sidebar: Resending and recalling messages 130

Key points 131

4   Store and access contact information   133

Saving and updating contact information. 134

    Creating contact records 135

    Address books 136

Communicating with contacts. 146

    Initiating communication from contact records. 146

    Sidebar: Conforming to address standards 147

    Selecting message recipients from address books. 148

Displaying different views of contact records. 149

    Sidebar: User-defined fields. 156

Printing contact records 157

Key points 165

5   Manage scheduling   167

Scheduling and changing appointments. 168

    Sidebar: Adding national and religious holidays to your calendar 174

    Sidebar: Creating an appointment from a message. 176

Scheduling and changing events. 177

Scheduling meetings. 178

    Sidebar: Updating and canceling meetings. 185

Responding to meeting requests 186

Displaying different views of a calendar 189

    Views 189

    Arrangements. 190

    Using the Date Navigator. 191

Key points 197

6   Track tasks   199

Creating tasks 200

     Creating tasks from scratch 201

     Creating tasks from Outlook items. 202

Updating tasks 210

Removing tasks and flagged items from task lists 212

Managing task assignments. 214

     Tasks you assign to others 214

     Tasks other people assign to you 216

Displaying different views of tasks 219

     Sidebar: Finding and organizing tasks 226

Key points 227

PART 2

Content management

7   Organize your Inbox   231

Working with Conversation view. 232

     Viewing conversations 233

     Conversation view settings. 234

     Managing conversations. 236

     Sidebar: Troubleshooting Conversation view 237

Arranging messages in different ways 237

     Sidebar: Marking messages as read or unread 244

Organizing items by using color categories 244

     Sidebar: Recording information by using Outlook notes 252

Organizing messages in folders. 253

Managing messages by using Quick Steps 257

Quickly locating messages 262

    Sidebar: Using Search Folders 264

    Sidebar: Deleting messages 265

Printing messages 268

Key points 273

8   Manage your calendar   275

Defining your available time. 276

Configuring time zones. 280

    Sidebar: Specifying appointment time zones 281

Working with multiple calendars. 282

    Displaying a co-worker's calendar 284

    Connecting to Internet calendars 284

Sharing calendar information. 290

    Sharing calendars with co-workers. 290

    Sharing calendar information outside of your organization. 294

Printing a calendar. 297

Key points 307

9   Manage contact records   309

Creating address books. 310

Importing and exporting contact records 315

Creating contact groups 325

Quickly locating contact information 332

    Sidebar: Sending business cards 336

Personalizing electronic business cards 337

Key points 343

10   Enhance message content   345

Personalizing the appearance of message text. 346
     Configuring message text formatting preferences 346
     Manually formatting message text. 352
     Configuring message signature preferences. 353
Inserting and modifying images 361
     Inserting pictures 361
     Sidebar: About online pictures. 363
     Inserting shapes 364
     Inserting screen images 366
Creating and formatting business graphics. 381
Changing message settings and delivery options 390
Key points 393

PART 3

Program management

11   Customize Outlook   397

Personalizing the Outlook program window. 398
Configuring Office and Outlook options 403
     Configuring Mail module options. 404
     Configuring Calendar module options. 415
     Configuring People module options 418
     Configuring Tasks module options 418
     Configuring search options 419
     Configuring language options. 421
     Configuring advanced options 422
Customizing the Quick Access Toolbar. 427
Customizing the ribbon. 433
     Sidebar: Customizing the status bar 439

Managing add-ins 440

        Sidebar: Creating Outlook forms. 442

Key points 443

12   Manage email settings   445

Creating and managing Quick Steps. 446

Creating rules to process messages 451

Blocking unwanted messages 459

        Working with junk email messages. 459

        Configuring junk email options. 463

Increasing email security. 467

        Digital signatures. 467

        Encryption. 474

        Plain text messages 475

        Information Rights Management 475

        Blocking external content. 476

Key points 477

13   Work remotely   479

Working with Outlook items while offline. 480

        Choosing to work offline 481

        Using public folders. 482

        Setting Cached Exchange Mode options. 485

        Managing an offline address book. 486

Managing download options for slow connections. 489

Automatically replying to messages. 491

Working with SharePoint site content 498

        Working offline with document library content. 499

        Importing SharePoint contact lists 503

        Connecting to a SharePoint calendar. 505

Key points 507

Glossary. 509

Keyboard shortcuts 517
    Outlook 2013 keyboard shortcuts 517
        Create Outlook items or files 517
        Navigate in Outlook 518
        Use the Outlook Backstage view 519
        Locate Outlook items 519
        Manage Outlook items 519
        Manage and format item content 520
        Work with the Mail module and email messages 521
        Work with the Calendar module and calendar items 522
        Work with the People module and contact records 523
        Work with the Tasks module and tasks 525
        Send and receive information 526
        Use development tools 527
    Office 2013 keyboard shortcuts 527
        Display and use windows 527
        Use dialog boxes 527
        Undo and redo actions 529
        Navigate the ribbon 529
        Move around in text or cells 529
        Move around in and work in tables 530
        Access and use panes and galleries 530
        Access and use available actions 530
        Find and replace content (when editing) 531
        Use the Help window 531

Index 533

About the authors 557

How to download your ebook 559

Survey page 560

Introduction

Part of the Microsoft Office 2013 suite of programs, Microsoft Outlook 2013 is a sophisticated communication-management program that helps you quickly and efficiently manage messages, schedules, address books, and other information. *Microsoft Outlook 2013 Step by Step* offers a comprehensive look at the features of Outlook that most people will use most frequently.

Who this book is for

Microsoft Outlook 2013 Step by Step and other books in the *Step by Step* series are designed for beginning to intermediate-level computer users. Examples shown in the book generally pertain to small and medium-sized businesses but teach skills that can be used in organizations of any size. Whether you are already comfortable working in Outlook and want to learn about new features in Outlook 2013 or you are new to Outlook, this book provides invaluable hands-on experience so that you can manage communications and information with ease.

How this book is organized

This book is divided into three parts. Part 1 explores the everyday experience of working in Outlook 2013. Part 2 discusses ways of managing content within Outlook to maximize your productivity. Part 3 delves into the management of Outlook itself, and ways of customizing program functionality and the appearance of the program window to fit the way you work. This three-part structure allows readers who are new to the program to acquire basic skills and then build on them, whereas readers who are comfortable with Outlook 2013 basics can focus on material that is of the most interest to them.

Chapter 1 contains introductory information that will primarily be of interest to readers who are new to Outlook or aren't familiar with the process of configuring Outlook to connect to an email account. If you are comfortable managing accounts in a recent version of Outlook, you might want to skip directly to Chapter 2.

This book has been designed to lead you step by step through all the tasks you're most likely to want to perform with Outlook 2013. If you start at the beginning and work your way through all the exercises, you will gain enough proficiency to be able to manage communications, contacts, tasks, and calendars. However, each topic is self-contained, so you can jump in anywhere to acquire exactly the skills you need.

Download the practice files

Before you can complete the exercises in this book, you need to download the book's practice files to your computer. These practice files can be downloaded from the following page:

http://aka.ms/Outlook2013sbs/files

IMPORTANT The Outlook 2013 program is not available from this website. You should purchase and install that program before using this book.

As you work through the exercises in this book, you will create Outlook items that you will use as practice files in later exercises. If you do not complete the earlier exercises, you can substitute Outlook items of your own and modify the exercise settings to fit.

The following table lists the practice files for this book.

Chapter	Use these files and items	Create these files and items
Chapter 1: Get started with Outlook 2013	*No practice files required*	None
Chapter 2: Explore Outlook 2013	*No practice files required*	None
Chapter 3: Send and receive email messages	We provide: NaturalGardening.pptx Procedures.docx	SBS First Draft message series SBS Tradeshow Schedule message
Chapter 4: Store and access contact information	*No practice files required*	Contact records for Ben Miller, Dean Halstead, Jill Frank, Lola Jacobsen, and Sarah Jones

Chapter	Use these files and items	Create these files and items
Chapter 5: Manage scheduling	*No practice files required*	SBS Lunch with Jane appointment SBS Pay Day event SBS Staff Meeting appointment SBS Study Session meeting
Chapter 6: Track tasks	You provide: SBS First Draft message SBS Tradeshow Schedule message	Flagged SBS First Draft message Flagged SBS Tradeshow Schedule message SBS Make Dinner Reservations task SBS Order Brochures task SBS Send Dinner Invitations task
Chapter 7: Organize your Inbox	You provide: SBS First Draft message series SBS Tradeshow Schedule message	SBS Messages folder
Chapter 8: Manage your calendar	*No practice files required*	Secondary calendar
Chapter 9: Manage contact records	We provide: JoanLambert.jpg SBSContacts.csv You provide: Contact records for Ben Miller, Dean Halstead, Jill Frank, Lola Jacobsen, and Sarah Jones	Contact records for Delphine Ribaute, Max Stevens, and Sara Davis SBS Contacts address book SBS Project Team contact group
Chapter 10: Enhance message content	We provide: Lighthouse.jpg	Casual email signature SBS Development Process message SBS Picture Tools message
Chapter 11: Customize Outlook	*No practice files required*	None
Chapter 12: Manage email settings	*No practice files required*	Flagged SBS Quick Message message SBS Messages folder SBS rule
Chapter 13: Work remotely	*No practice files required*	None

Your companion ebook

With the ebook edition of this book, you can do the following:

- Search the full text
- Print
- Copy and paste

To download your ebook, please see the instruction page at the back of the book.

Get support and give feedback

The following sections provide information about getting help with this book and contacting us to provide feedback or report errors.

Errata

We've made every effort to ensure the accuracy of this book and its companion content. Any errors that have been reported since this book was published are listed on our Microsoft Press site at oreilly.com, which you can find at:

http://aka.ms/Outlook2013sbs/errata

If you find an error that is not already listed, you can report it to us through the same page.

If you need additional support, email Microsoft Press Book Support at:

mspinput@microsoft.com

Please note that product support for Microsoft software is not offered through the addresses above.

We want to hear from you

At Microsoft Press, your satisfaction is our top priority, and your feedback our most valuable asset. Please tell us what you think of this book at:

http://www.microsoft.com/learning/booksurvey

The survey is short, and we read every one of your comments and ideas. Thanks in advance for your input!

Stay in touch

Let's keep the conversation going! We're on Twitter at: *http://twitter.com/MicrosoftPress*.

Basic skills

1 Get started with Outlook 2013   3

2 Explore Outlook 2013   39

3 Send and receive email messages   87

4 Store and access contact information   133

5 Manage scheduling   167

6 Track tasks   199

Chapter at a glance

Connect

Connect to email accounts,
page 8

Troubleshoot

Troubleshoot connection problems,
page 20

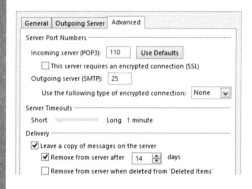

Work

Work in the Outlook 2013 user interface,
page 24

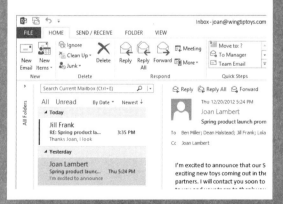

Learn

Get help with Outlook 2013,
page 33

Get started with Outlook 2013

IN THIS CHAPTER, YOU WILL LEARN HOW TO

- Identify new features of Outlook 2013.

- Connect to email accounts.

- Troubleshoot connection problems.

- Work in the Outlook 2013 user interface.

- Get help with Outlook 2013.

Bill Gates's dream of "a computer on every desktop" is becoming more and more of a reality—many people today work (and play) on computers both at work and at home. However, the digital world is rapidly expanding beyond that original dream—desktop computers turned out to be only the beginning. Laptops, netbooks, tablets, slates, and other portable computers, as well as smartphones such as Windows Phones, iPhones, and Android phones that run mobile applications are becoming a standard part of the productivity package. Electronic messaging—whether email, social network updates, instant messages, or text messages—keeps many of us in contact with colleagues, clients, friends, and family members for a dizzying portion of each day. For people who are dependent on electronic communications—and even more so for those who work in enterprises that use Microsoft Exchange Server, SharePoint, and Lync to manage collaboration—Microsoft Outlook 2013 offers an ideal solution. Outlook 2013 not only provides email functionality, but also integrates with instant messaging programs and Microsoft SharePoint resources. Outlook enables you to manage messaging and information—address books, calendars, task lists, and more—in one attractive interface. More importantly, Outlook makes this information immediately available to you when and where you need it. From one place, you can quickly store, organize, manage, and retrieve many types of information.

In an enterprise environment, Outlook interacts with Microsoft server products to provide unified communications services including real-time presence and status information, specialized functionality for internal messaging, access to fax messages and voice mail messages, offline access to SharePoint site content, and many other useful features.

You can use Outlook to:

- Send, receive, read, respond to, organize, and archive email messages.

- Create attractive business graphics and incorporate and edit external images in your communications.

- Send documents, spreadsheets, presentations, pictures, and other files as message attachments, and preview attachments you receive from other people.

- Schedule events, appointments, and meetings; invite attendees; and reserve conference rooms, projectors, and other managed resources.

- View upcoming appointments and tasks, and receive reminders for them.

- Share schedule information with other people, inside and outside your organization.

- Store contact information in a transferable and easily accessible format.

- Keep track of tasks you need to complete, schedule time to complete your tasks, and assign tasks to co-workers.

- Organize and easily locate information in messages, attachments, calendars, contact records, tasks, and notes.

- Filter out unwanted and annoying junk messages.

- Have information from favorite websites delivered directly to you.

In this chapter, you'll get an overview of the new features in Outlook 2013 to help you identify changes if you're upgrading from a previous version. Then you'll configure Outlook to connect to one or more email accounts, and explore the program's user interface. Finally, you'll learn how to get help with the program.

PRACTICE FILES You don't need any practice files to complete the exercises in this chapter.

Microsoft Office 2013 encompasses a wide variety of programs, including Microsoft Access 2013, Excel 2013, InfoPath 2013, Lync 2013, OneNote 2013, Outlook 2013, PowerPoint 2013, Publisher 2013, and Word 2013. Office is available in various editions that include different combinations of Office programs; you can also purchase most of the programs individually.

The programs in the Office suite are designed to work together to provide highly efficient methods of getting things done. You can install one or more Office programs on your computer, or work with online versions of some programs in a web browser. Some programs have multiple versions designed for different platforms. Although the core purpose of a program remains the same regardless of the platform on which it runs, the available functionality and the way you interact with the program might be different.

The program we work with and depict in images throughout this book is a desktop installation of the Outlook 2013 client application for Windows, which we installed directly on our computers. The standard client installation has all the available Outlook functionality. It is available as part of the Office 2013 suite of programs, as a freestanding program, or as part of an Office 365 subscription that allows users to install desktop programs from the Internet.

TIP Office 365 is a cloud-based solution that small, midsize, and large businesses can use to provide products and services to their employees through a subscription licensing program.

Outlook Web App

Outlook Web App is a browser-based version of Outlook that supports much of the desktop installation functionality. You can perform many of the same functions in Outlook Web App that you can in a desktop installation of Outlook, from within a web browser window. Outlook Web App is available as part of Office 365 subscriptions and Exchange Server installations. The functionality of Outlook Web App is dependent on the version you're using. Recent versions of Outlook Web App have an appearance and functionality similar to that of the Outlook 2013 client.

If Outlook Web App is available for your email account, you can access it by entering an organization-specific URL in a web browser or by clicking the Access This Account On The Web link on the Info page of the Backstage view of the Outlook client. The most recent version of Outlook Web App can be run with varying levels of functionality in the Windows Internet Explorer, Firefox, Safari, and Chrome web browsers on computers that run Windows, Mac OS, or Linux. The available functionality depends on the specific combination of web browser and operating system.

Identifying new features of Outlook 2013

Outlook 2013 builds on previous versions to provide powerful information-management and communication tools. If you're upgrading to Outlook 2013 from a previous version, you're probably most interested in the differences between the old and new versions and how they will affect you, and want to find out about them in the quickest possible way. In this section, we discuss features that are new in Outlook 2013 or have been removed from this version of Outlook.

Significant changes have been made from previous versions of Outlook. If you're upgrading from Outlook 2007 or Outlook 2003, you might find that some of the changes take a bit of getting used to—particularly the global incorporation of user interface elements such as the ribbon and the Quick Access Toolbar, and the movement of program-management functionality to the Backstage view. These elements have been carefully designed to provide intuitive access to tools and commands; however, you do have many options for personalizing your Outlook 2013 working environment to suit your preferences.

If you are upgrading from Outlook 2010, you will encounter the following new features in Outlook 2013:

- **Simplified user interface** Outlook 2013 has a sleek new look with subtle coloring and simplified iconography.

- **Folder Pane** The Folder Pane (formerly called the Navigation Pane) is now dedicated to the display of account folder structures, and no longer contains the module navigation links.

- **Navigation Bar** Outlook module links have moved from the former Navigation Pane to a separate Navigation Bar in the lower-left corner of the program window. The standard Navigation Bar contains text links and the compact Navigation Bar, which is on by default, contains only module buttons.

- **Message list functionality** It's now easier to manage messages directly from the message list. The default view displays the message subject, sender, and first line of content of each message. Many message status and content indicators and response options are available from the message list and from the Reading Pane. You can easily display only new messages by clicking the Unread button at the top of the message list.

- **Inline replies** By default, message responses are drafted directly in the Reading Pane so you don't have to manage an extra message window. If you prefer to work in a separate window, you can "pop out" the response draft.

- **Module preview** You can quickly peek at current information in the Calendar, People, or Tasks module by pointing to the module link or button on the Navigation Bar. You can pin these module "peeks" to the To-Do Bar.

- **Multiple-source contact information** In the new People Card view, a single contact record can display contact information about a person from multiple sources, including Outlook, Microsoft Lync, and social networks such as LinkedIn. You can initiate many types of interactions with a person directly from the contact card.

- **Site mailbox connections** If your organization uses shared site mailboxes on a SharePoint 2013 site, you can access messages and documents in site mailboxes of which you are a member directly from the Outlook Folder Pane.

- **Exchange ActiveSync support** You can connect to email accounts that support ActiveSync, such as a Windows Live Hotmail or Outlook.com account, without installing additional software. Then you can synchronize information such as Hotmail tasks with Outlook so that you can easily work with your business and personal accounts from one location.

- **Weather Bar** With this fun new addition to Outlook, you can display current weather conditions in the Calendar module. You can add multiple locations to the Weather Bar and easily display the current conditions for a location by selecting it from a list.

As is always the case with developing technologies, some features that were available in previous versions of Outlook are now redundant due to technological or procedural changes. Of these, features that we have discussed in earlier editions of this book and that have been modified include the Notes and Journal features. If you used these features in previous versions of Outlook, here's what you need to know:

- The Notes and Journal folders are still available in the Folder List, and the Notes module is available from the Navigation Bar.

- Notes and Journal options are not available in the Outlook Options dialog box.

- The automatic journaling functionality has been disabled. You can create Journal entries, but only manually.

- You can create new notes, but only with the default color and font settings.

The following table describes other features that have been discontinued or modified in Outlook 2013.

Feature	Description
Data files	Outlook 2013 does not support the creation of Outlook 97-2002 Data Files (.pst files). If you upgrade to Outlook 2013, existing .pst files are available from the Folder Pane. New Exchange Server account items are delivered to an offline Outlook Data File (.ost file). Cached Exchange Mode is on by default.
Importing and exporting	Options for importing Internet email account settings, messages, and addresses are discontinued. Options for exporting Outlook data as tab-separated values and directly to Microsoft Access and Excel are no longer supported.
Dial-up networking support	Outlook 2013 uses the network connections configured in Windows; it is not necessary to separately configure a dial-up connection in Outlook.
Exchange Server classic offline mode	This feature is discontinued. Exchange Server accounts can be used online or in Cached Exchange Mode.
Exchange Server Download Headers And Then Full Items mode	This feature has been discontinued. After you upgrade to Outlook 2013, if you had this option selected, it is automatically changed to Download Full Items

Connecting to email accounts

By using Outlook 2013, you can easily manage one or more email accounts and the information (such as calendar items and contact records) associated with those accounts. You can configure Outlook to connect to many different types of business and personal email accounts. If your organization uses Exchange Server, you can use Outlook to work with all the features of your Exchange account, including email, calendaring, contact tracking, task tracking, and notes. If your organization also uses Lync Server features, you can initiate audio and video calls, instant messaging sessions, online meetings, and more from Outlook 2013.

Although you don't have to connect to an email account to use Outlook, it is customary to do so. After you configure Outlook to connect to an account, you can easily manage the information stored with that account by using the Outlook features specifically designed for each type of information.

A default installation of Outlook 2013 supports the following types of email accounts:

- **Exchange** You can configure Outlook 2013 to connect to an Exchange account hosted on Exchange Server 2013, Exchange Server 2010, Exchange Server 2007, or Exchange Server 2003. If your organization uses any of these versions of Exchange Server, you can send mail within or outside of your organization's network. Messages are stored centrally on the Exchange server. They are also stored locally in a data file on your computer. Outlook synchronizes with the server when you're connected to it either over a corporate network or over the Internet, so you can work with existing Outlook items and create new items while working offline.

  In previous versions of Outlook and Exchange, you could connect to a corporate Exchange account only when your computer was connected to the corporate network. This required that you manually configure Outlook to connect to the corporate Exchange server either through a virtual private network (VPN) connection or by using Outlook Anywhere (a friendly name for a service otherwise known as *RPC over HTTP*) when you wanted to work in another location. More recent versions of Exchange automatically route all Outlook client access through Outlook Anywhere and do not require a direct corporate network connection.

  TIP Some Outlook features are dependent on the functionality of the specific version of Exchange hosting your email account. The functionality described in this book is specific to Exchange Server 2010 accounts. Outlook provides additional functionality in environments that include Lync Server and SharePoint.

- **Exchange ActiveSync–compatible service** Although this sounds quite technical, it's simply a description for an Internet-based email service such as Hotmail or Outlook.com. It is no longer necessary to install a separate connector in order to configure Outlook 2013 to connect to an account of this type.

- **Post Office Protocol (POP)** When connected to a POP account, Outlook downloads messages from your email server to your computer, and removes the original messages from the server after a specified length of time. You read and manage messages on your computer, and Outlook synchronizes with the server when it is connected.

- **Internet Message Access Protocol (IMAP)** When connected to an IMAP account, Outlook stores copies of messages on your computer, but leaves the originals on the email server. You read and manage messages locally, and Outlook synchronizes with the server when it is connected.

Before you can use Outlook to manage an email account, you need to configure the program to connect to the account. When you first start the program, the Microsoft Outlook Account Setup wizard guides you through an automated process. This process is a significant improvement over the manual account setup process of Outlook 2003 and earlier versions of Outlook, which required you to provide much more information. For many accounts, you need to supply only three pieces of information—your name, your email address, and your email account password—and the Account Setup wizard will handle the rest of the connection process for you. If the Account Setup wizard isn't able to configure Outlook to connect to your account, you can provide additional information to complete the process manually.

Configuring Outlook creates an Outlook Data File for each email account and an Outlook profile, which stores information about you and your email accounts. You can work with your profile from within Outlook or from the Mail control panel in Windows. Your profile includes information about your email account such as the user name, display name, server name, password, and where Outlook stores your data. You can connect to more than one email account per profile, to manage all your email communications through Outlook. If you want to, you can create multiple profiles that link to different email accounts or to different sets of email accounts, but it is no longer necessary to create multiple profiles to manage multiple accounts.

You can add multiple email accounts of any type to your Outlook profile, either during setup or at any time thereafter.

Adapting exercise steps

The screen images shown in this book were captured at a resolution of 1024 × 768, at 100 percent magnification. If your settings are different, the ribbon on your screen might not look the same as the one shown in this book. For example, you might have more or fewer buttons in each group, the buttons you have might be represented by larger or smaller icons than those shown, or a group might be represented by a button that you click to display the group's commands. As a result, exercise instructions that involve the ribbon might require a little adaptation. Our instructions use this format:

- On the **Insert** tab, in the **Illustrations** group, click the **Chart** button.

If the command is in a list, our instructions use this format:

- On the **Home** tab, in the **Filter Email** group, click the **Categorized** arrow and then, in the **Categorized** list, click **Any Category**.

TIP On subsequent instances of instructions located on the same tab or in the same group, the instructions are simplified to reflect that we've already established the working location.

If differences between your display settings and ours cause a button to appear differently on your screen than it does in this book, you can easily adapt the steps to locate the command. First click the specified tab, and then locate the specified group. If a group has been collapsed into a group list or under a group button, click the list or button to display the group's commands. If you can't immediately identify the button you want, point to likely candidates to display their names in ScreenTips.

If you prefer not to have to adapt the steps, set up your screen to match ours while you read and work through the exercises in this book.

In this book, we provide instructions based on the traditional keyboard and mouse input methods. If you're using Outlook on a touch-enabled device, you might be giving commands by tapping with a stylus or your finger. If so, substitute a tapping action any time we instruct you to click a user interface element. Also note that when we tell you to enter information in Outlook, you can do so by typing on a keyboard, tapping an on-screen keyboard, or even speaking aloud, depending on your computer setup and your personal preferences.

In this exercise, you'll configure Outlook to automatically connect to an Exchange Server account, and you'll manually configure the account settings.

TIP Although we demonstrate connecting to an Exchange account, the basic process is the same to connect to another type of email server. To connect to a POP or IMAP account, you should first read the topic "Connecting to Internet email accounts" in "Troubleshooting connection problems" later in this chapter.

SET UP You don't need any practice files to complete this exercise. You need your email account user name and password. If you are connecting to a POP account, an IMAP account, or an Exchange account that is hosted by an external service provider, you might also need to know the names and authentication requirements of your incoming and outgoing servers. These will be available from your email service provider.

1   Start Outlook by using one of the following methods:

■ On a computer that runs Windows 8, display the **Start** screen, enter Outlook, and then click the **Microsoft Outlook 2013** icon.

■ On a computer that runs Windows 7, click the **Start** button, click **All Programs**, click **Microsoft Office**, and then click **Microsoft Outlook 2013**.

TIP If the Email link at the top of the Start menu specifies Microsoft Outlook as your default email program, you can click that link instead.

2   The next step depends on whether Outlook is already configured.

■ If Outlook has not yet been configured, the **Microsoft Outlook Account Setup** wizard begins. On the **Welcome** page, and again on the **Add an Email Account** page, click **Next** to display the **Auto Account Setup** page of the **Add Account** wizard.

TIP To configure an Outlook profile without connecting to an email account, start the program, click Next on the Welcome page, click No and then Next on the Add An Email Account page, select the Use Outlook Without An Email Account check box, and then click Finish.

■ If an Outlook profile has already been configured, the program starts. Manually start the account configuration process by clicking the **File** tab at the left end of the ribbon to display the **Info** page of the **Backstage** view, and then clicking **Add Account** to display the **Auto Account Setup** page of the **Add Account** wizard.

TIP You control Outlook program settings from the Backstage view. For detailed information, see "Configuring Office and Outlook options" in Chapter 11, "Customize Outlook."

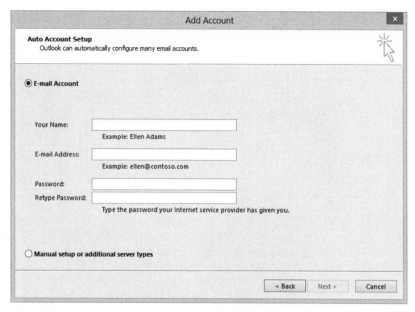

The Add Account wizard, which you can start from the Account Setup wizard or from the Info page of the Backstage view.

3 On the **Auto Account Setup** page of the **Add Account** wizard, enter your name, email address, and email account password in the text boxes provided. Then click **Next** to search your available networks and the Internet for the specified domain.

TIP The password characters you enter are hidden, so ensure that the Caps Lock key is not inadvertently active when you enter the password.

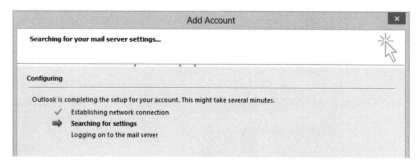

The wizard searches for the domain that hosts your account and attempts to log on to it by using the credentials you provided in step 3.

If the wizard locates an account matching the email address you entered, it attempts to log on by using the password you entered. If the connection is successful, a confirmation appears, along with additional account configuration options.

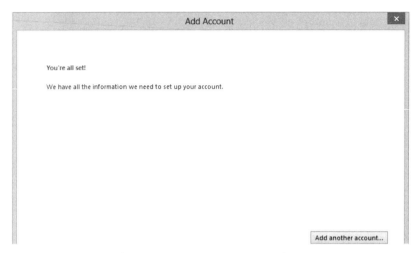

After successfully configuring a connection to an email account, you can connect to another account, or click Finish to begin using the account.

If the wizard is unable to connect to the account without further information, an error page appears.

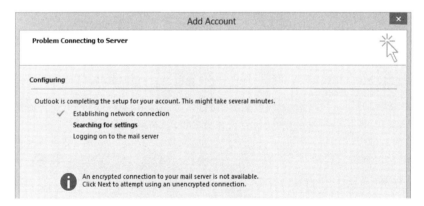

The specific message that appears might differ from the one shown here.

The next step depends on whether Outlook successfully connected to your account.

4   If the wizard successfully connected to your account, click **Finish**. Click the **File** tab to display the **Info** page of the **Backstage** view, click the **Account Settings** button, and then click **Account Settings**. In the **Account Settings** dialog box, double-click your account. Then skip to step 11 to practice configuring additional settings.

5   If the wizard didn't connect to your account, click **Back** to return to the **Auto Account Setup** page (shown in step 2 of this exercise). Then select the **Manual setup or additional server types** option, and click **Next** to display the **Choose Service** page.

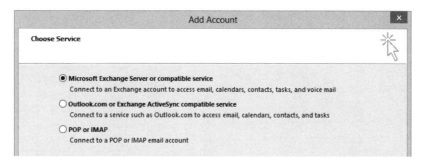

You can manually configure a connection to any of the account types supported by Outlook.

6   On the **Choose Service** page, click the type of account you're configuring (we chose **Microsoft Exchange**), and then click **Next**.

> **IMPORTANT** The screen that appears next varies based on the selected account type. If the screen that appears to you is not shown in this exercise, see "Troubleshooting connection problems" later in this chapter for more information.

7   On the **Server Settings** page, enter the name or address of your Exchange server (provided by your Exchange server administrator) and your user name (usually your email address) in the boxes provided, and then click **Check Name**.

8   If the **Connect to** dialog box appears, enter your logon information, and then click **OK** to contact the specified server. If the user name and password you provided match the information stored on the server, the wizard replaces your user name with your display name (as recorded in your organization's Global Address List) and underlines it. (This is known as *resolving the address*.)

     If the wizard is unable to validate the information, an error message appears. (This might occur if you're connecting to a corporate Exchange server over the Internet, and Outlook requires additional information to establish the connection.) Click **OK** in the message box to open a simple **Microsoft Exchange** dialog box that contains only a **General** page displaying the Exchange server and mailbox information. Then click **Cancel** to return to the **Server Settings** page.

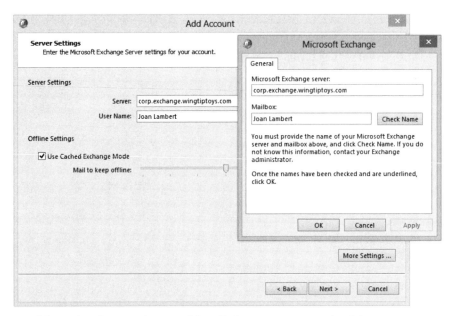

Possible results of attempting to validate Exchange account credentials.

If the wizard successfully resolves your server name and user name, you can begin using your account, or you can manually configure additional account settings. For the purpose of this exercise, we'll look at the manual configuration options.

9   On the **Server Settings** page, click **More Settings** to open the **Microsoft Exchange** account settings dialog box, displaying the **General** page. On this page, you can specify the name that identifies the account within Outlook (for example, on the title bar of the program window and in the Folder Pane). This setting does not affect the name that appears to message recipients.

10 Enter the name by which you would like to identify this account. For example, your name, the email address, or the company name that this account represents.

The General page of the Microsoft Exchange account settings dialog box.

Now we'll review the available settings.

11   Click the **Advanced** page tab. On this page, you can specify additional mailboxes
on the same Exchange server that you want to open in Outlook.

*If you are responsible for monitoring another mailbox, such
as a departmental mailbox, you can specify it here.*

SEE ALSO For information about Cached Exchange Mode, see "Working with Outlook
items while offline" in Chapter 13, "Work remotely."

12   On the **Advanced** page, click the **Outlook Data File Settings** button to display
information about the data file in which a copy of your email account information
is stored on your computer. The **Compact Now** button is not active until you start
using your account. (At this point, there's nothing in the data file to compact.)

You can reduce the data file size by compacting its contents.

13   Click the **Security** page tab. On this page, you can choose to help secure your locally stored account data by requiring logon credentials each time you start Outlook.

If other people have access to your computer, you can add an additional layer of security by instructing Outlook to access this account only if you enter the account credentials.

14   Click the **Connection** page tab. On this page, you can specify whether you want Outlook to connect to the Exchange server through your local area network or over the Internet.

Selecting this option causes Outlook to connect to the server over the Internet.

TIP If you are accustomed to using a previous version of Outlook, you might wonder where the network connection settings that were previously available from this page have gone. Outlook now uses the Windows network connection settings; you don't need to enter any additional information in the program configuration.

15   On the tabs of the **Microsoft Exchange** dialog box, enter any additional connection information provided to you by your email server administrator, and then click **OK**.

16   On the **Server Settings** page of the **Add Account** wizard, click **Next**. Then on the wizard's final page, click **Finish**. The **E-mail** page of the **Account Settings** dialog box might appear and display the new email account.

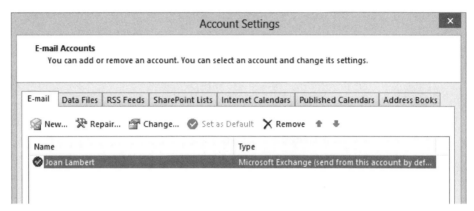

You can manage Outlook settings for all the email accounts, RSS feeds, SharePoint lists, calendars, and address books you connect to from the Account Settings window.

17   If the **Account Settings** dialog box opens, close it to display the Outlook program window.

While Outlook finishes configuring the connection to your account, a notice appears in the lower-right corner of the screen. After it connects to your account, any messages that you have appear in your Inbox.

TIP Outlook might prompt you to select update settings. Options include Use Recommended Settings, Install Updates Only, and Ask Me Later. The recommended settings install updates and connect your Office installation to a customer feedback program that permits Microsoft to gather data about typical usage. Your participation in the program is entirely anonymous and does not give Microsoft access to your personal information or to the contents of messages or of files stored on your computer.

✖ CLEAN UP You're now ready to begin using your email account!

Troubleshooting connection problems

The automatic account setup feature is very handy, but might not work every time. It is most successful when connecting to an on-premises Exchange account. When connecting to a remote Exchange server, to an Exchange account hosted by an external hosting company, or to a POP or IMAP account, manual configuration steps might be necessary.

Connecting to Exchange accounts

Here are some common error messages and problems you could encounter when you connect to an Exchange account, and how to address them:

- **Server certificate does not match site** If Outlook encounters security issues associated with the electronic file (digital certificate) that validates the mail server's identity —for example, if the digital certificate does not match the name of your domain— Outlook notifies you of this problem and lets you choose whether to proceed.

  If a Security Alert message box appears, you can click the View Certificate button to display the digital certificate of the mail server and verify that you know and trust the company that issued the certificate. If you want, you can install the certificate on your computer by clicking the Install Certificate button and following the steps in the Certificate Import wizard.

  SEE ALSO For more information about digital certificates, see "Increasing email security" in Chapter 12, "Manage email settings."

- **Encrypted connection not available** This message might appear if your Exchange account is with a hosted service provider. Outlook first tries to establish an encrypted connection to the server. If this attempt is not successful, Outlook notifies you of this problem and asks whether you want to try to establish an unencrypted connection.

  If you click Next to establish an unencrypted connection, Outlook might inadvertently configure the connection to your Exchange account as it would a connection to an IMAP or POP account. This configuration can result in a loss of functionality related to information, such as appointments and tasks, stored on the Exchange server. The more likely solution to this issue is to click the Back button, click the Manual Setup Or Additional Server Types option, click Next, and then manually enter the server and connection information for your account.

If you encounter either of these errors when connecting to an Exchange account, verify that you are using the correct internal server address method. For example, if your email address is *jane@adatum.com*, you might address your email server as *mail.adatum.com* or by an internal address, such as *ADATUMExchange.adatum.local*.

To successfully troubleshoot your connection issues, you will likely need to manually configure your server settings. This requires that you have additional information from your server administrator about your email account, including the names of the incoming and outgoing servers, and whether either of the servers requires additional authentication.

Connecting to Internet email accounts

If the Add Account wizard is unable to automatically configure a connection to your POP or IMAP account, you can manually configure the connection.

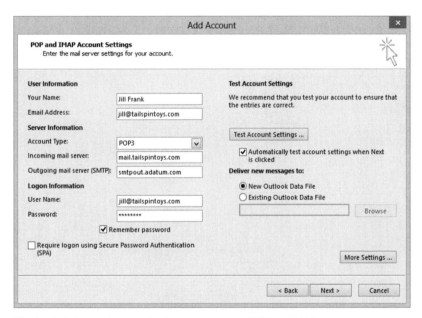

The basic information required to connect to a POP or IMAP account.

In addition to your name and email address, you must provide the following information, which you can obtain from your email service provider:

- **Account type** Choose POP3 or IMAP from the drop-down list.

- **Incoming and outgoing mail servers** Server addresses are usually entered in the format *server.domain.com*.

- **Account user name** Many providers require that you enter the entire email address for this parameter rather than only the name before the @ symbol.

- **Account password** Outlook disguises the password characters as asterisks.

- **Logon authentication requirements** Some mail servers require that you log on by using secure password authentication.

Click the More Settings button to open the Internet E-mail Settings dialog box in which you can enter additional information, such as the name by which you want to identify the account, the email address you want to appear when you reply to a message, and outgoing server authentication information.

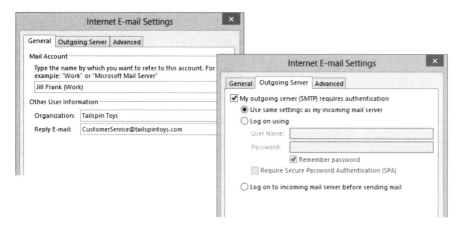

It might be necessary to supply additional server authentication information.

The default account settings are for unencrypted connections. Your mail account provider might require that you use encrypted connections for your incoming server, outgoing server, or both. Selecting the This Server Requires An Encrypted Connection check box on the Advanced page of the Internet E-mail Settings dialog box changes the Incoming Server port to 995 and directs email traffic through the HTTPS protocol rather than the HTTP protocol.

It is important to note that when connecting to a POP account, you can control the retention of messages on the email server. By default, messages downloaded from a POP server to your computer are removed from the server after 14 days. You can choose to leave the messages on the server permanently, leave them there for a specified amount of time, or leave them there until you delete them from Outlook.

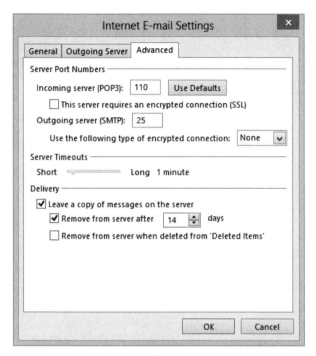

If you access your POP email account from multiple computers, you will probably want to leave messages on the server to ensure that they're available to you from all your computers.

TIP If you configure Outlook to connect to a POP account from a portable computer and experience difficulty sending email messages when connected to a public network (such as a hotel network), it might be because the network has blocked traffic on the default outgoing server port, port 25. If so, you can likely resolve the issue by changing the outgoing server port on the Advanced page of the Internet E-mail Settings dialog box for the account to port 80, 465, or 587.

After supplying the connection information for your email account and closing the Internet E-mail Settings dialog box, you can click Test Account Settings or Next on the POP And IMAP Account Settings page of the Add Account wizard to ensure that Outlook successfully connects to your incoming and outgoing servers.

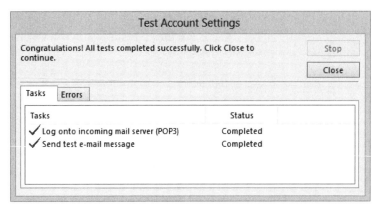

Validating the successful configuration of an Internet email account.

Working in the Outlook 2013 user interface

The goal of the Office 2013 working environment is to make working with Office documents, including Microsoft Word documents, Excel workbooks, PowerPoint presentations, Outlook email messages, and Access database tables, as intuitive as possible. To that end, each program in the Office system, including Outlook, has a similar user interface.

Unlike other Office programs, Outlook doesn't function for a single purpose or create a single category of files. You use it to create, organize, and track several types of information that are critical to keeping your daily life functioning smoothly. To minimize the work of dealing with such diverse items of information as email messages, contact records, appointments, tasks, and notes, Outlook provides a module for each type and presents each module in a similar interface, allowing you to work with different items of information in consistent ways.

As an information-management system, Outlook has more complex functionality than other Office applications; it also has more elements in its user interface. However, some are hidden by default, and you can choose the elements you want to display.

SEE ALSO For information about hiding and displaying user interface elements, see "Personalizing the Outlook program window" in Chapter 11, "Customize Outlook."

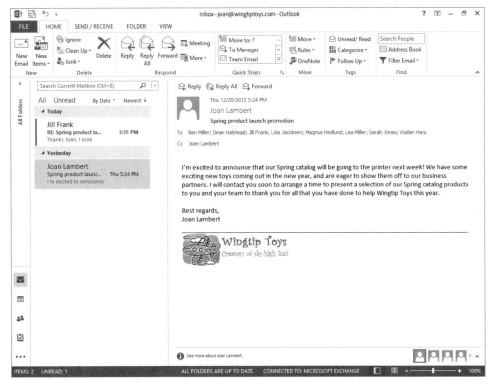

In the default configuration of the Outlook 2013 program window, many of the program tools are minimized or hidden.

The program window is bordered by the standard Office program window elements on the top and bottom:

- **Title bar** This bar across the top of the program window displays the name of the active account and provides tools for managing the program and the program window.

Program icon   Active account   Help button

Quick Access Toolbar   Ribbon Display Options button

The Outlook program window title bar.

At the left end of the title bar is the program icon, which you click to display commands to restore, move, size, minimize, maximize, and close the program window.

To the right of the program icon is the Quick Access Toolbar, which by default displays the Send/Receive Folders and Undo buttons. You can customize the Quick Access Toolbar to display any commands you want.

The program window and the windows in which you work with each type of Outlook item have individually configurable Quick Access Toolbars. For example, you can display commands specific to creating and formatting message content only in message item windows and commands specific to creating and managing tasks only in task item windows.

TIP You might find that you work more efficiently if you organize the commands you use frequently on the Quick Access Toolbar and then display it below the ribbon, directly above the workspace. For information, see "Customizing the Quick Access Toolbar" in Chapter 11, "Customize Outlook."

At the right end of the title bar are five buttons: the Microsoft Outlook Help button that opens the Outlook Help window; a Ribbon Display Options button that allows you to control the display of the ribbon; and the familiar Minimize, Maximize/Restore Down, and Close buttons.

SEE ALSO For information about the Outlook Help system, see "Getting help with Outlook 2013" later in this chapter.

- **Ribbon** Located below the title bar, the ribbon gathers all the commands for working with Outlook content together in a central location.

  SEE ALSO For more information, see "Working with the ribbon" later in this section.

- **Status bar** Across the bottom of the program window, this bar displays information about the current account and provides access to certain program functions.

The account information in the center is shown only for Exchange accounts.

SEE ALSO For information about modifying the indicators shown on the status bar, see the sidebar "Customizing the status bar" in Chapter 11, Customize Outlook."

By default, Outlook displays the Items In View, Unread Items In View, and Reminders indicators (whichever are valid) at the left end of the status bar. Each of these indicators displays at a glance the status of that feature; clicking the Reminders indicator displays the Reminders dialog box in which you can process active reminders. For Exchange accounts, the connection status is displayed in the center of the status bar.

The View Shortcuts, Zoom Slider, and Zoom Level controls are displayed at the right end of the status bar. The View Shortcuts toolbar includes buttons for the two primary program content views. The Zoom Slider and Zoom Level controls enable you to adjust the magnification of the Reading Pane.

SEE ALSO For information about the various ways you can view program window and item content, see Chapter 2, "Explore Outlook 2013." We discuss the module-specific views in Chapter 4, "Store and access contact information," Chapter 5, "Manage scheduling," Chapter 6, "Track tasks," and Chapter 7, "Organize your Inbox."

Working with the ribbon

You might be familiar with the ribbon command structure from other Office programs. Outlook differs from those in one respect—it has one ribbon for the program window, and a separate ribbon for each item window. As a result, each Outlook ribbon is simpler and contains fewer tabs than the ribbons in other programs.

The program window and each of the Outlook item windows have individually configurable ribbons that display content specific to the program or to the item type you're working with. All the ribbons share common structural features.

The Home tab of each ribbon displays the most frequently used commands.

TIP Your ribbons might look different from those shown in this book. You might have installed programs that add their own tabs to the ribbon, or your screen settings might be different. For more information, see "Ribbon appearance" later in this section.

- Across the top of the ribbon is a set of tabs. Clicking a tab displays an associated set of commands. The Home tab of each ribbon contains the most commonly used commands for the related item.

- On each tab, buttons representing commands are organized into named groups. The groups that appear on each tab, and the buttons that appear in each group, vary based on the active module or item.

- Depending on your screen resolution and the size of the program window, the commands in a group might be displayed as labeled buttons, as unlabeled icons, or as one or more large buttons that you click to display the commands within the group.

- You can point to any button to display a ScreenTip containing the command name, a description of its function, and its keyboard shortcut (if it has one).

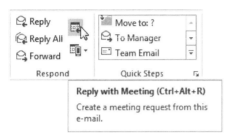

ScreenTips provide helpful information about buttons.

SEE ALSO For information about controlling the display and content of ScreenTips, see "Configuring Office and Outlook options" in Chapter 11, "Customize Outlook."

- Some buttons include an integrated or separate arrow. To determine whether a button and arrow are integrated, point to the button to display its border. If a button and arrow are integrated within one border, clicking the button displays a list of related options. If the button and arrow have separate borders, clicking the button carries out the default action indicated by the button's current icon. You can change the default action of the button by clicking the arrow and then clicking the action you want.

*The arrow of the Use Voting Buttons button is integrated,
and the arrow of the Permission button is separate.*

- Related but less common commands are not represented as buttons in a group. Instead, they're available in a dialog box or pane, which you display by clicking the dialog box launcher located in the lower-right corner of the group.

- To the right of the groups on the ribbon is the Collapse The Ribbon button. Clicking this button hides the commands but leaves the tab titles visible. When the groups are hidden, the Collapse The Ribbon button changes to the Pin The Ribbon button, which is shaped like a pushpin. You can click any tab title to temporarily display the groups, then click a ribbon command or click away from the ribbon to hide the groups again, or click the Pin The Ribbon button to permanently redisplay the groups.

KEYBOARD SHORTCUT Press Ctrl+F1 to unpin or pin the ribbon. For more information about keyboard shortcuts, see "Keyboard shortcuts" at the end of this book.

Module and item tabs

Commands related to working with the content of Outlook items are represented in function-specific groups on separate feature-specific tabs of the ribbon.

- The ribbon in each module includes four standard tabs: Home, Send/Receive, Folder, and View. The Home tab changes to reflect the commands necessary to manage items within the current module.

- The ribbon in each new Outlook item window includes an item-specific tab such as Message, Appointment, Contact, or Task. It also includes the Insert, Format Text, and Review tabs. The ribbon might also contain additional tabs specific to an item type, to a program installed on your computer, or to customizations you've made in the Outlook Options dialog box.

  SEE ALSO For information about adding standard tabs, removing standard tabs and groups, and creating custom tabs and groups, see "Customizing the ribbon" in Chapter 11, "Customize Outlook."

- When certain types of item content (such as tables, charts, and graphics) are active (selected), additional *tool tabs* appear at the right end of the ribbon. These tool tabs are indicated by colored headers and a colored bottom border, and they contain commands that are specific to working with the selected content. For example, when the cursor is in a table, the Design and Layout tool tabs for tables appear to the right of the Review tab. When a chart or chart element is selected, the Design, Layout, and Format tool tabs for charts appear to the right of the Review tab. Each of the available tool tab groups has a unique color so you can easily differentiate between them.

The ribbon was designed to make working with Outlook items and item content a natural extension of the way most people work. Commands for tasks you perform often are readily available, and even those you might use infrequently are easy to find.

For example, when a formatting option has several available choices, they are often displayed in a gallery of thumbnails. These galleries provide a visual array of the available choices. When a gallery contains more thumbnails than can be shown in the available ribbon space, you can display more content by clicking the scroll arrow or More button located on the right edge of the gallery.

If you point to a thumbnail in a gallery, the Live Preview feature shows you what that choice looks like if you apply it to the active content.

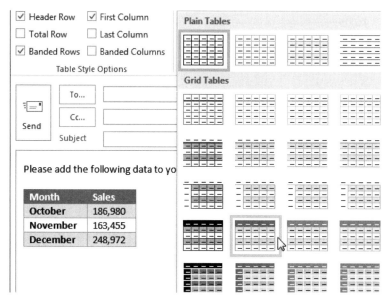

Live Preview shows the effect of clicking the thumbnail to which you are pointing.

TIP Some older commands no longer appear as buttons on the ribbon but are still available in the program. You can make these commands available by adding them to the Quick Access Toolbar. For more information, see "Customizing the Quick Access Toolbar" in Chapter 11, "Customize Outlook."

Ribbon appearance

The ribbon is dynamic, meaning that as its width changes, its buttons adapt to the available space. As a result, a button might be large or small, it might or might not have a label, or it might even change to a command on a menu. When sufficient horizontal space is not available to fully display the ribbon commands, small button labels disappear and entire groups of buttons might hide under one button that represents the entire group. Clicking the group button displays a menu of the commands available in that group. When the ribbon becomes too narrow to display all the groups, a scroll arrow appears at its right end. Clicking the scroll arrow displays the hidden groups.

The width of the ribbon depends on these three factors:

- **Program window width** Maximizing the program window provides the most space for the ribbon. To maximize the window, click the Maximize button, drag the borders of a non-maximized window, or drag the window title bar to the top of the screen until it resizes.

- **Screen resolution** Screen resolution is the size of your screen display expressed as *pixels wide × pixels high*. The greater the screen resolution, the greater the amount of information that will fit on one screen. Your screen resolution options are dependent on the display adapter installed in your computer, and your monitor. Common screen resolutions range from 800 × 600 to 2560 × 1600. The greater the number of pixels wide (the first number), the greater the number of buttons that can be shown on the ribbon.

  To change your screen resolution, first display the Screen Resolution control panel item (available by right-clicking the desktop and then clicking Screen Resolution). In the Screen Resolution window, click the Resolution arrow, click or drag to select the screen resolution you want, and then click Apply or OK.

- **The magnification of your screen display** If you increase the screen magnification in Windows, text and user interface elements are larger and therefore more legible, but fewer elements fit on the screen. You can set the magnification from 100 to 500 percent.

  You can change the screen magnification from the Display control panel item (available within the Appearance And Personalization group, or by right-clicking the desktop, clicking Personalization, and then clicking Display in the lower-left corner of the window). To change the screen magnification to a magnification that is available in the Display window, click that option. To select another magnification, click the Custom Sizing Options link and then, in the Custom Sizing Options dialog box, click the magnification you want in the list or drag the ruler to change the magnification even more (the cursor changes to a pointer to indicate that you're dragging). After you click OK in the Custom Sizing Options dialog box, the custom magnification is shown in the Display window along with any warnings about possible problems with selecting that magnification. Click Apply in the Display window to apply the selected magnification.

1

Working in the Backstage view

Commands related to managing Outlook and Outlook accounts are located in the Backstage view, which you display by clicking the File tab at the left end of the ribbon.

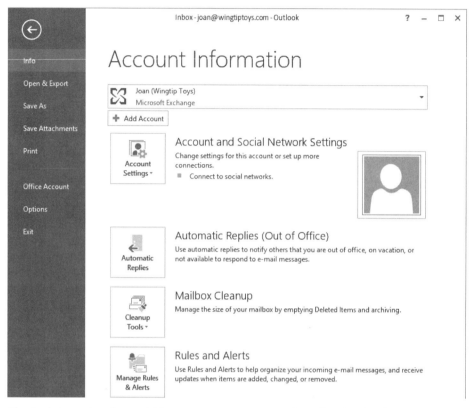

The Backstage view, from which you can manage accounts and customize the program.

TIP The contents of the Backstage view when opened from the program window are identical regardless of which module you're working in. However, the Automatic Replies button is available only for Exchange accounts.

Commands available in the Backstage view are organized on pages, which you display by clicking the page tabs in the colored left pane. The Backstage view of Outlook 2013 includes the following pages:

- **Info** Manage account settings, automatic replies, mailbox size, rules, and alerts.
- **Open & Export** Open an external calendar file, Outlook data file, or other Outlook user's folder in Outlook; import and export files, settings, and RSS feeds.

- **Save/Save As** Save the active or selected item as a file to a local, network, or Internet location.

- **Save Attachments** Save attachments to a local, network, or Internet location. (Available only when the active or selected item has attachments.)

- **Print** Select a printer, set print options, preview the effect of the applied options, and print module content or selected items.

- **Office Account** Access information about your Outlook or Office installation, manage product activation, product keys, user settings, and connected services.

The Backstage view also includes a link to the Outlook Options window, from which you can manage program settings, and links to close the active item or exit the program.

SEE ALSO For information about managing program settings, see "Configuring Office and Outlook options" in Chapter 11, "Customize Outlook."

You redisplay the program or item and the ribbon by clicking the Back arrow located above the page tabs or the Exit command at the bottom of the left pane.

Getting help with Outlook 2013

Whenever you have a question about Outlook 2013 that isn't answered in this book, your first recourse is the Outlook Help system. This system is a combination of articles, videos, and training tools available from the Office website for reference when you are online, and basic information stored on your computer for reference when you are offline.

You can find Help resources in the following ways:

- To find out about an item on the screen, you can point to the item to display a ScreenTip. For example, to display a ScreenTip for a button, point to the button without clicking it. The ScreenTip gives the button's name, the associated keyboard shortcut if there is one, and unless you specify otherwise, a description of what the button does when you click it.

- In the Outlook program window, you can click the Microsoft Outlook Help button (a question mark) near the right end of the title bar to open the Outlook Help window.

- In a dialog box, you can click the Help button near the right end of the dialog box title bar to open the Outlook Help window and display any available topics related to the functions of that dialog box.

In this exercise, you'll search for information by using Outlook Help.

SET UP You don't need any practice files to complete this exercise. With Outlook running, follow the steps.

1   Near the right end of the title bar, click the **Microsoft Outlook Help** button to open the **Outlook Help** window.

KEYBOARD SHORTCUT Press F1 to display the Outlook Help window.

TIP To switch between online and offline reference content, click the arrow to the right of Outlook Help and then click Outlook Help From Office.com or Outlook Help From Your Computer. You can print the information shown in the Help window by clicking the Print button on the toolbar to the left of the search box. You can change the font size of the topic by clicking the Use Large Text button on the toolbar.

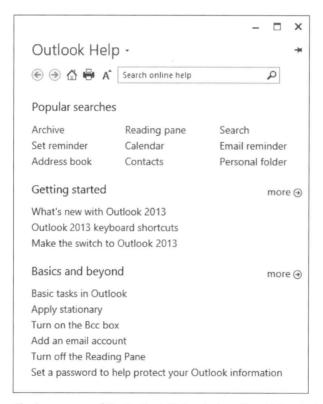

The home page of the Outlook Help window. Your Help window might look different from this one because the material on the Office website is regularly updated.

2   At the top of the **Outlook Help** window, in the search box, enter *printing* and then
     click the **Search** button (the magnifying glass) to display a list of topics related to
     printing Outlook items.

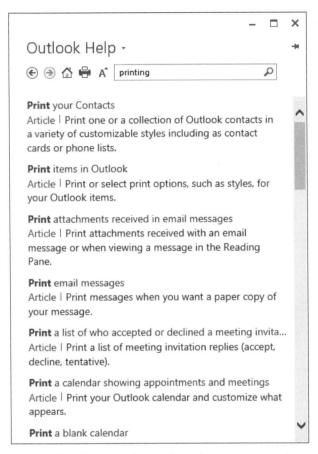

A typical list of Help topic search results.

3   Click the **Print your Contacts** link to display the corresponding article. Then scroll
     through the article and note the types of information it contains.

     TIP When section links appear in an article, you can click a link to move directly to
     that section of the article. You can click the Top Of Page link at the end of an article
     to return to the beginning. When Show All appears at the beginning of a Help topic,
     you can click it to display any hidden auxiliary information available in the topic, and
     then click Hide All to hide the information.

In the **Print** dialog box, you can also customize print styles or create your own unique styles with fonts and layouts that you design.

What do you want to do?

⇩ Print one contact
⇩ Print multiple contacts
⇩ Print all contacts

————— Section links

Print one contact

1. Click **People**.

    Mail Calendar People Tasks ⋯

2. In the Folder Pane, under **My Contacts**, click the contacts folder that contains the contact that you want to print.

————— Link to related information

3. Double-click the contact to open it.

4. Click the **File** tab.

5. Click **Print**.

6. Do one of the following:

A typical Help article.

4   Display related information by clicking any link identified by colored text.

5   In the **Search** box, enter services, and then press the **Enter** key to display topics related to the search term.

6   In the results list, click **Connect services to Office 2013** to display that topic.

7   At the left end of the toolbar, click the **Back** button to return to the topics you previously displayed.

❌ CLEAN UP Close the Outlook Help window when you finish exploring.

Key points

- You can configure Outlook to connect to Exchange, Exchange ActiveSync, POP, and IMAP accounts.

- You can configure multiple email accounts within one Outlook profile.

- The Add Account wizard can connect to many email accounts automatically. You need to provide only your email address and account password.

- You can manually configure account connection settings or additional server settings such as the time to retain Internet account email messages.

- Outlook organizes different types of information in modules.

- The Outlook user interface provides module-specific and item-specific command structures in the familiar ribbon interface.

- The Outlook Help window provides access to current information and training materials for many aspects of the program.

1

Chapter at a glance

Mail

Work in the Mail module,
page 45

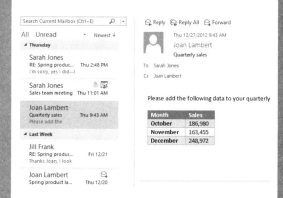

Calendar

Work in the Calendar module,
page 65

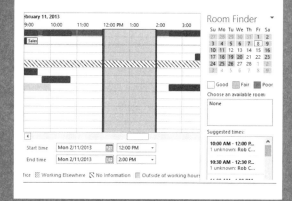

People

Work in the People module,
page 73

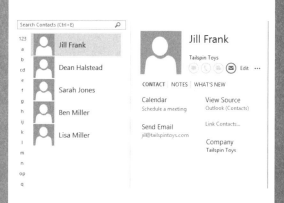

Tasks

Work in the Tasks module,
page 81

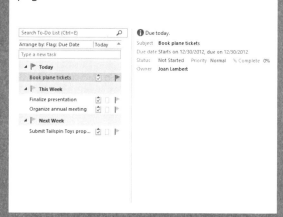

Explore Outlook 2013

2

IN THIS CHAPTER, YOU WILL LEARN HOW TO

- Work in the Outlook program window.

- Work in the Mail module.

- Work in the Calendar module.

- Work in the People module.

- Work in the Tasks module.

The Microsoft Outlook 2013 user interface includes many features and tools to help you easily store, find, and display information. Outlook functionality is divided among several modules that are specific to the content you work with in them, including Mail, Calendar, People, and Tasks. You display and work with one module at a time in the program window. The program window elements of each module present content-specific functionality.

The program window ribbon in each Outlook module displays commands specific to working with the Outlook items created and stored in that module. Similarly, the ribbon in each type of Outlook item window has a unique tab that displays commands specific to creating that type of item.

In this chapter, you'll first learn about the features and tools available in the Outlook program window. Then, you'll explore item window features in message windows, calendar item windows, contact record windows, and task windows.

PRACTICE FILES You don't need any practice files to complete the exercises in this chapter.

Working in the Outlook program window

The first time you start Outlook, the program window displays the contents of the Mail module in Reading view, which hides or minimizes many of the tools you can use to manage your messages and other Outlook items. (The other available program window layout is Normal view.) When you subsequently start Outlook, the program window displays the view and arrangement of the Mail module that was active when you closed the program.

TIP In Outlook, the named views control the way the program window is laid out rather than the way actual content is displayed. After choosing a view, you can display and hide program elements, and also control the way Outlook displays information in the content area, by using commands on the View tab.

Any modifications you make to the display of elements in the Outlook program window are visible in Normal view. You can switch between these standard views by clicking the buttons on the View Shortcuts toolbar near the right end of the status bar.

TIP In addition to the two program window layout views, each module has standard content area view options. For information about the available views, see the individual module sections later in this chapter.

Program window elements

You can individually control the display, and in some cases the location, of program window elements from the View tab. In addition to the title bar, ribbon, and status bar that are common to all Microsoft Office programs, the Outlook program window includes four areas in which you work with Outlook items.

- **Folder Pane** This collapsible pane appears on the left side of the Outlook program window in every module. Its contents change depending on the module you're viewing—it might display links to email folders, Microsoft SharePoint lists and libraries, external content, or view options. By default, the Folder Pane is minimized to display only favorite folders. The Folder Pane setting (Normal or Minimized) remains the same as you switch among modules.

  When the compact Navigation Bar is displayed, it is incorporated into the Folder Pane and displayed vertically when the Folder Pane is minimized or horizontally when the Folder Pane is open.

  SEE ALSO For more information, see "Navigation Bar" later in this section.

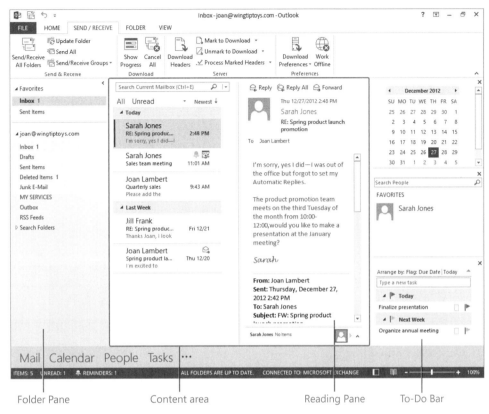

In the Mail module, the Outlook program window displays the message list and the Reading Pane.

- **Content area** The content area is the part of the program window bordered on the left by the Folder Pane and on the right by the To-Do Bar, when the To-Do Bar is displayed, or by the right side of the program window when it is not displayed. The content area displays the content of the selected module—your message list, calendar, contact records, or tasks—and can also host the Reading Pane.

- **Reading Pane** This optional pane can be displayed vertically or horizontally within the content area. Within the Reading Pane, you can preview and work with the content of a selected item, or display a full-featured preview of a file that is attached to an Outlook item (including Microsoft Word documents, Microsoft Excel worksheets, Microsoft PowerPoint presentations, and PDF files). The Reading Pane can also host the People Pane.

The Reading Pane can be displayed in any Outlook module but is displayed by default only in the Mail and Tasks modules.

SEE ALSO For information about working with the Reading Pane, see "Viewing messages and message attachments" in Chapter 3, "Send and receive email messages."

- **To-Do Bar** This optional pane displays the Calendar peek, People peek, and Tasks peek, or any combination of these that you choose. In Outlook 2013, the To-Do Bar can be either open or closed, but not minimized as it could be in previous versions of Outlook.

  The To-Do Bar can be displayed in any Outlook module, but is not displayed by default.

  SEE ALSO For information about working with tasks on the To-Do Bar, see "Displaying different views of tasks" in Chapter 6, "Track tasks."

TIP If you find that the default Outlook window layout isn't perfectly suited for the way you work, or you'd just like to try a different layout, there are many ways in which you can personalize the appearance and functionality of Outlook. For more information, see "Personalizing the Outlook program window" in Chapter 11, "Customize Outlook."

Navigation Bar

The Navigation Bar, which is new in Outlook 2013, is located near the lower-left corner of the program window, above the status bar. In previous versions of Outlook, the navigation controls were incorporated into the Folder Pane (formerly called the Navigation Pane). In Outlook 2013, the navigation controls are presented on the Navigation Bar, which can appear as a compact vertical or horizontal bar that displays only module icons, or as a larger horizontal bar with text labels.

The standard Navigation Bar is separate from the Folder Pane and does not change orientation. The compact Navigation Bar is incorporated into the Folder Pane and its orientation depends on whether the Folder Pane is minimized or expanded. To display more or fewer buttons on the vertical compact Navigation Bar, drag its top border up or down up. To display more or fewer buttons on the horizontal compact Navigation Bar, change the width of the Folder Pane.

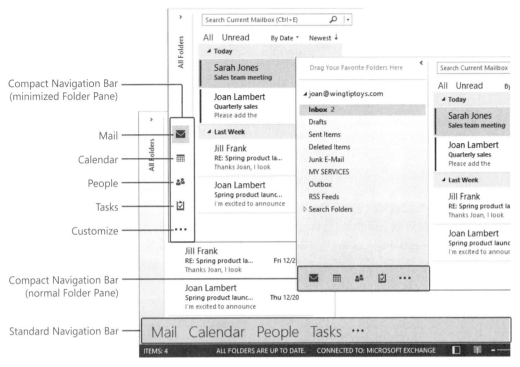

Compact Navigation Bar
(minimized Folder Pane)

Mail

Calendar

People

Tasks

Customize

Compact Navigation Bar
(normal Folder Pane)

Standard Navigation Bar

The appearances and elements of the Navigation Bar.

You can change the appearance of the Navigation Bar and the number and order of the modules that are displayed on it from the Navigation Options dialog box, which you access by clicking the ellipsis at the end of the Navigation Bar and then clicking Navigation Options.

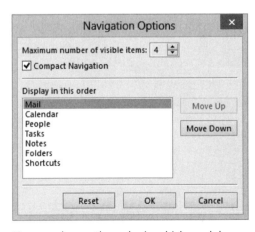

You can change the order in which modules appear on the Navigation Bar.

You can display any module by clicking the corresponding link or button on the Navigation Bar. If a module link or button doesn't appear on the Navigation Bar, click the ellipsis at the right end of the Navigation Bar, and then click the module name to display it.

KEYBOARD SHORTCUT Hold down the Ctrl key and then press 1 for Mail, 2 for Calendar, 3 for Contacts, 4 for Tasks, 5 for Notes, 6 for Folders, 7 for Shortcuts, or 8 for Journal to switch between modules. For more information about keyboard shortcuts, see "Keyboard shortcuts" at the end of this book.

You can "peek" at the current content of the Calendar, People, or Tasks module by pointing to the module link or button. The Calendar peek displays this month's Date Navigator and today's appointments, the People peek displays the contacts you've saved as favorites and a search box, and the Tasks peek displays your upcoming tasks and a new task entry box. Clicking the Dock The Peek button in the upper-right corner of any peek pane pins the peek to the To-Do Bar (and displays the To-Do Bar in the program window, if it wasn't already open).

Peeks display information that in previous versions of Outlook was shown only on the To-Do Bar.

Working in the Mail module

The Mail module is displayed by default when you start Outlook or when you click the Mail link or button on the Navigation Bar. By default, the Mail module displays the Folder Pane, Navigation Bar, message list, and Reading Pane. The appearance of the Folder Pane and Navigation Bar depends on the settings that you select. For the purposes of this topic, let's assume that the Folder Pane is open so that its content is visible, and the Navigation Bar is in its default compact state.

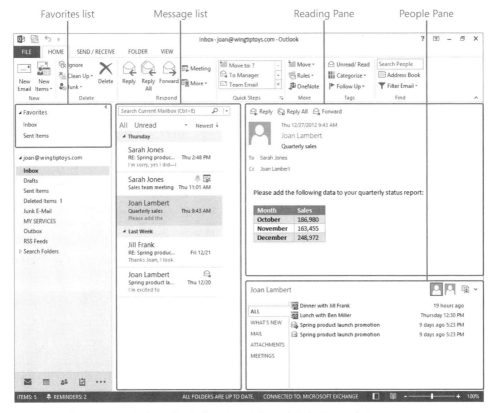

The Outlook program window, displaying the Mail module in Normal view.

Folder Pane content

In the Mail module, the Folder Pane displays the Favorites list and the folder structure of your mailbox (or mailboxes, if you have set up multiple email accounts). The folders you add to your Favorites list are displayed at the top of the Folder Pane when it is open, and on the minimized Folder Pane when it is minimized.

Until you add folders to your Favorites list, it displays the message Drag Your Favorite Folders Here. You can add a folder to the Favorites list by using any of these methods:

- Drag the folder to the Favorites list.

- Right-click the folder, and then click Show In Favorites.

- Click the folder, and then on the Folder tab, in the Favorites group, click the Show In Favorites button.

TIP If you have Outlook configured to connect to multiple email accounts, you might find it convenient and efficient to add the Inbox folders of each account to the Favorites list, so you can easily access all your messages in one location.

When you connect to any type of email account, these eight folders are available in each mailbox:

- **Inbox** By default, Outlook delivers new messages to this folder.

- **Drafts** Outlook stores temporary copies of in-progress messages in this folder, which is created the first time you save a message without sending it. Outlook might also create a draft for you while you work, if you don't send the message immediately.

  SEE ALSO For information about creating and working with message drafts, see "Creating and sending messages" in Chapter 3, "Send and receive email messages."

- **Sent Items** When you send a message, Outlook stores a copy of it in this folder. You can change this setting if you would prefer to store sent messages elsewhere or if you prefer to not store sent messages, but the safest option is to stick to this default setting.

- **Deleted Items** Outlook items that you delete from other folders are held in this folder. They are not deleted permanently until you empty the folder.

  SEE ALSO For information about deleting and restoring items, see the sidebar "Deleting messages" in Chapter 7, "Organize your Inbox."

- **Junk E-Mail** Outlook delivers messages blocked by the spam filter to this folder.

- **Outbox** Outlook holds outgoing messages in this folder while establishing a connection to your mail server.

- **RSS Feeds** Website information feeds you subscribe to are available from this folder. When you first start Outlook, you might find information feeds recommended by Microsoft here.

- **Search Folders** These folders contain up-to-date results of searches you've conducted for messages that match specific search criteria.

Other folders might be installed by your email service provider.

In previous versions of Outlook, you could display additional folders by clicking the Folders button at the bottom of what was then called the Navigation Pane. In Outlook 2013, you can display the Folder List by clicking the ellipsis at the end of the Navigation Bar and then clicking Folders (or by increasing the number of visible items on the Navigation Bar) so that the Folders button is visible, and then clicking the Folders button). The Folder List includes these additional folders for Exchange account mailboxes:

- **Calendar** Contains the contents of the Outlook Calendar module.

- **Contacts** Contains the contents of the Outlook People module.

- **Journal** Contains the contents of the Outlook Journal module.

- **Notes** Contains the contents of the Outlook Notes module.

- **Suggested Contacts** If you upgraded to Outlook 2013 from Outlook 2010, and already had this folder, which was created by the previous version of Outlook, the folder migrates to the new version. It contains a list of email addresses with which you've recently corresponded that are not in your primary address book.

- **Sync Issues** Contains a list of conflicts and communication failures on your mail server or in your mailbox.

- **Tasks** Contains the contents of the Outlook Tasks module.

- **User-created folders** Any calendar, contact, or task folders you create are visible in the Folder List displayed in the Folder Pane when you click Folders on the Navigation Bar.

- **Public Folders** If your organization uses Exchange public folders, a link to these appears at the same level as your mailbox (rather than within it).

If you connect or subscribe to any SharePoint lists or Internet calendars, links to these groups appear at the same level as your mailbox.

KEYBOARD SHORTCUT Press Ctrl+6 to display the Folder List in the Folder Pane.

Content area views

You can control the layout of the Mail module by displaying either Normal view or Reading view. As previously mentioned, Reading view minimizes the Folder Pane on the left and closes the To-Do Bar, if you have opened it. Reading view does not affect the display of the ribbon or of the People Pane.

In addition to these large-scale view controls, you can control the appearance of content in the content area by using the commands in the Current View and Arrangement groups on the View tab.

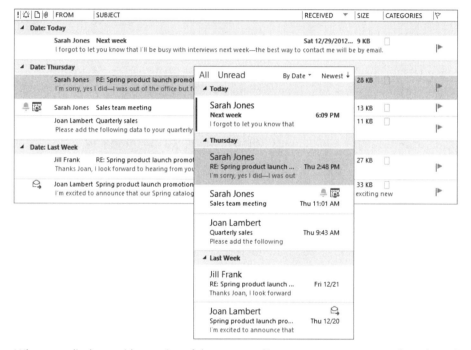

When you display a wider version of the message list, you can sort messages by column headers.

Three content area view options are available from the Change View list in the Current View group on the View tab:

- **Compact** Displays three rows of information in the message list, and opens the Reading Pane. The first row includes the name of the message sender followed by icons that represent message properties such as category, follow-up flag, importance, response status, reminder, and item type for items other than messages (such as meeting invitations). The second row contains the message subject and date or time of receipt. The third row contains a preview of the message content. A blue vertical bar in the left margin and bold blue second row indicate an unread message. This is the default view.

TIP You can change the number of rows of previewed content by selecting Off, 1 Line, 2 Lines, or 3 Lines from the Message Preview list on the View tab.

- **Single** Displays two rows of information in the message list, and maintains the Reading Pane. The first row includes icons that represent message properties, the message sender's name, the message subject, and the date or time of receipt.

- **Preview** Displays two rows of information in the message list, and closes the Reading Pane.

Regardless of the view you choose, when you point to an item in the message list, it displays active icons such as a follow-up flag and Delete button. The default Compact view of the message list is designed to provide the maximum amount of interaction with content, with the least number of clicks. As you use Outlook, experiment with the view options to find the one that works the best for you.

The ribbon

The ribbon in the Mail module includes the File tab and the four tabs that appear in all modules. The tab content differs in each module. The Mail module includes the following tabs:

- **Home** Includes commands you need for creating and managing email messages (but not message content). For an Internet email account, this tab also includes a Send/ Receive group.

The Home tab of the Mail module ribbon.

- **Send/Receive** Includes commands for synchronizing data in Outlook with data on your mail server. You can control how Outlook sends and receives messages, whether Outlook automatically downloads full messages or only message headers, and manual download processes. You can also choose to disconnect Outlook from the active

Internet connection if you want to work offline; for example, to stop sending and receiving messages while connected to the Internet.

The Send/Receive tab of the Mail module ribbon.

TIP The Work Offline button is available for Internet accounts that download content to your computer, and for Exchange accounts when you specify that Outlook should use Cached Exchange Mode for the account connection.

- **Folder** Includes commands for creating and managing folders in which you can store messages, calendar items, contact records, notes, tasks, and other Outlook items, in addition to Search Folders in which you can display up-to-date collections of messages that meet specific criteria. You can manage the contents of the folder and recover inadvertently deleted items; add a folder to the Favorites list; view messages that have been archived to an Exchange server; and control archive settings, folder access permissions, and the folder properties.

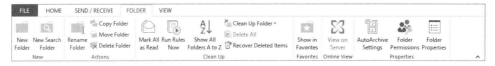

The Folder tab of the Mail module ribbon.

- **View** Includes commands for changing the way items are displayed in the content area; displaying, hiding, or changing the location of program window panes; and opening or closing secondary program windows.

The View tab of the Mail module ribbon.

Message windows

Outlook displays email messages (in addition to meeting requests and task assignments received from other Outlook users) in the Mail module. When you start Outlook, it displays the Inbox of your default email account. When you create a new message or open an existing message, it opens in a separate message window. The message window has its own ribbon and Quick Access Toolbar, separate from those in the Outlook program window. You can insert and format outgoing message content, modify the settings of outgoing messages, and take action with received messages by using the commands on the message window ribbon.

In Outlook 2013, when you respond to an existing message and the Reading Pane is open, the response message is drafted within the Reading Pane, and a Message tool tab that contains a limited selection of commands appears on the Mail module ribbon. You can draft and send the response from the Reading Pane, or if you'd prefer to work with it in a separate window with a full set of commands, you can do so by clicking the Pop Out button in the message draft.

SEE ALSO For information about changing the way Outlook handles new and original messages when you reply to or forward a message, see "Configuring Office and Outlook options" in Chapter 11, "Customize Outlook."

The layout of all message windows is similar. However, depending on whether you're working in a new message composition window or a message reading window, the content of the message window and the commands on the message window ribbon differ.

Message composition windows

When you're composing an original message, you work in a message composition window that is separate from the Outlook program window.

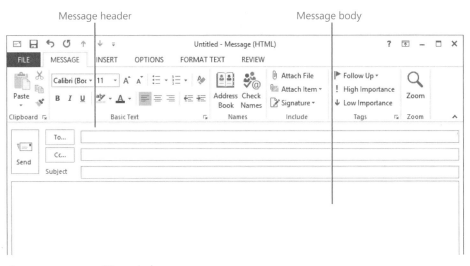

A message composition window.

The message composition window interface includes the following elements:

■ **Quick Access Toolbar** Provides access to the window-management menu (represented by a New Message icon) and the Save, Undo, Redo/Repeat, Previous Item, and Next Item buttons. The Save command is available in the Backstage view, but the other commands are not available either in the Backstage view or on the ribbon; they are available only from the Quick Access Toolbar.

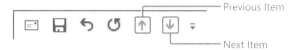

The Previous Item and Next Item buttons on the Quick Access Toolbar are inactive in a message composition window; they're active in a message reading window.

TIP You can add commands to the Quick Access Toolbar so that they are available regardless of which tab is currently active in the message composition window. Adding a command to the Quick Access Toolbar in a message composition window does not add it to the Quick Access Toolbar of any other Outlook item window (including the message reading window) or any other Office 2013 program window.

■ **Ribbon** Includes the File tab (your link to the Backstage view) and the Message, Insert, Options, Format Text, and Review tabs.

■ **Message header** Includes the To and Cc address fields and the Subject field, by default. If you configure Outlook to connect to multiple accounts, a From field appears above the To field. You can click the From button to select the account from which you want to send the message. You can also display the Bcc field in the message header by clicking that button in the Show Fields group on the Options tab.

SEE ALSO For information about the From field, see the sidebar "Managing multiple accounts" in Chapter 3, "Send and receive email messages."

■ **Message body** The area in which you create message content. The message body can include text, images, tables, charts, screen clippings, hyperlinks, and other types of content. An email message created in Outlook 2013 can include virtually any element that you can insert into a standard electronic document, such as a Word document.

■ **People Pane** Appears after you enter at least one message recipient; displays information about the intended message recipients. Clicking a recipient's icon displays information about previous communications with that person.

SEE ALSO For more information about the Bcc field, message header, message body, and People Pane, see "Creating and sending messages" in Chapter 3, "Send and receive email messages."

When opened from a message composition window, the Backstage view includes commands related to message management tasks, such as saving message and message attachments and closing, restricting permissions to, moving, resending, recalling, and printing messages.

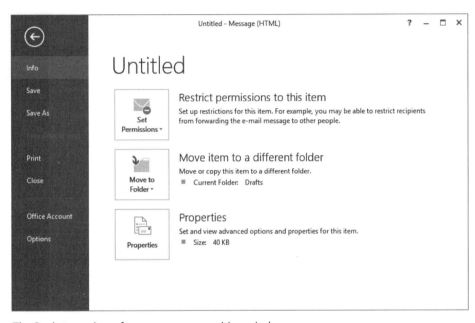

The Backstage view of a message composition window.

Commands on the ribbon of a message composition window are organized on five tabs:

- **Message** Includes a selection of the commands you are most likely to use when creating a new message, some of which are also available on other ribbon tabs. Specific to this tab are commands for inserting and validating email addresses, marking an outgoing message for follow-up, indicating the importance of an outgoing message to the message recipient, and magnifying the message content.

The Message tab of the message composition window ribbon.

- **Insert** Includes commands that are standard to all item-creation windows, for attaching items such as files and contact cards to the message, and for inserting specialized content such as email signatures, tables, images, links, and artistic text into the message body. In addition to the standard commands, the Insert Calendar command is available in the Include group on the Insert tab of the message composition window ribbon.

The Insert tab of the message composition window ribbon.

- **Options** Includes commands that are specific to the message composition window, for applying thematic formatting to message content, displaying less-frequently used address fields in the message header, and setting specialized message delivery options.

The Options tab of the message composition window ribbon.

- **Format Text** Includes commands that are standard to all item-creation windows, for manipulating and formatting characters and paragraphs; applying and working with Quick Styles and style sets; and finding, replacing, and selecting text and objects within a text box. In addition to the standard commands, commands for changing the message format are available in the Format group on the Format Text tab of the message composition window ribbon.

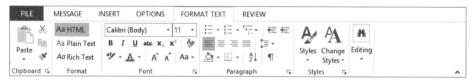

The Format Text tab of the message composition window ribbon.

SEE ALSO For information about formatting fonts, using styles, inserting various types of illustrations, setting permissions, and tracking messages, see Chapter 10, "Enhance message content."

- **Review** Includes commands that are standard to all item-creation windows, for working with the text in the message body, including checking spelling and grammar; researching word choices; tracking message content statistics (pages, words, characters, paragraphs, and lines); and translating content either directly or through an online service.

The Review tab of the message composition window ribbon.

TIP Depending on the programs you have installed on your computer, tabs and groups other than those described here might also appear on the ribbon.

Message reading windows

When you open a sent or received message in its own window rather than displaying it in the Reading Pane, you're working in a message reading window.

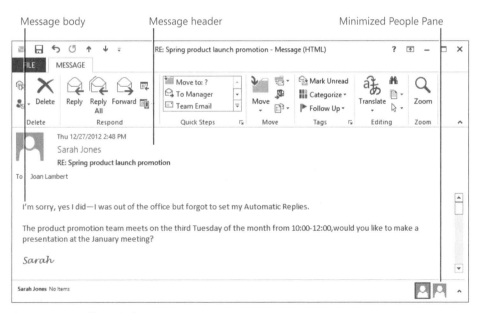

A message reading window.

The message reading window interface includes the following elements:

- **Quick Access Toolbar** Provides access to the window-management menu (represented by a Received Message icon) and the same commands as it does in the message composition window. The Previous Item and Next Item buttons are active.

- **Ribbon** Includes the File tab and a Message tab that contains a set of commands different from the commands on this tab in a message composition window. This tab includes commands for working with the active message, including deleting, responding to, moving, tagging, editing, and viewing it. The Message tab also includes the Quick Steps gallery of command combinations that you can use to accomplish multiple tasks with one click.

  SEE ALSO For information about Quick Steps, see "Managing messages by using Quick Steps" in Chapter 7, "Organize your Inbox" and "Creating and managing Quick Steps" in Chapter 12, "Manage email settings." For information about the elements of the ribbon in Outlook item windows, see "Working in the Calendar module," "Working in the People module," and "Working in the Tasks module," later in this chapter.

- **Message header** Displays the name and online status (if available) of the message sender and message recipients (those entered in the To and Cc boxes), along with the message subject and any message notifications, categories, or flags.

- **Message body** Displays the content of the message.

  TIP To edit message content—for example, to make notes to yourself about the message—click the Actions button in the Move group, and then click Edit Message. Make the changes you want, and then when you close the message, Outlook will prompt you to save your changes.

- **People Pane** Displays information about the message sender and the message recipients, including you.

When opened from a message reading window, the Backstage view includes the Set Permissions, Move To Folder, and Properties commands that are available from the message composition window, in addition to the commands related to recalling (available only if you are the message sender) and resending the message.

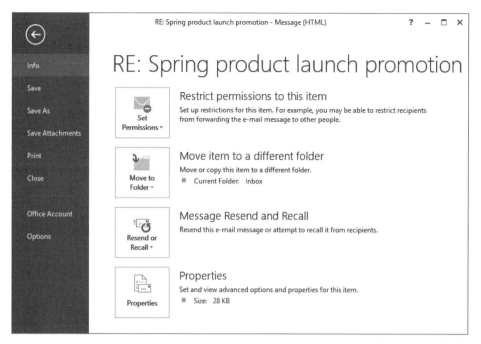

The Backstage view of a message reading window.

SEE ALSO For information about the Print commands and options, see "Printing messages" in Chapter 7, "Organize your Inbox." For information about moving Outlook items, see "Organizing messages in folders" in the same chapter. For information about setting advanced options and properties for a message, see "Changing message settings and delivery options" in Chapter 10, "Enhance message content." For information about restricting recipients from forwarding, copying, or printing messages you send, see "Increasing email security" in Chapter 12, "Manage email settings."

In this exercise, you'll take a tour of the window-management and content-management tools in a message composition window. Along the way, you'll work with commands on the ribbon, on the Quick Access Toolbar, and in the Backstage view.

➜ SET UP You don't need any practice files to complete this exercise. Display your Outlook Inbox, and then follow the steps.

1   On the **Home** tab, in the **New** group, click the **New Email** button to open an untitled message window with the cursor in the **To** box. Notice that the commands in the **Basic Text** group on the **Message** tab are inactive.

     KEYBOARD SHORTCUT Press Ctrl+Shift+M to create a message.

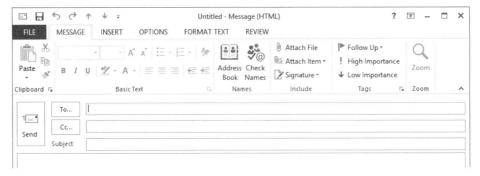

You can compose and send any standard email message by using only the commands available on the Message tab.

TIP Only the buttons for commands that can be performed on the currently selected message element are active.

2   Click to insert the cursor in the message body. Notice that additional commands on the ribbon become active.

TIP The Microsoft Office Clipboard is shared by the applications installed on your computer and might display content cut or copied from Outlook or from programs such as Word, Excel, or PowerPoint. For information about working with the Clipboard, refer to *Microsoft Word 2013 Step by Step* by Joan Lambert and Joyce Cox (Microsoft Press, 2013).

3   In the message body, enter Please respond to me as soon as possible by email, phone, or fax. Triple-click the inserted text to select the paragraph and display the **Mini Toolbar**.

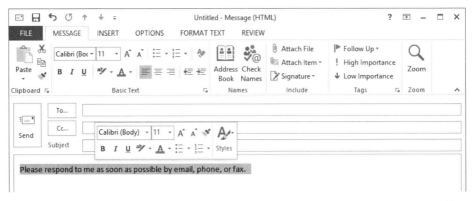

When you select content, the Mini Toolbar displays commands with which you can quickly format the selection or perform other actions depending on the type of content you select.

SEE ALSO For information about turning off the display of the Mini Toolbar, see "Configuring Office and Outlook options" in Chapter 11, "Customize Outlook."

4   On the **Mini Toolbar**, click the **Font** arrow, and then in the **Font** list, click **Arial Rounded MT Bold** to change the text to the selected font. (If the **Mini Toolbar** disappears before you can complete the step, use the commands in the **Basic Text** group on the **Message** tab.)

5   On the **Message** tab, in the **Basic Text** group, click the **Increase Font Size** button twice to increase the font size to **14** points, and then click the **Center** button to move the selected paragraph to the horizontal center of the message content pane.

KEYBOARD SHORTCUT Press Ctrl+> to increase the font size and Ctrl+E to center the paragraph.

6   Point to the other buttons in the **Basic Text** group, and note their functionality as described in the ScreenTips that appear. Then click the **Basic Text** dialog box launcher to open the **Font** dialog box.

The Font dialog box includes settings that aren't available from the Message tab.

7   On the **Font** page of the **Font** dialog box, in the **Effects** area, select the **Small caps** check box. Notice that the **Preview** area immediately reflects the change.

8   In the **Font** dialog box, click the **Advanced** tab. From the **Advanced** page, you can control character spacing and specific font characteristics.

The preview box demonstrates the effect of the currently selected font-formatting options.

9   In the **Character Spacing** area, in the **Scale** list, click **80%**.

10   In the lower-left corner of the dialog box, click the **Text Effects** button to open the **Format Text Effects** dialog box. On the **Text Fill & Outline** page, click the **Text Fill** and **Text Outline** headings to expand these sections. Notice the types of formatting you can apply from this page.

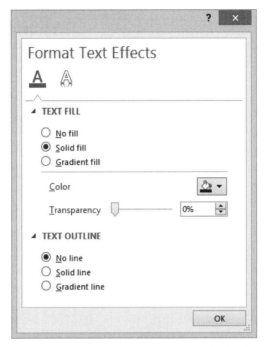

The Text Fill & Outline settings govern the basic appearance of the lettering.

11   In the **Text Fill** area, click the **Color** button, and then at the top of the **Theme Colors** palette, click the orange swatch (**Orange, Accent 2**).

12   At the top of the dialog box, click the **Text Effects** button (the button on the right) to display the **Text Effects** page, which contains the **Shadow**, **Reflection**, **Glow**, **Soft Edges**, and **3-D Format** settings. Click each of the headings to expand the sections and notice the many ways in which you can format the appearance of text within an email message.

    TIP You can't format the content of the message header fields.

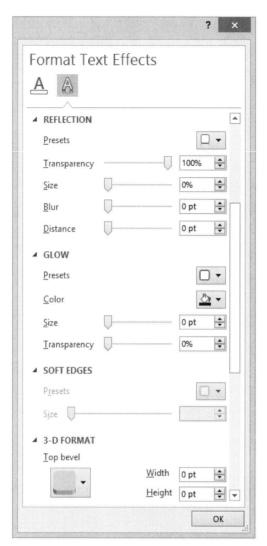

The Text Effects settings include many advanced options that add dimension to characters.

13   In the **Shadow** area, click the **Presets** button, and then in the **Presets** gallery, click the first shadow setting in the **Outer** section (**Offset Diagonal Bottom Right**). Notice that the individual **Shadow** settings change to reflect the preset shadow.

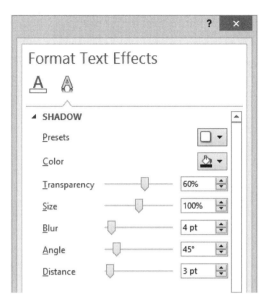

Each aspect of the shadow effect can be individually modified.

14   Click the **Color** button, and in the **Standard Colors** palette, click the **Red** swatch. Then click **OK** in the **Format Text Effects** dialog box, and again in the **Font** dialog box to change the message text to reflect your selected text formatting options.

15   In the message body, click away from the selected text to see the results of your formatting changes.

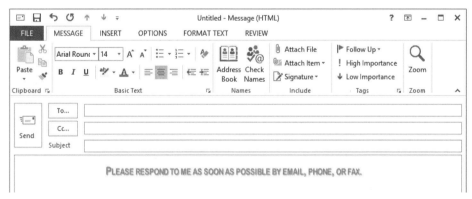

You can further modify the look of the selected text by using the options in the Basic Text group.

16   In the message window, explore the commands on the **Insert**, **Options**, **Format Text**, and **Review** tabs. Notice that many of the commands available on these tabs are also available from the **Message** tab. We work with these commands later in this chapter and throughout this book.

17   At the right end of the ribbon, click the **Collapse the Ribbon** button to hide the groups so that only the tabs are visible.

      KEYBOARD SHORTCUT   Press Ctrl+F1 to collapse or display the ribbon.

18   On the **Quick Access Toolbar**, click the **Undo** button to revert the formatting you applied from the **Text Effects** dialog box.

      KEYBOARD SHORTCUT   Press Ctrl+Z to undo the most recent change.

19   On the collapsed ribbon, click the **Format Text** tab, and then in the **Font** group, click the **Clear All Formatting** button to revert the text to its original font and size.

      TIP   Clicking a tab on the minimized ribbon temporarily expands it so that you can perform a single command. You can collapse the ribbon without performing an action by clicking anywhere away from it or by pressing Esc. Double-clicking a tab or clicking the Expand The Ribbon button restores the ribbon to its maximized state.

20   Click the **File** tab to display the **Info** page of the **Backstage** view. Then in the left pane, click **Close**.

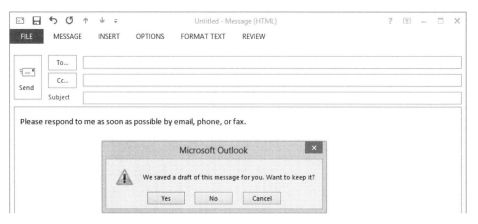

Outlook prompts you to save or discard the draft message.

      SEE ALSO   For information about message drafts, see "Creating and sending messages" in Chapter 3, "Send and receive email messages."

21   In the **Microsoft Outlook** message box, click **No** to close the message window.

✖ CLEAN UP   Open a new message window, click the Ribbon Display Options button to the right end of the title bar, click Show Tabs And Commands, and then close the message window to reset the ribbon before continuing to the next exercise.

Working in the Calendar module

You can display the Calendar module by clicking the Calendar link or button on the Navigation Bar.

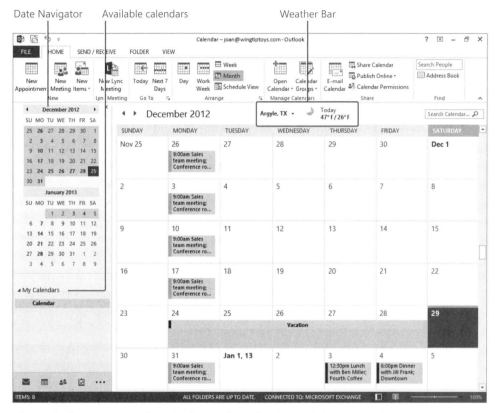

Date Navigator · Available calendars · Weather Bar

The Outlook program window, displaying the Calendar module in Normal view.

Calendar module content

As with the other Outlook modules, the Calendar module has a Reading view, which displays only the content area and the minimized Folder Pane, and Normal view, which displays any elements that you choose.

In the Calendar module, the Folder Pane displays the Date Navigator and a list of calendars that you can use. The list might include only the default Outlook Calendar, or it might include custom calendars you create, calendars that are shared with you by other Outlook users, and Internet Calendars or SharePoint Calendars that you connect to.

The content area displays your calendar for a period of time that you select. The default time period is one month; however, you will frequently find it more useful to display only a day or a week at a time, to have a closer look at your activities for those time periods. You can display a single day, your specified work week, a seven-day period, a month, or a schedule view that shows a close-up view of a six-hour time period.

You can display the content for each time period in Calendar view, Preview view, List view, and Active view. These options are available from the Change View list in the Current View group on the View tab.

The ribbon in the Calendar module includes the File tab and the four standard module tabs:

- **Home** Includes the commands you need for creating calendar items, displaying specific views of the calendar, managing other calendars and calendar groups, and sharing the calendar with other people.

The Home tab of the Calendar module ribbon.

TIP The commands in the Lync Meeting group function only if Microsoft Lync is part of your organization's collaboration environment. Lync provides the capability not only to commence real-time text, audio, video, and collaboration sessions with other people in your organization, but also to invite internal and external attendees to online meetings.

- **Send/Receive** Includes commands for synchronizing Outlook with your email accounts. This set of commands is common to the Send/Receive tab in all modules.

The Send/Receive tab of the Calendar module ribbon.

- **Folder** Includes commands for creating and working with calendars. From this tab, you can create a new calendar, manipulate an existing calendar, share a calendar with other Outlook users and specify what each user can do with the shared calendar, open a calendar that you're not currently connected to, and control the behind-the-scenes behavior of a calendar.

The Folder tab of the Calendar module ribbon.

TIP From a structural point of view, a calendar is simply a folder that contains calendar items. By virtue of specifying the Calendar type of folder, it is subject to the display options allocated to calendars and is managed with other calendars. For information about creating calendars, see "Working with multiple calendars" in Chapter 8, "Manage your calendar."

- **View** Includes commands for viewing and arranging calendar items, changing the layout and appearance of the Calendar module, displaying missed reminders, opening multiple calendars in separate windows, and closing open calendar item windows.

The View tab of the Calendar module ribbon.

SEE ALSO For information about calendar views, see "Displaying different views of a calendar" in Chapter 5, "Manage scheduling." For information about changing default settings for the Calendar module, see "Configuring Office and Outlook options" in Chapter 11, "Customize Outlook."

Calendar item windows

We refer to a window in which you create or respond to an appointment as an appointment window, to a meeting as a meeting window, and to an event as an event window; collectively, we refer to these windows as *calendar item windows*. Like the message windows, the calendar item windows contain their own commands arranged on the ribbon.

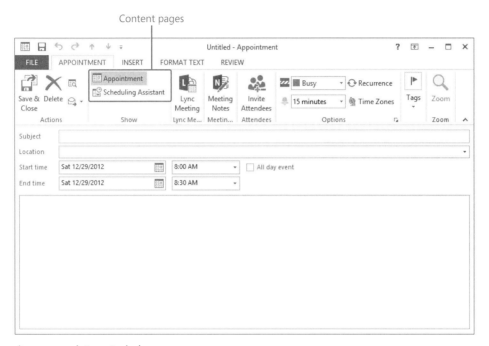

A new appointment window.

Each calendar item window includes two pages:

- **Appointment** On this page, you can perform all the necessary tasks related to creating and managing the item content.

- **Scheduling/Scheduling Assistant** On this page, you can view the schedules of other people in your organization who you want to invite to a meeting or event.

   TIP The name of this page varies depending on the type of account for which you're creating the calendar item.

The calendar item window interface includes the Quick Access Toolbar, the ribbon, and the content area that displays the appointment, message, or event information.

When opened from a calendar item window, the Backstage view includes commands related to managing calendar items, such as saving items and attachments and closing, moving, and printing items.

The Backstage view of an appointment window.

Commands on the ribbon of a calendar item window are organized on four tabs: a main tab specific to the type of calendar item and the Insert, Format Text, and Review tabs. The latter three tabs are identical to those of other item windows.

The commands you use to create and manage calendar items are available on the main tab. The tab name changes (Appointment, Meeting, or Event) depending on the type of item you're creating and whether you invite other people to attend. Regardless of the tab name, commands are organized on the tab in six groups: Actions, Show, Attendees, Options, Tags, and Zoom. You can create a calendar item by using only the commands available on this tab. The tab also includes groups for Lync and Microsoft OneNote if these programs are installed on your computer; you can use the commands in these groups to facilitate the relationship between Outlook calendar items and that program.

TIP The Insert, Format Text, and Review tabs of the calendar item windows contain the same commands as they do in other types of item windows.

In this exercise, you'll take a tour of the calendar item window elements that differ from the message windows discussed earlier in this chapter. You'll also learn about the differences between the types of calendar items.

SET UP You don't need any practice files to complete this exercise; just follow the steps.

1   On the **Navigation Bar**, click the **Calendar** button to open the **Calendar** module and display the calendar associated with your default email account in the **Calendar** pane.

KEYBOARD SHORTCUT Press Ctrl+2 to display the Calendar module.

TIP If you want to work in two modules at the same time, you can open a module in a second instance of Outlook by right-clicking the module link or button on the Navigation Bar and then clicking Open In New Window.

2   On the **Home** tab, in the **New** group, click the **New Appointment** button to open an untitled appointment window.

KEYBOARD SHORTCUT Press Ctrl+Shift+A to create an appointment from any Outlook module.

3   On the **Appointment** tab, in the **Attendees** group, click the **Invite Attendees** button to change the appointment window to a meeting window and display the **Room Finder** pane.

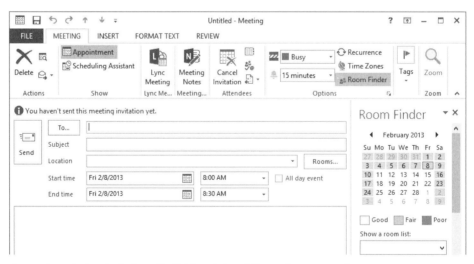

A meeting window includes a To field and the ability to locate meeting resources.

TIP If the Room Finder pane doesn't open automatically, click the Room Finder button in the Options group on the Meeting tab to display it.

The meeting request header includes a To field in addition to the Subject and Location fields present in the Appointment and Event windows. You can invite attendees by entering them in the To field, by clicking the To button and selecting them from an address list, or by entering them in the All Attendees list on the Scheduling Assistant page.

4   Enter one or more contact names or email addresses in the **To** box. Then on the **Meeting** tab, in the **Show** group, click the **Scheduling** or **Scheduling Assistant** button to display information about the available time of the requested meeting attendees in the meeting window.

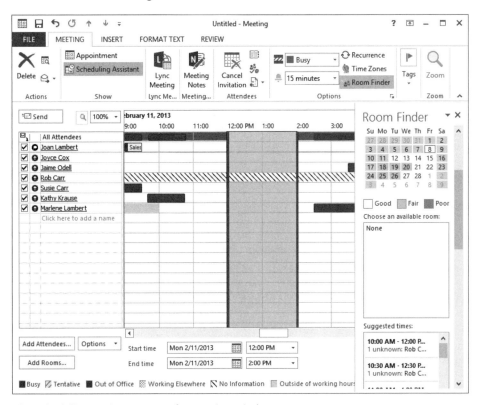

The Scheduling Assistant page of a meeting window.

5   Familiarize yourself with the information on the **Scheduling Assistant** page. Then close the meeting window without saving the meeting.

6   On the **Home** tab of the **Calendar** module, in the **New** group, click **New Items**, and then click **All Day Event** to open an untitled event window.

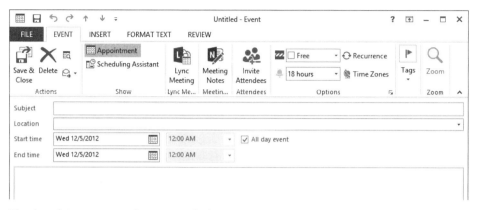

The Appointment page of an event window.

TIP You can also open an Event window by selecting the All Day Event check box in the header of an appointment window.

The Event tab contents are nearly identical to the Appointment tab contents—the only change is that on the Event tab, in the Options group, your time is shown as Free by default rather than Busy, and the reminder is set to display 18 hours prior to the event rather than 15 minutes.

TIP You can invite people to an event in the same way you do to a meeting, by clicking the Invite Attendees button from within an event window.

7   In the **Start time** area, clear the **All day event** check box to change the event to an appointment.

8   On the **Appointment** tab, in the **Options** group, click the **Time Zones** button to display a new field containing the time zone for each of the start and end times. With this useful feature, you can schedule an appointment that crosses time zones—for example, a flight from New York to London.

SEE ALSO For more information about displaying more than one time zone in your calendar, see "Configuring time zones" in Chapter 8, "Manage your calendar."

✖ CLEAN UP Click the Time Zones button to hide the time zone settings if you don't want to display them. Then close the appointment window without saving your changes.

Working in the People module

You can display the People module by clicking the People link or button on the Navigation Bar.

Contact index

The default view of the People module displays contact information in People cards.

TIP Clicking a letter or letter pairing on the contact index scrolls the Contacts pane to display contact records that begin with that letter. You can add a second contact index that displays the Arabic, Cyrillic, Greek, Thai, or Vietnamese alphabet by clicking the button at the bottom of the contact index and then clicking the language you want.

People module content

As with the other Outlook modules, the People module has a Reading view, which displays only the minimized Folder Pane and the content area, and Normal view, which displays any elements that you choose.

In the People module, the Folder Pane displays your available address books—the Contacts address book, any custom address books you create, address books shared with you by co-workers, and address books containing contacts from social networks that you connect to. The content area includes the contact list and Reading Pane.

In the People module, the content area displays the contact records saved in the currently selected address book. The default view of contact records in Outlook 2013 is a new format named People cards, but you can choose among several standard views, including business cards, text-only cards, and various lists.

SEE ALSO For more information, see "Displaying different views of contact records" in Chapter 4, "Store and access contact information."

The ribbon in the People module includes the File tab and the four standard module tabs:

- **Home** Includes the commands you need for creating, managing, and viewing contact records, and for initiating communication with contacts. You can select contacts for a mail-merge process, send contact information to OneNote, share contacts with other Outlook users, and tag contact records in ways that enable you to better locate or manage them.

The Home tab of the Contacts module ribbon.

- **Send/Receive** Identical to that in the Calendar and Tasks modules.

- **Folder** Provides the same functionality as it does in the Calendar and Tasks modules, but is specific to contact records.

- **View** Provides the same functionality as it does in the Mail and Tasks modules. The content of the Arrangement gallery is specific to contact records.

The View tab of the Contacts module ribbon.

TIP The Arrangement commands are available only when you display contact records in a list view.

Contact record windows

When you create a contact record or display the contact record for a person or group of people, it opens in a contact record window. The contact record window has its own ribbon and Quick Access Toolbar, separate from those in the Outlook program window and other types of item windows. You can insert, format, and work with information in a contact record or contact group record by using the commands on the contact record window ribbon.

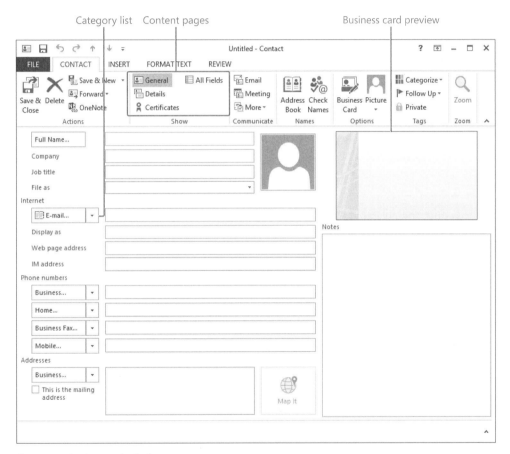

A new contact record window.

TIP You save information in a field by entering it into the corresponding text box. Outlook saves the information you enter as data attached to the item, and uses it in various ways. Some types of fields have special rules attached that affect the appearance of the data in the field. For example, phone number fields in contact records automatically format the numbers you enter to match a standard (123) 456-7890 format.

The contact record window interface includes the Quick Access Toolbar, the ribbon, and the People Pane, in addition to the content area that displays the contact record information.

When opened from a contact record window, the Backstage view includes commands related to managing contact records, such as saving contact records and contact record attachments and closing, moving, and printing contact records.

TIP The commands available in the Backstage view of a contact record window are identical to those in the Backstage view of an appointment window. For more information, see "Working in the Calendar module" earlier in this chapter.

Commands on the ribbon of a contact record window are organized on four tabs:

- **Contact** Includes commands that are specific to managing and working with contact records. Commands include those for managing the contact record, switching among the contact record pages, communicating with the contact, accessing and verifying saved contact information, and personalizing a contact's electronic business card. This tab also includes commands for assigning a category or follow-up flag to a contact record, preventing other Outlook users from viewing the contact record when connected to your account, and changing the magnification level of the notes pane within the contact record window.

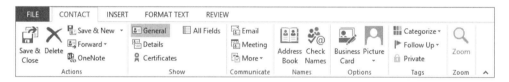

The Contact tab of the contact record window ribbon.

TIP The commands you use for managing contact records are available on only the Contact tab.

- **Insert** Includes the same standard commands as the Insert tab of a message composition window ribbon. The commands on the Insert tab of the contact record window ribbon, other than those in the Include group, apply only to the content of the notes pane.

SEE ALSO For information about inserting various graphic elements, see Chapter 10, "Enhance message content."

- **Format Text** Includes the same standard commands as the Format Text tab of a message composition window ribbon. The commands on the Format Text tab of the contact record window ribbon, other than the Paste commands and the Select command, apply only to the content of the notes pane.

- **Review** Includes the same standard commands as the Review tab of a message composition window ribbon. The commands on the Review tab of the contact record window ribbon, other than the Research and Thesaurus commands, apply only to the content of the notes pane.

TIP In earlier versions of Outlook, the People module was named the Contacts module. Remnants of the previous naming convention can be found throughout the program. In this book, we frequently refer to people whose contact information you have stored in Outlook as *contacts*. We assure you, however, that contacts are people too!

SEE ALSO For information about changing the default settings for the People module, see "Configuring Office and Outlook options" in Chapter 11, "Customize Outlook."

In this exercise, you'll familiarize yourself with the types of information you can store in a contact record and the customizations you can make to the way Outlook manages contact records.

 SET UP You don't need any practice files to complete this exercise; just follow the steps.

1   On the **Navigation Bar**, click the **People** button to display the **People** module. The content area displays the **People** view of contacts saved in your primary address book (or the last address book you viewed).

     KEYBOARD SHORTCUT Press Ctrl+3 to display the People module.

2   On the **Home** tab, in the **New** group, click the **New Contact** button to open a new, blank contact record window displaying the **General** page of the contact record. The cursor is automatically active in the **Full Name** box, so you can immediately begin entering a contact's information.

     KEYBOARD SHORTCUT Press Ctrl+Shift+C to create a contact record from any Outlook module.

TIP An arrow to the right of a field name indicates that the displayed field is one of a group of related fields that you can display in that location, one at a time. For example, the arrow next to the email address field indicates that there are multiple email address fields; clicking the arrow displays a list. Clicking a field in the list displays it in place of the previous related field.

3   On the **Contact** tab, in the **Show** group, click **Details** to display the optional fields for business and personal information that you might want to save as part of a contact record.

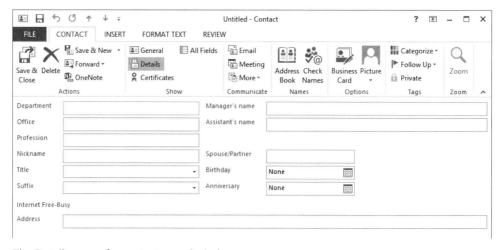

The Details page of a contact record window.

4   In the **Show** group, click **Certificates** to display digital IDs that you can use to encrypt messages you send to this contact.

SEE ALSO For information about digital IDs, see "Increasing email security" in Chapter 12, "Manage email settings."

5   In the **Show** group, click **All Fields** to display the **All Fields** page of the contact record window. The default view displays custom fields that you define yourself, none of which are present in the default contact record window.

SEE ALSO For information about defining custom fields, see the sidebar "User-defined fields" in Chapter 4, "Store and access contact information."

6 Click the **Select from** arrow, and scroll the list to note the many categories on which you can filter the information displayed on the **All Fields** page. Then in the **Select from** list, click **Phone number fields** to filter the page to display all the types of phone numbers that might be included in this contact record.

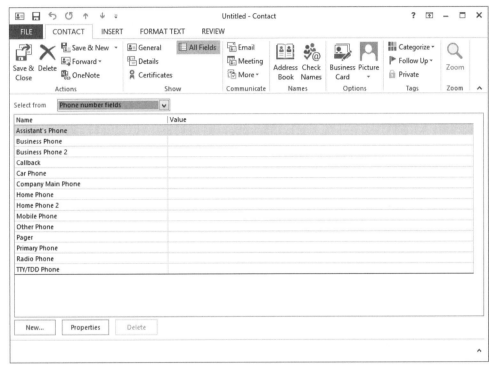

The All Fields page of a new contact record, displaying the available fields that are formatted to contain phone numbers.

Although these fields aren't all displayed on the General page of a contact record, you can still save the information by entering it directly into the Value cell of a field on the All Fields page. The information is then available for you to use in another format, such as in a mail merge process, or to display on a custom contact form.

7 In the **Show** group, click **General** to return to the primary page of the contact record window.

8 In the **Communicate** group, click **More** to display the **More** list, which shows the types of communication you can initiate with a contact from his or her contact record.

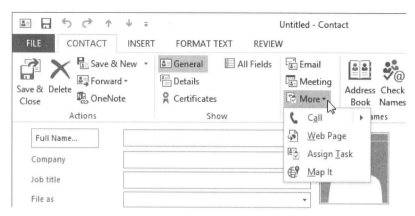

When a contact record includes an address, you can quickly locate the address in Bing Maps by clicking Map It on the More menu.

KEYBOARD SHORTCUT Press Ctrl+F to create an email message with the selected contact record attached. Press Ctrl+Shift+X to open the webpage associated with the contact record.

9   Click to position the cursor in the **Notes** box of the contact record. Then click the **Insert**, **Format Text**, and **Review** tabs in turn to see the available commands. Notice that the commands on these tabs are identical to those in a message window; you can insert and format any of the standard Office graphic elements in the notes that you save with a contact record.

> **TIP** Many commands on the Insert, Format Text, and Review tabs of a contact record window are unavailable when the cursor is located anywhere other than in the notes pane.

10   In the left pane of the **Backstage** view of the contact record, click **Close**. Then in the **Microsoft Outlook** message box that asks whether you want to save changes, click **No**.

> **TIP** By clicking Close in the Backstage view or on the menu that opens when you click the Outlook icon at the left end of the title bar, or by clicking the Close button at the right end of the title bar, you have the option to not save changes to the contact record. Clicking the Save & Close button in the Actions group on the Contact tab saves the contact record without further prompting.

✖ CLEAN UP If you created a contact record while experimenting in the contact record window that you don't want to keep, right-click the contact record in the Contacts pane, and then click Delete.

Working in the Tasks module

You can display the Tasks module by clicking the Tasks link or button on the Navigation Bar.

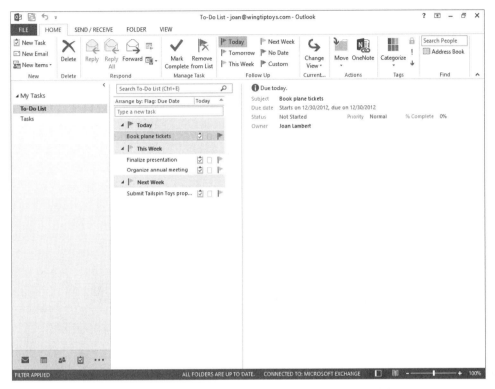

The Outlook program window, displaying the To-Do List in the Tasks module.

Tasks module content

As with the other Outlook modules, the Tasks module has a Reading view, which displays only the minimized Folder Pane and the content area, and Normal view, which displays any elements that you choose.

The Folder Pane in the Tasks module displays the two basic task list variations you can display in the content area: the default To-Do List view and the Tasks view. (These views are represented as folders although both display different views of the same tasks, much like a Search Folder.) It also contains any custom task folders you create. The content area displays the selected folder content.

- **To-Do List** Displays tasks organized by default in groups by due date (you can reorder the tasks any way you want), and the Reading Pane, in which you can preview the details of any selected task. This is the default view.

- **Tasks** Displays a list of task details in columns. Each task is preceded by a check box so that you can easily indicate when the task is complete. The Reading Pane is hidden by default, so you must open a task item (or display the Reading Pane) to display additional details.

TIP In addition to these standard views, you can display tasks filtered and organized in many other ways, by selecting a view from the Change View gallery. For more information, see "Displaying different views of tasks" in Chapter 6, "Track tasks."

The ribbon in the Tasks module includes the File tab and the four standard module tabs:

- **Home** Includes the commands you need to create, manage, and view tasks, and to initiate communication with contacts. You can assign tasks to co-workers and work with tasks assigned to you, send task information to a OneNote notebook, and tag tasks in ways that enable you to better locate or manage them.

The Home tab of the Tasks module ribbon.

- **Send/Receive** Identical to that of the Calendar and People modules.

- **Folder** Provides the same functionality as it does in the Calendar and People modules, but is specific to task items.

TIP Many of the Actions commands are available only when you select a custom folder (a folder that you create, rather than the To-Do List or Tasks folders created by Outlook)

- **View** This tab provides the same functionality as it does in the Mail and People modules. The content of the Arrangement gallery is specific to tasks.

The View tab of the Tasks module ribbon.

Task windows

The window in which you create or manage a task is a task window. Like the message, contact record, and calendar item windows, the task window includes the Quick Access Toolbar, a unique set of commands arranged on the ribbon, and the content area that displays the task information.

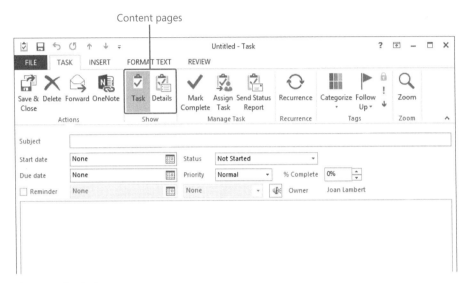

A new task window.

When opened from a task window, the Backstage view includes commands related to managing tasks, such as saving, closing, moving, and printing tasks.

TIP The commands available in the Backstage view of a task window are identical to those in the Backstage view of an appointment window. For more information, see "Working in the Calendar module" earlier in this chapter.

Commands on the ribbon of a task window are organized on the four standard tabs: Task, Insert, Format Text, and Review. The commands you use to create and manage most tasks are available on the Task tab. Commands include those for managing and assigning the task, sending the task to a OneNote notebook, and switching among the task pages. This tab also includes commands for assigning a category or follow-up flag to a task, preventing other Outlook users from viewing the task details when connected to your account, and changing the magnification level of the notes pane (not of the task window).

The Insert, Format Text, and Review tabs are identical to those of other item windows. The commands for inserting, modifying, and formatting elements apply only to content in the notes pane of the Task window.

In this exercise, you'll take a tour of the Tasks module and look at features in the task window that differ from those in the message, calendar item, and contact record windows.

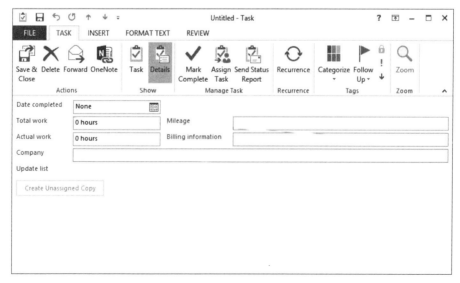

SET UP You don't need any practice files to complete this exercise; just follow the steps.

1   On the **Navigation Bar**, click the **Tasks** button to open the **Tasks** module and display the **To-Do List** view of your task list.

2   On the **Home** tab, in the **New** group, click the **New Task** button to open an untitled task window.

KEYBOARD SHORTCUT Press Ctrl+Shift+K to create a task from any Outlook module.

3   Familiarize yourself with the fields in the task window.

The Subject field is the only field in which you must enter text to create a task. If you enter an end date, Outlook adds the task to the appropriate Due Date category (Today, Tomorrow, This Week, Next Week, or a custom category based on the date). Leaving the Due Date set to None adds the task to the No Date category.

TIP You can easily move a task to a different Due Date category by clicking the task in the To-Do List, in the Tasks list, or on the To-Do Bar, and then clicking the time-frame you want in the Follow Up group on the Home tab of the Tasks module.

4   On the **Task** tab, in the **Show** group, click the **Details** button.

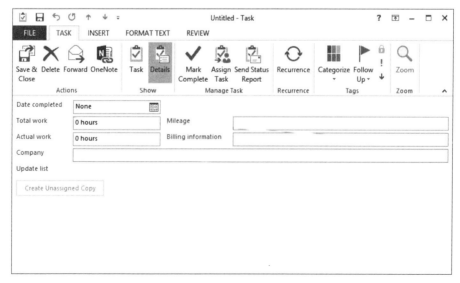

The Details page displays the additional fields of information you can save with the task.

5   Notice the type of information you can track on the **Details** page, which could be useful when tracking billable tasks for clients.

TIP The default detail fields in the Task window are somewhat generic. Consider whether your organization would benefit from tracking information such as this. If the default fields don't fit your needs, you can create a custom form to track exactly the information that is necessary for your needs.

❌ CLEAN UP Close the task window.

SEE ALSO For information about changing the default settings for the Tasks module, see "Configuring Office and Outlook options" in Chapter 11, "Customize Outlook."

Key points

- The Outlook program window includes eight areas in which you work with Outlook or with your Outlook items: the title bar, the ribbon, the Folder Pane, the content area, the Reading Pane, the To-Do Bar, the Navigation Bar, and the status bar.

- You give commands from the ribbon and from the Quick Access Toolbar.

- Outlook stores information in individual modules that have unique user interface characteristics.

- Each module and each type of item window have individually configurable ribbons and Quick Access Toolbars to streamline the user interface. You can make the commands you want available specifically where you want them.

- The different item windows share certain common tabs, but each has a main tab that contains all the commands you need when creating or working with a basic Outlook item of that type.

Chapter at a glance

Create

Create and send messages,
page 88

Attach

Attach external content to messages,
page 103

View

View messages and message attachments,
page 108

Respond

Respond to messages,
page 123

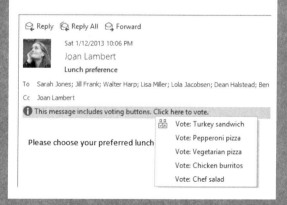

Send and receive email messages

IN THIS CHAPTER, YOU WILL LEARN HOW TO

- Create and send messages.

- Attach external content to messages.

- View messages and message attachments.

- View message participant information.

- Respond to messages.

Although Microsoft Outlook 2013 is an excellent tool for managing your schedule, contact records, and task lists, the primary reason most people use Outlook is to send and receive email messages. Over the past decade, email (short for *electronic mail*) has become an accepted and even required form of business communication. And of course, many people use email to keep in touch with friends and family, either from work or from home. Outlook makes it easy to connect to multiple email accounts, either on a business network or over the Internet, and provides all the tools you need to send, respond to, organize, filter, sort, find, and otherwise manage email messages.

When sending email messages from Outlook, you can format the text to suit your preferences, and include attachments such as documents, workbooks, and images. You can also personalize your message by embedding images, business graphics, and automatic signatures; setting message options such as voting buttons, importance, sensitivity, and reminders; and requesting electronic receipts when a message is delivered or opened.

Outlook 2013 has many features that make it easy to display and track information about the people you correspond with, particularly if your organization uses Microsoft Exchange Server and Microsoft Lync. These features include presence icons that indicate whether a person is currently available, information cards that appear when you point to a name in an email message header, and the People Pane that tracks interactions of all types that you have with people with whom you correspond.

In this chapter, you'll create, send, and view messages, with and without attachments. You'll view information about message participants. Then you'll reply to and forward messages.

Creating and sending messages

Creating an email message is a relatively simple process. You will usually provide information in the following fields:

- **To** Enter the email address of the primary message recipient(s) in this field. This is the only field that is absolutely required to send a message.

- **Subject** Enter a brief description of the message contents or purpose in this field. The subject is not required, but it is important to provide information in this field, both so that you and the recipient can identify the message and so that the message isn't blocked as suspected junk mail by a recipient's email program. Outlook will warn you if you try to send a message with no subject.

- **Message body** Enter your message to the recipient in this field, which is a large text box. You can include many types of information, including formatted text, hyperlinks, and graphics in the message body.

TIP In this chapter and throughout this book, for expediency's sake, we sometimes refer to email messages simply as *messages*. When referring to other types of messages we use full descriptions such as *instant messages* or *text messages*.

Addressing messages

Addressing an email message is easy: just insert the intended recipient's email address (or name, if he or she is in your address book) into an address box in the message header of a message composition window. You can enter email recipients into any of three address boxes:

- **To** Use for primary message recipients. Usually, these are the people you want to respond to the message. Each message must have at least one address in the To box.

- **Cc** Use for "courtesy copy" recipients. These are usually people you want to keep informed about the subject of the email message but from whom you don't require a response.

- **Bcc** Use for "blind courtesy copy" recipients. These are people you want to keep informed, but whom you want to keep hidden from other message recipients. Bcc recipients are not visible to any other message recipients and therefore aren't included in message responses unless specifically added to one of the address boxes in the response message.

  TIP The To and Cc address boxes are always displayed in the message header. The Bcc address box is not displayed by default. You can display it in the message header by clicking the Bcc button, located in the Show Fields group on the Options tab of the message composition window.

You can insert an email address into an address box in the following ways:

- Enter the entire address.

- Enter part of a previously used address and then select the address from the Auto-Complete List that appears.

  SEE ALSO For information about the Auto-Complete List, see "Troubleshooting message addressing" later in this section.

- Click the address box label to display the Select Names dialog box, in which you can select one or more addresses from your address book(s).

  SEE ALSO For information about address books, see "Saving and updating contact information" in Chapter 4, "Store and access contact information."

TIP Responding to a received message automatically fills in one or more of the address boxes in the new message window. For information, see "Responding to messages" later in this chapter.

If your email account is part of an Exchange network, you can send messages to another person on the same network by typing only his or her email alias—for example, *joan*; the at symbol (@) and domain name aren't required. If you enter only the name of a person whose email address is in your address book, Outlook associates the name with the corresponding email address, a process called *resolving the address*, before sending the message.

KEYBOARD SHORTCUT Press Ctrl+K to initiate address resolution. For more information about keyboard shortcuts, see "Keyboard shortcuts" at the end of this book.

Depending on the method you use to enter a message recipient's name or email address into an address box, Outlook either resolves the name or address immediately (if you chose it from a list of known names) or resolves it when you send the message. The resolution process for each name or address has one of two results:

- If Outlook successfully resolves the name or address, an underline appears below it. If the name or address matches one stored in an address book, Outlook replaces your original entry with the content of the Display As field in the contact record, and then underlines it.

  SEE ALSO For information about contact record fields, see "Saving and updating contact information" in Chapter 4, "Store and access contact information."

- If Outlook is unable to resolve the name or address, the Check Names dialog box opens, asking you to select the address you want to use.

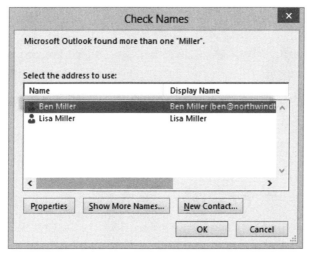

The Check Names dialog box might display No Suggestions, names that match the entry, or contact options saved in the contact record for the entered name.

In the Check Names dialog box, you can select from the suggested options, or do one of the following:

- Click **Properties** to learn more about the selected option.

- Click **Show More Names** to display your default address book.

- Click **New Contact** to create a new contact record in your default address book, directly from the dialog box.

Troubleshooting message addressing

Outlook 2013 includes many features intended to simplify the process of addressing messages to recipients. As with any tool, these features can sometimes be more difficult to use than you'd like. In this section, we discuss troubleshooting tips for some common problems.

Troubleshooting the Auto-Complete List

As you enter a name or an email address into the To, Cc, or Bcc box, Outlook displays matching addresses in a list. You can insert a name or address from the list into the address box by clicking it or by pressing the arrow keys to select it and then pressing Tab or Enter.

Sometimes the Auto-Complete List might contain incorrect or outdated addresses—for example, if you have previously sent a message to an incorrect email address, or if a person changes his or her email address. The list might also contain people with whom you no longer correspond. If you don't remove incorrect or outdated addresses from the list, it can be easy to mistakenly accept Outlook's suggestion and send a message to the wrong address.

To clean up the Auto-Complete List:

1   In the list, point to the name or address you want to remove.

2   Click the **Delete** button (the X) that appears to the right of the name or address.

You can modify the Auto-Complete List settings in the Send Messages section of the Mail page of the Outlook Options dialog box as follows:

- To prevent the Auto-Complete List from appearing when you enter an address, clear the **Use Auto-Complete List to suggest names...** check box.

- To remove all entries from the Auto-Complete List (and start the list from scratch) click the **Empty Auto-Complete List** button, and then click **Yes** in the dialog box that appears.

SEE ALSO For more information, see "Configuring Office and Outlook options" in Chapter 11, "Customize Outlook."

Troubleshooting multiple recipients

By default, Outlook requires that you separate multiple email addresses with semicolons. If you separate multiple addresses by pressing the spacebar or the Enter key, Outlook replaces the space or carriage return with a semicolon before sending the message. If you separate multiple addresses by using a comma (which might seem to be the more natural action), Outlook treats the addresses as one address and displays an error message when you try to send the message.

You can instruct Outlook to accept commas as address separators by selecting the Commas Can Be Used To Separate Multiple Message Recipients check box in the Send Messages section of the Mail page of the Outlook Options window.

Troubleshooting address books

By default, Outlook first searches your Global Address List (the corporate directory provided with an Exchange account, if you're working with one), and then searches the contact records stored in the People module of your default account. If an email address isn't located in one of those locations, Outlook may search other address books such as those containing contact records stored with secondary email accounts or custom address books that you create.

If you have multiple address books, particularly multiple address books associated with multiple accounts, Outlook does not, by default, search all of the address books and therefore might not locate an email address you have saved.

To change the order in which Outlook searches the address books, or to add address books to the search list, follow these steps:

1 On the **Home** tab of the program window, in the **Find** group, click **Address Book**.

2 In the **Address Book** window, on the **Tools** menu, click **Options**.

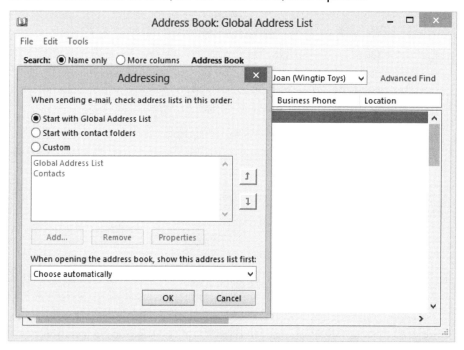

You can designate the order in which Outlook searches for contacts in existing address books.

3   In the **Addressing** dialog box, click **Custom**. Then do any of the following:

- To search additional address books, click **Add**. Then in the **Add Address List** dialog box, click the address list you want to add, click **Add**, and click **Close**.

- To change the order in which Outlook searches the address books in the list, click an address book and then click the **Move Up** or **Move Down** button.

- If you're uncertain which address book is represented by a list entry, click the address book and then click **Properties** to display the account name and folder name of the address book.

4   In the **Addressing** dialog box, click **OK**, and then close the **Address Book** window.

Entering content

If you have an Internet connection, you can send email messages to people within your organization and around the world by using Outlook, regardless of the type of email account you have. Outlook can send and receive email messages in three message formats:

- **HTML** Supports paragraph styles (including numbered and bulleted lists), character styles (such as fonts, sizes, colors, weight), and backgrounds (such as colors and pictures). Most (but not all) email programs support the HTML format. Programs that don't support HTML display these messages as Plain Text.

- **Rich Text** Supports more paragraph formatting options than HTML, including borders and shading, but is compatible only with Outlook and Exchange Server. Outlook converts Rich Text messages to HTML when sending them outside of an Exchange network.

- **Plain Text** Does not support the formatting features available in HTML and Rich Text messages but is supported by all email programs.

Email message content isn't limited to simple text. You can create almost any type of content in an email message that you can in a Microsoft Word document. Because Outlook 2013 and Word 2013 share similar commands, you might already be familiar with processes for creating content such as lists and tables.

You can personalize your messages by using an individual font style or color and by inserting your contact information in the form of an email signature or business card. (You can apply other formatting, such as themes and page backgrounds, but these won't always appear to email recipients as you intend them to, and they can make your communications appear less professional.)

TIP You can specify different email signatures for new messages and for replies and forwarded messages. For example, you might want to include your full name and contact information in the signature that appears in new messages, but only your first name in the signature that appears in replies and forwarded messages. For more information, see "Personalizing the appearance of message text" in Chapter 10, "Enhance message content."

You can format the text of your message to make it more readable by including headings, lists, or tables, and you can represent information graphically by including charts, pictures, clip art, and other types of graphics. You can attach files to your message and link to other information, such as files or webpages.

For the purposes of this book, we assume that you know how to enter, edit, and format content by using standard Word techniques, so we don't discuss all of them in this book. We demonstrate many of these techniques within the step-by-step exercises, though, so be alert for any new features that you aren't yet familiar with.

SEE ALSO For extensive information about entering and editing content and about formatting content by using character and paragraph styles, Quick Styles, and themes, refer to *Microsoft Word 2013 Step by Step*, by Joan Lambert and Joyce Cox (Microsoft Press, 2013).

Saving and sending messages

At regular intervals while you're composing a message (every three minutes, by default), Outlook saves a copy of the message in the Drafts folder. This is intended to protect you from losing messages that are in progress. If you close a message that hasn't yet had a draft saved, Outlook gives you the option of saving one. You can manually save a message draft at any time by clicking the Save button on the Quick Access Toolbar in the message window.

KEYBOARD SHORTCUT Press Ctrl+S to save a draft email message.

To resume working on a message that's been saved as a draft and closed, display the Mail module, and click the Drafts folder in the Folder Pane. Then double-click the message you want to work on to open it in its own window, or continue composing the message directly in the Reading Pane.

After you finish composing a message, you can send it by clicking the Send button located in the message header or by pressing Ctrl+Enter. (The first time you press this key combination, Outlook asks whether you want to designate this as the keyboard shortcut for sending messages.) When you send the message, Outlook deletes the message draft, if one exists, and stores a copy of the sent message in the Sent Items folder.

TIP Each account you access from Outlook has its own Drafts folder and its own Sent Items folder. Outlook automatically saves draft messages and sent messages in the folder affiliated with the email account in which you compose or send the message. You can change the frequency and the location in which Outlook saves message drafts from the Mail page of the Outlook Options dialog box. For more information about this dialog box, see "Configuring Office and Outlook options" in Chapter 11, "Customize Outlook."

In this exercise, you'll compose an email message, save an interim message draft, and then send the message.

 SET UP **You don't need any practice files to complete this exercise. Display your Inbox in Normal view, ensure that the Folder Pane is open, and then follow the steps.**

1   On the **Home** tab, in the **New** group, click the **New Email** button to open a new message window.

    TIP From the New Items menu, you can create any type of Outlook item, such as an appointment, contact, fax, message, note, or task, or an organizational item such as a contact group or data file, without leaving the module you're working in.

2   In the **To** box, enter your own email address.

3   In the **Subject** box, enter **SBS Tradeshow Schedule**.

    TIP The subject of this message begins with *SBS* (for *Step by Step*) so that you can easily differentiate it from other messages in your Inbox and Sent Items folders and can locate it later.

4   At the right end of the message window title bar, click the **Close** button.

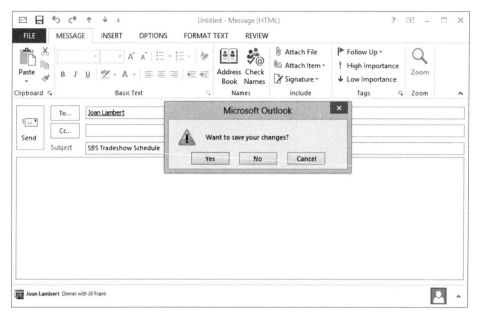

If you close a message composition window before sending the message, Outlook prompts you to save a draft.

5   In the **Microsoft Outlook** message box, click **Yes** to save a draft and close the message window. In the **Folder Pane**, the number in the unread message counter to the right of the **Drafts** folder increases.

Now we'll modify the saved message draft.

6   In the **Folder Pane**, click the **Drafts** folder to display your message and its current content. Notice that the cursor is active in the **Reading Pane**, and a **Message** tool tab appears on the ribbon. The tool tab contains only the most frequently used commands from the message composition window ribbon.

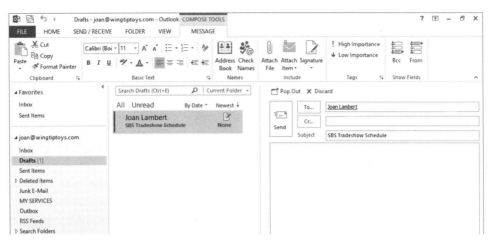

In Outlook 2013, you can compose message drafts directly in the Reading Pane.

7   In the **Reading Pane**, click in the content pane of the message draft. Enter The
following people will be working at the tradeshow: and press the **Enter** key
twice. Then enter Jaime, Kathy, Marlene, and Susie, pressing **Enter** once after each
of the first three names, and twice after the fourth one. Notice that the list of names
is currently unformatted.

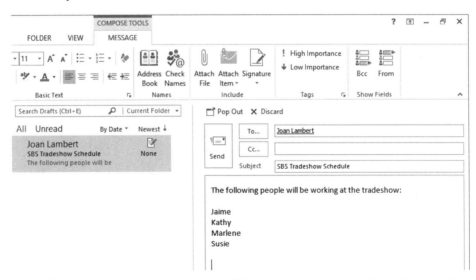

*The updated message draft contents are visible in the message composition window and in
the message list.*

8   Select the list of names. Then on the **Mini Toolbar** that appears, click the **Bullets** button (not its arrow) to convert the list of names to a simple bulleted list.

> **TIP** The Bullets button and other paragraph-formatting commands are also available in the Basic Text group on the Message tool tab.

9   With the bulleted list still selected, click the **Bullets** arrow. Notice the types of bullets available in the **Bullet Library** gallery. You can change the list to use any of these bullets by clicking the bullet you want.

10 On the **Bullets** menu, point to **Change List Level** to display a menu that illustrates bullets used by a multilevel list. You can demote (or promote) a list item to any of nine levels, differentiated by the bullet character and indent level.

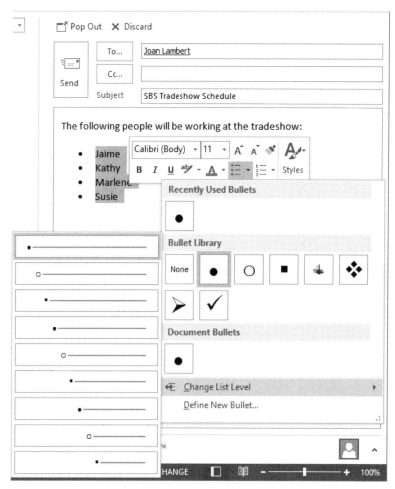

You can format message content in the message composition window just as you can in Word.

11   Press **Esc** three times, or click in a blank area of the message composition window, to hide the **Mini Toolbar** and its menus without making changes.

12   Press **Ctrl+End** to move the cursor to the end of the message. Enter Promotional giveaways will be as follows: and then press **Enter** twice.

Now let's insert a table. Notice that the Insert Table command does not appear on the Message tool tab when you're working in the embedded message draft.

13   In the upper-left corner of the embedded message composition window, click the **Pop Out** button to display the message in an individual window with the full ribbon.

14   On the **Insert** tab, in the **Tables** group, click the **Table** button.

15   In the **Table** gallery, point to the third cell in the second row to display a live preview of a three-column by two-row table at the cursor location in the message window.

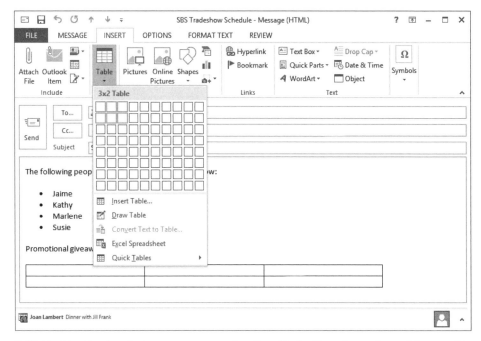

With the Live Preview feature, you can preview the effect of inserting or formatting graphic elements before you commit to the change.

16   Click the selected cell to insert the table in the message content area. The cursor is active in the first table cell.

17 Enter the following information in the table, pressing **Tab** to move between table cells. Notice that the table and table content are currently unformatted.

9:00-11:00   12:00-2:00   3:00-5:00

Mouse pads   T-shirts   Pens

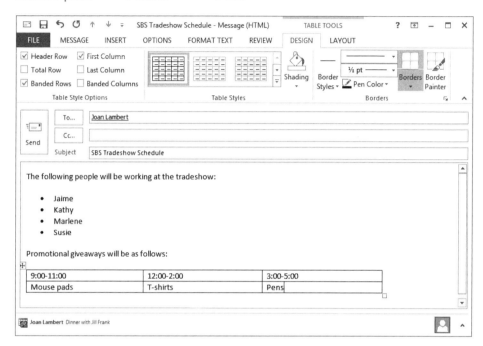

While the table is active, the Design and Layout tool tabs appear on the ribbon.

18 With the cursor still active in the lower-right table cell, click the **More** button in the **Table Styles** gallery on the **Design** tool tab to display the **Table Styles** menu. A box around the first thumbnail in the gallery indicates the formatting of the active table.

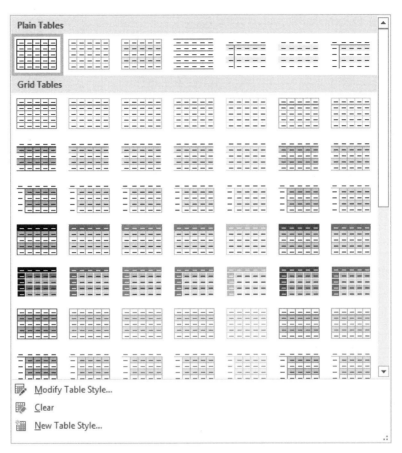

The Table Styles menu includes a gallery of table formats and related commands.

19   In the **List Tables** section of the gallery, point to the third thumbnail in the third row (**List Table 3 – Accent 2**) to preview the table with the style applied, and then click the thumbnail to apply the selected table style.

> **TIP** You can change many aspects of the table formatting by selecting or clearing check boxes in the Table Style Options group on the Design tool tab.

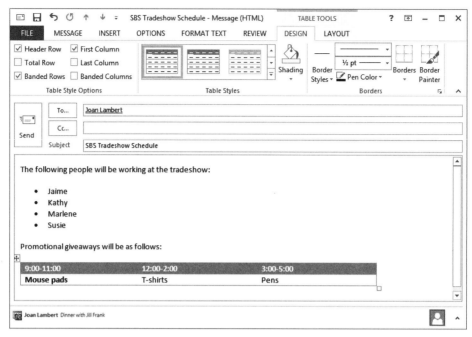

The message is now ready to send.

20   In the message header, click the **Send** button to close the message window, send the message, and remove the message draft from the **Drafts** folder.

KEYBOARD SHORTCUT   Press Ctrl+Enter to send a message.

21   When Outlook receives the message, a desktop alert appears in the upper-right corner of the program window.

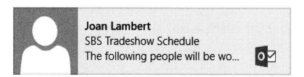

You can open or delete a message by using the commands that appear when you point to a desktop alert.

22   In the **Folder Pane**, click the **Inbox** folder and, if necessary, click the received message in the message list to display it in the **Reading Pane**.

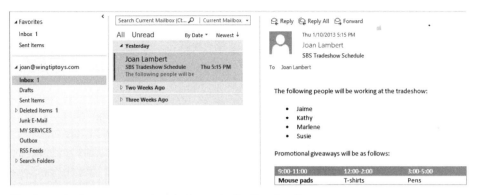

The formatted message content is shown in the Reading Pane.

23   In the **Folder Pane**, click the **Sent Items** folder to verify that the sent message is in this folder.

❌ CLEAN UP Display your Inbox. Retain the SBS Tradeshow Schedule message in your Inbox and Sent Items folders for use in later exercises.

Attaching external content to messages

A convenient way to distribute a file (such as a Microsoft PowerPoint presentation, Excel workbook, Word document, or picture) is by attaching the file to an email message. Message recipients can preview or open the file from the Reading Pane, open it from the message window, forward it to other people, or save it to their computers.

TIP You can also email Microsoft Office files directly from the Office program you create them in, by using commands in the Backstage view. For example, to send a Word document, open the document, display the Share page of the Backstage view, and then click the Email button. Word offers the options of sending the document as an attached Word document, PDF file, or XPS file (Word converts the file for you before sending it), sending a link to the document (if it's saved in a shared location), or sending the document to a fax machine.

Managing multiple accounts

If you have configured Outlook to connect to multiple email accounts, you need to ensure that the message is being sent from the correct account.

By default, Outlook assumes that you intend to send a message from the account you're currently working in. If you begin composing a message while viewing the Inbox of your work account, for example, Outlook selects the work account as the message-sending account. If you reply to a message received by your personal account, Outlook selects the personal account as the message-sending account.

You can easily change the message-sending account. When Outlook is configured to use multiple accounts, a From button appears in the message header.

TIP If Outlook is configured to connect to only one account, you can display the From button by clicking From in the Show Fields group on the Options tab of a message composition window.

Clicking the From button displays a list of active accounts from which you can choose. If the account from which you want to send the message doesn't appear in the list, you can specify another account; however, you must have permission to send messages from that account.

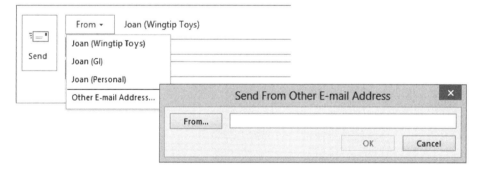

In this exercise, you'll send two files as attachments to an email message.

 SET UP You need the Procedures document and the NaturalGardening presentation located in the Chapter03 practice file folder to complete this exercise. Display your Inbox, and then follow the steps.

1   On the **Home** tab, in the **New** group, click the **New Email** button.

2   In the **To** box of the new message window, enter your own email address.

TIP If you completed the previous exercise, Outlook displays your email address in the Auto-Complete List as you begin typing. You can insert the address by clicking it or by pressing the Down Arrow key to select it (if necessary) and then pressing Enter.

3   In the **Subject** box, enter **SBS First Draft**.

4   In the content pane, enter Here is some information for your review. Then press **Enter** to move to the next line.

5   On the **Message** tab, in the **Include** group, click the **Attach File** button to open the **Insert File** dialog box and display the contents of your **Documents** library.

3

   TIP The Attach File button is also available in the Include group on the Insert tab.

6   Navigate to the **Chapter03** practice file folder. In the **Chapter03** folder, click the **NaturalGardening** presentation, hold down the **Ctrl** key, click the **Procedures** document, and then click **Insert**. Notice that the **Attached** box containing the files appears in the message header.

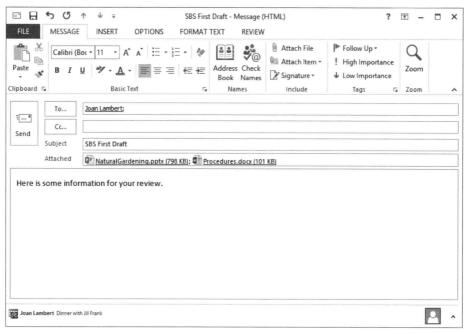

Information about file attachments is visible to the sender and to the recipient.

7   Send the message.

❌ **CLEAN UP** When you receive the SBS First Draft message in your Inbox, retain it for use in later exercises.

Working with new mail notifications

When new messages, meeting requests, or task assignments arrive in your Inbox, Outlook alerts you in several ways so that you can be aware of email activity if you are using another application or if you've been away from your computer.

- A desktop alert appears on your screen for a few seconds, displaying the sender's information, the message subject, and the first few words of the message.

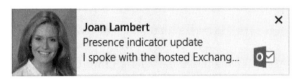

You can open the message from the desktop alert.

- A chime sounds.

- A New Mail Message icon appears on the Outlook taskbar button.

- You can configure Outlook to briefly change the shape of the mouse pointer to an envelope.

You can configure the individual notification options from the Mail page of the Outlook Options dialog box.

TIP In previous versions of Outlook, you could respond to or delete a message by clicking buttons in the desktop alert. You could also change the location, transparency, and length of time desktop alerts appear. In Outlook 2013, you have none of these options; the only configuration available for desktop alerts is whether to display them.

Troubleshooting file types and extensions

By default, Windows does not display file extensions in File Explorer windows or dialog boxes such as the Insert File dialog box. You can usually differentiate file types by their icons—for example, in the preceding exercise, the blue Word icon precedes the Procedures document name, and the red PowerPoint icon precedes the NaturalGardening presentation name.

TIP In Windows 8, File Explorer has replaced Windows Explorer. Throughout this book, we refer to this browsing utility by its Windows 8 name. If your computer is running Windows 7, use Windows Explorer instead.

In a dialog box such as the Insert File dialog box, you can display the file type by clicking the Change Your View arrow on the toolbar and then clicking either Details or Tiles; each of these views includes the Type field.

TIP Many picture files are large, requiring a lot of bandwidth to send and a lot of storage space to receive. Instead of opening a message and then attaching a full-size picture file to it, you can send and simultaneously resize a picture from File Explorer by right-clicking the picture file, clicking Send To, and then clicking Mail Recipient. In the Attach Files dialog box that appears, choose from among five picture size options; the corresponding file size appears when you select a picture size. Then click Attach to create an email message with the resized file attached.

TIP If you want to send personalized copies of the same email message to several people, you can use the mail merge feature of Word 2013. For more information, refer to *Microsoft Word 2013 Step by Step* by Joan Lambert and Joyce Cox (Microsoft Press, 2013).

Viewing messages and message attachments

Each time you start Outlook and connect to your email server, any new messages received since the last time you connected appear in your Inbox. Depending on your settings, Outlook downloads either the entire message to your computer or only the message header, which provides basic information about the message, such as:

- The item type (message, meeting request, task assignment, and so on).
- Who sent it.
- When you received it.
- The subject.

Icons displayed in the message header indicate optional information such as:

- The most recent response action taken.
- Whether files are attached.
- If it has been digitally signed or encrypted.
- If the sender marked it as being of high or low importance.

TIP If a message contains external content, which many marketing email messages do, the external content will be automatically downloaded only if your security settings are configured to permit this. Otherwise, you can click the InfoBar to download the external content.

There are three standard views of the message list:

- **Compact** This view displays two lines of message properties, including the read status, subject, sender, time received, whether files are attached to the message, and any color categories or follow-up flags associated with the message. This is the default view.
- **Single** This one-line view displays the importance, reminder, item type or read status, whether files are attached to the message, sender, subject, received, size, category, and follow-up flags. The Reading Pane is open by default in this view.
- **Preview** This view displays from one to four lines of information about each message. For every message, Preview view displays the same information as Single view. For each unread message, Preview view also displays a part of the message content— specifically, the first 255 characters (including spaces). If a message contains fewer than 255 characters, *<end>* appears in the preview text. The Reading Pane is closed by default in this view.

These three standard views are available from the Change View gallery on the View tab.

Messages that you haven't yet read are indicated in the message list by vertical blue lines on the left edge and bold blue header text. When you open a message, Outlook indicates that you have read it by removing the blue indicators and changing the header font in the message list from bold to normal.

SEE ALSO For more information, see the sidebar "Marking messages as read or unread" in Chapter 7, "Organize your Inbox."

You can view the text of a message in several ways:

- You can open a message in its own window by double-clicking its header in the message list.

- You can read a message without opening it by clicking its header once in the message list to display the message in the Reading Pane.

- You can display the first three lines of each unread message under the message header by using the Preview feature. Scanning the first three lines of a message frequently gives you enough information to make basic decisions about how to manage it. The only drawback is that in Preview view, each unread message takes up five lines rather than the two lines in the default Messages view, so fewer messages are visible on your screen at one time.

SEE ALSO For information about turning on specific view features, see "Arranging messages in different ways" in Chapter 7, "Organize your Inbox."

You can view message attachments in several ways:

- You can preview certain types of attachments (including Word documents, Excel workbooks, PowerPoint presentations, and PDF files) directly in the Reading Pane by clicking the attachment (one time) in the message header.

  When you click the attachment, the message text is replaced by a preview of the attachment contents, and the Attachments tool tab appears on the ribbon. To redisplay the message content, click the Message button that appears to the left of the attachments in the message header.

3

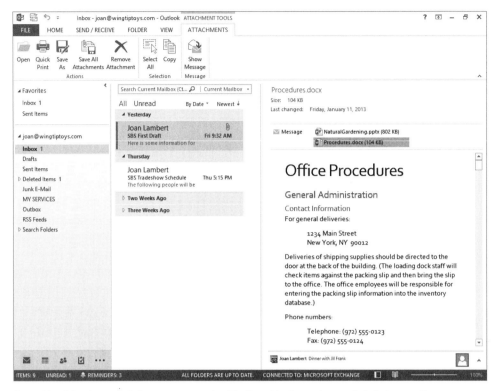

From the Attachments tab, you can work with the attachment or switch between the message content and attachment preview.

TIP You can turn off the Attachment Preview feature from the Attachment Handling page of the Trust Center window, which you open from the Outlook Options dialog box. For information about Trust Center settings, see "Configuring Office and Outlook options" in Chapter 11, "Customize Outlook."

■ You can open the attachment in the program assigned to that file type from the Reading Pane or from an open message window by double-clicking the attachment in the message header.

■ You can save the attachment to your hard disk and open it from there. This strategy is recommended if you suspect an attachment might contain a virus, because you can scan the file for viruses before opening it (provided that you have a virus scanning program installed).

If you receive a contact record or business card as a message attachment, you can add it to your primary address book by dragging the attachment from the email message to the Contacts link or button on the Navigation Bar. To add the contact record to a secondary address book, expand the folder structure in the Folder Pane and drag the attachment to that folder.

If you want to concentrate on reading messages without the distraction of other information typically presented in the Outlook program window, you can quickly reconfigure the program window to optimize message reading by clicking the Reading button on the status bar, to the left of the zoom controls.

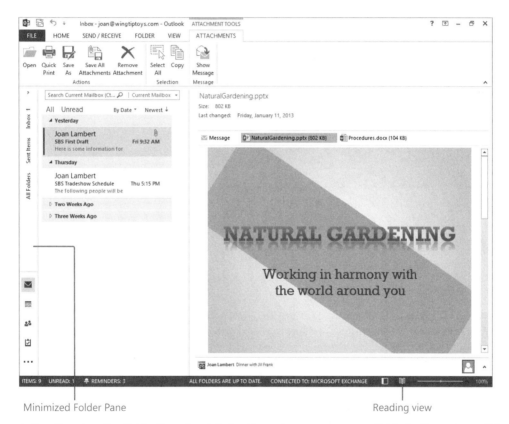

Minimized Folder Pane   Reading view

In Reading view, the Folder Pane is minimized to make more space available for the message list and Reading Pane.

Viewing conversations

Conversation view was first introduced in Outlook 2007 as a way of grouping a series of received messages that stem from the same original message. This feature made it easy to locate various responses to a message and to identify separate branches of a conversation (referred to as *message threads*). The original Conversation view has been expanded to present an even clearer method of tracking message threads and to include not only received messages but also sent messages. Conversation view is a useful organizational tool that you can use to more easily manage all the information associated with a particular subject.

In Conversation view, a conversation of multiple messages is indicated by an arrow to the left of the conversation message header. You can click the arrow once to display all the unique messages in the conversation, and again to display all the messages, including your sent messages. You can manage Conversation view from the Messages group on the View tab.

SEE ALSO For more information about Conversation view, see "Working with Conversation view" in Chapter 7, "Organize your Inbox."

Viewing content in the Reading Pane

You will frequently read and work with messages and other Outlook items in the Reading Pane. You can display the Reading Pane to the right of or below the module content pane.

You might find it difficult to read the text in the Reading Pane at its default size, particularly if your display is set to a high screen resolution, as is becoming more and more common. You can change the size of the content displayed in the Reading Pane by using the Zoom controls located at the right end of the program window status bar to change the pane's magnification level.

In the program window, the Zoom controls change the size of the content in the Reading Pane.

SEE ALSO For information about modifying Reading Pane functionality, see "Configuring Office and Outlook options" in Chapter 11, "Customize Outlook."

You can change the magnification of a message in the Reading Pane in the following ways:

- To set a specific magnification level, click the **Zoom level** button to open the **Zoom** dialog box.

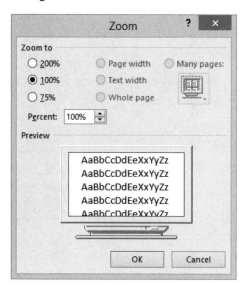

Select one of the three predefined magnification levels, or enter a specific magnification level in the Percent box.

- To change the zoom level in 10-percent increments, click the **Zoom Out** and **Zoom In** buttons.

- To quickly change the zoom level to any setting between 10 percent and 500 percent, move the **Zoom** slider to the left or right.

You can scroll through a long message in the Reading Pane in the following ways:

- Scroll at your own pace by dragging the vertical scroll bar that appears at the right side of the Reading Pane.

- Move up or down one line at a time by clicking the scroll arrows.

- Move up or down one page at time by clicking above or below the scroll box.

- Move up or down one page at a time by pressing the Spacebar. When you reach the end of a message by using this feature, called Single Key Reading, pressing the Spacebar again displays the first page of the next message. This option is very convenient if you want to read through several consecutive messages in the Reading Pane, or if you find it easier to press the Spacebar than to use the mouse.

In this exercise, you'll preview and open a message and two types of attachments.

SET UP You need the SBS First Draft message you created earlier in this chapter to complete this exercise. If you did not create that message, you can do so now, or you can substitute any received message with an attachment in your Inbox. Display your Inbox in Normal view, and then follow the steps.

1   On the **View** tab, in the **Current View** group, click the **Change View** button, and then click **Preview** to close the **Reading Pane**, and display the first 255 characters of each message in the **Inbox** below the message header.

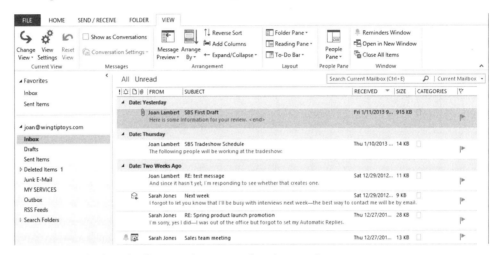

Preview view displays the first 255 characters of each unread message.

2   Locate the **SBS First Draft** message in your **Inbox**, and then click the message to display the message content in the **Reading Pane**.

3   Note the following below the message header: a **Message** button (which looks more like just the word *Message* than it does like a button), and, depending on the width of your **Reading Pane**, either the names of both attachments or the name of one of the attached files, and an **Attachment** icon (a paper clip) followed by the number **2**.

TROUBLESHOOTING If you are working through this exercise with a message that does not have an attachment, the header does not include the elements described in step 3.

4   On the **View** tab, in the **Change View** list, click **Single**.

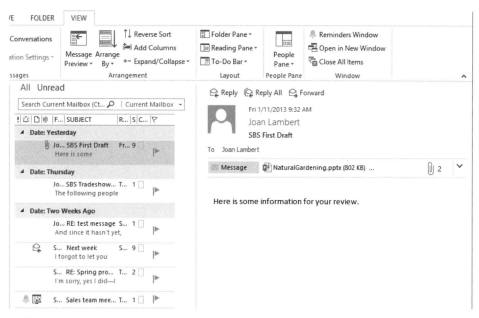

In Single view, the preview text is removed and the Reading Pane reopens.

5   Click the **Attachment** icon one time to display both attachments
    (**NaturalGardening.pptx** and **Procedures.docx**).

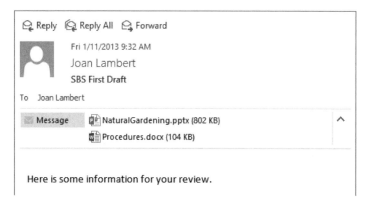

Pointing to the Message button displays the number of attached files. Pointing to an attachment displays information about that file. The same information is displayed in the user interface.

TIP If more files are attached than can be displayed in the attachment list, you can scroll the list by using the scroll bar to the right of the list.

6   Click the **Procedures.docx** attachment once to preview the fully formatted Word 2013
    document in the **Reading Pane**. Notice that the document information replaces the
    message header.

7   Scroll through the document in the **Reading Pane**. Notice that elements such as hyperlinks are active and available.

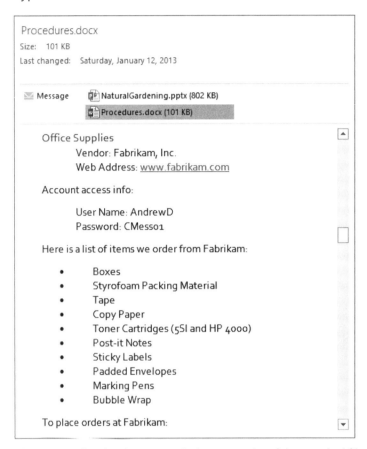

The message header changes to display properties of the attached file.

TIP If preview software for a selected file type hasn't been installed, Outlook won't be able to preview a file of that type in the Reading Pane. Clicking certain types of attachments displays a warning message asking you to confirm that the content comes from a trusted source. You can click Preview File to continue. You can give Outlook permission to skip the warning message for files of this type by clearing the Always Warn Before Previewing This Type Of File check box and then clicking Preview File.

8   Click the **Natural Gardening.pptx** attachment to display the title slide of the presentation in the **Reading Pane**. The presentation includes animated elements, and therefore the first slide is blank until you click it in the **Reading Pane**. You can run the animations and move among the presentation's slides by clicking the slide in the preview area.

9   In the preview area, click the slide to run the first animation. Click the slide a second time to run the second animation, and a third time to advance the presentation to the second slide, exactly as it would if you were displaying the slide show in PowerPoint.

10 At the bottom of the vertical scroll bar, click the **Next** button (the arrow) once to advance to the third slide without displaying the animated elements on the second slide. Then click the slide in the preview area once to display the first animated element on the slide.

When previewing a PowerPoint presentation, you can navigate through the presentation by clicking the presentation or the Next button.

11 In the **Reading Pane**, click the **Message** button (or, in the **Message** group on the **Attachments** tab, click **Show Message**) to redisplay the message content in the **Reading Pane**.

12   In the **Reading Pane**, double-click the **NaturalGardening.pptx** attachment (or, in the **Actions** group on the **Attachments** tab, click **Open**) to start PowerPoint and open the presentation.

> **SEE ALSO** For information about and tutorials for using PowerPoint 2013, refer to *Microsoft PowerPoint 2013 Step by Step* by Joyce Cox and Joan Lambert (Microsoft Press, 2013).

13   Close the presentation to return to your **Inbox**.

14   In the message list, double-click the **SBS First Draft** message to open the message in its own window. The **Message** button and attachments are shown below the message header in the message window, as they are in the **Reading Pane**.

15   In the message window, click the **Procedures.docx** attachment once. The **Attachments** tool tab appears on the ribbon, and a preview of the document appears in the message content pane exactly as it did in the Reading Pane.

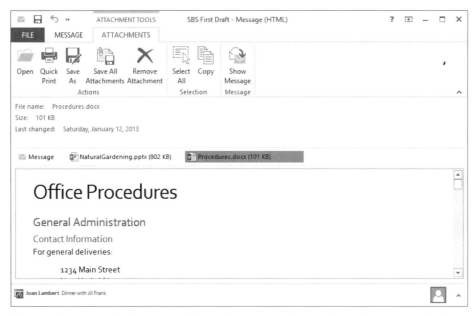

You use the same techniques to preview and open attachments from the message window that you do from the Reading Pane.

✖ CLEAN UP Close the SBS First Draft message window, and retain it in your Inbox for use in later exercises. On the View tab of the program window, in the Current View group, click Compact in the Change View gallery, and then click Reset View.

Viewing message participant information

After you receive a message (or after Outlook validates a recipient's name in a message that you're sending), you can easily display contact information and a history of your communications with that person.

Presence icons

Outlook uses presence information provided by programs such as Microsoft Lync Server and Office Communications Server. If presence information is available, a square presence icon appears in the Reading Pane or message window to the left of each message participant's name, and a rectangular icon to the left of each contact picture, when shown in a message. The presence icon (casually referred to as a *jelly bean* or *chiclet*) is color-coded to indicate the availability or online status of the message participant, as follows:

- **Green** The person is online and available.
- **Red** The person is busy, in a conference call, or in a meeting.
- **Dark red with a white bar** The person does not want to be disturbed.
- **Yellow** The person is away or has not been active online for a certain length of time (usually five minutes).
- **Gray** The person is offline.
- **White** The person's presence information is not known.

TIP This same set of presence icons is used in Outlook, Microsoft SharePoint, and Lync to provide a consistent user experience. We don't display the presence icons in all the graphics in this book, but we do display some in this topic.

Contact cards

Pointing to a message participant's name displays an interactive contact card of information that includes options for contacting the person by email, instant message, or phone; for scheduling a meeting; and for working with the person's contact record.

Pinning the contact card keeps it open even if you send or close the email message.

Clicking the Open Contact Card button displays a more extensive range of information and interaction options.

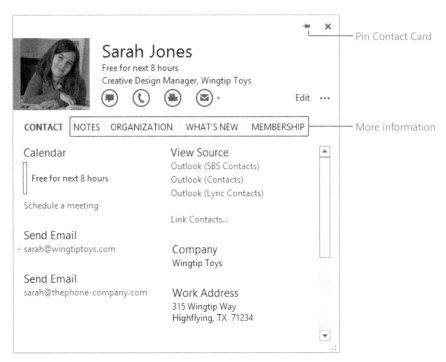

From the expanded contact card, you can view the contact's position within the organization and which distribution lists he or she is a member of.

TIP A distribution list is a membership group created through Exchange and available from an organization's Global Address List. You can't create distribution lists, but you can create contact groups, which are membership groups saved in the Outlook Contacts module. For more information, see "Creating contact groups" in Chapter 9, "Manage contact records."

Clicking any of the blue links initiates contact with the person through the stored phone number or email address, initiates a meeting request, or, if the person is in your address book, opens his or her contact record.

The Organization tab displays information about the person's manager and direct reports. The What's New tab displays social updates. The Membership tab displays information about distribution lists the contact is a member of. This information is available only for Exchange accounts.

The People Pane

The People Pane at the bottom of the message window displays extensive information about your previous communications with each message participant.

In its minimized state, the People Pane displays small thumbnails that represent each message participant. If a person's contact record includes a photograph, the photo appears in the People Pane. If no photograph is available, a silhouette of one person represents an individual message participant, and a silhouette of three people represents a distribution list.

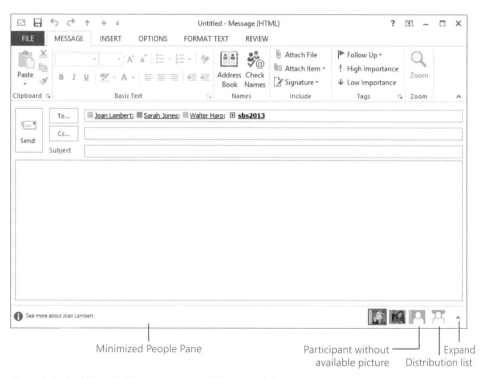

Minimized People Pane   Participant without —— available picture | Expand Distribution list

The minimized People Pane shows small images of the conversation participants.

You can expand the People Pane by clicking the Expand button at the right end of the pane, by dragging the horizontal bar at the top of the pane, or by clicking Normal in the People Pane list on the View tab. The People Pane can occupy only a certain percentage of the message window, so the amount you can manually adjust the height of the People Pane to is dependent on the height of the message window.

In its expanded state, the People Pane displays either large thumbnails or a tabbed break-down of communications for each message participant.

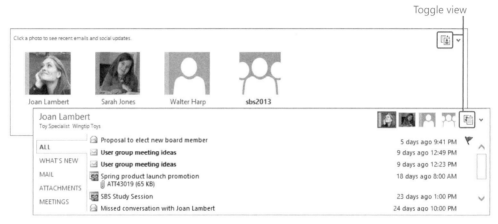

The expanded People Pane displays either participant images or a history of interactions with the selected participant.

You can switch between the simple view and the detailed view by clicking the Toggle button located near the right end of the expanded People Pane header.

The All Items tab of the detailed view displays all your recent Outlook interactions with the selected person. If you're looking for a specific item, such as a meeting request or a docu-ment attached to a message, you can filter the item list by clicking any of the tabs to the left of the list.

TIP The detailed People Pane is available for all types of email accounts. The images in this book depict the People Pane for an Exchange account. The People Pane for a POP3 account is identical except that the tabs are labeled with words only, rather than icons and words.

Troubleshooting the People Pane

When working with an Exchange account, you can display the People Pane in detailed view only if the Cached Exchange Mode feature is enabled. If the Toggle button isn't visible in the expanded People Pane when you're viewing an Exchange account message, the likely problem is that Cached Exchange Mode is not enabled.

To enable Cached Exchange Mode, follow these steps:

1. On the **Info** page of the **Backstage** view of the Outlook program window, click **Account Settings**, and then in the list that appears, click **Account Settings**.

2. On the **E-mail** page of the **Account Settings** dialog box, click your Exchange account, and then click **Change**.

3. On the **Server Settings** page of the **Change Account** wizard, select the **Use Cached Exchange Mode** check box, click **Next**, and then on the wizard's final page, click **Finish**.

The Toggle button should now be visible in the header of the expanded People Pane.

Responding to messages

You can respond to most email messages that you receive by clicking a response button either in the Reading Pane, in the message window, or in the Respond group on the Message tab.

The most standard response to a message is a reply. When you reply to a message, Outlook fills in one or more of the address boxes for you, as follows:

- **Reply** Creates an email message, addressed to only the original message sender, that contains the original message text.

- **Reply All** Creates an email message, addressed to the message sender and all recipients listed in the To and Cc boxes, that contains the original message text. The message is not addressed to recipients of blind courtesy copies (Bcc recipients).

- **Reply with Meeting** Creates a meeting invitation addressed to all message recipients. The message text is included in the meeting window content pane. Outlook suggests the current date and an upcoming half-hour time slot for the meeting.

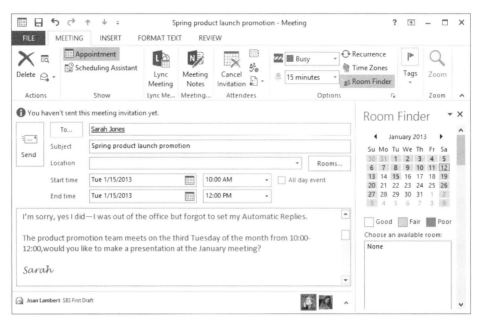

A meeting invitation created from a message.

Message replies include the original message header and text, preceded by a space in which you can respond. Replies do not include any attachments from the original message.

You can add, change, and delete recipients from any reply before sending it.

You can forward a received message to any email address (regardless of whether the recipient uses Outlook) provided the message was not sent with restricted permissions. Outlook 2013 has the following message-forwarding options:

- **Forward** Creates a new message that contains the text of the original, and retains any attachments from the original message.

- **Forward As Attachment** Creates a blank message that contains no text but includes the original message as an attachment. The original message text and any attachments are available to the new recipient when he or she opens the attached message.

Both types of forwarded messages include the original message header and text, preceded by a space in which you can add information. Forwarded messages include attachments from the original message.

When you forward a message, Outlook does not fill in the recipient boxes for you.

If you reply to or forward a received message from within the message window, the original message remains open after you send your response. You can instruct Outlook to close original messages after you respond to them—you'll probably be finished working with the message at that point. To do so, display the Mail page of the Outlook Options dialog box, select the Close Original Message Window When Replying Or Forwarding check box in the Replies And Forwards area, and then click OK.

TIP When responding to an email message, take care to use good email etiquette. For example, if your response is not pertinent to all the original recipients of a message, don't reply to the entire recipient list, especially if the message was addressed to a distribution list that might include hundreds of members.

You can prevent other people from replying to all recipients of a message you send by addressing the message to yourself and entering other recipients in the Bcc box. Then the recipient list will not be visible to anyone.

SEE ALSO For information about restricting recipients from copying, printing, or forwarding messages, see "Increasing email security" in Chapter 12, "Manage email settings."

If your organization has the necessary unified communications infrastructure, you may also have these additional response options:

- **Call or Call All** Initiates a Voice over IP (VoIP) call from your computer to the phone number of the original message sender or sender and other message recipients.

- **Reply with IM or Reply All with IM** Opens an instant messaging window with the message sender or sender and other recipients as the chat participants.

TROUBLESHOOTING The response options available in your Outlook installation might vary from those described here. The available response options for your installation will appear in the Respond group on the Message tab of the message window or the Home tab of the program window.

Nonstandard messages have alternative response options, such as the following:

- A meeting request includes options for responding to the request.

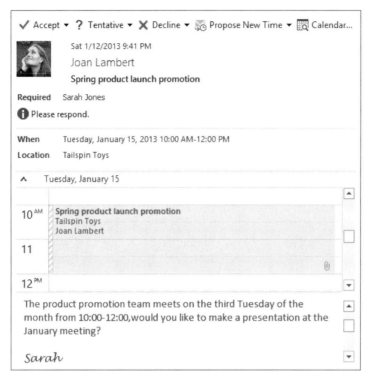

Responding to a meeting request from the Reading Pane.

SEE ALSO For information about meeting requests, see "Scheduling meetings" in Chapter 5, "Manage scheduling."

- A task assignment includes options for accepting or declining the assignment.

Responding to a task assignment from the Reading Pane.

SEE ALSO For information about task assignments, see "Managing task assignments" in Chapter 6, "Track tasks."

- If a message contains voting buttons, you can respond by opening the message, clicking the Vote button in the Respond group on the Message tab, and then clicking the response you want to send. Or you can click the InfoBar (labeled *Click here to vote*) in the Reading Pane and then click the response you want.

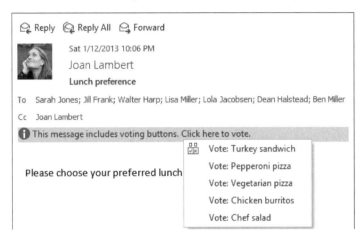

Voting from the Reading Pane.

SEE ALSO For information about polling other Outlook users in your organization, see "Changing message settings and delivery options" in Chapter 10, "Enhance message content."

In this exercise, you'll reply to and forward a message that has an attachment.

SET UP You need the SBS First Draft message you created earlier in this chapter to complete this exercise. If you did not create that message, you can do so now, or you can substitute any received message with an attachment in your Inbox. Display your Inbox, and then follow the steps.

1   Open the **SBS First Draft** message in a message window. Notice that the message includes two attachments, and the message window ribbon displays only the **Message** tab containing all the commands you use with a received message.

2   On the **Message** tab, in the **Respond** group, click the **Reply** button to create a response already addressed to you (the original sender). If the message had been sent to any other people, the reply would not include them. The *RE:* prefix appears at the beginning of the message subject to indicate that this is a response to an earlier

message. Note that the response does not include the original attachments (and in fact there is no indication that the original message had any). The original message, including its header information, appears in the content pane, separated from the new content by a horizontal line.

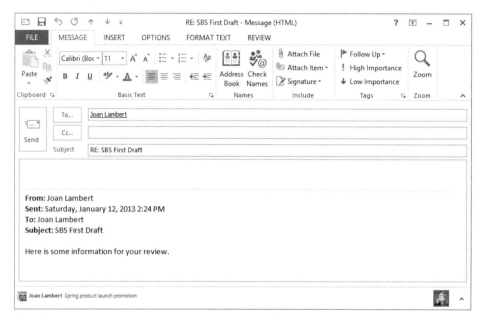

Replying to a message generates a new message addressed to the original sender.

3   With the cursor at the top of the content pane, enter the following sentence:

We'll need to get approval from the Marketing team before proceeding.

4   In the response header, click the **Send** button to send the reply, which appears in your **Inbox** as the active message in the **SBS First Draft** conversation. The original message remains open on your screen.

5   In the original message, in the **Respond** group, click the **Forward** button to create a new version of the message that is not addressed to any recipient. The **FW:** prefix at the beginning of the message subject indicates that this is a forwarded message. The files that were attached to the original message appear in the **Attached** box. The message is otherwise identical to the earlier response. You address and send a forwarded message as you would any other.

TROUBLESHOOTING If the original message closes, select the message in your Inbox and then click the Forward button in the Respond group on the Home tab.

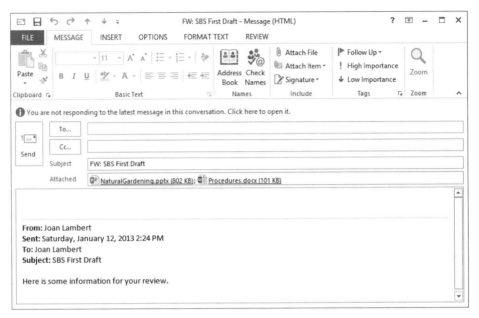

The MailTip at the top of the message header indicates that another message (your response) has been added to the conversation, so the message you're forwarding isn't the most current message in the conversation.

6   With the cursor active in the **To** box, enter your email address.

7   Click to position the cursor at the top of the content pane, and then enter the following sentence:

Don't forget to review these!

8   Send the message, and then close the original message window.

9   When the second message appears in your **Inbox**, compare the two messages and note the similarities and differences. For example, the **Subject** prefixes are different, and the forwarded message includes the original message attachments.

✕ CLEAN UP Close any open message windows. Retain the SBS First Draft conversation for use in exercises in later chapters.

Resending and recalling messages

If you want to send a new version of a message you've already sent—for example, a status report in which you update details each week—you can *resend* the message. Resending a message creates a new version of the message with none of the extra information that might be attached to a forwarded message. To resend a message, follow these steps:

1 From your **Sent Items** folder, open the message you want to resend. (Or, if you copied yourself on the message, you can open it from your **Inbox**.)

2 On the **Message** tab, in the **Move** group, click the **More Move Actions** button, and then in the list, click **Resend This Message**.

Outlook creates a new message form identical to the original. You can change the message recipients, subject, attachments, or content before sending the new version of the message.

If, after sending a message, you realize that you shouldn't have sent it—for example, if the message contained an error or was sent to the wrong people—you can *recall* it by instructing Outlook to delete or replace any unread copies of the message. To recall a message, follow these steps:

1 From your **Sent Items** folder, open the message you want to recall.

2 On the **Message** tab, in the **Move** group, click the **More Move Actions** button, and then click **Recall This Message**.

3 In the **Recall This Message** dialog box, click the option to delete unread copies of the message or the option to replace unread copies with a new message, and then click **OK**.

You will receive a notification for each of the original message participants telling you whether the recall was successful for that participant. The message recall operation works only for participants with Exchange accounts. Participants with Internet email accounts and participants who have already opened the original message will end up with both the original message and the recall message.

TROUBLESHOOTING You may want to test the message recall functionality within your organization before you have occasion to need it. Only unread messages can be recalled.

Key points

- You can easily create email messages that include attachments.

- By default, messages you receive appear in the message list in your Inbox.

- You can display the first few lines of each message in Preview view, open a message in its own window, or preview messages in the Reading Pane. You can also preview message attachments in the Reading Pane.

- You can reply to the message sender only or to the sender and all other recipients. You can also forward a message and its attachments to other people.

3

Chapter at a glance

Save

Save and update contact information,
page 134

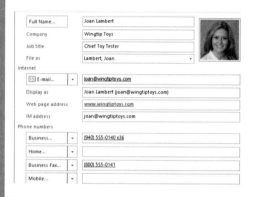

Communicate

Communicate with contacts,
page 146

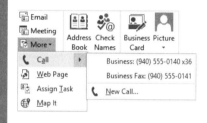

Display

Display different views of contact records,
page 149

Print

Print contact records,
page 157

Store and access contact information

4

IN THIS CHAPTER, YOU WILL LEARN HOW TO

- Save and update contact information.

- Communicate with contacts.

- Display different views of contact records.

- Print contact records.

Having immediate access to current, accurate contact information for the people you need to interact with—by email, phone, mail, or otherwise—is important for timely and effective communication. You can easily build and maintain a detailed contact list, or address book, in the Microsoft Outlook 2013 People module. From your address book, you can look up information, create messages, and share contact information with other people. You can also keep track of your interactions with a person whose contact information is stored in Outlook.

If you need to take contact information with you in a non-electronic format, you can print an address book or selected contact records, in many different formats.

In this chapter, you'll create and edit contact records and view them in different ways. Then you'll discover how to initiate communications with people from contact records or from an address book. Finally, you'll print a contact record and a list of contact information.

PRACTICE FILES You don't need any practice files to complete the exercises in this chapter.

Saving and updating contact information

You save contact information for people and companies by creating a contact record in an address book.

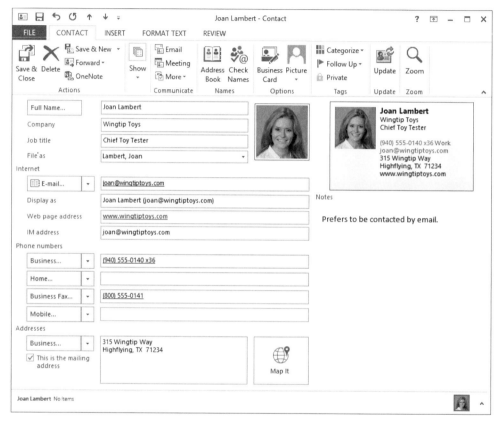

A typical contact record for a business contact.

TIP You can create a personalized electronic business card for yourself or for any of your contacts. For information, see "Personalizing electronic business cards" in Chapter 9, "Manage contact records."

On the General page of a contact record, you can store the following types of contact information:

- Name, company name, and job title
- Business, home, and alternate addresses
- Business, home, mobile, pager, and other phone numbers
- Business, home, and alternate fax numbers
- Webpage address (URL), instant messaging (IM) address, and up to three email addresses

  TIP If you need to store more than three email addresses for a contact, you can do so by creating a custom contact record form.

- Photo, company logo, or other identifying image
- General notes, which can include text and illustrations such as photos, clip art images, SmartArt diagrams, charts, and shapes

On the Details page of a contact record, you can store personal and organization-specific details, such as the following:

- Professional information, including department, office location, profession, manager's name, and assistant's name
- Personal information, including nickname, spouse or partner's name, birthday, anniversary, and the title (such as Miss, Mrs., or Ms.) and suffix (such as Jr. or Sr.) for use in correspondence

Creating contact records

You typically create a contact record by displaying the address book to which you want to add the contact record in the People module and then clicking the New Contact button in the New group on the Home tab. In the contact record window that opens, you insert the information you want to save. After you save the contact record, it appears in the contact list.

You can create a contact record that contains only one piece of information (for example, a name or company name), or as much information as you want to include. You can quickly create contact records for several people who work for the same company by cloning the company information from an existing record to a new one. And of course, you can add to or change the information stored in a contact record at any time.

The order in which Outlook displays contact records in the contact list is controlled by the File As setting. By default, Outlook files contacts by last name (Last, First order). If you prefer, you can change the order for new contacts to any of the following:

- First Last
- Company
- Last, First (Company)
- Company (Last, First)

To set the filing order for all your contacts, display the People page of the Outlook Options dialog box, click the Default "File As" Order arrow and select an order from the list. You can change the filing order for an individual contact by selecting the order you want in the File As list in the contact record.

TIP In addition to creating individual contact records, you can create groups of contacts so that you can manage messaging to multiple people through one email address. For information, see "Creating contact groups" in Chapter 9, "Manage contact records."

Address books

Outlook stores contact information from different sources in separate address books. Some are created by Outlook, some by your email server administrator, and others by you.

Contacts address books

Outlook creates a Contacts address book for each account you connect to. These address books are available from the My Contacts list in the Folder Pane of the People module.

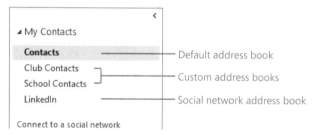

The Folder Pane of the People module displays a list of all your address books.

The Contacts address book of your default email account is your main address book, and it is the address book that appears by default in the People module. The Contacts address book is empty until you add contact records to it.

Custom address books

You can create address books in addition to those associated with email accounts; for example, you might want to keep contact information for family and friends in an address book separate from client contact information, or you might maintain an address book for clients that meet specific criteria.

You create an address book by creating a folder and specifying that the folder will contain contact items.

An address book is a folder designed specifically to contain contact records and contact groups.

When you display the Folder List in the Folder Pane, your custom address books appear along with other folders you create, and you can organize them in the same manner— for example, at the same level as your Inbox, as a subfolder of the Contacts address book, or inside a project folder. All address books are available from the My Contacts list in the Folder Pane of the People module.

SEE ALSO For information about creating address books, see "Organizing messages in folders" in Chapter 7, "Organize your Inbox."

TIP If your organization stores contact information in a SharePoint contact list, you can import the list contents from SharePoint into Outlook as an address book. For more information, see "Working with SharePoint site content" in Chapter 13, "Work remotely."

Global Address Lists

If you have a Microsoft Exchange Server account, you also have access to an official address book called the Global Address List (or *GAL*). The GAL is maintained by your organization's Exchange administrator and includes information about individuals within your organization, distribution lists, and resources (such as conference rooms and media equipment) that you can reserve when you schedule meetings. It can also include organizational information (each person's manager and direct subordinates) and group membership information (the distribution lists each person belongs to).

The GAL doesn't appear in the My Contacts list shown in the Folder Pane of the People module. To display the GAL, click the Address Book button in the Find group on the Home tab of the People module or the Address Book button in the Names group on the Message tab of a message composition window. Outlook users can view the GAL but not change its contents. Only an Exchange administrator can modify the GAL.

In this exercise, you'll create and edit a contact record in your main address book.

 SET UP You don't need any practice files to complete this exercise. Display the People module, and then follow the steps.

1   On the **Home** tab, in the **New** group, click the **New Contact** button to open a new contact record window.

2   In the **Full Name** box, enter Sarah Jones, and then press the **Tab** key to move the cursor to the **Company** box. Notice that Outlook transfers the name to the **File as** box, and displays it in the default order (**Last, First**). The name also appears on the contact record window title bar and in the business card representation.

    SEE ALSO For information about changing the default order, see "Configuring Office and Outlook options" in Chapter 11, "Customize Outlook."

3   In the **Company** box, enter Wingtip Toys.

4   In the **Job title** box, enter Creative Design Manager.

5   In the **Internet** area of the form, enter sarah@wingtiptoys.com in the **E-mail** box, and press **Tab**. Notice that Outlook formats the email address as a hyperlink and enters the name and email address in the **Display as** box. This box indicates the way the contact will appear in the headers of email messages you exchange with this contact.

6   In the **Display as** box, select the email address inside the parentheses and replace it with the designator work.

7   Click the **E-mail** arrow (not the button) to display a list of the email address fields available in the contact record.

Groups of related contact information fields are indicated by an arrow button to the right of the field name.

8   In the **E-mail** list, click **E-mail 2** to change the displayed email address and display name.

9   In the **E-mail 2** field, enter sarah@thephone-company.com, and then press **Tab** to populate the **Display as** field with information for this email address. Although the field name doesn't change to indicate it, this information is specific to the **E-mail 2** field.

10   In the **Display as** box, select the email address inside the parentheses and then enter personal. Notice that the business card representation in the upper-right corner of the contact card displays both email addresses, but not their labels.

11   In the **Web page address** box, enter www.wingtiptoys.com. Outlook formats the URL as a hyperlink.

12   In the **Phone numbers** section of the form, enter 9405550140 in the **Business** box, and then press **Tab**. Notice that Outlook formats the string of numbers in standard telephone number format.

13   In the **Addresses** area, click in the text box to the right of **Business**, enter 315 Wingtip Way, press the **Enter** key, and then enter Highflying, TX 71234.

TIP In a new contact record, a selected check box to the left of the Business address field indicates that it is the default mailing address for the contact.

14   Click the **Business** arrow to display the list of address labels, and then click **Home** to indicate the address information you want to enter.

15   In the text box, enter 111 Magnolia Lane, press **Enter**, and then enter Flower Hill, TX 71235. The contact record now contains both business and personal contact information.

TIP If you enter multiple addresses for a contact and want to specify one as the default mailing address, display that address and then select the This Is The Mailing Address check box.

SEE ALSO For information about adding an image to a contact record, see "Personal-izing electronic business cards" in Chapter 9, "Manage contact records."

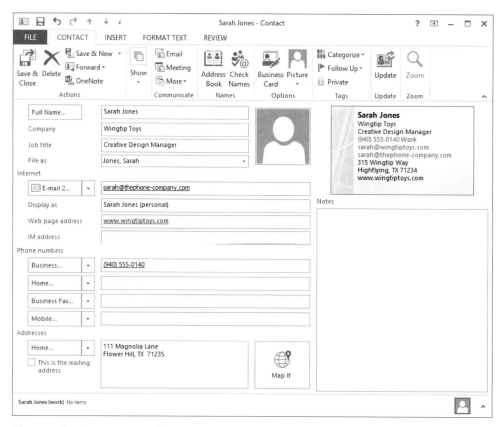

The completed contact record.

16   On the **Contact** tab, in the **Actions** group, click the **Save & Close** button to close the
      contact record window. The contact list now includes the new contact record for
      Sarah Jones, shown in the default **People** view.

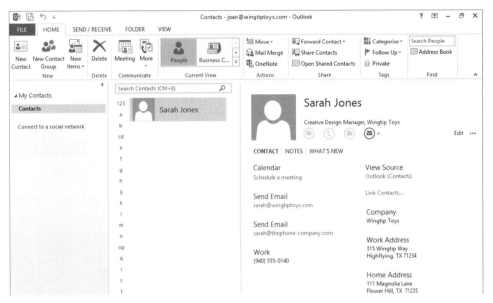

A People card view of the new contact record is visible in the contact list.

17   In the contact list, double-click the entry for **Sarah Jones** to open the **People** card
      that contains her information. This card format is new in Outlook 2013; it cleanly
      displays the available information exactly as it appears in the Reading Pane.

      TIP You can assign follow-up flags to contact entries, and link contact entries to
      email messages, appointments, tasks, and other Outlook items. For more informa-
      tion, see "Creating tasks" in Chapter 6, "Track tasks." You can open a contact record in
      the original multipage contact record window by first displaying the People module
      in a view other than People view, and then double-clicking the contact record. You
      can view all items linked to a contact on the Activities page of the contact record
      window.

18   In the **Reading Pane**, click **Edit**, and then scroll to the bottom of the pane.

      TIP You can edit a contact record directly in the Reading Pane or you can open it in a
      separate window by double-clicking it in the contact list.

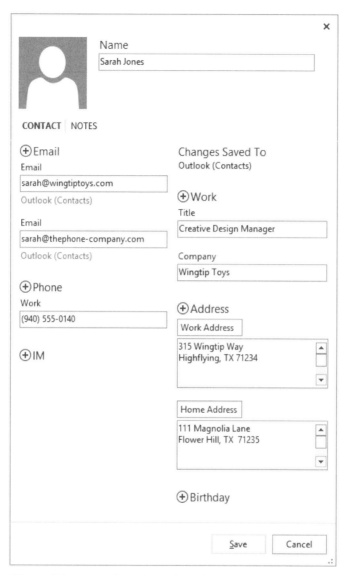

When editing a People card, you have fewer options than when editing a standard contact record.

19   Click the plus sign to the left of **Birthday**, click the **Birthday** arrow, scroll the calendar to **January**, and then click **23** to display January 23 of the current year in the **Birthday** box.

> **TIP** The birthday or anniversary date you select in the calendar defaults to the current calendar year.

20 In the **Birthday** box, replace the current year with 1979.

21 In the lower-right corner of the **Reading Pane**, click the **Save** button.

22 In the contact list, click the **Sarah Jones** contact record. On the **Home** tab, in the **New** group, click the **New Items** button, and then click **Contact from the Same Company** to create a new contact record that already contains the company name, webpage address, business phone number, and business address from the **Sarah Jones** contact record. Because no person's name has been provided, the **File as** name is currently set to the company name.

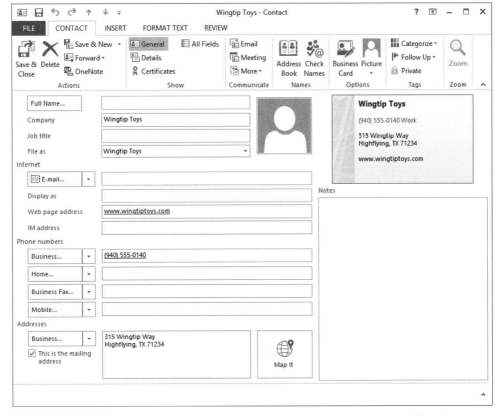

Without any changes, the new contact record could be saved as a contact record for the company rather than for a specific person.

23 In the **Full Name** box, enter Lola Jacobsen, and in the **Job title** box, enter Sales Associate.

24 In the **E-mail** box, enter lola@wingtiptoys.com. Leave the default **Display as** text.

25 Save and close the open contact record.

26 Create a new contact record and enter the following information:

- Full name: Ben Miller

- Company: Fabrikam, Inc.

- Job title: Manufacturing Manager

- Email address: ben@fabrikam.com

- Webpage address: www.fabrikam.com

27 After you enter the contact information, click the **Save & New** arrow (not the button) in the **Actions** group on the **Home** tab, and then click **Contact from the Same Company** to create a new contact record for Fabrikam, Inc.

28 Populate this contact record and create one more, to create contact records for the following people:

Full name	Company	Job title	Email address
Dean Halstead	Fabrikam, Inc.	Quality Control Manager	dean@fabrikam.com
Jill Frank	Fabrikam, Inc.	Sales Associate	jill@fabrikam.com

29 Save and close the open contact records. The contact list now includes the five records you've created. Notice that the contact records appear in **File as** (last, first) order rather than in order by first name, even though the first name appears first in the contact list.

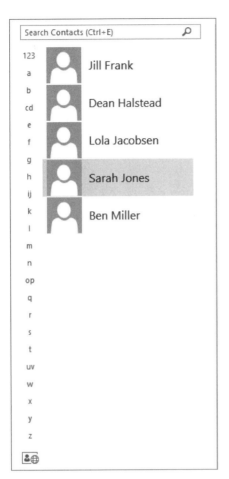

If an address book contains a lot of records, you can quickly scroll to those filed by a specific letter by clicking that letter in the contact index.

❌ CLEAN UP Save and close any open contact records to return to the contact list. Retain the Jill Frank, Dean Halstead, Lola Jacobsen, Sarah Jones, and Ben Miller contact records for use in later exercises.

Communicating with contacts

Saving contact information for people in a physical or an electronic address book is useful because it centralizes the information in one place so that you no longer have to remember the information or where to find it. The added benefit of saving contact information in an Outlook address book is that it makes the process of initiating communication with a contact much more efficient.

Initiating communication from contact records

Contact records are useful not only for storing information; you can also initiate a number of actions that are specific to a selected contact. Commands for initiating communication are available in the Communicate group on the Contact tab of an open contact record or in the header of a People card.

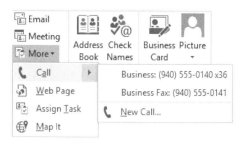

The commands available in the Communicate group may vary based on your specific Outlook configuration.

You can perform many actions from within a contact record window (but not in a People card) by using the commands in the Communicate group on the Contact tab, including the following:

- Create an email message addressed to the contact by clicking the Email button.

- Create a meeting request that includes the contact by clicking the Meeting button.

- Initiate a chat session with the contact by clicking the Reply With IM button (if it is available in your organization's environment).

- Place a call to the contact by clicking the Call arrow and then, in the list, clicking the phone number you would like Outlook to dial (requires unified communications).

- Display the contact's website by clicking the Web Page button.

- Create a task assigned to the contact by clicking the Assign Task button.

- Display a map of the contact's address by clicking the Map It button.

If Microsoft OneNote 2013 is installed on your computer, you can create a OneNote notebook entry that is linked to the contact record by clicking the OneNote button in the Actions group on the Contact tab.

Conforming to address standards

When you enter information in a contact record, Outlook verifies that the information conforms to expected patterns. If Outlook detects possible irregularities, a related dialog box opens, prompting you to enter information into a standard template.

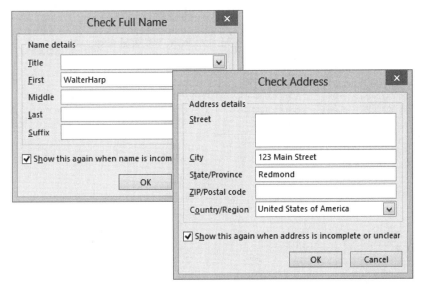

The Check Full Name and Check Address dialog boxes fit contact information into standard patterns.

The intention of these dialog boxes is to verify that you have usable contact information available. If you determine that the information in the dialog box is correct as-is, you can click Cancel to close the dialog box without making changes.

TIP You can create a contact record for the sender of a message you have received by right-clicking the sender's name in the message header—either in the Reading Pane or the open message item—and then clicking Add To Outlook Contacts. Outlook creates a contact record with the name and email address already filled in. Add any other information you want to record, and then save the contact record.

Selecting message recipients from address books

When you send an email message to a person whose contact information is stored in one of your address books, you can quickly address the message to that person by entering his or her name exactly as it appears in the address book and letting Outlook validate the address. If you don't know the exact spelling of the name, follow these steps:

1 In the message composition window, click the **Address Book** button in the **Names** group on the **Message** tab to open the **Select Name** dialog box.

2 In the **Address Book** list, click the arrow, and then click the address book you want to search.

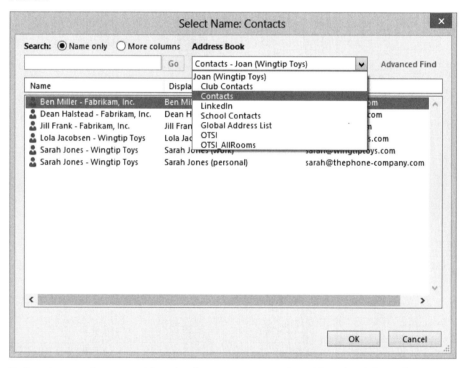

To insert names from an address book, you must open the address book from the message composition window.

3   Scroll through the **Name** list, and locate the person's name. If you have multiple email addresses saved for that person, the name will appear once for each email address.

   TIP You can enter the first few letters of the person's name to scroll to entries beginning with those letters.

4   To add the person in the **To** box as a primary message recipient, double-click the name, or click it and then press **Enter**. To add the person as a secondary or private recipient, click in the **Cc** or **Bcc** box at the bottom of the dialog box and then double-click the name, or click it and press **Enter**.

   TIP If you click the To, Cc, or Bcc box in the message header before clicking the Address Book button, double-clicking the name adds the person to that box. You can also click the Cc or Bcc box and then click the adjacent button to open the Select Names dialog box with that box active.

5   After selecting all message recipients from the address book, click **OK** to close the **Select Names** dialog box and return to the message composition window.

SEE ALSO For information about creating email messages, see "Creating and sending messages" in Chapter 3, "Send and receive email messages."

Displaying different views of contact records

You can view all your address books in the People module. You can also display a list of the contacts in an address book, including those in your organization's Global Address List, in one of these ways:

- Click the **Address Book** button in the **Find** group on the **Home** tab of the program window in any module to open the **Address Book** window.

- Click the **Address Book** button in the **Names** group on the **Contact** tab of a contact record window to open the **Select Name** dialog box.

Expand the Address Book list, and then click the name of the address book whose contents you want to display.

In the People module, you can view an address book in many different formats. You can choose any standard view from the Current View gallery on the Home tab.

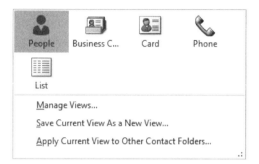

The standard view options for the People module.

Each view presents information from your contact records either as cards or in a list:

- **People** Displays only contact names in the contact list, and the available information for the selected contact in the Reading Pane. Contact names are displayed in alphabetical order by first or last name, depending on the File As selection. This view displays information about the contact from multiple sources. For example, if you have an Outlook contact record for a person you network with on LinkedIn and Facebook, the People card displays a compilation of the information from all three locations. This view, which is new in Outlook 2013, is the default view.

- **Business Card** Displays the business card associated with each contact record—either the default card created by Outlook or a custom card if you have one. Business cards are displayed in the alphabetical order specified by the File As selection.

- **Card** Displays contact information as truncated business cards that include limited information, such as job title and company name.

- **Phone** Displays a columnar list that includes each contact's name, company, and contact numbers. You can choose the grouping you want from the Arrangements gallery on the View tab.

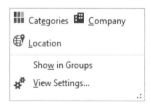

Buttons in the gallery on the Arrangements menu of the People module are available only while contact records are displayed in a list view.

- **List** Displays a columnar list with contact records arranged in groups. You can choose the grouping you want from the Arrangements gallery on the View tab.

  In any list view, you can expand and collapse the groups or select and take action on an entire group of contacts. You can also enter information directly into any contact record field displayed in the list.

You can search and filter your contact records in any view by using the Instant Search feature from the search box at the top of the content area. You can sort contact records by any displayed column in a list view by clicking the column header.

KEYBOARD SHORTCUT Press Ctrl+E to move to the search box in the active module. For more information about keyboard shortcuts, see "Keyboard shortcuts" at the end of this book.

You can change the fields displayed in each view; the way records are grouped, sorted, and filtered; the display font; the size of business cards; and other settings to suit your preferences. You can personalize a view from the Advanced View Settings dialog box, which you open by clicking View Settings in the Current View group on the View tab.

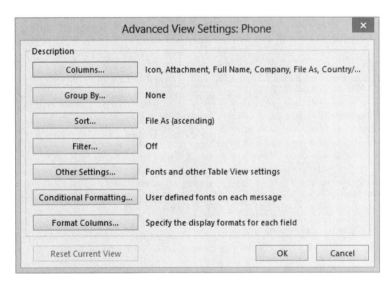

The options available in the Advanced View Settings dialog box vary depending on the currently displayed view.

TIP From the Advanced View Settings dialog box, you can undo your changes to the currently displayed view by clicking the Reset Current View button, which is available only when the default settings for the view have been changed.

In this exercise, you'll look at different views of contact records within the contact list, add and remove columns in a list view, and reset a customized view.

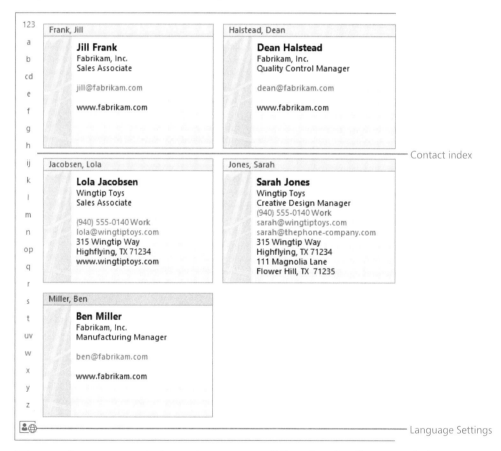

SET UP This exercise uses the contact records you created in the exercise "Saving and updating contact information," earlier in this chapter. If you didn't complete that exercise, you can do so at this time or use contact records of your own. Display the People module, and then follow the steps.

1   On the **Home** tab, in the **Current View** gallery, click the **Business Card** button to display standard business cards for each contact (in addition to any personalized business cards you may have created). The cards are organized by **File as** name.

2   On the contact index located to the right of the contact list, click the letter **m** to scroll the contact list to the business card for **Ben Miller** (or the first contact record in your **People** module that is filed under **m**).

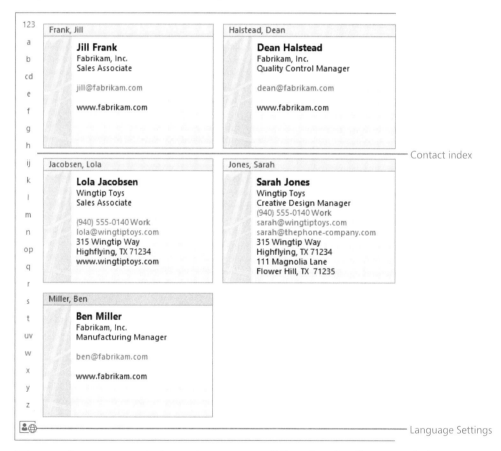

When you have many contact records, you can scroll them by using the contact index.

3   In the **Current View** gallery, click the **Card** button.

4   If the card columns are not wide enough to display the information saved with the
     contact records, click the **Zoom In** button at the right end of the status bar until the
     information is visible. Notice that Outlook displays the contact records in a compact
     card-like format that includes only text and no additional graphic elements.

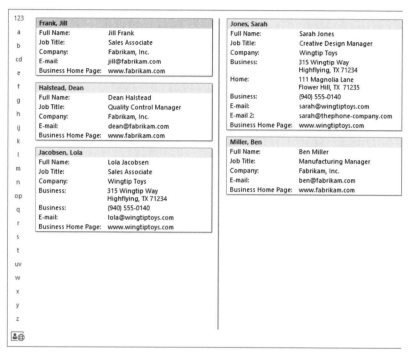

Card view displays all the available primary contact information.

5   In the **Current View** gallery, click the **Phone** button to display your contact records in
     a grid of columns and rows organized in ascending order based on the **File as** column.

6   Click the **Full Name** column heading to sort the contact records in ascending order
     based on the **Full Name** field, as indicated by the upward-pointing sort arrow to the
     right of the column heading. You can reverse the sort order by clicking the active
     heading again.

	FULL NAME ▲	COMPANY	FILE AS		COUNTRY/REGION	BUSINESS PHONE	BUSINESS FAX
	Click here to add a new ...						
	Ben Miller	Fabrikam, Inc.	Miller, Ben				
	Dean Halstead	Fabrikam, Inc.	Halstead, Dean				
	Jill Frank	Fabrikam, Inc.	Frank, Jill				
	Lola Jacobsen	Wingtip Toys	Jacobsen, Lola		United States of Am...	(940) 555-0140	
	Sarah Jones	Wingtip Toys	Jones, Sarah		United States of Am...	(940) 555-0140	

Click any column header to sort by that column or to reverse the sort order.

TIP You can add a contact to your address book in any list view by clicking the box under the Full Name header (labeled Click Here To Add A New Contact) and entering the contact's information.

7   Click the **Company** column heading to sort the contact records in ascending order based on the **Company** field.

8   Right-click the **Company** column header, and then click **Field Chooser** to open the **Field Chooser** window.

9   Scroll down the field list until the **Job Title** field is visible. Drag the **Job Title** field from the **Field Chooser** window to the column heading area, and when the red arrows indicate that it will be inserted between the **Company** and **File as** fields, release the mouse button. Notice that the list view now includes a column that displays the **Job Title** for each contact.

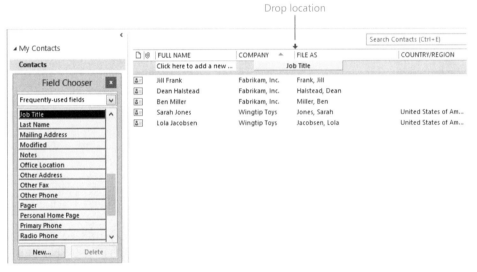

You can add any field to a list view from the Field Chooser.

10   Point to the column separator between **Job Title** and **File as**. When the cursor changes to a double-headed arrow, double-click to change the column width to accommodate its contents.

11   Drag the **Country/Region** column header down from the column heading row until a black X appears. Then release the mouse button to remove the **Country/Region** column from the list view.

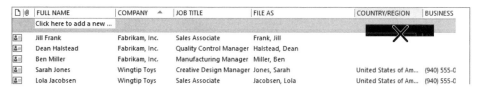

You can remove a column from a list view by dragging its column header away from the column header row.

4

12   On the **View** tab, in the **Current View** group, click the **Reset View** button. Then in the **Microsoft Outlook** dialog box that asks whether you want to reset the view to its original settings, click **Yes** to return the **Phone** view to its original settings.

13   Close the **Field Chooser** window. Then in the **Current View** gallery, click the **List** button to display the final standard view of your contact records. Notice that the contact records are currently grouped by company.

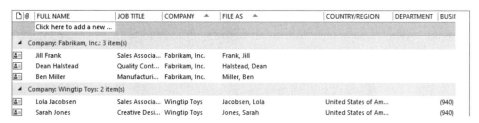

List view displays contact records grouped by whatever field you choose.

❌ CLEAN UP Return the People module to the default People view. Retain the Jill Frank, Dean Halstead, Lola Jacobsen, Sarah Jones, and Ben Miller contact records for use in later exercises.

User-defined fields

If you'd like to save information that doesn't fit into the default contact record fields, you can create a custom field. A custom field can contain information such as text, numbers, percentages, currency, Yes/No answers, dates, times, durations, keywords, and formulas.

You can create a custom information field from any view of the All Fields page of the contact record window by clicking the New button in the lower-left corner of the page and then specifying the name, type, and format of the field in the New Column dialog box that opens.

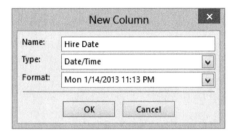

Custom fields can be formatted to contain many specific types of information.

Custom fields appear when you filter the All Fields page on User-Defined Fields In Folder. When you enter information in the custom field for a specific contact, it also appears in the User-Defined Fields In This Item list within that contact record.

Printing contact records

You can print an address book or individual contact records, either on paper or to an electronic file (such as a PDF file or an XPS file), from any address book view. Depending on the view, Outlook offers a variety of print styles, such as those described in the following table.

Style	Description	Available in these views
Card	Contact information displayed alphabetically in two columns. Letter graphics appear at the top of each page and the beginning of each letter group.	Business Card, Card, People
Small Booklet	Contact information displayed alphabetically in one column. Formatted to print eight numbered pages per sheet. Letter graphics appear at the top of each page and the beginning of each letter group, and a contact index at the side of each page indicates the position of that page's entries in the alphabet.	Business Card, Card, People
Medium Booklet	Contact information displayed alphabetically in one column. Formatted to print four numbered pages per sheet. Letter graphics appear at the top of each page and the beginning of each letter group, and a contact index at the side of each page indicates the position of that page's entries in the alphabet.	Business Card, Card, People
Memo	Contact information displayed under a memo-like header that contains your name. One record per sheet.	Business Card, Card, People
Phone Directory	Contact names and phone numbers displayed in two columns. Letter graphics appear at the top of each page and the beginning of each letter group.	Business Card, Card, People
Table	Contact information displayed in a table that matches the on-screen layout.	Phone, List

You can customize the layout of most of the default print styles, in addition to saving custom print styles.

4

In this exercise, you'll set up Outlook to print a phone list and then to print individual address cards.

SET UP This exercise uses the contact records you created in the exercise "Saving and updating contact information," earlier in this chapter. If you didn't complete that exercise, you can do so at this time or use contact records of your own. Display the People module in Card view, and then follow the steps.

IMPORTANT To fully complete this exercise, you must have a printer installed. If you don't have a printer installed, you can perform all the steps of the exercise other than printing.

1 Display the **Print** page of the **Backstage** view.

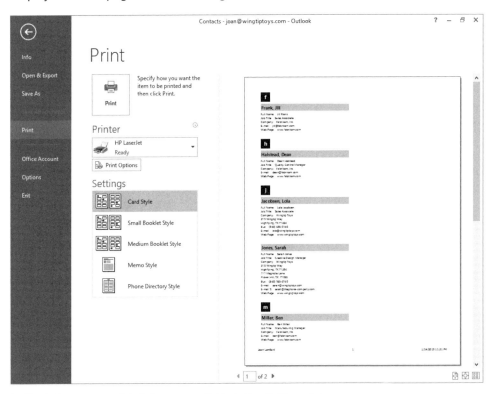

In Card view, many print styles are available in the Settings list.

TIP The Backstage view on your computer reflects your individual printer settings and might display other print options than those shown here.

The preview pane displays the way the cards will appear if printed in the default Card Style, with the current settings. The page indicators at the bottom of the preview pane indicate that the cards will be printed on two pages.

2 In the lower-right corner of the preview pane, click the **Multiple Pages** button to display both pages in the preview pane. The second page contains a series of lines and illegible text.

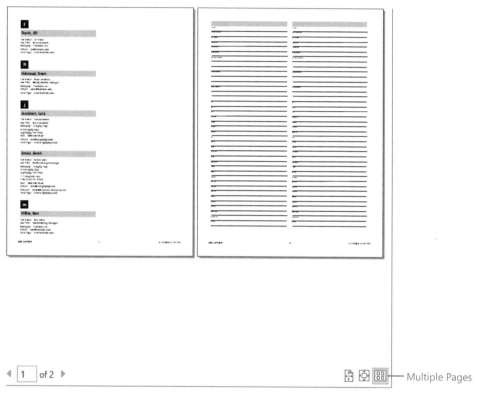

◀ | 1 | of 2 ▶   🔲 🔳 🔳 —— Multiple Pages

The second page of the Card Style printout provides space for you to enter additional contact information.

3 In the lower-right corner of the preview pane, click the **Actual Size** button to display a full-size version of the document in the preview pane. The magnified text is large enough to read.

4 At the bottom of the preview pane, to the right of the number of pages, click the right arrow to display the second page, which provides an area for you to record information about an additional contact, in the preview pane. Outlook refers to this page of the print style as a *blank page*.

5   In the middle pane, click **Print Options** to open the **Print** dialog box and display the options for the **Card Style** print style.

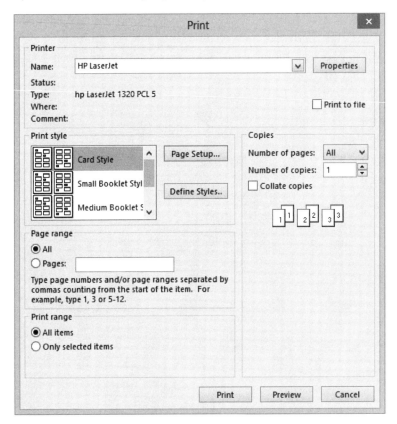

When printing contact records in the Card Style print style, you can select specific contact records (items) to be printed.

6   With **Card Style** selected in the **Print style** box, click **Page Setup** to display the **Format** page of the **Page Setup: Card Style** dialog box.

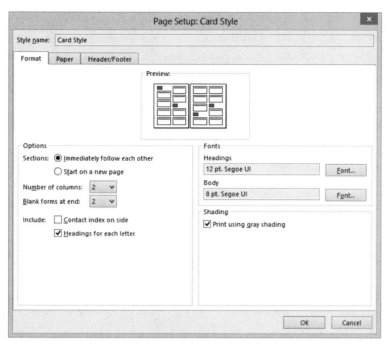

The Page Setup dialog box contents vary depending on the selected print style.

7   Review the settings available on each of the dialog box pages. For all print styles, you can change the fonts, paper size, page orientation and margins, header and footer, and other basic settings. For this print style, you can also change the layout of cards on the page, the number of blank forms to be printed, and how the alphabetical division of the cards is indicated.

8   In the **Options** area of the **Format** page, click **None** in the **Blank forms at end** list. Select the **Contact index on side** check box, and then clear the **Headings for each letter** check box.

9   Click **OK** in the **Page Setup** dialog box, and then click **Preview** in the **Print** dialog box to display in the preview pane the previously selected **Actual Size** view of the card list. Note that it's now only one page.

10   In the lower-right corner of the preview pane, click the **One Page** button to display in the preview pane the entire card list as it will appear when printed.

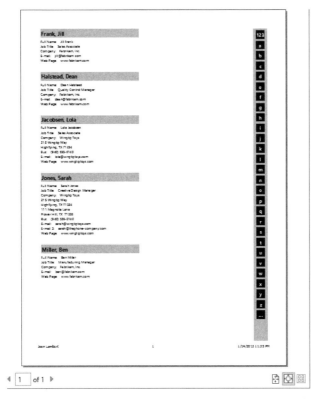

Alphabetical headings no longer precede the contact record cards.

11   If you want to print the card list, click the **Print** button. After printing the card list, Outlook returns to the **People** module.

12   On the **Home** tab, in the **Current View** gallery, click the **List** button.

13   In the contact list, click the **Lola Jacobsen** contact record to select it, press and hold the **Ctrl** key, and then click the **Sarah Jones** contact record to add it to the selection.

14   Display the **Print** page of the **Backstage** view. Notice that the **Settings** list displays only two options—**Table Style** and **Memo Style**. **Memo Style** is selected by default.

15   If a **Preview** button appears in the preview pane, click it to preview the selected contact records.

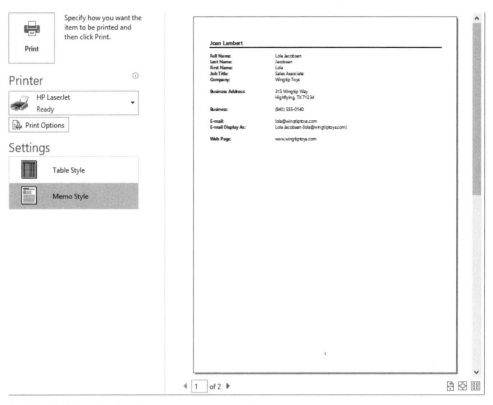

By default, Memo Style prints one contact record per page.

16   In the **Settings** list, click **Table Style**. The preview of **Table Style** indicates that all contact records will be printed rather than only the two you selected.

17   In the middle pane, click **Print Options** to open the **Print** dialog box and display the options for the **Table Style**.

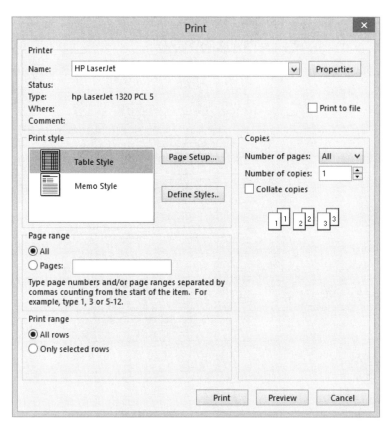

When printing contact records in Table Style, you can select specific items to be printed.

18 In the **Print range** area, click **Only selected rows**. Then click **Preview** to reflect your change.

19 If you want to print the selected records, click the **Print** button.

20 Experiment with the other ways in which you can print your contact records and your address book.

✖ CLEAN UP Return to the default People view or your preferred view of the People module before continuing to the next chapter. Retain the Jill Frank, Dean Halstead, Lola Jacobsen, Sarah Jones, and Ben Miller contact records for use in exercises in later chapters.

Key points

- You can create and access different types of address books, including the Global Address List provided by your Exchange Server account, your main address book, and any custom address books that you create.

- Contact records can include names, email and IM addresses, phone numbers, mailing addresses, birthdays, and other information.

- You can display contact records in many different views. In card views, you can move among records by clicking the contact index. In list views, you can sort records by any field.

- You can print your address book or individual contact records in several formats.

4

Chapter at a glance

Schedule

Schedule and change appointments,
page 168

Meet

Schedule meetings,
page 178

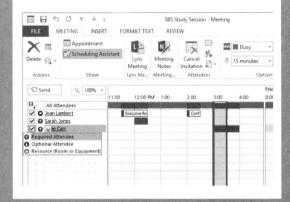

Respond

Respond to meeting requests,
page 186

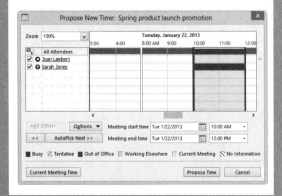

Display

Display different views of a calendar,
page 189

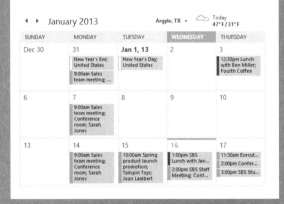

Manage scheduling

5

IN THIS CHAPTER, YOU WILL LEARN HOW TO

- Schedule and change appointments.
- Schedule and change events.
- Schedule meetings.
- Respond to meeting requests.
- Display different views of a calendar.

You can use the Microsoft Outlook 2013 calendar to organize your daily activities and to remind you of important tasks and events. If you're a busy person and use the Outlook calendar to its fullest potential, it might at times seem as though the calendar runs your life—but that isn't necessarily a bad thing! Using the calendar effectively can help you stay organized, on time, and on task. You can schedule and track appointments, meetings, and events, and block time as a reminder to yourself to take care of tasks. And because you can also set up Outlook on your mobile device, you can be assured of having up-to-date schedule information available wherever and whenever you need it.

If you have a Microsoft Exchange Server account, a calendar is part of that account. Some Internet accounts will also have calendars as part of the profile. When you configure Outlook to connect to a different type of account, Outlook connects to the calendar as well. If you don't have a calendar as part of your account, Outlook creates a blank calendar for you. You can easily schedule appointments, events, and meetings on any Outlook calendar.

In this chapter, you'll schedule an appointment and an event on your own calendar and work with appointment options, including recurrence, reminders, and availability. You'll schedule a meeting with another person, and learn about responding to, updating, and canceling meeting requests. Then you'll experiment with different ways of viewing your calendar to find the view that is most effective for your daily working style.

PRACTICE FILES You don't need any practice files to complete the exercises in this chapter.

Scheduling and changing appointments

Appointments are blocks of time you schedule for only yourself (as opposed to meetings, to which you invite other Outlook users). An appointment has a specific start time and end time (as opposed to an event, which occurs for one or more full 24-hour periods).

To schedule an appointment, you enter, at the minimum, a subject and time in an appointment window. The basic appointment window also includes a field for the appointment location and a notes area in which you can store general information, including formatted text, website links, and even file attachments so that they are readily available to you at the time of the appointment.

When creating an appointment, you indicate your availability (referred to as *Free/Busy time*) by marking it as Free, Working Elsewhere, Tentative, Busy, or Out Of Office. The appointment time is color-coded on your calendar to match the availability you indicate. Your availability is visible to other Outlook users on your network, and is also displayed when you share your calendar or send calendar information to other people.

TIP When viewing your calendar in Day, Work Week, or Week view, each item on your Outlook task list appears in the Tasks section below its due date. You can schedule specific time to complete a task by dragging it from the Tasks area to your calendar.

SEE ALSO For information about adding the contents of a received message to your calendar, see the sidebar "Creating an appointment from a message" later in this chapter. For information about assigning appointments to categories, see "Organizing items by using color categories" in Chapter 7, "Organize your Inbox." For information about sharing your calendar with other Outlook users on your network and about sending your schedule information in an email message, see "Sharing calendar information" in Chapter 8, "Manage your calendar."

By default, Outlook displays a reminder message 15 minutes before the start time of an appointment—you can change the reminder to occur as far as two weeks in advance, or you can turn it off completely if you want to. If you synchronize your Outlook installation with a mobile device, reminders also appear on your mobile device. This is very convenient when you are away from your computer.

If you have the same appointment on a regular basis—for example, a monthly haircut or a weekly exercise class—you can set it up in your Outlook calendar as a *recurring appointment*. A recurring appointment can happen at almost any regular interval, such as every Tuesday and Thursday, every other week, or the last day of every month. Configuring an appointment recurrence creates multiple instances of the appointment in your calendar at the time interval you specify. You can set the appointment to recur until further notice, to end after a certain number of occurrences, or to end by a certain date. The individual appointments are linked. When making changes to a recurring appointment, you can choose to update all occurrences or only an individual occurrence of the appointment.

You can specify the time zone in which an appointment starts and ends. You might want to set different starting and ending time zones if, for example, your "appointment" is an airplane flight with departure and arrival cities located in different time zones, and you want the flight to show up correctly wherever you're currently located.

In this exercise, you'll schedule an appointment and a recurring appointment, and you'll update appointments by using commands in the appointment window.

 SET UP You don't need any practice files to complete this exercise. Display the Calendar module, and then follow the steps.

1   In the **Date Navigator** at the top of the **Folder Pane**, click tomorrow's date to display the **Day** view for that day.

> **SEE ALSO** For information about the default Calendar module view and the Date Navigator, see "Displaying different views of a calendar" later in this chapter.

2   In the calendar, point to the **12:00 P.M.** time slot (or, if you already have an appointment scheduled at 12:00 P.M., to another time when you have 30 minutes available).

3   Click once to activate the time slot.

4   Enter **SBS Lunch with Jane**, and then press **Enter** to create a half-hour appointment beginning at 12:00 P.M.

> **TIP** The subject of each appointment, meeting, or event you create while working through the exercises in this book begins with *SBS* so that you can easily differentiate the practice items you create from other items on your calendar.

5   Drag the appointment from the **12:00 P.M.** time slot to the **1:00 P.M.** time slot (or, if you already have an appointment scheduled at 1:00 P.M., to another time when you have an hour available) to change the appointment start time.

6   Click the appointment once to select it and display handles on the top and bottom of the calendar entry, if necessary. Point to the bottom handle, and when the pointer changes to a double-headed arrow, drag down one time slot so that the appointment ends at **2:00 P.M.**

7   Point to the appointment on the calendar to display the basic appointment information.

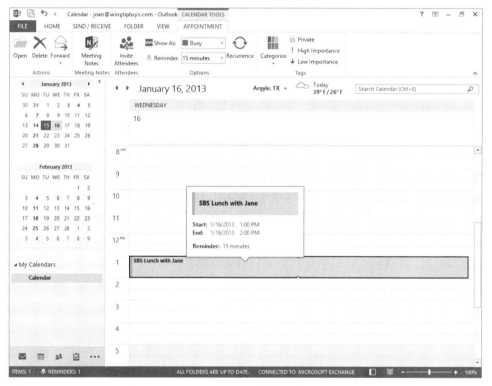

The most common appointment settings are available on the Appointment tool tab.

8   Double-click the **SBS Lunch with Jane** appointment to open the appointment in its own window. (If the appointment window is not already maximized, maximize the window to expose more of the ribbon buttons.) The subject, date, and times are set according to the information you entered in the calendar.

Now we'll add more details to the appointment and change the default settings from within the appointment window.

9   In the **Location** box, enter Fourth Coffee.

10 On the **Appointment** tab of the appointment window (not the Appointment tool tab in the Calendar module), in the **Options** group, click the **Show As** arrow, and then in the list, click **Out of Office**.

11 In the **Options** group, click the **Reminder** arrow, and then in the list, click **1 hour**.

12 In the **Tags** group (or the **Tags** list, if the group is minimized under a button), click the **Private** button to hide the appointment details from anyone you share your calendar with.

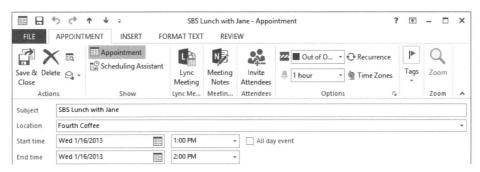

All these settings other than the location are available from the Appointment tool tab in the Calendar module.

13 In the **Actions** group, click the **Save & Close** button to close the appointment window and apply your changes to the appointment shown on the calendar. The settings on the **Appointment** tool tab also reflect the changes you made to the appointment.

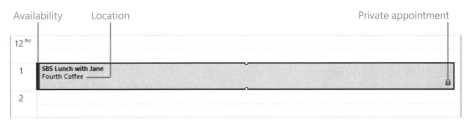

Your availability is indicated by the colored bar on the left side of the appointment.

14 Double-click the **2:00 P.M.** time slot to open an appointment window with the appointment start time set to **2:00 P.M**. and the end time set 30 minutes later. Because this immediately follows the lunch appointment you just created, the InfoBar at the top of the meeting window indicates that the meeting is adjacent to another on your calendar.

15 In the **Subject** box, enter SBS Staff Meeting. In the **Location** box, enter Conference room. Then in the notes area, enter Bring status reports.

16 On the **Appointment** tab, in the **Options** group, click the **Recurrence** button to open the **Appointment Recurrence** dialog box. The default appointment recurrence is weekly on the currently selected day of the week.

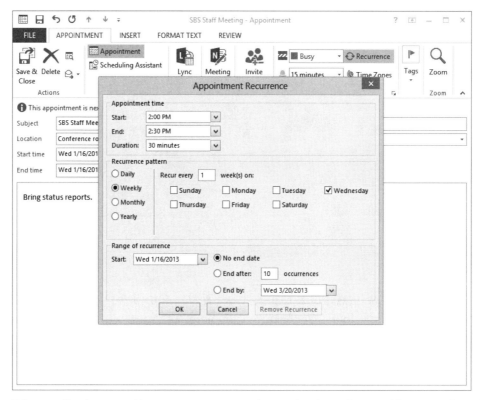

When configuring a weekly recurrence, you can change the times, days, and frequency from the Appointment Recurrence dialog box.

17 In the **End** list, click **4:00 PM (2 hours)**. In the **Range of recurrence** area, click **End after**, and then in the box, replace **10** with 2.

18 Click **OK** in the **Appointment Recurrence** dialog box to replace the **Start Time** and **End Time** fields in the appointment window with the recurrence details.

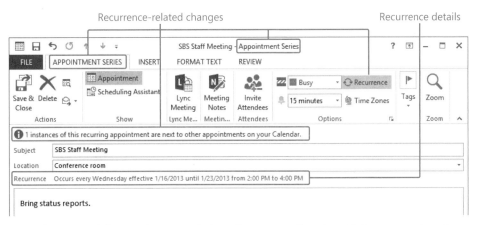

Several aspects of the appointment window change to reflect that this is now a series of recurring appointments.

19   On the **Appointment Series** tab, in the **Actions** group, click the **Save & Close** button to add the new appointments to your calendar.

20   If necessary, scroll the calendar to display the entire appointment.

The circling arrow icon at the right end of the time slot indicates that it's a recurring appointment.

21   In the **Date Navigator**, click the weekday of the appointment in each of the next two weeks and verify that the appointment appears on your calendar next week, but not the following week.

❌ CLEAN UP Retain the SBS Lunch with Jane and SBS Staff Meeting appointments on your calendar for use as practice files later in this chapter.

Adding national and religious holidays to your calendar

You can easily add the holidays of a specific country or religion to your Outlook calendar. To do so, follow these steps:

1   Display the **Calendar** page of the **Outlook Options** dialog box.

2   In the **Calendar Options** section, click the **Add Holidays** button to open the **Add Holidays to Calendar** dialog box.

The holidays of more than 110 countries are available to add to your calendar.

3   Select the check boxes of the locations or religions whose holidays you want to add to your calendar, and then click **OK**.

TIP If you've already added the holidays for a selected country to your calendar, Outlook prompts you to verify that you want to install a second instance of each holiday. Assuming that you do not want to do this, click No.

4   After Outlook adds the selected country's holidays to your calendar, click **OK** in the confirmation message box and in the **Outlook Options** dialog box.

Outlook assigns a color category named *Holiday* to all the local holidays it adds to your calendar. To view all the holidays on your calendar, enter *category:holiday* in the Search box. Note that Outlook adds each holiday for the next 20 years to the calendar, so the entire list of results might not be displayed immediately (only the first 200 results). If the search returns more than 200 results, add search criteria to narrow down the field or click the More link at the end of the search results list to display the entire list.

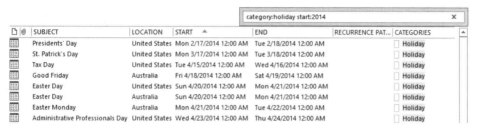

You can narrow your search by using the Search tool tab or entering criteria in the search box.

SEE ALSO For information about categories, see "Organizing items by using color categories" in Chapter 7, "Organize your Inbox." For information about Outlook search functionality, see "Quickly locating messages" in the same chapter.

To remove national holidays from your calendar, follow these steps:

1 Use the **Search** function to locate the holidays you want to remove. (Expand the search if necessary to locate all instances of the holidays.)

2 Select individual holidays you want to remove; or click any holiday in the list to activate the list, and then press **Ctrl+A** to select all the holidays in the search results.

3 Press the **Delete** key.

TIP If you inadvertently add two sets of holidays from one country to the calendar, the easiest way to rectify the situation is to remove all of that country's holidays and then add them again.

Creating an appointment from a message

Some email messages that you receive might result in your wanting or needing to schedule an appointment on your calendar based on the information in the message. For example, if a friend or co-worker sends you a message that contains the details of the grand opening for a local art gallery, you can add that information to your calendar. Outlook provides a convenient method of creating a calendar item (an appointment, event, or meeting request) based on an email message; you simply drag the message to the Calendar link or button on the Navigation Bar. When you release the mouse button, an appointment window opens, already filled in with the message subject as the appointment subject, the message text in the content pane, and any message attachments attached to the appointment. The start and end times are set to the next half-hour increment following the current time. You can convert the appointment to an event or meeting in the same way that you would create an event or meeting from within the Calendar module. You can retain any or all of the message information as part of the calendar item so that you (or other meeting participants) have the information on hand when you need it. After creating the calendar item, you can delete the actual message from your Inbox.

To create an appointment from an email message:

1   Drag the message from the message list to the **Calendar** link or button on the **Navigation Bar**.

2   After the cursor changes to display a plus sign, release the mouse button to create an appointment based on the message. You can convert the appointment to an event by selecting the **All day event** check box, or convert it to a meeting by inviting other people to attend. You can edit the information in the content pane without affecting the content of the original message, and you can move or delete the original message without affecting the appointment.

3   In the appointment window, click the **Save & Close** button to save the appointment to your calendar.

SEE ALSO For information about adding message content to your To-Do List, see "Creating tasks" in Chapter 6, "Track tasks."

Scheduling and changing events

Events are day-long blocks of time that you schedule on your Outlook calendar, such as birthdays, payroll days, or anything else occurring on a specific day but not at a specific time. In all other respects, creating an event is identical to creating an appointment, in that you can specify a location, indicate recurrence, indicate your availability, and attach additional information to the event item.

You can create an event directly on the calendar when viewing your calendar in Month, Week, Work Week, or Day view.

In this exercise, you'll schedule an event and convert it to a recurring event by using the commands in the Calendar module.

 SET UP You don't need any practice files to complete this exercise. Display the Calendar module in Calendar view. Then follow the steps.

1   In the **Date Navigator** at the top of the **Folder Pane**, click the first day of the next month to display the **Day** view of that day.

2   In the calendar, point to the space below the day header and above the time slots that contains the date. This is the event slot.

3   Click once to activate the event slot. Enter SBS Pay Day, and then press **Enter**.

4   On the **Appointment** tool tab, in the **Options** group, click the **Recurrence** button to open the **Appointment Recurrence** dialog box. The default recurrence for events is the same as for appointments—weekly on the currently selected day of the week. Note that the **Start** and **End** times are set to **12:00 AM** and the **Duration** to **1** day, indicating that this is an all-day event.

5   In the **Recurrence pattern** area, click **Monthly**. You can schedule a monthly event to recur on a specific date of the month or on a selected (first, second, third, fourth, or last) day of the month. Monthly events can recur every month or less often (for example, every third month).

> **TIP** If you have an Exchange account and a mobile device that supports connections to Exchange accounts (such as a Windows Phone), it's easy to keep your calendar and reminders at your fingertips wherever you are by configuring your mobile device to connect to your Exchange account.

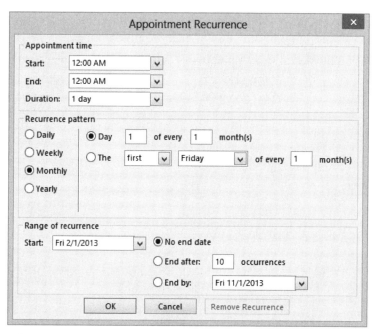

When configuring a monthly recurrence, you can change the day or date, frequency, and duration from the Appointment Recurrence dialog box.

6   Click **OK** in the **Appointment Recurrence** dialog box to create an appointment on the first day of every month for an indefinite period.

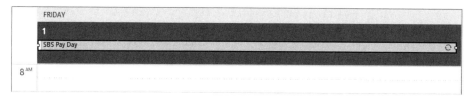

In Day view, events appear above the schedule for the day.

✖ CLEAN UP Retain the SBS Pay Day event in your calendar for use as a practice file later in this chapter.

Scheduling meetings

A primary difficulty when scheduling a meeting is finding a time that works for all the people who need to attend it. Scheduling meetings through Outlook is significantly simpler than other methods of scheduling meetings, particularly when you need to accommodate the schedules of several people. Outlook displays the individual and collective schedules of people within your own organization, and of people outside of your organization who have published their calendars to the Internet. You can review attendees' schedules to locate a time when everyone is available, or have Outlook find a convenient time for you.

You can send an Outlook meeting invitation (referred to as a *meeting request*) to anyone who has an email account—even to a person who doesn't use Outlook. You can send a meeting request from any type of email account (such as an Exchange account or an Internet email account).

The meeting window has two pages: the Appointment page and the Scheduling Assistant page. The Appointment page is visible by default. You can enter all the required information directly on the Appointment page, or use the additional features available on the Scheduling Assistant page to find the best time for the meeting.

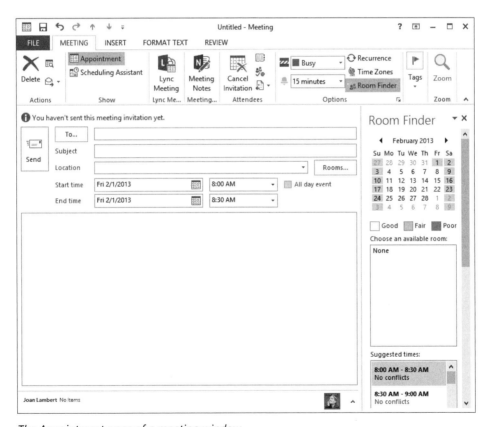

The Appointment page of a meeting window.

The Room Finder is open by default on the right side of each page of the meeting window. This handy tool helps you to identify dates and times that work for the greatest number of attendees, in addition to available locations. The monthly calendar at the top of the Room Finder indicates the collective availability of the group on each day, as follows:

- Dates that occur in the past and nonworking days are unavailable (gray).

- Days when all attendees are available are Good (white).

- Days when most attendees are available are Fair (light blue).

- Days when most attendees are not available are Poor (medium blue).

TIP All the capabilities of the Room Finder are available for Exchange accounts, but functionality is limited for other types of accounts. You can display or hide the Room Finder pane by clicking the Room Finder button in the Options group on the Meeting tab.

Managed conference rooms that are available at the indicated meeting time are shown in the center of the Room Finder. At the bottom of the Room Finder pane, the Suggested Times list displays attendee availability for appointments of the length of time you have specified for the meeting.

Selecting a date in the calendar displays the suggested meeting times for just that day. (Scheduling suggestions are not provided for past or nonworking days.) Clicking a meeting time in the Suggested Times list updates the calendar and the meeting request.

People you invite to meetings are referred to as *attendees*. By default, the attendance of each attendee is indicated as Required. You can inform noncritical attendees of the meeting by marking their attendance as Optional. You can invite entire groups of people by using a contact group or distribution list. You can also invite managed resources, such as conference rooms and audio/visual equipment, that have been set up by your organization's Exchange administrator.

A meeting request should have at least one attendee other than you, and must have a start time and an end time. It should also include a subject and a location, but Outlook will send the meeting request without this information if you specifically allow it. The body of a meeting request can include text and web links, and you can also attach files. This is a convenient way to distribute meeting information to attendees ahead of time.

The secondary page of the meeting window is the Scheduling Assistant page, if your email account is part of an Exchange Server network. Otherwise, the secondary page is the Scheduling page, which doesn't include the Room Finder feature.

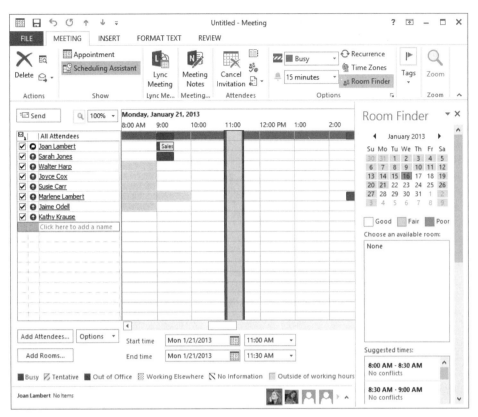

If you're organizing a meeting for a large number of people, you can view collective information about their schedules on the Scheduling or Scheduling Assistant page.

The Scheduling and Scheduling Assistant pages include a group schedule that shows the status of each attendee's time throughout your working day. Outlook indicates your suggested meeting time on the group schedule. If free/busy information is available for meeting attendees, the status is indicated by the standard free/busy colors and patterns that match the legend at the bottom of the page. If no information is available (either because Outlook can't connect to an attendee's calendar or because the proposed meeting is further out than the scheduling information stored on the server), Outlook shows the time with gray diagonal stripes. The row at the top of the schedule, to the right of the All Attendees heading, indicates the collective schedule of all the attendees.

TIP You can enter additional attendees in the To box on the Appointment page or in the All Attendees list on the Scheduling or Scheduling Assistant page. You can also add attendees by clicking the To button on the Appointment page or the Add Attendees button on the Scheduling or Scheduling Assistant page, and then selecting attendees from an address box.

You can change the time and duration of the meeting to work with the displayed schedules by selecting a different time in the Start Time and End Time lists, by dragging the vertical start time and end time bars in the group schedule, or by clicking the time you want in the Suggested Times list.

SEE ALSO For information about creating a meeting request from an email message, see the sidebar "Creating an appointment from a message" earlier in this chapter.

Outlook tracks responses from attendees and those responsible for scheduling the resources you requested, so you always have an up-to-date report of how many people will attend your meeting. The number of attendees who have accepted, tentatively accepted, and declined the meeting request appears in the meeting header section when you open a meeting in its own window.

In this exercise, you'll create and send a meeting request.

 SET UP You don't need any practice files to complete this exercise. Display your default calendar and inform two co-workers or friends that you are going to practice inviting them as attendees to a meeting. Ask the attendees not to respond to the meeting request that they receive. Then follow the steps.

1   In the **Date Navigator**, click the next work day's date. Then in the calendar, click the **3:00 P.M.** time slot (or if you have a conflicting appointment, click a time when you have 30 minutes available).

2   On the **Home** tab, in the **New** group, click the **New Meeting** button to open an untitled meeting window. The selected date and times are shown in the **Start time** and **End time** boxes above the notes pane.

3   In the **To** box, enter the email address of the first co-worker or friend with whom you arranged to practice.

4   In the **Subject** box, enter SBS Study Session.

5   In the **Location** box, enter Test meeting to indicate that the meeting request is for testing purposes only. You have now provided all the standard information for a meeting request.

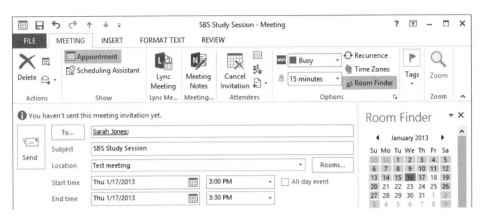

A basic meeting request.

6   On the **Meeting** tab, in the **Show** group, click the **Scheduling Assistant** button.
      Notice that the **All Attendees** list on the **Scheduling Assistant** page includes you
      and the attendee you entered in the **To** box (showing the attendee's email address
      or, if the attendee has an entry in your **Address Book**, the associated name). The
      icon next to your name, a magnifying glass in a black circle, indicates that you are
      the meeting organizer. The icon next to the attendee's name, an upward-pointing
      arrow in a red circle, indicates that he or she is a required attendee.

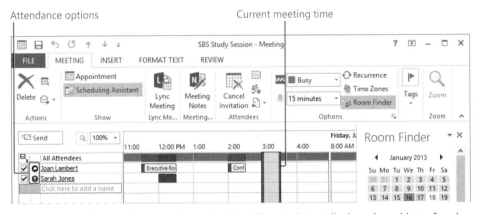

*When you are the meeting organizer, the Scheduling Assistant displays the subject of each
appointment on your schedule that is not marked as Private.*

7   If necessary, scroll to the bottom of the **Room Finder** to display the **Suggested times**
      list. The times shown are based on your schedule and the schedule information that is
      available for the first attendee.

8   In the **All Attendees** list, click **Click here to add a name**, enter the email address of the second person with whom you arranged to practice, and then press **Tab** to update the **Suggested times** list in the **Room Finder** to reflect any schedule conflicts for the second attendee.

9   Click the **Required Attendee** icon to the left of the second attendee's name to expand a list of attendance options.

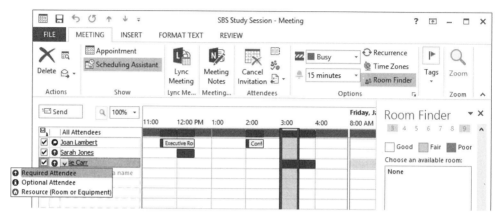

You can extend a courtesy invitation to optional attendees.

10   In the list, click **Optional Attendee** to indicate that you're sending the meeting request for his or her information, but he or she does not need to attend.

11   In the group schedule, experiment with changing the meeting time and duration by dragging the start time bar and the end time bar. Then in the **Suggested times** list, select a meeting time that works for all three attendees and move the start time and end time bars to the selected time slot. You can change the **Show As** and **Reminder** settings, create recurrences, assign color categories, and make any other changes you want. The availability specified in the **Show As** list will apply to all attendees who accept your meeting request.

12   After you select the meeting time you want, click the **Appointment** button in the **Show** group. Notice that on the **Appointment** page, the second attendee has been added to the **To** box, and the **Start time** and **End time** boxes display the meeting time you selected.

13   Verify the meeting details, and then click the **Send** button to add the meeting to your calendar, and send the meeting request to your co-workers or friends.

✖ CLEAN UP   Remind your attendees not to respond to the meeting request. Retain the SBS Study Session meeting in your calendar for use in later exercises.

Updating and canceling meetings

You might find it necessary to change the date, time, or location of a meeting after you send the meeting request. As the meeting organizer, you can change any information in a meeting request at any time, including adding or removing attendees, or canceling the meeting.

To edit a meeting request, double-click the meeting on your calendar. If the meeting is one of a series (a recurring meeting), Outlook prompts you to indicate whether you want to edit the meeting series or only the selected instance of the meeting. Make the changes you want, and then send the meeting update to the attendees. Each attendee will receive a meeting update message.

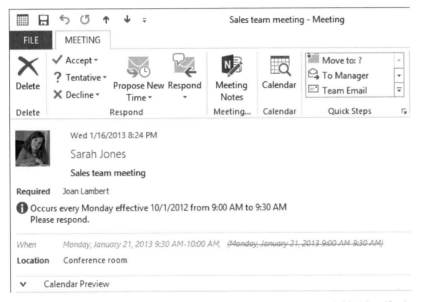

Changes to meeting details are tracked so that attendees can quickly identify them.

To cancel a meeting, click the meeting on your calendar, or open the meeting window, and then click the Cancel Meeting button in the Actions group on the Meeting or Meeting Series tab.

After you edit or cancel a meeting, Outlook sends an updated meeting request to the invited attendees to keep them informed. If the only change you make is to the attendee list, Outlook gives you the option of sending an update only to the affected attendees.

Responding to meeting requests

When you receive a meeting request from another Outlook user, the meeting appears on your calendar with your time scheduled as Tentative. Until you respond to the meeting request, the organizer doesn't know whether you plan to attend.

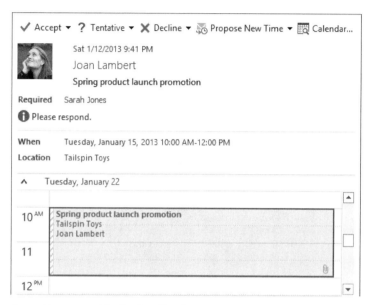

A meeting request in the Reading Pane.

You can respond to a meeting request in one of these four ways:

- Accept the request. Outlook deletes the meeting request and adds the meeting to your calendar.

- Tentatively accept the request, which indicates that you might be able to attend the meeting but are undecided. Outlook deletes the meeting request and shows the meeting on your calendar as tentatively scheduled.

- Propose a new meeting time. Outlook sends your request to the meeting organizer for confirmation and shows the meeting with the original time on your calendar as tentatively scheduled.

- Decline the request. Outlook deletes the meeting request and removes the meeting from your calendar.

If you don't respond to a meeting request, the meeting remains on your calendar with your time shown as tentatively scheduled and the meeting details in gray font rather than black.

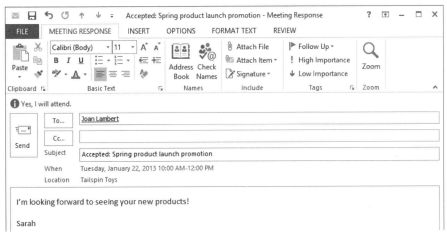

	MONDAY	TUESDAY	WEDNESDAY	THURSDAY	FRIDAY
	21	22	23	24	25
8 AM					Working from home
9	Sales team meeting;				
10		Spring product launch promotion Tailspin Toys Joan Lambert			
11					
12 PM	Lunch break (offline		Lunch break (offline	Lunch break (offline	Lunch t
1					

Tentatively scheduled time is indicated by diagonal striping in the left margin of the time block.

If you're unsure whether a meeting time works for you, you can click the Calendar Preview link in the meeting request to display your calendar for the time period immediately surrounding the meeting, or you can click the Calendar button at the top of the meeting request to open your default calendar for the suggested meeting day in a separate window.

When accepting or declining a meeting, you can choose whether to send a response to the meeting organizer. If you don't send a response, your acceptance will not be tallied, and the organizer will not know whether you are planning to attend the meeting. If you do send a response, you can add a message to the meeting organizer before sending it.

You can add a note to the meeting organizer or attach a document that pertains to the meeting subject.

To respond to a meeting request:

1   In the meeting window, in the **Reading Pane**, or on the shortcut menu that appears when you right-click the meeting request, click **Accept**, **Tentative**, or **Decline**.

2   Choose whether to send a standard response, a personalized response, or no response at all.

To propose a new time for a meeting:

1   In the meeting window or in the **Reading Pane**, click **Propose New Time**, and then in the list, click **Tentative and Propose New Time** or **Decline and Propose New Time** to open the **Propose New Time** dialog box.

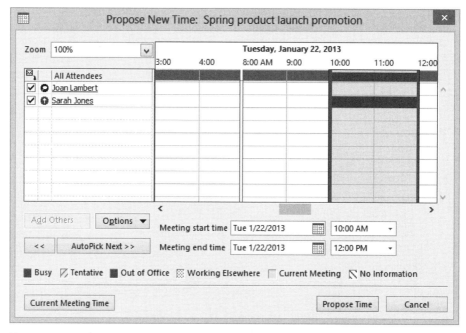

You can respond to a meeting request by proposing a different meeting time.

2   In the **Propose New Time** dialog box, change the meeting start and end times to the times you want to propose, either by dragging the start time and end time bars or by changing the date and time in the lists, and then click the **Propose Time** button.

3   In the meeting response window that opens, enter a message to the meeting organizer if you want to, and then click **Send** to send your response and add the meeting to your calendar as tentatively scheduled for the original meeting time. If the meeting organizer approves the meeting time change, you and other attendees will receive updated meeting requests showing the new meeting time.

Displaying different views of a calendar

You can select a view and an arrangement for the display of your calendar. The default view is Calendar, and the default arrangement is Day. Most exercises in this chapter have shown the calendar in this default view and arrangement, which we refer to simply as *Day view*.

TIP Because Outlook coordinates your scheduled tasks with your calendar, you can display your daily task list for each day shown when the calendar is in Day view, Work Week view, or Week view. You can drag tasks from the daily task list to the calendar to allocate time for completing the tasks, and you can track your progress by marking tasks as complete when you finish them.

Views

The Calendar module offers four distinct views of content, which are available from the Change View list in the Current View group on the View tab. These views are:

- **Calendar** This is the standard view in which you display your Outlook calendar. In the Day, Work Week, or Week arrangement, Calendar view displays the subject, location, and organizer (if space allows) of each appointment, meeting, or event, in addition to the availability bar and any special icons, such as Private or Recurrence.

- **Preview** In the Day, Work Week, or Week arrangement, Preview view displays more information, including information from the notes area of the appointment window, as space allows.

- **List** This list view displays all appointments, meetings, and events on your calendar.

- **Active** This list view displays only future appointments, meetings, and events.

When working in a list view, you can group calendar items by selecting a field from the Arrangement gallery on the View tab.

IMPORTANT In this book, we assume you are working in Calendar view, and refer to the standard Calendar view arrangements as *Day view*, *Work Week view*, *Week view*, *Month view*, and *Schedule view*. For information about changing and resetting views, see "Displaying different views of contact records" in Chapter 4, "Store and access contact information."

Arrangements

By default, your calendar displays the Month arrangement of Calendar view. However, this arrangement limits the number of calendar items visible on each day and the amount of detail visible for each calendar item.

TIP You can point to any calendar item to display the item details.

To help you stay on top of your schedule, you can display several different arrangements of your calendar:

- **Day** Displays one day at a time separated into half-hour increments.

- **Work Week** Displays only the days of your work week. The default work week is Monday through Friday from 8:00 A.M. to 5:00 P.M. Time slots that fall within the work week are white on the calendar; time slots outside of the work week are colored.

    SEE ALSO For information about modifying the days and hours of the work week shown in Outlook, see "Defining your available time" in Chapter 8, "Manage your calendar."

- **Week** Displays one calendar week (Sunday through Saturday) at a time.

- **Month** Displays one calendar month at a time, in addition to any preceding or following days that fall into the displayed weeks.

- **Schedule view** Displays a horizontal view of the calendar for the selected time period. This view is very useful for comparing limited time periods for multiple calendars, such as the members of a calendar group.

    SEE ALSO For information about calendar groups, see "Sharing calendar information" in Chapter 8, "Manage your calendar."

You switch among arrangements by clicking the buttons in the Arrangement group on the View tab of the Calendar module ribbon.

TIP If you've made changes to any view (such as the order in which information appears) and want to return to the default settings, click the Reset View button in the Current View group on the View tab. If the Reset View button is unavailable, the view already displays the default settings.

You can use these additional tools to change the time period shown in the calendar:

- Display the previous or next time period by clicking the Back button or the Forward button next to the date or date range in the calendar header.

- Display the current day by clicking the Today button in the Go To group on the Home tab.

- Display a seven-day period starting with the current day by clicking the Next 7 Days button in the Go To group on the Home tab.

- Display week numbers to the left of each week in Month view and in the Date Navigator. If you implement this option, you can click the week tab to display that week.

    TIP Specific weeks are referred to in some countries by number to simplify the communication of dates. (For example, you can say you'll be out of the office "Week 24" rather than "June 7–11.") Week 1 is the calendar week in which January 1 falls, Week 2 is the following week, and so on through to the end of the year. Because of the way the weeks are numbered, a year can end in Week 52 or (more commonly) in Week 53. To display week numbers in the Date Navigator and in the Month view of the calendar, select the Show Week Numbers... check box on the Calendar page of the Outlook Options dialog box.

Using the Date Navigator

You can use the Date Navigator to change the day or range of days shown on the calendar.

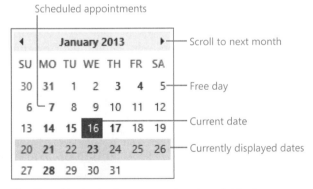

The Date Navigator is a compact and useful tool.

The current date is indicated by a blue square. The date or dates currently displayed in the calendar are indicated by light blue highlighting. Bold dates indicate days with scheduled appointments, meetings, or events.

You can display a specific day, week, or month in the calendar by selecting it in the Date Navigator. Use these techniques to work with the Date Navigator:

- To display a day, click that day.

  If you're displaying the calendar in Day, Work Week, or Week view, the day appears and is highlighted in the current view. If you're displaying the calendar in Month view, the display changes to Day view.

- To display a week, point to its left margin and then when the cursor points to the week, click in the margin. Or, if you display week numbers in the Date Navigator and Calendar, click the week number to display that week.

  In any calendar view, selecting a week in the Date Navigator changes the display to Week view.

- To display a month, click the Previous or Next button to scroll one month back or forward, or click the current month name and hold down the mouse button to display a range of months, point to the month you want to display, and then release the mouse button. To scroll beyond the seven-month range displayed by default, point to the top or bottom of the month list.

  In Month view, scrolling the month displays the entire month; in Day view, the Date Navigator displays the same date of the selected month; in Week or Work Week view, it displays the same week of the selected month.

By default, the Outlook 2013 Calendar module displays the current month and next month in the Date Navigator at the top of the Folder Pane. You can display more or fewer months by changing the width or height of the area allocated to the Date Navigator.

When the Date Navigator displays more than one month, each month shows either five or six weeks at a time—whichever is necessary to show all the days of the currently selected month in a Sunday through Saturday calendar format and to match the height of any other month displayed next to it. Only the first and last months include the days of the preceding or following month (in gray).

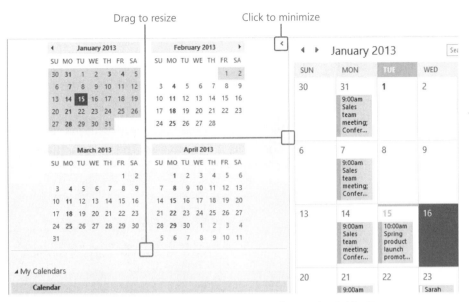

Drag to resize   Click to minimize

You can allocate up to 50 percent of the program window to the Folder Pane.

In this exercise, you'll first display different periods of time in your calendar and reset a customized view to its default settings. Then you'll change the display of the Daily Task List and of the To-Do Bar. Finally, you'll navigate through your calendar by using the Date Navigator, and display different levels of information about scheduled appointments and events.

SET UP You need the SBS Staff Meeting appointment you created in a previous exercise in this chapter. If you did not complete that exercise, you can do so now, or use any appointments, meetings, or events on your own calendar. Display the Calendar module, and then follow the steps.

1   On the **Home** tab, in the **Arrange** group, click the **Work Week** button to display your currently configured work week in the calendar and highlight the corresponding days in the **Date Navigator**. The first time slot of your defined work day appears at the top of the pane.

KEYBOARD SHORTCUT Press Ctrl+Alt+2 to display your calendar in the Work Week arrangement. For more information about keyboard shortcuts, see "Keyboard shortcuts" at the end of this book.

2   On the **View** tab, in the **Layout** group, click the **Daily Task List** button and then click **Normal** to display the task list area below the calendar.

3   Scroll the calendar to display one hour prior to the start of your work day. Notice that time slots within your work day are white; time slots outside of your work day are shaded.

4   On the **Home** tab, in the **Go To** group, click the **Today** button. If the calendar wasn't previously displaying the current week, it does so now. The times displayed remain the same. The current day and the current time slot are highlighted.

In this view, you can display your entire work week at one time.

5 On the **View** tab, in the **Arrangement** group, click the **Day** button to display only today's schedule, with the **Daily Task List** still open below the calendar.

6 In the **Layout** group, click the **Daily Task List** button, and then in the list, click **Minimized** to change the **Daily Task List** to a single row below the calendar. The minimized **Daily Task List** displays a count of your total, active, and completed tasks for the day.

7 In the **Date Navigator** at the top of the **Folder Pane**, point to the left edge of a calendar row that contains one or more bold dates. When the cursor changes to point toward the calendar, click once to display the selected seven-day week in the calendar.

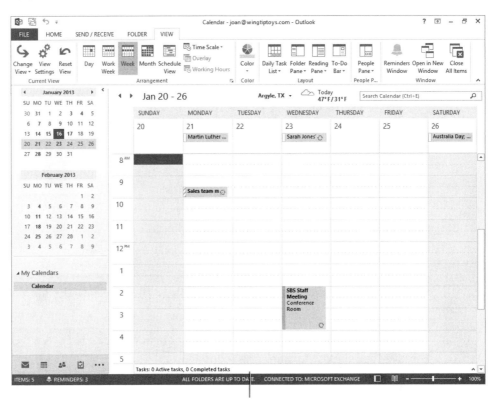

Minimized Daily Task List

The days shown in the calendar are shaded in the Date Navigator.

8   On the **Home** tab, in the **Arrange** group, click the **Month** button to display your calendar for the month. Alternating months are shaded to provide an obvious visual indicator of the change. The **Daily Task List** is not available in **Month** view.

KEYBOARD SHORTCUT Press Ctrl+Alt+4 to display your calendar in the Month arrangement.

You can display a different month by scrolling the calendar, or by clicking the month you want to view in the Date Navigator.

9   To the left of the date range in the calendar header, click the **Forward** button to move the calendar forward one month.

10   On the **View** tab, in the **Current View** group, click the **Change View** button and then in the gallery, click **Preview** to display additional details on the monthly calendar.

11   Use any of the available navigation methods to display a week that contains one of the **SBS Staff Meeting** appointments. Notice that the calendar displays the notes saved with the recurring appointment.

12   Display the day on which the **SBS Staff Meeting** appointment occurs in the **Day** arrangement, which in **Preview** view also displays the meeting notes.

In Preview view, the calendar displays any notes saved with the appointment.

13 In the **Change View** gallery, click **Calendar** to return the calendar to its default settings. Then in the **Current View** group, click **Reset View** to return to the default calendar state.

❌ CLEAN UP Retain the SBS Staff Meeting appointment on your calendar for use in exercises in later chapters.

Key points

- You can create and manage appointments and all-day events in your calendar.

- Other people in your organization can find out whether you are free, busy, or out-of-office by reviewing the appointments, events, and meetings scheduled in your calendar.

- You can personalize the display of your available working hours, and mark appointments as private to hide the details from other people.

- You can use Outlook to set up meetings, invite participants, and track their responses.

- Outlook can identify a meeting time based on participants' schedules.

- If your organization is running Exchange Server, you can use the Scheduling Assistant features to quickly identify meeting times of a specific duration during which your planned attendees are available.

- You can display many different views of your calendar. You can change the dates and date ranges displayed in the calendar by using the Date Navigator, by using navigational buttons located in the calendar header, or by using commands on the ribbon.

Chapter at a glance

Create

Create tasks,
page 200

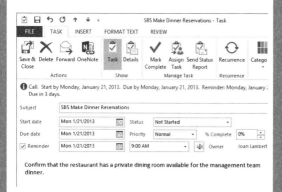

Remove

Remove tasks and flagged items from
task lists, page 212

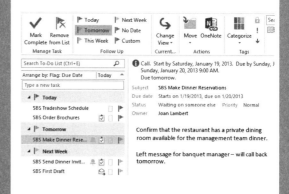

Manage

Manage task assignments,
page 214

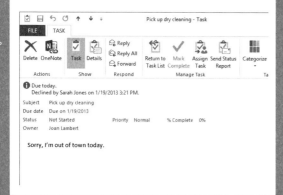

Display

Display different views of tasks,
page 219

Track tasks

6

IN THIS CHAPTER, YOU WILL LEARN HOW TO

- Create tasks.

- Update tasks.

- Remove tasks and flagged items from task lists.

- Manage task assignments.

- Display different views of tasks.

Many people keep one or more task lists going at all times, listing things to do, things to buy, people to call, and other tasks. You might cross off tasks as you complete them, transfer unfinished tasks to other lists, create multiple lists for multiple purposes, or follow a specialized system designed by an efficiency expert. You probably write these task lists on pieces of paper, even though you've undoubtedly experienced the pitfalls of that age-old system. Paper crumples and tears, and paper lists have a special knack for getting lost. If you have a smartphone, you might use one of the many built-in note-taking apps to keep the list in electronic format on your phone, but then you also have to keep it up to date.

If you use Microsoft Outlook 2013 on a daily basis, you might find it far easier to use the built-in task-tracking functionality. You can add tasks, flag messages for follow-up, assign due dates, receive reminders, and mark tasks as complete when you finish them. You can even assign tasks to other people, and if those people use Outlook, you can view their progress on assigned tasks as they track progress milestones.

You can view the task list associated with your default email account in several locations within Outlook, including the Tasks module, the Tasks peek, the Daily Task List that appears in selected calendar views, and the Outlook Today page. You can create and view additional task lists as well. For example, you might want to keep a business-related task list and a personal task list, or an individual task list and a shared task list.

SEE ALSO For information about the Daily Task List, see "Displaying different views of a calendar" in Chapter 5, "Manage scheduling." For information about the Tasks peek, see "Personalizing the Outlook program window" in Chapter 11, "Customize Outlook."

In this chapter, you'll create tasks from scratch and flag items to add them to your task list. You'll delegate tasks to other people and manage task assignments. You'll also review different ways of arranging, organizing, and locating tasks, and you'll remove tasks from your list by marking them as complete or by deleting them.

PRACTICE FILES The exercises in this chapter use Outlook items you created in exercises in previous chapters. If an exercise requires an item that you don't have, you can complete the exercise in which you create the item before beginning the exercise, or you can substitute a similar item of your own.

Creating tasks

If you use your Outlook task list to its fullest potential, you'll frequently add tasks to it. You can create one-time or recurring tasks from scratch in different ways, accept a task assignment from someone else, or add an existing Outlook item (such as a message) to your task list. Regardless of how or where you create a task, all tasks and flagged messages are moderated by the Tasks module and displayed in various views, including the To-Do List and Tasks folders in the Tasks module, the Tasks peek available in any module, and the Daily Task List available in the Calendar module.

TIP For information about the To-Do list and Tasks folders, see "Displaying different views of tasks" later in this chapter.

You can attach files to task items, and you can include text, tables, charts, illustrations, hyperlinks, and other content in the task window content pane by using the same commands you use in other Outlook item windows and in other Microsoft Office 2013 programs, such as Microsoft Word. You can also set standard Outlook item options such as recurrence, color categories, reminders, and privacy.

Creating tasks from scratch

You can create a task item from scratch by entering the task information in a task window or in the entry box provided at the top of any of the task list views (in the Tasks module, in the Tasks peek, or in the Daily Tasks List). The amount of information you can enter when creating the task item varies based on the location in which you create it.

When you create a task item, the only information you really need is the subject. As with many other types of Outlook items, you can set several options for tasks to make it easier to organize and identify tasks.

- **Start date and due date** You can display tasks on the various Outlook task lists on either the start date or the due date. The color of the task flag indicates the due date.

- **Status** You can track the status of a task to remind yourself of your progress. Specific status options include Not Started, In Progress, Completed, Waiting On Someone, or Deferred. You also have the option of indicating what percentage of the task is complete. Setting the percentage complete to 25%, 50%, or 75% sets the task status to In Progress. Setting it to 100% sets the task status to Complete.

- **Priority** Unless you indicate otherwise, a task is created with a Normal priority level. You can set the priority to add a visual indicator of a task's importance. Low priority displays a blue downward pointing arrow and High priority displays a red exclamation point. You can sort and filter tasks based on their priority.

- **Recurrence** You can set a task to recur on a regular basis; for example, you might create a Payroll task that recurs every month. Only the current instance of a recurring task appears in your task list. When you mark the current task as complete, Outlook creates the next instance of the task.

- **Category** Tasks use the same category list as other Outlook items. You can assign a task to a category to associate it with related items such as messages and appointments.

- **Reminder** You can set a reminder for a task in the same way you do for an appointment. The reminder appears until you dismiss it or mark the task as complete.

  TIP By default, Outlook doesn't set a reminder for tasks. You can turn on reminders from the Outlook Options dialog box. For more information, see "Configuring Office and Outlook options" in Chapter 11, "Customize Outlook."

- **Privacy** Marking a task as private ensures that other Outlook users to whom you delegate account access can't see the task details.

From any view of the task list, you can assign the task to a category, change the due date, add a reminder, mark the task as complete, or delete the task entirely. To access these commands, right-click the task name, category, or flag, and then click the option you want. None of the options are required, but they can be helpful to you when sorting, filtering, and prioritizing your tasks.

TIP The fields available in the Tasks List vary based on the list view you're displaying. For information about the available views, see "Displaying different views of tasks" later in this chapter.

Creating tasks from Outlook items

You frequently need to take action based on information you receive in Outlook—for example, information in a message or in a meeting request. You might want to add information from another Outlook item to your task list, to ensure that you complete any necessary follow-up work.

Depending on the method you use, you can either create a new task from an existing item or simply transfer the existing item to your task list by flagging it.

To create a new task from a message, contact record, or note:

- Drag the item to the **Tasks** link or button on the **Navigation Bar**, and when a plus sign appears next to the cursor, release the mouse button.

  This method opens a task window that already has information filled in from the original item. You can change settings, add information and attachments, assign the task to other people, and make other changes.

To transfer an existing email message to your task list without creating an individual task:

- In the **Mail** module, point to a message in the message list, and then click the flag icon that appears.

  This method, referred to as *flagging a message for follow-up*, adds the message to your task lists by using the default due date, and adds an InfoBar to the message. However, it does not create a separate task item, so to retain the task, you must retain the message; you can move the message between mail folders, but deleting the message also deletes it from the task list.

TIP Flagged messages appear on your task list under the default due date header. You can change the default due date by configuring the Quick Click flag either from the Tasks page of the Outlook Options dialog box or from the shortcut menu that appears when you right-click a message flag.

- In the **Mail** module, point to a message in the message list, right-click the flag icon that appears, and then click a specific due date: **Today**, **Tomorrow**, **This Week**, **Next Week**, **No Date**, or **Custom** (which you can use to set specific start and end dates).

- Drag the message to the **Tasks** peek on the **To-Do Bar** and drop it under the heading for the due date you want to assign to it. (If the desired due date doesn't already have a heading in the task list, drop the message under another heading and then assign the due date you want.)

  This method adds the message to your task list but doesn't create a separate task item.

You can flag a contact record for follow-up by clicking the contact record in the contact list and then clicking the Follow-Up button in the Tags group on the Home tab.

If you frequently want to create message-based tasks with special settings, such as a task with the original message attached to it, with specific follow-up settings or categories, and with specific assignments, you can create a Quick Step to accomplish all of these steps with one click.

SEE ALSO For information about Quick Steps, see "Managing messages by using Quick Steps" in Chapter 7, "Organize your Inbox" and "Creating and managing Quick Steps" in Chapter 12, "Manage email settings."

In this exercise, you'll pin the Tasks peek to the To-Do Bar, flag a message for follow-up, and create tasks from the To-Do Bar and from the Tasks module.

➜ SET UP This exercise uses the SBS Tradeshow Schedule and SBS First Draft messages you created in Chapter 3. If you didn't create those messages, you can do so now, or you can substitute any messages in your Inbox. Display your Inbox, ensure that the message list and Reading Pane are open, and then follow the steps.

1 On the **Navigation Bar**, point to **Tasks**, and then in the upper-right corner of the **Tasks** peek, click the **Dock the peek** button to pin the **Tasks** peek (which contains any existing tasks or flagged items) to the **To-Do Bar** at the right side of the program window. Display or hide other areas of the **To-Do Bar** as you want.

TIP In Outlook 2013, the To-Do Bar displays the Calendar, People, and Tasks areas in whatever order you select them. To arrange them in a specific order, clear all the check marks and then select the areas in the order you want to display them. Drag the borders between the areas to allocate space among them and display more or less of each area.

> **IMPORTANT** In the remainder of this exercise, we refer to performing actions in the Tasks peek. Although you could perform these steps from the Navigation Bar, for the purposes of this exercise, we mean the Tasks peek that you pinned to the To-Do Bar in step 1.

2   Locate the **SBS Tradeshow Schedule** message. In the message list, point to the message, and then click the flag icon that appears. The flag remains visible in the message list, follow-up information appears below the message header in the **Reading Pane**, and **SBS Tradeshow Schedule** appears in the **Today** category in the **Tasks** peek.

TIP If necessary, minimize the Folder Pane so that the Reading Pane contents are visible.

Minimized Folder Pane   Follow-up flag   Follow-up information   Flagged item

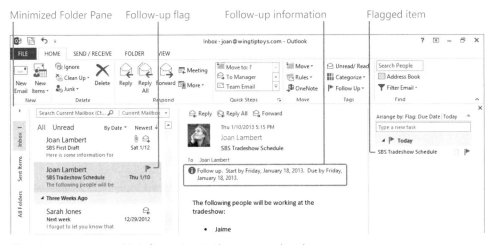

Flagging a message adds information to the message header.

3   On the **To-Do Bar**, point to the **SBS Tradeshow Schedule** task to display a tooltip that contains the start date, the reminder time, the due date, the folder in which the message appears, and any categories assigned to the message.

4   Double-click the **SBS Tradeshow Schedule** task to open the flagged message in a message window. The message header indicates that you need to follow up on this message. The start and due dates given are today's date.

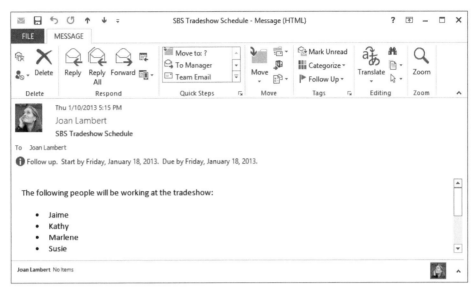

The ribbon of the flagged message includes only message commands; it does not have additional task-related tabs or commands.

5   Close the message window.

6   In the message list, locate the **SBS First Draft** message. Drag the message from the message list to the **Tasks** peek on the **To-Do Bar**, and release the mouse button when the red horizontal insertion line indicates that the item will be inserted immediately after the **SBS Tradeshow Schedule** item. Notice that the flag icon is now visible on the **SBS First Draft** message in the message list.

7   On the **To-Do Bar**, in the **Tasks** peek, right-click (don't click) the red flag to the right of the **SBS First Draft** message to display a list of due date options. Because a task has been activated, the **Task List** tool tab appears on the ribbon.

TROUBLESHOOTING Clicking an active flag marks the item as complete in the Inbox, and removes it from the Tasks peek. For more information, see "Removing tasks and flagged items from task lists" later in this chapter.

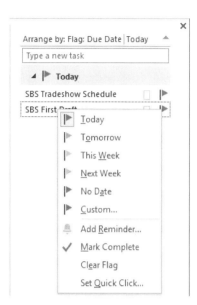

*It's easy to change the due date of a task or the follow-up
date for a flagged message from the Tasks peek.*

8   In the **Tasks** peek, click **Next Week** to move the message under the corresponding
due date heading in the list. In the message list and in the **Tasks** peek, the flag to the
right of the **SBS First Draft** message changes from red to light pink. In the **Reading
Pane**, the start and due dates change.

TIP Flagging a task for completion This Week or Next Week sets the start date to
the first working day of the specified week and the due date to the last working day
of the week. (Therefore, changing a due date from Today to This Week has no effect
if today is the last day of the work week.) The default work week is Monday through
Friday but the start and due dates reflect your own work week configuration. For information about changing the days and times of your work week, see "Defining your
available time" in Chapter 8, "Manage your calendar."

9   In the **Tasks** peek, click **Type a new task**, enter SBS Order Brochures, and then
press **Enter** to add the task to the **Today** section of the task list.

TIP The tasks you create while working through the exercises in this book begin with
SBS so that you can differentiate them from any real tasks you create.

10   On the **Navigation Bar**, click the **Tasks** button to open the **Tasks** module, displaying
the **To-Do List** folder. (If the **Folder Pane** is minimized, expand it to display the
folders in the **My Tasks** list.)

An icon to the right of the **SBS Order Brochures** task indicates that it is a standard task item. Other icons might indicate whether a flagged message is read or unread and whether you've replied to or forwarded the message.

11 In the task list, click **SBS Tradeshow Schedule** to display the flagged message contents and the response options in the **Reading Pane**. Notice that all the commands on the **Home** tab of the **Tasks** module are available for the selected item.

12 In the task list, click **SBS Order Brochures** to display the task item contents in the **Reading Pane**. Notice that some commands in the **Respond** group become unavailable, and you can't edit the task settings directly in the **Reading Pane**.

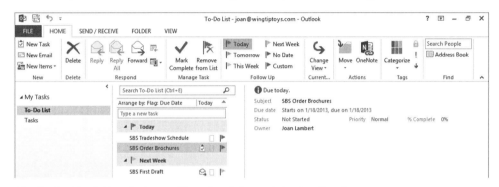

The To-Do List folder displays a filtered task list and the Reading Pane.

13 At the top of the task list, click **Type a new task**, enter SBS Make Dinner Reservations, and then press **Enter** to add the task in the **Today** section of the task list.

14 Double-click the **SBS Make Dinner Reservations** task to open it in a task window.

15 On the **Task** tab, in the **Tags** group, click the **Follow Up** button, and then click **Custom**.

16 In the **Custom** dialog box that opens, select **Call** in the **Flag to** list, then click the **Start date** arrow and in the calendar that opens, click the next **Monday** to change both the start date and the end date.

You can set custom flags and reminders.

17 Select the **Reminder** check box, and in the list of times, click **9:00 AM**. Then click **OK** to update the task header.

18 In the notes pane below the task header, enter Confirm that the restaurant has a private dining room available for the management team dinner.

> **TIP** The outline surrounding the notes pane might not be visible when editing a task or contact record. However, the notes pane is still there and it will become active when you click in it.

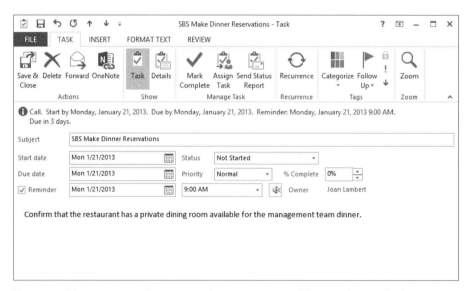

You can add many types of content to the notes pane and format the text in the notes pane.

19 On the **Task** tab, in the **Actions** group, click the **Save & Close** button.

20   On the **Home** tab, in the **New** group, click the **New Task** button.

KEYBOARD SHORTCUT Press Ctrl+Shift+K to create a new task from any module. For more information about keyboard shortcuts, see "Keyboard shortcuts" at the end of this book.

21   In the **Subject** box, enter SBS Send Dinner Invitations.

22   Click the button at the right end of the **Start date** box, and on the calendar that appears, click the **Tuesday** that follows the Monday you selected for the **SBS Make Dinner Reservations** task.

23   Click the **Due date** button, and on the calendar that appears, click the **Wednesday** that follows the start date.

TIP You can't assign to a task a due date that has already passed.

24   Select the **Reminder** check box. Notice that the default reminder time available from the task item (**8:00 AM**) is different from that available in the **Custom** dialog box (**4:00 PM**).

6

25   In the notes pane, enter the following sentence:

Invite all management team members and their spouses.

26   In the **Actions** group, click the **Save & Close** button to add the task to your task list.

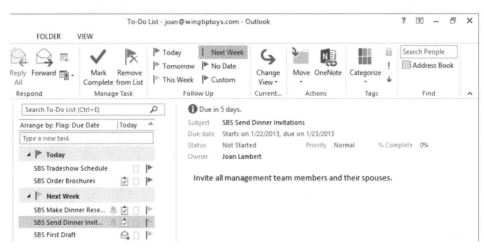

A bell next to a task name indicates that a reminder is set for the task.

❌ CLEAN UP Retain the SBS Order Brochures, SBS Make Dinner Reservations, and SBS Send Dinner Invitations tasks, and the flagged SBS Tradeshow Schedule and SBS First Draft messages, for use in later exercises.

Updating tasks

Tasks generally appear on the Outlook task lists by start date or due date. You can change the details or dates of a task, or track the progress you've made on it.

To update the status of a task:

1. Open the task window.

2. In the **% Complete** list, enter or select (by clicking the arrows) the percentage of the project you estimate as complete to change the status to reflect your selection. Tasks that are **0%** complete are **Not Started**, tasks that are **1%** to **99%** complete are **In Progress**, and tasks that are **100%** complete are **Completed**.

3. If you want to manually change the task status—for example, to **Deferred** or **Waiting on someone else**—click that option in the **Status** list.

4. Save and close the task to update the task both in your own task list and in the task originator's task list.

You can't track the status of a flagged message.

In this exercise, you'll update the status and due date of a task on your task list.

 SET UP You need the SBS Make Dinner Reservations task you created earlier in this chapter to complete this exercise. If you didn't create that task, you can do so now, or you can substitute any task in your default task list. Display the To-Do List folder in the Tasks module, and then follow the steps.

1. In the task list, double-click the **SBS Make Dinner Reservations** task. For the purposes of this exercise, assume that you are waiting for the banquet manager to confirm whether a private dining room is available. You want to update the task to reflect your progress, change the task due date, and also remind yourself to call again if you don't hear from her by the end of the day.

2. Note the original start and due dates, which you set to the next Monday. Click the **Start date** arrow, and then below the calendar, click **Today**. Notice that the due date also changes to today.

3. Click the **Due date** arrow, and then on the calendar, click tomorrow's date.

4. Click the **Status** arrow, and then in the list, click **Waiting on someone else**.

5. In the **% Complete** box, enter or select (by clicking the arrows) **25%.**

6   In the notes pane, click at the end of the existing note, press **Enter** twice, and then enter the following sentence:

Left message for banquet manager – will call back tomorrow.

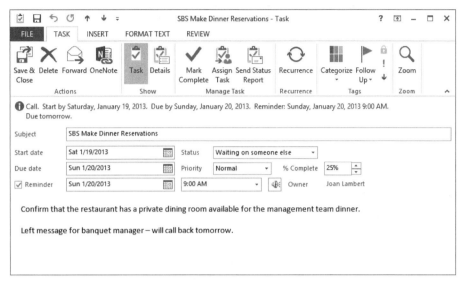

You can easily update a task to reflect its current completion status.

7   On the **Task** tab, in the **Actions** group, click the **Save & Close** button.

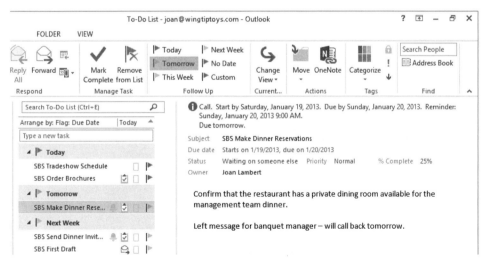

The changes you made in the task window are reflected in the task list and Reading Pane.

❌ CLEAN UP Retain the SBS Make Dinner Reservations task for use in later exercises.

Removing tasks and flagged items from task lists

When you complete a task or follow up on a flagged item, you have three options for managing its presence on your task list: marking the task or flagged item as complete, removing the flag from a flagged item, or deleting the task or flagged item entirely.

Marking a task or flagged item as complete retains a record of the item on your task list. Completed tasks are visible only in certain task list views.

To mark a task as complete:

- In the **Tasks** module, click the task to make it active, and then on the **Home** tab, in the **Manage Task** group, click the **Mark Complete** button.

- In views that include a check box preceding the task subject (most list views), select the check box to delete the task.

- In views that include a colored flag, click the flag once.

- In any view, right-click the task, and then click **Mark Complete**.

- In the task window, change the **Status** to **Completed** or the **% Complete** setting to **100%**.

Whichever method you use, when you display an unfiltered view of your task list, the completed task is crossed through, the Complete check box is selected, and the flag changes to a check mark. In the task window for the completed task, Status is set to Completed and % Complete is set to 100%. (In other words, doing any one thing accomplishes all the others.)

Completed tasks are hidden in many views, but you can display them if you want to.

After you mark an instance of a recurring task as complete, Outlook generates a new instance of the task at whatever interval you specified when creating the task.

Removing the flag from a flagged item such as a message or contact record retains the item in its original location but removes it from your task list entirely.

To remove the flag from an item:

- In the **Tasks** module, click the flagged item to select it, and then click the **Remove from List** button in the **Manage Tasks** group on the **Home** tab.

- In the **Tasks** peek, click the flagged item, and then click the **Remove from List** button in the **Manage Tasks** group on the **Task List** tool tab.

- In either location, right-click the flagged item, click **Follow-up**, and then click **Clear Flag**.

Deleting a task or flagged item moves the task or the original item to the Deleted Items folder; it is permanently deleted when you empty that folder. No record of it remains on your task list or in its original location (such as your Inbox).

To delete a task or flagged item:

- In the **Tasks** module, click the task to make it active and then on the **Home** tab, in the **Delete** group, click the **Delete** button.

- In any view, right-click the task, and then click **Delete**.

6

Managing task assignments

You can assign tasks from your Outlook task list to other people within and outside of your organization (and other people can assign tasks to you). Outlook indicates assigned tasks in your task list by adding a blue arrow pointing to a person on the task icon, similar to that of a shared folder in Windows Explorer.

Tasks you assign to others

You can assign tasks to people on your Microsoft Exchange Server network, to people on other Exchange Server networks, and to people running email programs other than Outlook.

- When you assign a task to a person on your Exchange Server network, Outlook sends a task request, similar to a meeting request, to the person you designated. The assignee can accept or decline the task assignment by clicking the corresponding button in the Reading Pane or in the task window header. Outlook indicates the status of the task in your task list as Assigned.

- When you assign a task to a person who is on another Exchange Server network or is using an email program other than Outlook, Outlook sends a message that the assignee can respond to manually. Until you change the task status, it is shown in the open task window as Waiting For Response From Recipient, rather than Assigned.

When you assign a task, you can choose whether to keep a copy of the task on your own task list or transfer it entirely to the assignee's task list. Either way, the task remains on your own task list until accepted, so you won't lose track of it. (If the recipient declines the task, you can return it to your task list or reassign it.)

TIP You can assign only actual task items; you can't assign flagged messages that appear in your task list. The items you've assigned are visible only when you choose to include them in your view of the task list.

After you assign a task to someone else, ownership of the task transfers to that person, and you can no longer update the information in the task window. (The assignee becomes the task owner and you become the task originator.) If you keep a copy of the task on your task list, you can follow the progress as the assignee updates the task status and details, and you can communicate information about the task to the owner by sending status reports. Unless you choose otherwise, Outlook automatically sends you a status report on an assigned task when the assignee marks the task as complete.

To delegate a task to another Outlook user:

1   Open the task in the task window. On the **Task** tab, in the **Manage Task** group, click the **Assign Task** button.

2   In the **To** box that appears in the task header, enter the name or email address of the person you want to assign the task to.

3   Review the task subject, dates, status, priority, and completion settings and ensure that they are as you want them—after you assign the task, you will no longer be able to change the task details.

4   If you do not want to keep a copy of the assigned task on your task list or receive a status report when the task is complete, clear the corresponding check box.

5   In the task header, click the **Send** button. If a message box notifies you that the task reminder has been turned off, click **OK** to send the task request and notify you when the assignee accepts or declines the task.

You can view the status of tasks you have assigned to other people by displaying your task list in Assignment view.

SEE ALSO For information about task list views, see "Displaying different views of tasks" later in this chapter.

The assignee receives a task request that he or she can accept or decline. Either action generates a response message to you. As with meeting requests, the task request recipient has the option of sending a message with the response.

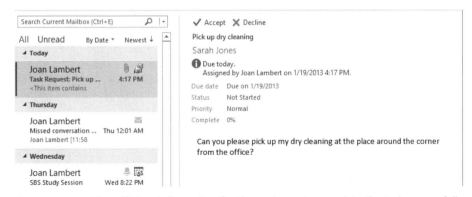

Be sure to provide sufficient information for the assignee to complete the task successfully.

TIP Only Exchange users have the Accept and Decline options in the task request message; Internet email account users do not.

If you assign a task and the assignee declines the assignment, the task doesn't automatically return to your task list; you need to either reclaim the task (return it to your own task list) or reassign it.

To reclaim or reassign a declined task:

1   Open the declined task assignment (indicated in your Inbox by a task icon with a red X).

The Manage Task group on the Task tab of the ribbon includes commands specific to managing the declined task.

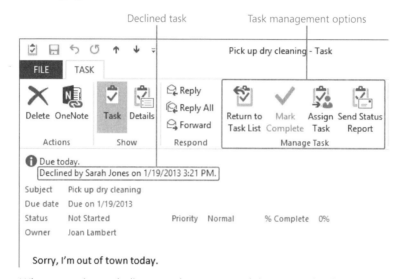

When an assignee declines a task, you can reclaim or reassign it.

2   In the **Manage Task** group, click the **Return to Task List** button to reclaim the task, or the **Assign Task** button to reassign it.

Tasks other people assign to you

When another person assigns a task to you, you receive a task request.

To accept, decline, respond to, or reassign a task request:

1   Accept or decline the task from the **Reading Pane**, or open the task request to see additional options for managing the task request on the **Task** tab of the task window ribbon.

KEYBOARD SHORTCUT Press Alt+C to accept a task request; press Alt+D to decline a task request.

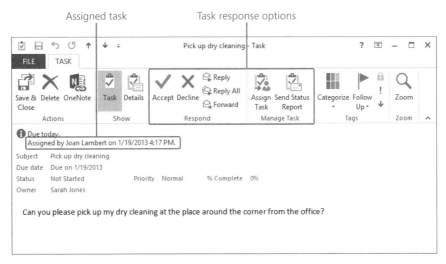

You can respond in several ways to a task assignment.

2   Take one of the following actions:

- In the **Respond** group, click the **Accept** button to accept the task or the **Decline** button to decline the task, and send the associated response to the task owner.

- In the **Respond** group, click **Reply** to send a message to the task owner without accepting or declining the task, or the **Forward** button to forward the task content to another person without reassigning the task.

- In the **Manage Task** group, click the **Assign Task** button, and follow the process described earlier in this topic to assign the task to another person.

You can update the details of a task assigned to you by someone else in the same way that you do tasks that you create.

To send a status report about a task assigned to you by someone else:

1   Open the task window.

2   On the **Task** tab, in the **Manage Task** group, click the **Send Status Report** button to generate an email message that has the task information in the **Subject** field and message body.

3   Address the message to the people you want to send the report to, and then send the message.

In this exercise, you'll assign a task to another person.

 SET UP You need the SBS Send Dinner Invitations task you created earlier in this chapter to complete this exercise. If you didn't create that task, you can do so now, or you can
substitute any task in your default task list. Choose a co-worker or other email contact
to practice assigning tasks to, and let him or her know to expect a task assignment. Then
display the To-Do List folder in the Tasks module, and follow the steps.

1 In the task list, double-click the **SBS Send Dinner Invitations** task to open the task in
a task window.

2 In the **Manage Task** group, click the **Assign Task** button to display a **To** box and **Send**
button in the task header. Notice that the **Manage Task** group now includes only the
Cancel Assignment button.

3 In the **To** box, enter the email address of the person to whom you want to assign the
task. Note that the **Keep an updated copy of this task on my task list** and **Send me**
a status report when this task is complete check boxes are selected by default.

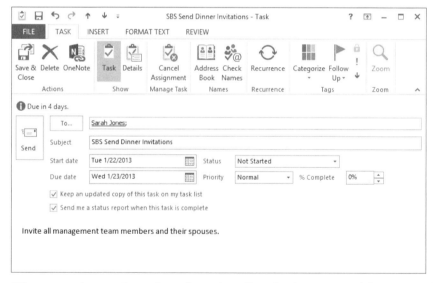

When you assign a task, you have the option of keeping it on your task list or removing it.

4 In the task header, click the **Send** button. A message box notifies you that the task
reminder previously set for this task will be turned off when you assign it to another
person.

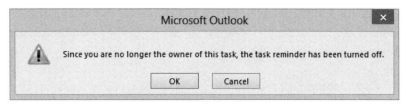

Assigning a task cancels any reminders that you have set for yourself.

5   Click **OK** in the message box to send the task request.

6   Ask the task request recipient to accept the task. Outlook notifies you when the assignee accepts or declines the task.

❌ CLEAN UP Retain the assigned SBS Send Dinner Invitations task for use in later exercises.

Displaying different views of tasks

Outlook 2013 makes it simple to keep your task list at your fingertips. You can view tasks in several different locations, including the following:

- In the Tasks module, you can display the To-Do List folder, which includes both tasks and flagged messages, or the Tasks folder, which includes only tasks. Outlook provides many options for viewing and arranging the contents of each folder.

  TIP The Tasks folder is the default folder in which Outlook stores task items. You can create additional folders to contain task items if you want to. The To-Do List folder is a virtual folder (like a Search Folder) that displays the contents of your Tasks folder plus any items you flag for follow-up. The To-Do List folder doesn't contain unique copies of the task items.

- In any module, you can display the Tasks peek on the To-Do Bar. The Tasks peek displays a task list in which tasks are grouped and sorted by due date. (You can also sort this list by category, start date, folder, type, or importance, or you can create a custom arrangement.) You can scroll through the list to display all your tasks or collapse the groups you don't want to view. To increase the space available for your task list, you can close or reduce the height of other To-Do Bar elements.

SEE ALSO For information about the To-Do Bar, including changing the type and amount of content displayed, see "Personalizing the Outlook program window" in Chapter 11, "Customize Outlook."

▪ In the Calendar module, the Daily Task List appears below the calendar in Day, Work Week, or Week view. When expanded, the Daily Task List displays the tasks due, including the category and task type, during the displayed time period. In Day view, the start date, due date, and reminder time also appear.

TIP If you don't see the Daily Task List in Day, Work Week, or Week view, click the Daily Task List button in the Layout group on the View tab, and then click Normal.

Like the Folder Pane and the People Pane, you can minimize the Daily Task List so that it displays only the number of active and completed tasks and provides more space for you to work. You can switch between views of the Daily Task List by clicking the Minimize or Expand button on its header.

You can schedule a specific block of time to complete a task by dragging it from the Daily Task List to your calendar.

▪ On the Outlook Today page, the tasks due today are listed in the Tasks area. (This page was at one time the "home page" of Outlook.) You display the Outlook Today page by clicking your email account in the Folder Pane.

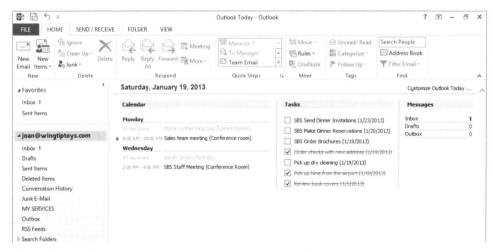

The Outlook Today page summarizes your upcoming activities.

So far in this chapter, we've been working in the To-Do List folder of the Tasks module, which displays both tasks and flagged messages. When you prefer to work with only task items, you can do so in the Tasks folder. In each folder, you can select a *view* and an *arrangement* of the folder content. The view filters the content and the arrangement orders the filtered content.

Outlook includes 11 built-in views, which are available in the Change View gallery; you can access this gallery from the Current View group on the Home tab or on the View tab.

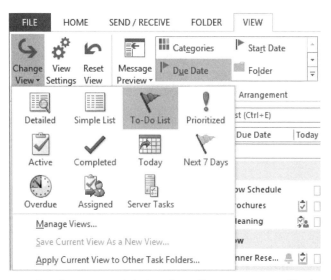

By using the commands below the gallery, you can modify the current view, create a new view, or apply the view to other task folders.

The available views include Active, Assigned, Completed, Detailed, Next 7 Days, Overdue, Prioritized, Server Tasks, Simple List, Today, and To-Do List. Detailed view displays all active and completed items in list format; most of the other views display only the items corresponding to the view name (for example, Active view displays only the active items in the folder and Completed view displays only the completed items).

The default view for the To-Do List folder is (somewhat confusingly) To-Do List view; this view displays a simple item list grouped by the selected arrangement, with the Reading Pane open on the right. The Reading Pane is not open by default in the other views. If you want, you can display it at the bottom of the task list so that you don't lose horizontal screen space and obscure task details.

The default view for the Tasks folder is Simple List view. This view displays the subject, due date, categories, and flags for each folder item and a check box that you can select to indicate that an item has been completed.

From the Arrangements gallery in the Arrangement group on the View tab, you can arrange items within the selected view by Assignment, Categories, Due Date, Folder, Importance, Modified Date, Start Date, or Type. Alternatively, you can manually reorder the tasks in any list view by clicking the heading of the field you want to sort on. You can add and remove fields from the list view by using the Field Chooser, in the same way that you would from the list view of contact records.

SEE ALSO For information about organizing tasks in custom folders, see the sidebar "Finding and organizing tasks" later in this chapter. For information about adding and removing fields in a list view, see "Displaying different views of contact records" in Chapter 4, "Store and access contact information."

Completed tasks remain in the Tasks folder until you delete them, so they are available there if you want to view them.

In this exercise, you'll look at different views of tasks and flagged messages within the Tasks module.

 SET UP This exercise uses the SBS Order Brochures, SBS Make Dinner Reservations, and SBS Send Dinner Invitations tasks, and the SBS First Draft and SBS Tradeshow Schedule flagged messages you created and assigned earlier in this chapter. If you didn't create those tasks and messages, you can do so now, or you can substitute any tasks and flagged messages in your task list. Display the To-Do List folder in the Tasks module, and then follow the steps.

1   Notice that in the lower-left corner of the window, the words **Filter Applied** appear at the left end of the status bar to indicate that the **To-Do List** folder is displaying a filtered view of the available items (in this case, only active items).

The default view of the To-Do List folder displays only active items.

2   On the **Home** tab, in the **Current View** group, click the **Change View** button to expand the **Change View** gallery. **To-Do List** is selected to indicate the current view of the folder contents.

3   In the **Change View** gallery, click **Detailed** to close the **Reading Pane** and display a list view of the active and completed tasks and flagged messages, with many task fields visible as list columns. Notice that the filter notification no longer appears at the left end of the status bar, because we are displaying all tasks.

The Detailed view of your tasks and flagged messages includes those tasks you've completed.

4   In the **Folder Pane**, click **Tasks** to display only task items in the list; flagged messages are absent. In the **Current View** group, click the **Change View** button and notice that **Simple List** is selected to indicate the current view of the folder contents. The arrow on the **Due Date** header indicates the current order of the items.

You can change the sort order by clicking the column headers.

5   On the **View** tab, in the **Arrangement** gallery, click the **More** button to expand the menu and display additional arrangements.

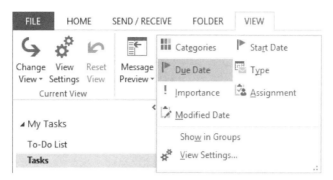

The Arrangement menu options are valid for any view.

6   In the **Arrangement** gallery, first click **Assignment**, and then expand the menu again
     and click the **Show in Groups** command beneath the gallery to group tasks that you
     own separately from tasks that you have assigned to other people.

     TIP If you have assigned a task to multiple people, the task appears in a group for
     each assignee.

You can group tasks by the current arrangement.

7   On the **View** tab, in the **Current View** group, in the **Change View** gallery, click **Active**
     and notice that the view displays only the active tasks assigned to you (even though
     the task you assigned is not yet complete).

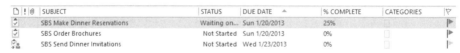

The list headers change to display information pertinent to the selected view.

8   In the **Change View** gallery, click **To-Do List** to display in the content area all the active tasks in the same format as in the default view of the **To-Do List** folder. Note that because we're currently displaying the **Tasks** folder, the list doesn't include flagged messages.

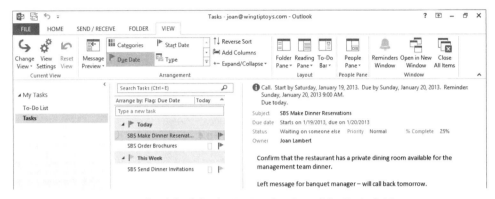

The Reading Pane is open by default in the To-Do List view of the Tasks folder.

9   In the **Change View** gallery, click **Simple List**. In the **Current View** group, click **Reset View**. Then click **Yes** in the dialog box that appears, to return the **Tasks** folder to its default settings.

10 In the **Folder Pane**, click **To-Do List**. In the **Change View** gallery, click **To-Do List** to return the folder to its default settings.

✖ CLEAN UP Retain the SBS Order Brochures, SBS Make Dinner Reservations, and SBS Send Dinner Invitations tasks, and the flagged SBS Tradeshow Schedule and SBS First Draft messages, for use in exercises in later chapters.

Finding and organizing tasks

You can use the Outlook Search feature to quickly locate tasks by searching for specific text or for item properties. To search for text, enter the word or other information you want to find in the Search box at the top of the module content area, in any folder or view. To search for properties, click in the Search box and then specify the properties by using the commands on the Search tool tab that appears. Outlook filters the folder items as you enter the criteria, displaying only those containing the search criteria you enter, and highlighting matching content in the results.

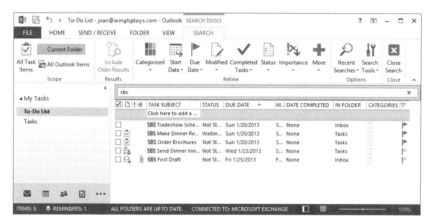

You can modify your search by using the tools on the Search tool tab.

TIP To help you organize and locate tasks, you can assign color categories to them. For information about using color categories, see "Organizing items by using color categories" and "Quickly locating messages" in Chapter 7, "Organize your Inbox."

If your task list gets too big, or if you want to maintain separate task lists for different purposes, you can organize tasks into separate folders. To create a task folder:

1 On the **Folder** tab, in the **New** group, click the **New Folder** button.

2 In the **Create New Folder** dialog box, enter the name and select the location of the folder.

3 In the **Folder Contains** list, click **Task Items**, and then click **OK**.

TIP If you drag a task into a Mail, Calendar, Contact, or Note Items folder, a message, meeting, contact, or note window opens with the task's subject entered in the Subject field and details of the task in the message body or notes pane.

Key points

- You can create tasks for yourself and assign tasks to other people.

- Outlook displays tasks in the Tasks module, in the Daily Task List in the Calendar module, and on the To-Do Bar, which is available from any Outlook module.

- You can organize tasks by grouping them in additional task folders or by assigning color categories to them.

- When you assign tasks, Outlook sends a task request to the designated person, who can accept or decline the task. If you keep a copy of the assigned task, it is updated when the person you assigned the task to updates the original.

- You can update tasks assigned to you and send status reports to the person who assigned the task.

- A task can have a status of Not Started, Deferred, Waiting, Complete, or the percentage of the task that has been completed.

- You can create one-time or recurring tasks. Outlook creates a new occurrence of a recurring task every time you complete the current occurrence.

- You can set a reminder to display a message at a designated time before a task is due.

- When you complete a task, you can mark it as complete, remove it from your task list, or delete it.

6

Content management

7 Organize your Inbox   231

8 Manage your calendar   275

9 Manage contact records   309

10 Enhance message content   345

Chapter at a glance

View

Work with Conversation view,
page 232

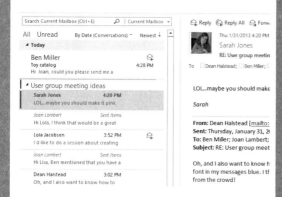

Organize

Organize items by using color categories,
page 244

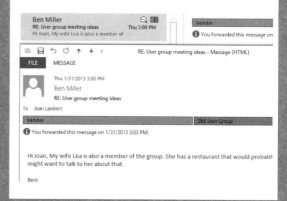

Manage

Manage messages by using Quick Steps,
page 257

Locate

Quickly locate messages,
page 262

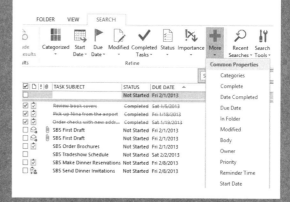

Organize your Inbox 7

IN THIS CHAPTER, YOU WILL LEARN HOW TO

- Work with Conversation view.

- Arrange messages in different ways.

- Organize items by using color categories.

- Organize messages in folders.

- Manage messages by using Quick Steps.

- Quickly locate messages.

- Print messages.

You can use Microsoft Outlook 2013 to manage multiple email accounts, including multiple Microsoft Exchange Server accounts and their associated contacts, calendars, and other elements. Even if you use Outlook only for sending and receiving email messages, you can rapidly build up a mass of messages that make it difficult to locate information. Fortunately, Outlook is designed to act as a complete information-management system; it provides many simple yet useful features that you can use to organize messages and other Outlook items and to quickly find information you need.

Outlook 2013 automatically handles certain types of organization for you. You can organize items in Outlook by storing related items in folders and by assigning color categories to related items of all types. Outlook makes it easy to follow related messages from multiple people by displaying the messages in Conversation view. With Outlook Search, you can quickly locate items that contain specific content or meet specific criteria; you can save search results as Search Folders in which you can view up-to-date search results at any time.

In this chapter, you'll work with Conversation view to locate unique and redundant messages in a related series of messages. You'll display the messages in your Inbox in a variety of arrangements and organize messages by assigning color categories and by moving them to folders. You'll work with the built-in Quick Steps. You'll filter and find messages by using the Search feature, and use Search Folders. Finally, you'll preview, print, and delete messages.

Working with Conversation view

Conversation view is an alternative arrangement of messages grouped by subject. All the messages with the same subject appear together in your Inbox (or other message folder) under one conversation header.

Collapsed conversations

Recent participants

Unread message indicator

Until you expand the conversation header, the entire conversation takes up only as much space in your Inbox as a single message would.

The conversation header provides information about the messages within the conversation, including the number of unread messages and whether one or more messages includes an attachment, is categorized, or is flagged for follow up.

When you receive a message that is part of a conversation, the entire conversation moves to the top of your Inbox and the new message appears when you click the conversation header. When a conversation includes unread messages, a blue vertical line appears to the left of the header and the conversation subject is in bold blue font, just as an unread message would appear. When you have multiple unread messages, the number is indicated in parentheses following the subject. The senders of the unread messages are listed below the subject.

TIP Conversation view is not turned on by default in Outlook 2013. You can turn it on by selecting the Show As Conversations check box in the Messages group on the View tab, or by clicking the header at the top of the message list and then clicking Show As Conversations to place a check mark next to the menu option.

When an email conversation involves more than two people, particularly if it is addressed to a large distribution list, it frequently happens that more than one person responds to the same message, and other people respond to each of those messages. Multiple conversations emerge from the primary conversation in a process that you might think of as branches growing out from a tree—each can split into additional branches that are farther and farther from the trunk (the original message). A conversation that contains multiple branches is called a *split conversation*.

Viewing conversations

You can display differing levels of messages within a conversation, as follows:

- Click the conversation header or the **Expand Conversation** button to the left of the conversation header once to display the most recent message in the **Reading Pane** and to display all the unique messages in the conversation—the most recent message in each thread—in the message list. Reading only these messages will give you all the information that exists in the conversation.

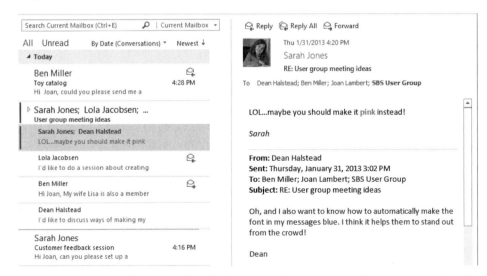

When a conversation is expanded to display only unique messages, the conversation header displays recent participants and the subject.

■ Click the **Expand Conversation** button again to expand the conversation to display all messages in the conversation, including messages from your **Sent Items** folder. (If you click the conversation header a second time, Outlook clears the **Reading Pane**.)

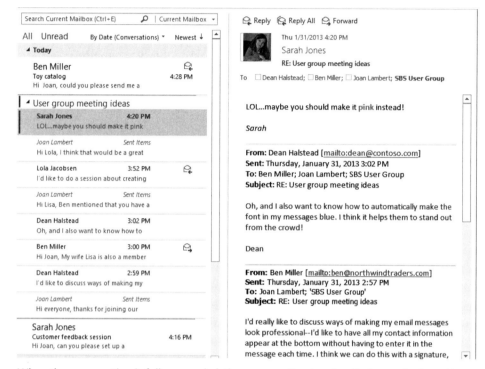

When the conversation is fully expanded, the conversation header displays only the subject.

Conversation view settings

As with other features of Outlook 2013, you can modify the way Conversation view displays messages to suit the way you work. You make changes to Conversation view by turning features on and off on the Conversation Settings menu in the Messages group on the View tab.

Conversation view settings include:

■ **Show Messages from Other Folders** By default, Conversation view displays messages stored in any folder, including sent messages that are stored in the Sent Items folder. (Within the expanded conversation, sent messages are indicated by italic font.) You can turn off this setting to display only messages from the current folder.

- **Show Senders Above the Subject** By default, when a conversation is collapsed, the conversation header displays the names of all the conversation participants above the conversation subject; when the conversation is fully expanded, the conversation header displays only the subject. This setting reverses the order of the information in the conversation header; the names of the conversation participants are displayed above the conversation subject. In some cases, such as when Outlook displays a message on the second line, the subject might not be visible at all.

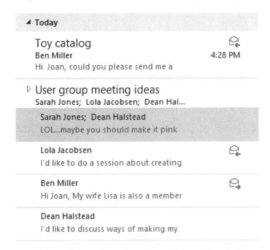

Turning off the Show Senders Above The Subject setting emphasizes the conversation subject.

- **Always Expand Conversations** This setting causes Outlook to display all messages in a conversation when you click the Expand Conversation button or conversation header once.

- **Use Classic Indented View** This setting causes Outlook to indent older messages within individual message threads to show the progression of the thread. This setting is not as effective as the default for displaying split conversations because a message might be at the root of multiple branches but can appear only once in the message list.

TIP In Outlook 2010, unique and redundant messages were indicated by dots of different colors and sizes, and individual message threads were connected by the dots. Outlook 2013 does not use this same system of visual thread indicators; you must independently differentiate between the indent levels.

Managing conversations

Although the most apparent function of conversations is the grouping of related messages, its greatest usefulness is as a message-management tool. It can be especially handy for Outlook users within large organizations that use distribution lists to disseminate information to a large group of people. When hundreds of message recipients use the Reply All function to respond to a message, your Inbox can quickly become cluttered. Outlook tracks conversations by subject and provides tools for managing conversations, regardless of whether you display the messages in Conversation view.

With Conversation view, you can manage all the messages within a conversation as a group. You can do this by clicking the conversation header to effectively select all the messages in the conversation (they won't appear selected, but, for example, moving the conversation header to another folder moves all the individual messages in the conversation) and then applying your action. Or you can use these very useful conversation-management tools:

- **Ignore Conversation** This command moves the selected conversation and any related messages you receive in the future directly to the Deleted Items folder.

  KEYBOARD SHORTCUT Press Ctrl+Del to ignore the currently active conversation. For more information about keyboard shortcuts, see "Keyboard shortcuts" at the end of this book.

  TIP Be cautious when using the Ignore Conversation command. Outlook identifies conversations based on message subjects. If you receive unrelated messages in the future that have the same message subject as a conversation that you've chosen to ignore, you won't receive those messages.

- **Clean Up Conversation** This command deletes redundant messages—messages whose text is wholly contained within later messages—from a conversation. By default, Outlook doesn't clean up categorized, flagged, or digitally signed messages. You can modify conversation clean-up settings on the Mail page of the Outlook Options dialog box.

  SEE ALSO For information about modifying mail settings, see "Configuring Office and Outlook options" in Chapter 11, "Customize Outlook."

Troubleshooting Conversation view

As with many features, Conversation view has its fans and its detractors. Many Outlook users appreciate the efficiency and space-savings of the automatically grouped messages; others worry that this feature might hide individual messages that they haven't yet read. Because Conversation view displays only unique messages until you fully expand the conversation, a specific message that you're looking for might not be immediately visible. If this happens, you can turn off Conversation view (by clearing the Show In Conversations check box in the Conversation group on the View tab) and then use one of the following methods to locate the message you want to find:

- Sort the messages by subject, and then type the first few letters of the message subject to scroll those messages to the top of the message list.

- Enter the subject into the Search box at the top of the message list and then specify any other criteria (such as the sender or date) of the message that you're looking for to narrow the results.

After using either of these methods to display a set of messages, visually scan the messages to locate the one you're looking for.

Arranging messages in different ways

As the number of messages in your Inbox increases, it can be challenging to keep track of them. You can arrange, group, and sort messages in Outlook to help you quickly determine which are the most important, decide which can be deleted, and locate any that need an immediate response.

SEE ALSO For information about the available message folder views, see "Viewing messages and message attachments" in Chapter 3, "Send and receive email messages."

You can view a message list in Compact view, Single view, or Preview view. Regardless of the view you're displaying, you can arrange messages and conversations within the message list by choosing a standard arrangement from the Arrange By menu in the Arrangement group on the View tab.

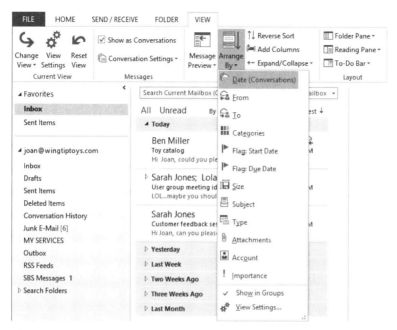

The Arrange By menu provides a variety of options for arranging your messages.

Alternatively, you can click the current arrangement in the message list header, and then click the arrangement or option you want.

The menu displayed when you click the message list header is the same as the Arrange By menu, with the addition of the Show As Conversations command.

By default, Outlook displays messages arranged by date, from newest to oldest. Alternatively, you can arrange items by any of the following attributes:

- **Account** Messages are grouped by the email account to which they were sent. This is useful if you receive messages for more than one email account in your Inbox (for example, if you receive messages sent to your POP3 account within your Exchange account mailbox).

- **Attachments** Messages are grouped by whether they have attachments and secondarily by date received.

- **Categories** Messages are arranged by the category you assign them to. Messages without a category appear first. Messages assigned to multiple categories appear in each of those category groups.

- **Flag: Start Date or Due Date** Unflagged messages and messages without specific schedules appear first. Messages that you've added to your task list with specific start or due dates are grouped by date.

- **From** Messages appear in alphabetical order by the message sender's display name. If you receive messages from a person who uses two different email accounts, or who sends messages from two different email clients (for example, from Outlook and from Windows Mail), the messages will not necessarily be grouped together.

- **Importance** Messages are grouped by priority: High (indicated by a red exclamation point), Normal (the default), or Low (indicated by a blue downward-pointing arrow).

- **To** Messages are grouped alphabetically by the primary recipients (the addresses or names on the To line). The group name exactly reflects the order in which addresses appear on the To line. Therefore, a message addressed to *Bart Duncan; Lukas Keller* is not grouped with a message addressed to *Lukas Keller; Bart Duncan*.

- **Size** Messages are grouped by size of the message, including any attachments. Groups include Huge (1–5 MB), Very Large (500 KB–1 MB), Large (100–500 KB), Medium (25–100 KB), Small (10–25 KB), and Tiny (less than 10 KB). This feature is useful if you work for an organization that limits the size of your Inbox, because you can easily locate large messages and delete them or move them to a personal folder.

- **Subject** Messages are arranged alphabetically by their subjects and then by date. This is similar to arranging by conversation except that the messages aren't threaded.

- **Type** Items in your Inbox (or other folder) are grouped by the type of item—for example, messages, encrypted messages, message receipts, meeting requests and meeting request responses, tasks, Microsoft InfoPath forms, and server notifications.

7

After arranging the items in your message list, you can change the sort order of the arrangement by clicking the sort order indicator that appears to the right of the message list header.

Two options that affect the way messages appear within an arrangement are conversations and grouping. Grouping, which is turned on by default, gathers messages that fit within specific arrangement categories under arrangement-specific headings so that you can manage common messages as one. For example, when messages are arranged by date, they are grouped by date: groups include each day of the current week, Last Week, Two Weeks Ago, Three Weeks Ago, Last Month, and Older. Each group has a header. You can expand or collapse an individual group by clicking the arrow to the left of the group name in the header. You can collapse the group containing the currently selected item by pressing the Left Arrow key, and you can expand a selected group by pressing the Right Arrow key. You can expand or collapse all groups by choosing a command from the Expand/Collapse list in the Arrangement group on the View tab.

Regardless of the view and arrangement you choose, you can sort messages by any visible column simply by clicking its column heading (and reverse the sort order by clicking the column heading a second time). You can change the displayed columns from the Show Columns dialog box, which you display by clicking the Add Columns button in the Arrangement group on the View tab.

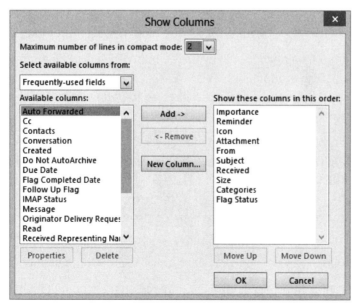

You can control the information shown in the message list and display up to 20 lines of a message in Compact view.

Outlook displays the selected columns in the order shown in the list on the right side of the Show Columns dialog box. If displaying all the columns requires more space than is available, only some of the columns will be visible. If necessary, you can change the number of lines shown to accommodate more columns. However, you are likely to find that one of the standard views fits your needs.

In a list view, you can control the arrangement, sorting, grouping, visible columns, and other settings from the shortcut menu that appears when you right-click any column header.

In this exercise, you'll change the arrangement, sort order, and grouping of messages, and filter the Inbox to display only specific messages. Then you'll restore the default settings.

➡ SET UP You don't need any specific practice files to complete this exercise; just use the messages in your Inbox. Display your Inbox, and then follow the steps.

1   On the **View** tab, in the **Arrangement** group, click the **Arrange By** button, and then in the list, click **From** to rearrange and group the messages in your **Inbox** alphabetically by sender.

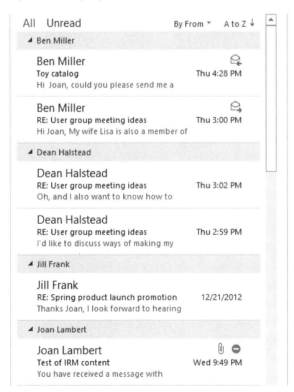

The Sort Order indicator changes to match the selected arrangement.

2   In the message list header, click **A to Z** to reverse the order of the messages. The sort order indicator label changes to **Z to A**.

3   In the message list header, click **By From**, and then in the list, click **Subject** to rearrange and group the messages by subject, in alphabetical order.

4   In the **Arrangement** group, on the **Expand/Collapse** menu, click **Collapse All Groups** to hide the messages and display only the message subjects.

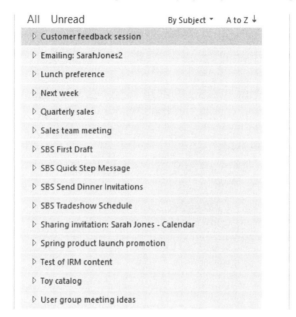

Collapsing groups of messages displays only the group headers.

5   On the **Home** tab, in the **Find** group, click the **Filter Email** button to display a list of message attributes by which you can quickly filter the current folder contents.

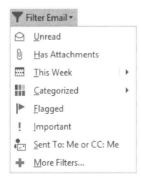

The options shown in the Filter Email list are also present on the Search tool tab.

6   In the **Filter Email** list, click **Unread** to activate the search feature and apply the specified filter. (If you have no unread messages in your Inbox, it appears to be empty.) Notice that the selected arrangement, by subject, is still in effect.

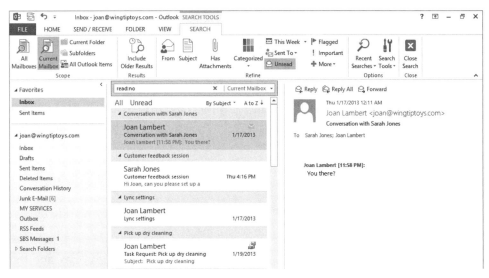

The Search box and Search tool tab indicate the applied filter.

TIP The quickest way to display only unread messages is to click Unread at the top of the message list. This convenient filter is new in Outlook 2013. When you use this method to filter a folder, the word *Unread* is blue and the word *All* is black. If you are unable to locate a message that you've read, ensure that All is selected at the top of the message list.

7   On the **Search** tab, in the **Close** group, click the **Close Search** button to remove the filter and return to the previous arrangement.

8   Experiment with the available arrangement, sorting, and grouping options.

9   On the **View** tab, in the **Current View** group, click the **Reset View** button, and then click **Yes** in the **Microsoft Outlook** dialog box to return the message list to its original arrangement: grouped by date.

❌ CLEAN UP Arrange your Inbox content in the way that works best for you. Retain the default view settings before continuing, if you want them to match those shown in the rest of this book.

Marking messages as read or unread

When a new message arrives in your Inbox, a blue vertical line and bold blue header text indicate that you haven't yet opened the message—its status is *unread*. When you open a message in a message window or preview it for a certain length of time in the Reading Pane, its status changes to *read*. The header is no longer bold, and its icon depicts an open envelope.

You might want to change the status of a message from read to unread, to remind you to revisit it, or from unread to read, if you know from the message subject that you don't need to take action on it.

You can manually change the status of a message by using these methods:

- Point to the message in the message list, and then click the wide blue vertical bar that appears at the left edge of the message.

- Click a message in the message list or select multiple messages, and then on the **Home** tab, in the **Tags** group, click the **Unread/Read** button.

- Right-click a message or one of a group of selected messages in the message list, and then click **Mark as Read** or **Mark as Unread**.

- Right-click a folder in the **Folder Pane**, and then click **Mark All as Read**. (There is no option to mark the folder contents as unread.)

  KEYBOARD SHORTCUTS Press Ctrl+Q to mark a message as read. Press Ctrl+U to mark a message as unread.

Organizing items by using color categories

To help you more easily locate Outlook items associated with a specific subject, project, person, or other attribute, you can create a category specific to that attribute and assign the category to any related items. You can assign a category to any type of Outlook item, such as a message, an appointment, a contact record, or a note. For example, you might assign contact records for customers to a Customers category, or contact records, messages, and meetings associated with a specific project to a category named for the project.

Outlook uses color categories, which combine named categories with color bars to provide an immediate visual cue when you view messages in your Inbox, appointments on your calendar, and other information. Depending on the view of the Outlook items, the category might be indicated by a simple colored block or a large colored bar.

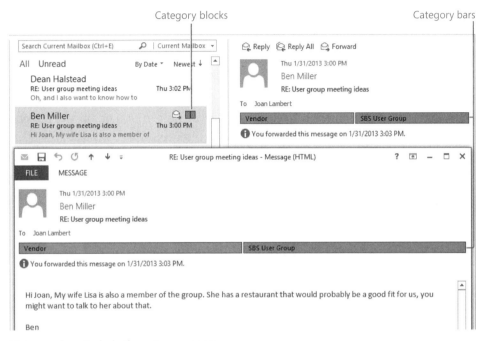

Category bars include the category name.

TIP You can locate, sort, and filter Outlook items by category. For information, see "Quickly locating messages" later in this chapter.

Outlook 2013 comes with six preconfigured color categories that are associated only with the color names. You can rename these six categories and create new categories. Each category can have the following elements:

- **Name** The category name can be one simple word or a long, descriptive phrase. The first 32 characters of the category name are visible in the Color Categories dialog box, but pointing to a truncated name displays the entire name in a ScreenTip.

- **Shortcut key** You can assign any of the 11 available keyboard shortcut combinations (Ctrl+F2 through Ctrl+F12) to the individual color categories.

- **Color** You can assign any of the 25 available colors to a category, or you can choose not to assign a color and to rely only on the name to distinguish between categories. When you assign a category that doesn't have an associated color to an Outlook item, the color block or color bar is shown as white. You can assign one color to multiple color categories.

If you don't rename a standard color category before assigning it for the first time, Outlook gives you the option of renaming the category the first time you use it.

Outlook users with Exchange, IMAP, or POP accounts can designate one category as the Quick Click category. Outlook assigns the Quick Click category by default when you simply click the category block or column associated with an item. (Category blocks appear in the message header in Single view and Preview view.) Until you select a Quick Click category, clicking the blank category blocks has no effect. You can set or change the Quick Click category by clicking Set Quick Click on any one of the Categorize menus and then making your selection in the Set Quick Click dialog box that appears.

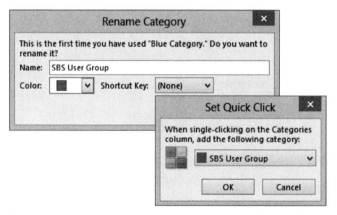

You can personalize categories and apply them with one click or by using a keyboard shortcut.

TIP You can also set the Quick Click category from the Advanced page of the Outlook Options dialog box. For more information, see "Configuring Office and Outlook options" in Chapter 11, "Customize Outlook."

You can apply color categories to a selected item or items by using any of these methods:

- In any mail or contact folder, click the **Categorize** button in the **Tags** group on the **Home** tab, and then in the list, click the category you want.

- In any calendar, click the **Categorize** button in the **Tags** group on the tool tab (such as **Appointment** or **Meeting**) that appears for the selected item, and then click the category you want.

- In any message list, click the blank block in the **Categories** column to assign the Quick Click category.

- In any folder, right-click an item or a selection of items, point to **Categorize**, and then click the category you want.

You can assign an unlimited number of categories to a message, but only the three most recently assigned appear in the message list. The colors representing all the assigned categories appear in the Reading Pane.

To quickly view the items assigned to a specific category, you can group items by category or include the category in a search. In a list view of any module, you can sort and filter by category. On the To-Do Bar, you can arrange flagged messages and tasks by category.

TIP You can instruct Outlook to automatically assign a category to an incoming message that meets specific criteria by creating a rule. For more information, see "Creating rules to process messages" in Chapter 12, "Manage email settings."

In this exercise, you'll change the name and color of an existing category, assign a shortcut key to a category, and create categories. Then you'll categorize a message, and experiment with organizing your Inbox contents by using categories.

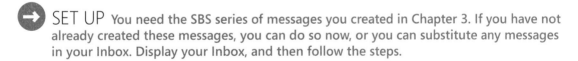 SET UP You need the SBS series of messages you created in Chapter 3. If you have not already created these messages, you can do so now, or you can substitute any messages in your Inbox. Display your Inbox, and then follow the steps.

1 In the message list, click the **SBS Tradeshow Schedule** message.

2　On the **Home** tab, in the **Tags** group, click the **Categorize** button to display the available categories in the **Categorize** list. Notice that you can remove all categories from a selected message or group of messages by clicking **Clear All Categories**.

If you haven't yet worked with categories, only the six standard categories, named by color, are available.

3　In the **Categorize** list, click **All Categories** to open the **Color Categories** dialog box in which you can select, modify, and create categories.

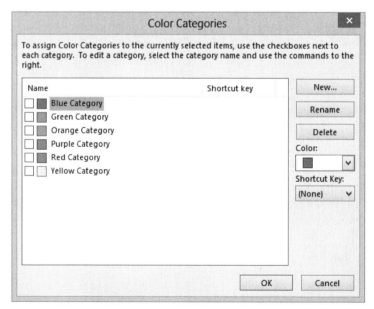

You can rename any of the standard color categories or create new color categories.

4   In the **Color Categories** dialog box, with the **Blue Category** name (not its check box) selected, click the **Rename** button, enter Management, and then press **Enter** (don't click OK) to change the category name. (If you have already renamed the standard categories, you can either create or rename a different category.)

      TIP The category order doesn't immediately change, but the next time you display the categories in a list or dialog box, they will be in alphabetical order.

5   With the **Management** category still selected, click the **Color** arrow, and then in the lower-right corner of the color palette, click the **Dark Maroon** swatch to change the color associated with the **Management** category.

6   Select the **Orange Category** name, and then repeat step 4 to change the category name to Travel Required.

7   In the **Color Categories** dialog box, click the **New** button to open the **Add New Category** dialog box.

8   In the **Name** box, enter Marketing. In the color palette, click the **Dark Green** swatch. Then click the **Shortcut Key** list to display the keyboard shortcuts reserved for color categories.

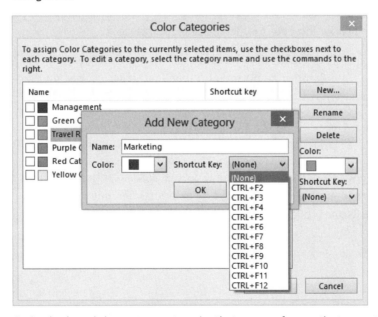

Assign keyboard shortcuts to categories that you use frequently, to save time.

9   In the **Shortcut Key** list, click **Ctrl+F2**. Then in the **Add New Category** dialog box, click **OK** to add the new category to the list of color categories. Notice that its check box is selected, indicating that it has been assigned to the currently selected message.

10   In the **Color Categories** dialog box, click the **Green Category** name (not its check box), click **Delete**, and then in the **Microsoft Outlook** dialog box confirming that you want to delete the category, click **Yes**.

      KEYBOARD SHORTCUT Press Alt+D to delete the selected category from the Color Categories dialog box.

11   In the **Color Categories** dialog box, click **OK** to assign the new **Marketing** category to the **SBS Tradeshow Schedule** message. A dark green category block appears in the message header, and the associated category bar appears at the top of the message in the **Reading Pane**.

12   Right-click the **SBS Tradeshow Schedule** message header, click **Categorize**, and then click **Travel Required** to assign a second category to the message. Notice that the **Categorize** menu displays the current color category options in alphabetical order.

13   In the message list, click the **SBS First Draft** message, and then press **Ctrl+F2** to assign the **Marketing** category to the selected message.

14   Click either of the **SBS First Draft** response messages. On the **Home** tab, in the **Tags** group, click the **Categorize** button and then, in the list, click **Management** to assign the **Management** category to the selected message.

      TIP If you have Conversation view turned on, the conversation header displays the two color category blocks assigned to the individual messages in the conversation.

15   On the **View** tab, in the **Arrangement** group, click **Arranged By**, and then click **Categories** to arrange the messages by category, beginning with the uncategorized messages (**None**), followed by the categorized messages in alphabetical order by category.

16   In the message list header, click **A to Z** to reverse the sort order so that the categorized messages appear at the top of the list.

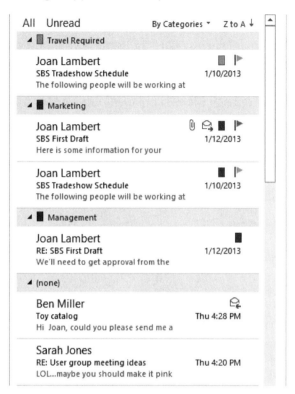

Messages that have multiple categories assigned appear in each of the category groups.

❌ CLEAN UP Reset the view before continuing to the next exercise. Retain the SBS series of messages for use in later exercises.

Recording information by using Outlook notes

You can store miscellaneous information such as reminders, passwords, account numbers, and processes by saving them in electronic notes. Because your notes are available to you from wherever you access Outlook, this can be a very convenient way of retaining information you might need later. And because you're less likely to accidentally delete a note than a message, it is safer than sending information to yourself in an email message.

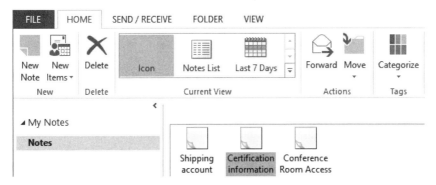

You can categorize notes and organize them in folders.

TIP The first time you access the Notes module, you must do so from the Folder List in the Folder Pane or by clicking Ctrl+5. Thereafter, you can also access it by clicking the ellipsis at the end of the Navigation Bar and then clicking Notes.

You can enter only text into a note; you can't format the text or include graphic elements. Notes do support hyperlinks; if you enter a website address and then press Enter, the website address will change to blue underlined text to indicate that it is a hyperlink. You can click the hyperlink to open the website or page in your default web browser.

Although notes are a type of Outlook item, they don't appear in the same type of windows as messages, appointments, contact records, and tasks. Instead, they appear in the form of "sticky notes." By default, note icons and sticky note representations are a pale yellow color, like the color of standard paper sticky notes. When you assign a category to a note, the note color changes to the category color.

You can view, sort, and organize notes in the same way you do other Outlook items. The standard views include Icons, Notes List, and Last 7 Days.

As with other Outlook items, if you're looking for a specific piece of information in a note, you can quickly locate it by entering a search word or phrase in the Search Notes box at the top of the content area.

To store information in a note:

1 Display the **Notes** module.

2 On the **Home** tab, in the **New** group, click the **New Note** button to display a new note. The current date and time appear at the bottom.

3 Enter the subject or title of the note, press **Enter**, and then enter the information you want to store into the note. The first line of the note becomes its subject.

4 To save and close the note, click the **Close** button in the upper-right corner to display the note in the content area. Only the subject is visible. You can access the stored information by opening the note.

Organizing messages in folders

After you read and respond to messages, you might want to keep some for future reference. You can certainly choose to retain them all in your Inbox if you want, but as the number of messages in your Inbox increases to the thousands and even tens of thousands, it might quickly become overwhelming. (Yes, faithful reader, it happens to the best of us!) To keep your Inbox content low and avoid an accumulation of unrelated messages, you can organize messages into folders. For example, you can keep messages that require action on your part in your Inbox and move messages that you want to retain for future reference into other folders.

TIP Because the Outlook Search function provides the option of searching within all folders containing items of a particular type, you can easily locate a message that's been moved to a folder without having to remember which folder it's in. For more information, see "Quickly locating messages" later in this chapter.

Popular personal-organization experts advocate various folder structures (for paper folders and email message folders) as an important part of an organizational system. You can apply any of these ideas when you create folders in Outlook, or you can use any other structure that works for you. For example, you might create folders that designate the level of action required, create a folder for each project you're working on, or create a folder to store all messages from a specific person, such as your manager, regardless of the message subject.

When you create a folder by clicking the New Folder button on the Folder tab of any module, you specify the location of the folder within your existing Outlook folder structure and the type of items you want the folder to contain. You can create folders to contain the following types of items:

- Calendar items
- Contact items
- InfoPath Form items
- Journal items
- Mail and Post items
- Note items
- Task items

The selection you make governs the folder icon that precedes its name in the Folder Pane, the folder window layout, the ribbon tabs and commands available in the folder, and the content of the Folder Pane when displaying the folder.

You can move messages to folders manually, or if your organization is running Exchange, you can have the email system move them for you. You can automatically move messages to another folder by creating a rule—for example, you can automatically move all messages received from your manager to a separate folder. You can also set up different rules that go into effect when you're away from the office.

SEE ALSO For information about automatically moving messages, see "Creating rules to process messages" in Chapter 12, "Manage email settings."

In this exercise, you'll create a folder and then use different methods to move messages to the folder.

 SET UP You need the SBS series of messages you worked with in the previous exercise. If you have not already created these messages, you can do so now, or you can substitute any messages in your Inbox. Display your Inbox, and then follow the steps.

1   On the **Folder** tab, in the **New** group, click the **New Folder** button to open the
    Create New Folder dialog box.

    KEYBOARD SHORTCUT Press Ctrl+Shift+E to open the Create New Folder dialog box.

*The default settings in the Create New Folder dialog box
match the active module at the time you create the folder.*

TROUBLESHOOTING If your default data file (the file in which your messages are
stored) is a personal folder on your hard disk, the first item in the Select Where To
Place The Folder box is Personal Folders.

2   In the **Name** box, enter SBS Messages. In the **Select where to place the folder**
    box, click your mailbox (at the very top of the list). Then, with **Mail and Post Items**
    selected in the **Folder contains** list, click **OK** to create the folder.

    TIP The name of this folder begins with *SBS* so that you can easily differentiate it
    from other folders in your mailbox.

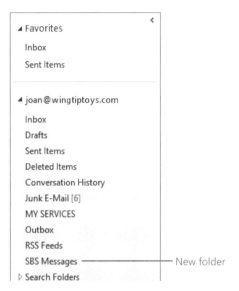

The new folder appears in the Folder Pane at the same
level as your Inbox, rather than as a subfolder.

3   In the message list, locate the **SBS First Draft**, **RE: SBS First Draft**, and **FW: SBS First
Draft** messages.

4   Drag the **SBS First Draft** message from the message list to the **SBS Messages** folder
in the **Folder Pane** to move the message.

5   Click the **RE: SBS First Draft** message to select it. Then on the **Home** tab, in the **Move**
group, click the **Move** button to display a menu of folders and options.

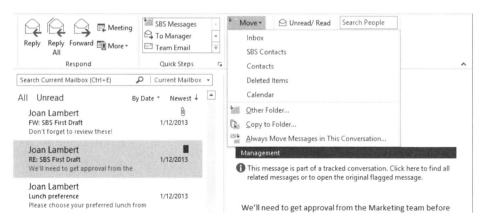

The Move list automatically includes folders that you create.

6   On the **Move** menu, click **SBS Messages** to move the selected message from the **Inbox** to the **SBS Messages** folder.

7   Right-click the **FW: SBS First Draft** message, click **Move**, and then click **SBS Messages** to remove the conversation from the **Inbox**.

>   **TIP** When Conversation view is turned on, moving the last message of a conversation from a folder removes the conversation from that folder.

8   In the **Folder Pane**, click the **SBS Messages** folder to display its contents.

9   Click or right-click the message list header, click **Show as Conversations**, and then click **This Folder** to arrange only these messages as a conversation.

✖ CLEAN UP Retain the SBS Messages folder and its contents for use in later exercises.

Managing messages by using Quick Steps

Outlook 2013 includes many features designed to increase the efficiency with which you perform tasks. With the Quick Steps feature available in the Mail module, you can perform multiple processes on one or more email messages with only one click. For example, you can reply to an email message and delete the original message, or you can flag a message for follow-up and move it to a specific folder.

Quick Steps are available from the Quick Steps group on the Home tab of the Mail module, and from the shortcut menu that appears when you right-click a message or group of messages.

Outlook provides standard Quick Steps that perform common functions.

TIP If you connect to multiple accounts, the Quick Steps in each Mail module are specific to that account. Only the Quick Steps that can be performed on the selected message or messages will be shown as available.

You can use the built-in Quick Steps, or create your own, to accomplish as many as 12 tasks at once.

A default Outlook installation includes these five Quick Steps:

- **Move To** Moves the selected message to a folder that you specify the first time you use the Quick Step and marks the message as read. After you specify the folder, the Quick Step name changes to include the folder name.

- **To Manager** Forwards the selected message to a person or people you specify the first time you use the Quick Step. You can edit the Quick Step to include Cc and Bcc recipients, a specific message subject, a follow-up flag, a level of importance, and specific message text, and to send the message one minute after you click the Quick Step command.

- **Team Email** Creates a message to a person or people you specify the first time you use the Quick Step. You can edit the Quick Step to include Cc and Bcc recipients, a specific message subject, a follow-up flag, a level of importance, and specific message text, and to send the message one minute after you click the Quick Step command.

- **Done** Moves the selected message to a folder that you specify the first time you use the Quick Step, marks the message as read, and marks the message as complete so that a check mark is displayed in the follow-up flag location.

- **Reply & Delete** Creates a response to the original message sender and immediately deletes the original message.

    TROUBLESHOOTING The Reply & Delete Quick Step deletes the original message before you send the reply. If you close the response message composition window without sending it, the original message will no longer be in your Inbox. If you want to respond to the original message, you first need to retrieve it from your Deleted Items folder.

For each of the built-in Quick Steps, you can change its name; edit, add, and remove actions; and specify tooltip text that appears when you point to the Quick Step in the Quick Steps gallery. You can assign shortcut keys (Ctrl+Shift+1 through Ctrl+Shift+9) to up to nine Quick Steps.

TIP You can create new Quick Steps to simplify the performance of many types of message-management actions. For more information, see "Creating and managing Quick Steps" in Chapter 12, "Manage email settings."

In this exercise, you will set up and use a built-in Quick Step.

SET UP Use the SBS Tradeshow Schedule message you worked with earlier in this chapter and the SBS Messages folder you created in the previous exercise. If you did not create these practice files, you can do so now or substitute any message and folder in your Inbox. Display your Inbox, locate the SBS Tradeshow Schedule message, and then follow the steps.

1   On the **Home** tab, in the **Quick Steps** gallery, click **Move to: ?**. Because you haven't yet configured a destination folder for this Quick Step, the **First Time Setup** dialog box opens.

Some generic Quick Steps require that you supply information the first time you use them.

2   In the **Move to folder** list, click **SBS Messages**. (If that folder doesn't appear in the list, click **Other Folder**. Then in the **Select Folder** dialog box, click the **SBS Messages** folder and click **OK**.) The name of the Quick Step in the **Name** box changes from *Move To: ?* to **SBS Messages**.

3   In the **First Time Setup** dialog box, click the **Options** button to open the **Edit Quick Step** dialog box. The built-in Quick Step contains two actions (**Move to folder** and **Mark as read**). You can modify the existing actions and add actions to the Quick Step.

The built-in Move To Quick Step includes two actions.

4   In the **Tooltip text** box, select the existing text and then enter **Move and mark as read**.

5   In the **Edit Quick Step** dialog box, click **Save** to change the name of the Quick Step in the **Quick Step** gallery from **Move To: ?** to **SBS Messages**.

6   In the message list, click the **SBS Tradeshow Schedule** message to select it.

7　In the **Quick Steps** gallery, point to **SBS Messages** to display the custom tooltip below the ribbon.

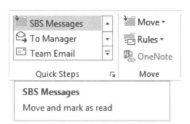

You can supply custom tooltip text for any Quick Step.

8　In the **Quick Steps** gallery, click **SBS Messages** to remove the selected message from the message list.

9　In the **Folder Pane**, click the **SBS Messages** folder to verify that Outlook moved the message to the designated folder.

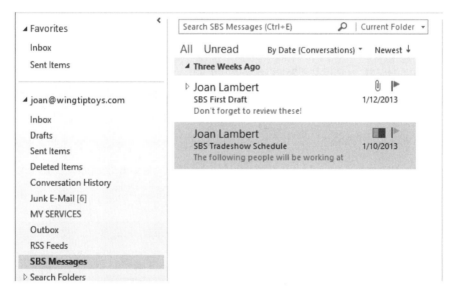

The categories and follow-up flag of the moved message are intact.

CLEAN UP Retain the SBS Messages folder and its contents for use in later exercises.

Quickly locating messages

The Outlook Search feature is based on the search technology that is built into the Windows operating system. Using the Windows Search technology, you can find any file on your computer that contains a specified search term—whether in a file or folder name; in document or workbook content; in an email message within Outlook; in a message attachment; in a picture, music, or video file; or other types of content. (As a matter of fact, if you prefer to do so, you can conduct all of your Outlook searches from the Windows Start menu.)

You can use the Search feature to locate specific terms in any Outlook item. Although you can search for items in the Calendar, People, Tasks, and Notes modules, you most often use it to locate messages in your Inbox and other mail folders. The Search feature can locate search terms in a message or in a file attached to a message. As you enter a search term in the Search box located at the top of the content area in any module, Outlook filters the items to show only those items in the module that contain the search term and highlights the search term in the list of results.

Outlook first displays up to 30 "recent results." Clicking the More link at the bottom of the list or the Include Older Results button in the Results group on the Search tool tab displays additional results within the selected search scope.

You can narrow the results by expanding the search term or by specifying other search criteria, such as the sender, the recipient (whether the message was addressed or only copied to you), a category assigned to the item, or whether the message contains attachments.

The Search tool tab appears when you activate the Search box in any Outlook module. You can enter search terms into the Search box and refine your search by using the commands on the Search tool tab.

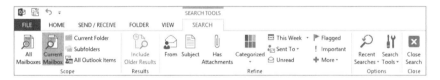

The Search tool tab appears when you click in a Search box or filter the contents of a folder.

When searching any folder, you can use the commands on the Search tool tab to set the scope of the search and to more closely define the search specifications. You can also return to the results of previous searches.

The buttons available in the Scope and Refine groups vary based on the type of folder you're searching. The Scope group always offers the options of the current folder, all sub-folders, all folders of the current type, and all Outlook items. The commands in the Refine group change to reflect common properties of items stored in the current folder type. The most common properties are shown as buttons in the Refine group; additional properties are available for selection from the More list.

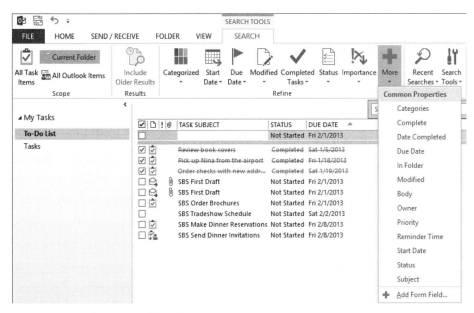

You can search for an item based on any property.

When you click a button in the Refine group or a property in the More list, that property appears in the Search box with a placeholder for you to specify the value you're looking for. As you define the criteria for a search, Outlook filters out all messages that don't match, which makes it easier to find what you're looking for. And here's the neat thing: Outlook searches not only the content of the email message header and the message itself, but also the content of message attachments. So if the search term you're looking for is in a Microsoft Word document attached to a message, the message is included in the search results.

TIP If your organization uses public folders (a feature of Exchange) you can use these same tools to search a public folder, but the content isn't filtered instantly; you must press Enter or click the Search button to get the same results as you would in a standard account folder.

Using Search Folders

A Search Folder displays all the messages in your mailbox that match a specific set of search criteria, no matter which folders the messages are actually stored in. When you create a Search Folder, it becomes part of your mailbox and is kept up to date. The Search Folder module is located in the Folder Pane, within your top-level mailbox, at the same level as the Inbox.

By default, Outlook 2013 includes one standard Search Folder: Unread Mail. (If your environment includes Microsoft Lync you might also have Search Folders for Missed Calls and Missed Conversations.) If you want quick access to messages that fit a specific set of criteria, you can create a custom Search Folder. To do so, follow these steps:

1 Display any mail folder.

2 On the **Folder** tab, in the **New** group, click **New Search Folder** to open the **New Search Folder** dialog box.

   KEYBOARD SHORTCUT Press Ctrl+Shift+P to open the New Search Folder dialog box.

Search Folder categories include Reading Mail, Mail From People And Lists, Organizing Mail, and Custom.

3   In the **New Search Folder** dialog box, select the type of **Search Folder** you want to create, and then click **OK**. You can choose from the standard options presented or click **Create a Custom Search Folder** to specify other search options.

You can make changes to the contents of an existing Search Folder by right-clicking the folder and then clicking Customize This Search Folder.

Outlook automatically keeps Search Folder contents up to date. The names of folders containing unread or flagged items are bold, with the number of unread items after the folder name. The names of folders whose contents are not up to date are italic. To update a Search Folder, click the folder name.

Each message in your mailbox is stored in only one folder (such as your Inbox), but it might appear in multiple Search Folders. Changing or deleting a message in a Search Folder changes or deletes the message in the folder in which it is stored.

Deleting messages

When you delete a message, contact record, or any other item, Outlook temporarily moves it to the Deleted Items folder of your mailbox. You can open the folder from the Folder Pane, view items that have been deleted but not purged, and restore items (undelete them) by moving them to other folders.

KEYBOARD SHORTCUT Press Shift+Delete to permanently delete a message from a message list without first moving it to the Deleted Items folder.

By default, Outlook does not permanently delete items until you purge them from the Deleted Items folder. You can empty the entire Deleted Items folder manually or automatically, or you can permanently delete individual items from it.

To manually empty the Deleted Items folder, right-click the Deleted Items folder in the Folder Pane, and then click Empty Folder. To automatically empty the Deleted Items folder each time you exit Outlook, select the Empty Deleted Items Folder When Exiting Outlook check box on the Advanced page of the Outlook Options dialog box.

7

In this exercise, you'll use the Search feature to locate a specific message in your Inbox.

 SET UP Use the series of messages and the SBS Messages folder you worked with earlier in this chapter. If you didn't create those practice files, you can do so at this time or substitute messages and a folder of your own. Display your Inbox and the Reading Pane, and then follow the steps.

1   In the **Search** box at the top of the message list, enter the. As you enter the text, the **Search** tool tab appears on the ribbon, and options for refining your search appear below the **Search** box.

KEYBOARD SHORTCUT Press F3 or Ctrl+E to move the cursor to the Search box.

Selecting an option other than Keyword enters the alternative search criterion (and term) in the Search box.

Outlook filters the messages in your Inbox to include only those that contain the word *the*, and highlights all occurrences of the word in the message list and in the active message.

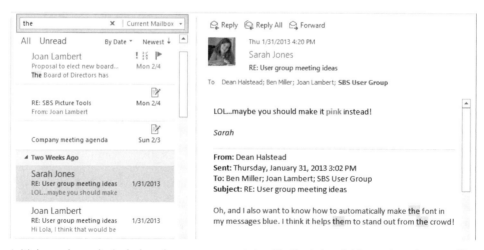

Initial search results include only messages contained in the Inbox folder and not in any of its subfolders or any other mailbox folders.

In the lower-left corner of the program window, the status bar displays the number of messages included in the search results.

2   On the **Search** tab, in the **Refine** group, click the **Subject** button to add the subject criterion to the **Search** box and prompt you to enter keywords that should appear in the **Subject** field of all search results.

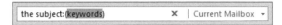

You replace the placeholder with the words you want to find in the subject field.

3   With **keywords** highlighted, enter SBS to instantly update the search results to display only the messages in your **Inbox** that contain the word *the* and have *SBS* somewhere in the **Subject** field.

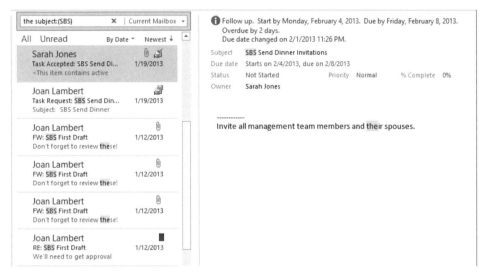

If you've followed along with all the exercises in this chapter, it's likely that the current search returns no results.

4   On the **Search** tab, in the **Scope** group, click the **All Mailboxes** button to display all the sent, received, and copied messages created in previous exercises.

KEYBOARD SHORTCUT   Press Ctrl+Alt+Z to expand a search to include subfolders. Press Ctrl+Alt+A to expand a search to include all items of the current type.

5   In the message list header, click **By Date**, and then click **Folder** to identify the search results by location.

6   In the **Options** group, click the **Recent Searches** button so you can view your recent searches and use the same search again at another time.

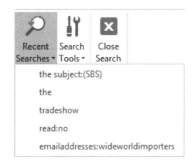

Clicking a previous set of search criteria reruns that search against your current items.

7 Experiment with locating information by specifying criteria. When you finish, click the **Close Search** button to remove the filter and redisplay the **Inbox** message list.

KEYBOARD SHORTCUT Press Esc to clear the search results.

✕ CLEAN UP Retain the SBS Messages folder and its contents for use in later exercises.

Printing messages

Although electronic communications certainly have less environmental impact than paper-based communications, you might at times want or need to print an email message—for example, if you want to take a hard copy of it to a meeting for reference, or if you keep a physical file of important messages or complimentary feedback. You can print the message exactly as it appears in your Inbox or embellish it with page headers and footers. Outlook prints the message as shown on the screen, including font and paragraph formats.

In this exercise, you'll preview a message as it will appear when printed, add a page header, and then print the message.

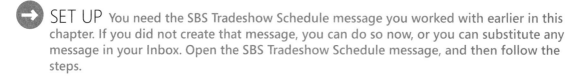

IMPORTANT To fully complete this exercise, you must have a printer installed. If you don't have a printer installed, you can perform all steps of the exercise other than printing.

➜ SET UP You need the SBS Tradeshow Schedule message you worked with earlier in this chapter. If you did not create that message, you can do so now, or you can substitute any message in your Inbox. Open the SBS Tradeshow Schedule message, and then follow the steps.

1 In the message window, display the **Print** page of the **Backstage** view.

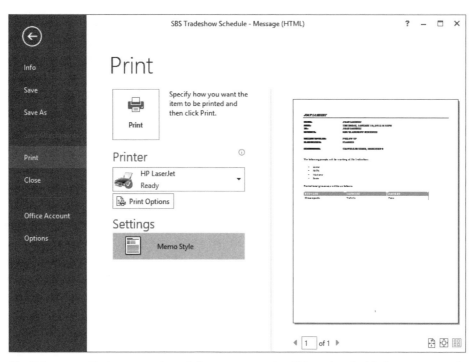

The Print page displays a preview of the message as it will be printed with the current settings.

The right pane displays the message as it will appear when printed, if you click the Print button without changing the settings shown in the center pane. If necessary, you can adjust the following settings:

- **Printer** Select an installed printer or add a new one.

- **Print Options** Change the default printing options in the Print dialog box before printing. You can also change an existing print style (the way the message is presented on the printed page) or create a new one.

- **Settings** Choose from the existing print styles available for the selected message or other Outlook item. The default print style is Memo style, which prints your name, the message header information, and then the message content.

2   Click the **Print Options** button to open the **Print** dialog box and display your default printer settings, which you can change before printing. Clicking **OK** prints the message with the current settings.

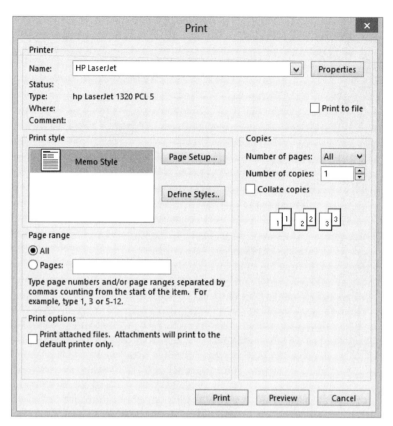

You can print the contents of any attachments with the message.

3   In the **Print** dialog box, click **Page Setup** to open the **Page Setup: Memo Style** dialog box. You can change the font, paper size, page margins, header, and footer from this dialog box.

4   On the **Format** page of the dialog box, click the **Font** button to the right of the **Title** setting. In the **Font** dialog box that opens, click **Impact** in the **Font** list, click **Oblique** in the **Font style** list, and then click **OK**.

5   Click the **Font** button to the right of the **Fields** setting. In the **Font** dialog box, click **Impact** in the **Font** list, and then click **OK**.

6   In the **Page Setup: Memo Style** dialog box, click **OK**, and then in the **Print** dialog box, click **Preview**.

7 In the lower-right corner of the **Print** page of the **Backstage** view, click the **Actual Size** button to display the message at 100 percent of its size. The right pane of the **Print** page displays the message as it will appear when printed, with the header text in the selected font. Notice that the **Print Options** button is shaded to indicate that the options have been modified.

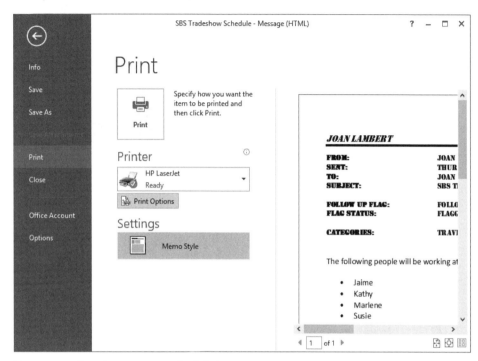

You can preview the message at its full size.

TIP If a message will be longer than one page when printed with the current settings, you can click the Multiple Pages button to preview all pages of the message at the same time. You might find this useful when, for example, you want to check page breaks or scan a document for a particular element.

8 Click **Print Options**, click **Page Setup**, and then in the **Page Setup: Memo Style** dialog box, click the **Paper** tab to display the available options.

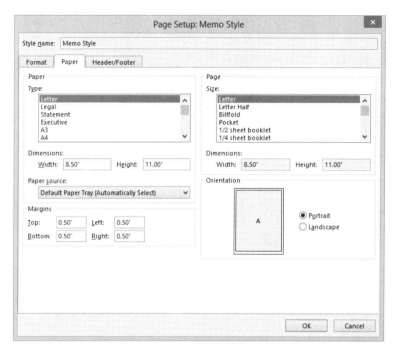

In addition to choosing the paper size, you can select the number of pages that will be printed on each sheet of paper, and set the page margins and the orientation.

9   Click the **Header/Footer** tab.

10   In the **Header** area, enter For Your Information in the center box, and then click the **Font** button above the box. In the **Font** dialog box, in the **Size** area, click **16**, and then click **OK**. The text you entered doesn't reflect the font size change, but the **Header** box to the left of the **Font** button indicates the current font selection.

11   In the **Footer** section, select the default text (the page number) that appears in the center box. Then in the **AutoText** box that appears near the bottom of the **Page Setup** dialog box, click the **User Name** button (labeled with a person's profile) to print the previously specified text at the top of the page and your name (or user name, if different) at the bottom.

12   In the **Page Setup** dialog box, click **OK**, and then in the **Print** dialog box, click **Print** to print the message, including your custom header and footer, to the active printer.

✖ CLEAN UP If you don't want to retain the custom header and footer as part of the standard message printing template, remove them from the Memo Style. Then close the SBS Tradeshow Schedule message.

Key points

- You can filter and locate messages in your mailbox by using the Search feature.

- You can group and sort messages by sender, time, subject, size, category, or any other field.

- You can assign color-coded categories to messages and then group and sort items by using color categories. You can use the default Outlook categories or tailor them to fit your needs.

- You can record miscellaneous information in electronic notes. You can categorize, search, display, and sort notes, and send notes to other people.

- You can create folders to organize your mail, and move items to folders manually or automatically.

- You can print a message when you need a paper copy. You can select from several print styles and make modifications to the print styles to suit your needs.

- When you delete a message or other Outlook item, it moves to the Deleted Items folder and is not permanently deleted until you empty the folder.

7

Chapter at a glance

Define

Define your available time,
page 276

Configure

Configure time zones,
page 280

Share

Share calendar information,
page 290

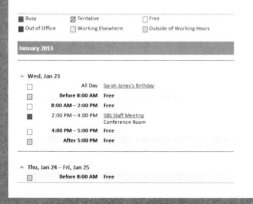

Print

Print a calendar,
page 297

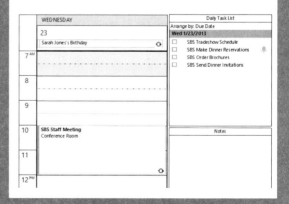

Manage your calendar 8

IN THIS CHAPTER, YOU WILL LEARN HOW TO

- Define your available time.

- Configure time zones.

- Work with multiple calendars.

- Share calendar information.

- Print a calendar.

Using the Microsoft Outlook 2013 calendar is a big step toward efficient time management. The Outlook calendar differentiates between working time and nonworking time—only working time is available to co-workers when they schedule meetings with you through Outlook. If the default working times set by Outlook don't match your actual work schedule, you can change the Work Week settings. You can also configure the Outlook calendar to track your schedule in two time zones and smoothly switch between time zones when you travel.

In addition to the default Outlook calendar, you can create, import, link to, subscribe to, and manage other calendars within the Calendar module. Other calendars might include Microsoft Exchange Server account calendars that Outlook creates, secondary calendars you create within your Outlook configuration, calendars other people share with you, and online calendars that you download or subscribe to. In the Calendar module, you can view either discrete or compiled views of information stored in multiple calendars.

You can share your calendar information with other people in several ways; for example, you can share an entire calendar or only selected information with people inside or outside of your organization.

If you need to access your calendar information when you're away from your computer, and don't have access to it from a mobile device, or if you want to share calendar information with other people in a hardcopy form, you can print out the information for specific date ranges. Outlook offers many different formats for printed calendars; you can choose the print style and level of detail that fit your needs.

In this chapter, you'll define your work time and learn how to configure Outlook for use in multiple time zones. You'll examine the different types of secondary calendars, and experiment with the different ways you can display and switch among multiple calendars. You'll also share selected calendar information by embedding it in an email message. Finally, you'll print daily and monthly calendars.

PRACTICE FILES You don't need any practice files to complete the exercises in this chapter.

Defining your available time

In your Outlook calendar, the time that you indicate you are available for other people to schedule meetings with you is referred to as your *work week*. The calendar timeslots within your work week are colored differently from those outside of your work week, and are the only timeslots made available to people on your network when they are searching for a time to meet with you.

By default, the Outlook work week is defined as from 8:00 A.M. to 5:00 P.M. (in your local time zone), Monday through Friday. You can change this to match your individual work schedule. In Outlook 2013, you can specify a start time and end time for your standard work day, specify the days of the week that you work, and specify the day of the week that you'd like to appear first when you display only the work week in your calendar.

You define your work week in the Work Time area on the Calendar page of the Outlook Options dialog box.

SEE ALSO For more information about locating available meeting times, see "Scheduling meetings" in Chapter 5, "Manage scheduling."

In this exercise, you'll view and change your work week.

 SET UP You don't need any practice files to complete this exercise. Display your calendar, turn off the Daily Task List, and then follow the steps.

1   On the **Home** tab, in the **Arrange** group, click the **Work Week** button.

Let's maximize the space available to view your work week.

2   On the **View** tab, in the **Layout** group, click the **Daily Task List** button, and then click **Off**.

3   In the **Layout** group, click the **Folder Pane** button, and then click **Minimized**.

4   If the **Reading Pane** or **To-Do Bar** is open, turn it off by using the commands in the **Layout** group.

5   Scroll up and down the calendar page to display the beginning and end of the work day. Notice that time slots during working hours are white, and time slots during nonworking hours are shaded.

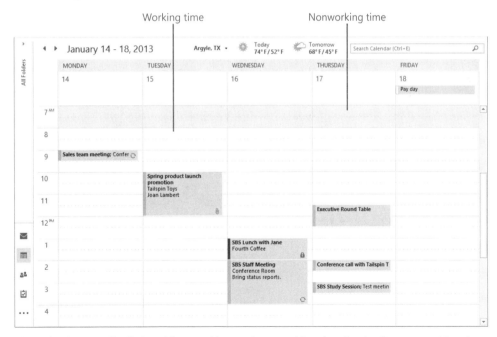

The calendar visually distinguishes working and nonworking time by shading nonworking time.

TROUBLESHOOTING If your work week does not match the default days and times described here, work through this exercise by using your own settings.

6   On the **Home** tab, click the **Arrange** dialog box launcher to display the **Calendar** page of the **Outlook Options** dialog box. The work week settings are located in the **Work time** section at the top of the page.

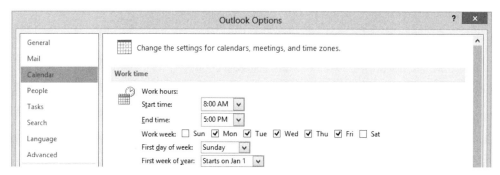

The default work week settings.

For the purposes of this exercise, assume that you work as a catering manager in a restaurant. You start work at 12:00 P.M. and finish at 8:00 P.M. You work Wednesday through Sunday, and have Monday and Tuesday off.

7   In the **Start time** list, click **12:00 PM**.

8   In the **End time** list, click **8:00 PM**.

9   In the **Work week** area, select the **Sun** and **Sat** check boxes, and clear the **Mon** and **Tue** check boxes.

10 In the **First day of week** list, click **Wednesday**.

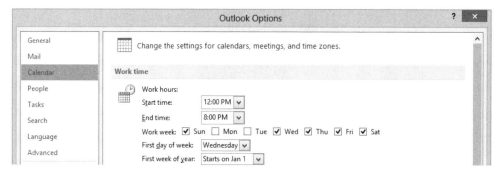

You can define the days and times that you are available to meet with co-workers.

11 In the **Outlook Options** dialog box, click **OK** to display the modified work week.

Nonworking time   Working time

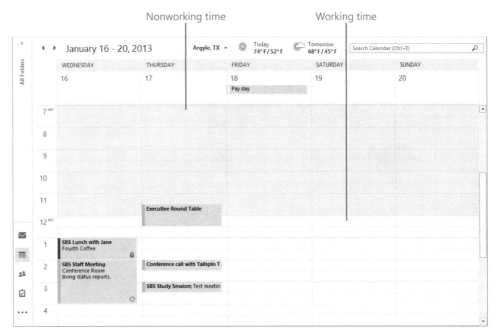

Your working time now starts at noon on Wednesday through Sunday.

TROUBLESHOOTING Outlook doesn't allow you to define a workday that crosses midnight or to define different start and end times for different days.

❌ CLEAN UP Use the methods you learned in this exercise to configure your work week the way you want it before continuing to the next exercise.

Configuring time zones

When you travel with your portable computer to locations in other time zones, you'll probably change the time zone on your computer to match the time zone you're in. You can do this from Windows or from Outlook. When you change the time zone, information—such as the receipt time of email messages and appointment times—changes to match the new time zone; if you display the clock in the Windows Taskbar notification area, the time shown there also changes.

To change the time zone of your computer from Outlook:

1 Display the **Calendar** page of the **Outlook Options** dialog box.

2 In the **Time zones** area, in the first **Time zone** list, click the time zone you want. Then click **OK** to close the dialog box.

When you prepare to travel, or if you schedule meetings involving participants in different time zones, you might want to configure Outlook to display two time zones in your calendar. Outlook then displays the two time zones in Day view, Work Week view, and Week view.

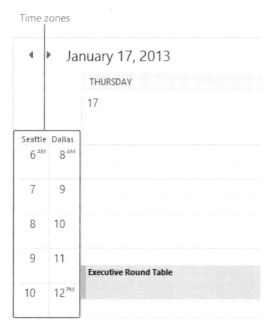

You might label a time zone with a city name or time zone name; use whatever is most meaningful to you.

To simultaneously display two time zones in your calendar:

1   Display the **Calendar** page of the **Outlook Options** dialog box.

2   In the **Time zones** area, select the **Show a second time zone** check box. Then in the second **Time zone** list, click the additional time zone you want to display.

3   Enter a label for each time zone in the corresponding **Label** box. Then click **OK** to close the dialog box.

TIP When you display two time zones in your Outlook calendar, you can quickly change the time zone of your computer by clicking the Swap Time Zones button in the Outlook Options dialog box.

Specifying appointment time zones

When you schedule an appointment or meeting, you have the option of specifying the time zone—for both the start time and the end time of the appointment or meeting. If you travel frequently, you might find that it is worth your time to do this. Here's an example of why you would want to do this:

Imagine that you live in Dallas, Texas (in the Central Time Zone). You have a meeting that occurs every Wednesday at noon. You travel to Seattle, Washington (in the Pacific Time Zone, two hours earlier than Central Time) for one week. When you arrive in Seattle, you change the time zone of your computer to Pacific Time. The appointments on your calendar shift to accommodate the time zone change. Your Wednesday meeting now appears on the calendar at 10:00 A.M. You call in to the meeting at the appropriate time.

During the meeting, you learn of a client presentation that will occur at 2:00 P.M. the following Tuesday. You enter the presentation as an appointment on your calendar at 2:00 P.M. Tuesday, but you do not specify the time zone of the presentation.

When you return to Dallas, you change the time zone of your computer to Central Time. On Wednesday morning, you look at your calendar and find out that you need to attend the client presentation. The presentation is on your calendar for 4:00 P.M. When you arrive at the client site, the presentation has already ended. Because you didn't specify the time zone of the appointment, the appointment time shifted by two hours when you returned to Dallas.

8

Working with multiple calendars

The Calendar button or link on the Navigation Bar connects to the calendar of your default email account. You can also display the following types of calendars in the Calendar module:

- **Calendars of your other email accounts** These are available automatically when you configure Outlook to connect to an account.

- **Custom calendars** You create a calendar in the same way that you do a folder that contains mail, contact records, or other items.

- **Calendars of people within your organization** Within an organization that uses Exchange, you can display the availability of your co-workers, individually or in a group, without special permission.

- **Shared calendars** Other Outlook users can share their calendars with you.

- **SharePoint site calendars** You can connect a SharePoint calendar to Outlook.

- **Internet calendars** You can subscribe to or import calendars from the Internet.

All these types of calendars are available to you from the Folder Pane in the Calendar module or the Folder List in the Mail module. You can display these calendars in the following ways:

- In the Calendar module, the Folder Pane displays a list of the available calendars. You display or hide a calendar by selecting or clearing its check box.

Available calendars in the Folder Pane of the Calendar module.

■ In the Mail module, calendars are shown in the expanded Folder List. You display a calendar in the Calendar module by clicking it in the Folder List.

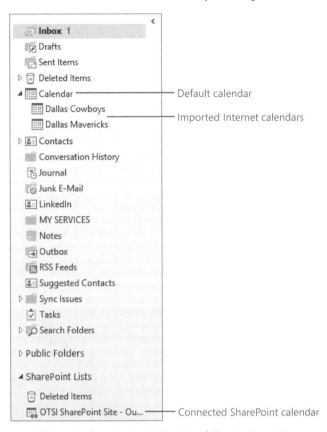

Available calendars in the Folder List of the Mail module.

You can display calendars individually, or you can display more than one calendar at a time. For example, you might have separate business and personal calendars and want to view them together. You can view multiple calendars next to each other, or you can overlay them to display a composite view of the separate calendars. When you view and scroll through multiple calendars, they all display the same date or time period.

You can copy items from one time, date, or calendar to another, by holding down the Ctrl key and dragging the original item to the location to which you want to copy it.

SEE ALSO For information about Internet calendars, see "Connecting to Internet calendars" later in this section. For information about connecting to SharePoint calendars, see "Working with SharePoint site content" in Chapter 13, "Work remotely."

Displaying a co-worker's calendar

Co-workers within an organization that uses Exchange can share full or partial details of their calendars with each other. Even if they don't, you can display a co-worker's availability by opening his or her calendar in Outlook. The default settings permit co-workers to view the time and availability (such as Busy or Out Of Office) of appointments and meetings for other members of their Exchange organization. This information, which is also used by the Scheduling Assistant, permits you to locate times that are suitable for meeting with co-workers.

SEE ALSO For information about sharing your calendar with co-workers and requesting that they share theirs with you, see "Sharing calendar information" later in this chapter.

To display a co-worker's calendar in your Outlook Calendar module, follow these steps:

1 In the **Calendar** module, on the **Home** tab, in the **Manage Calendars** group, click **Open Calendar**, and then click **From Address Book**.

2 In the **Select Name** dialog box displaying your organization's Global Address List (GAL), locate the person whose calendar you want to display. Double-click his or her name to insert it in the **Calendar** box, and then click **OK**.

The calendar appears in the Calendar module content area and in the list of Shared Calendars in the Folder Pane (even though its owner hasn't officially shared it with you). If you close the calendar, it remains in the Shared Calendars list so you can easily redisplay it.

Connecting to Internet calendars

A variety of specialized calendars, such as those that track professional sports schedules, holidays, entertainment, and scientific data, are available online. (For example, your local school district or sports team might offer an Internet calendar on its website that you can import or subscribe to.)

Internet calendars are files that have the extension .ics. You can locate Internet calendars by searching from a web browser, by locating links on the websites of specific organizations, or by visiting a calendar-sharing website such as iCalShare (located at *www.icalshare.com*).

You can work with an Internet calendar in one of two ways:

- **Subscribe to the calendar** You receive updates from the calendar publisher as they occur, but you can't change the calendar data.

- **Import the calendar** You can interact with a local copy of the calendar in Outlook. You can change the calendar data, but you won't receive any updates provided by the calendar publisher.

Most Internet calendars are accompanied by a link or button that you can click to start the subscription or import process. If the Internet calendar you want to connect to doesn't provide a simple method, you can manually connect to it.

To manually import or subscribe to an Internet calendar, follow these steps:

1   On the Internet, locate the calendar you want to connect to and copy the address of its .ics file.

2   Display the **Calendar** module. On the **Home** tab, in the **Manage Calendars** group, click the **Open Calendar** button and then, in the list, click **From Internet**.

3   In the **New Internet Calendar Subscription** dialog box, enter the address of the .ics file, and click **OK**. Then in the **Microsoft Outlook** message box that asks whether you want to add the calendar to Outlook and subscribe to updates, click **Yes** to display the selected Internet calendar and add it to the **Other Calendars** list in the **Folder Pane**.

You can display Internet calendars within the Calendar module as you would any other. You can modify aspects of an Internet calendar in Outlook, such as its location, color, or name, and you can share it with another person or delete it. You perform these actions by right-clicking the calendar name in the Folder Pane or its tab in the content area, and then clicking the applicable command.

8

In this exercise, you'll create custom calendars and then view multiple calendars in Side-By-Side mode, Overlay mode, and Schedule View.

SET UP You need access to multiple calendars to complete this exercise. Display your calendar in Month view, and then create, import, subscribe to, or share one or more additional calendars. For best results, display a month on which one or more appointments, meetings, or events appear on each calendar.

1 In the **Folder Pane**, in the **My Calendars** area, ensure that the check box for your default calendar (simply titled **Calendar**) is selected. Then in the **Other Calendars** or **Shared Calendars** area, select the check box for at least one additional calendar.

   TIP Outlook displays a calendar named Calendar for each account to which you connect. When you connect to multiple accounts, Outlook appends the associated email address to the calendar name in the Folder Pane so you can differentiate between them.

   By default, Outlook displays the calendars side by side and in different colors. Notice that in **Side-By-Side** mode, each calendar tab has a **Close** button (an X) near its right edge. The tab of each calendar other than your default calendar has a **View in Overlay Mode** button (a left-pointing arrow) near its left edge.

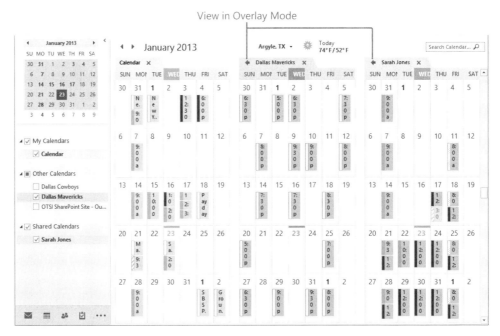

The order of the calendars in the Folder Pane and the content area is the same; your default calendar always appears first.

TIP For the purpose of this exercise, we reduced the height of the Date Navigator section of the Folder Pane.

2   On the **Home** tab, in the **Arrange** group, click the **Week** button. Notice that the views of all the displayed calendars change. Then click the **Back** or **Forward** button to the left of the date range and notice that the calendars remain synchronized.

3   Click the **Calendar** tab to make your default calendar the active calendar. Then on the tab of each secondary calendar, click the **View in Overlay Mode** button. The secondary calendars overlap your default calendar. The **Search** box indicates the active calendar. Each of the overlapping calendar tabs now has a **View in Side-By-Side Mode** button (a right-pointing arrow) near its left edge.

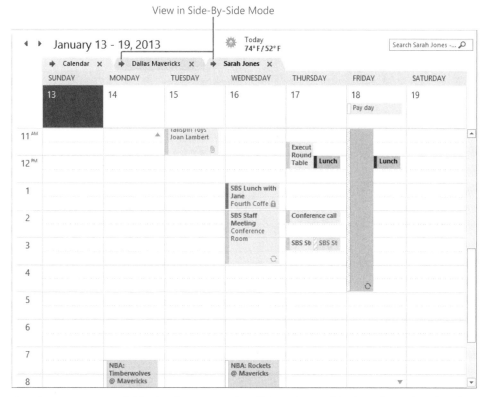

Appointments on overlaid calendars appear in a lighter font and in the color assigned to that calendar.

4   Click any calendar item to bring that calendar to the top of the stack.

5   On each of the secondary calendars, click the **View in Side-By-Side Mode** button to return to the standard display.

6   On the **Home** tab, in the **Arrange** group, click the **Schedule View** button to change the calendars to a horizontal format that displays appointments and meetings, but not events. A timeline above the calendar indicates the date and time being displayed.

> **KEYBOARD SHORTCUT** Press Ctrl+Alt+5 to switch to Schedule View. For more information about keyboard shortcuts, see "Keyboard shortcuts" at the end of this book.

7   If necessary, click the **Zoom Out** button (the minus sign) near the right end of the status bar to display several hours of each calendar. Click the scroll bar or drag the scroll box below the calendar to change the displayed time period. Notice that this view displays only your working hours; calendar items outside of your working hours are not visible.

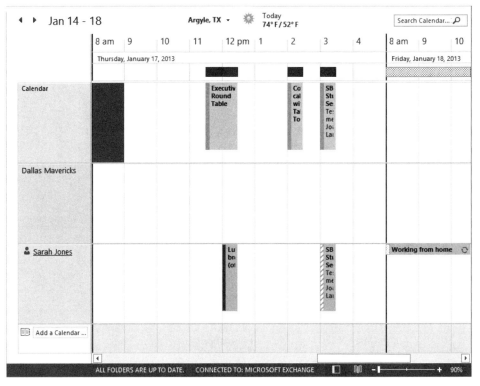

In Schedule View, you can view and compare appointments on multiple calendars.

TIP By default, Schedule View is active only when from one to four calendars are available. You can modify this setting in the calendar options. For more information, see "Configuring Office and Outlook options" in Chapter 11, "Customize Outlook."

8   In the **Arrange** group, click the **Work Week** button to return to **Side-By-Side** mode. If you changed the zoom level of the calendar in **Schedule View**, the side-by-side view of the calendar reflects your change.

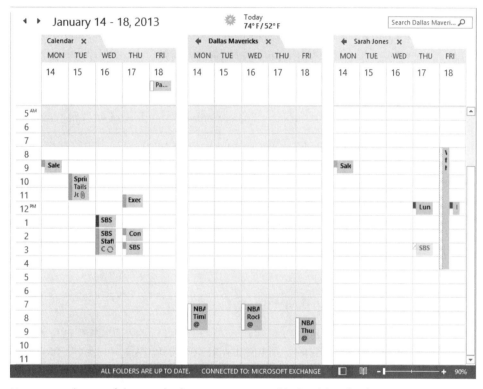

You can apply any of the standard arrangements to side-by-side calendars.

9   Close each secondary calendar by clicking the **Close Calendar** button at the right end of its tab or by clearing its check box in the **Folder Pane**.

❌ CLEAN UP Reset the Calendar view to return to the default calendar display and zoom level.

Sharing calendar information

Co-workers can view your available working time when they schedule meetings with you or view your calendar through Outlook. If you want to share more information with co-workers or with people outside of your organization, you have several options for doing so.

- You can allow selected co-workers to view calendar item details by sharing your calendar with them.

- You can allow selected co-workers to view your entire calendar and to make appointments and respond to meeting requests on your behalf by delegating control of the calendar to them.

- You can publish your calendar to the Office.com website or to a corporate web server and then share the published calendar with any person who has access to the Internet.

- You can send a professional graphic representation of your appointments during a selected date range by email to any person who uses an HTML-capable email program (not only people who use Outlook), including colleagues, friends, and family members.

The options for sending, sharing, and publishing calendar information are available from the Share group on the Home tab of the Calendar module.

Sharing calendars with co-workers

If your email address is part of an Exchange network, you can give permission to other people on your network to view, modify, or create items within a calendar or any other type of Outlook folder. The level of access each co-worker has is governed by the permissions you assign to him or her.

Using this method, you can share your default calendar or a secondary calendar that you create, import, or subscribe to.

To share a calendar with a co-worker:

1 In the **Calendar** module, display the calendar you want to share.
2 On the **Home** tab, in the **Share** group, click the **Share Calendar** button to create a message, called a *sharing invitation*.

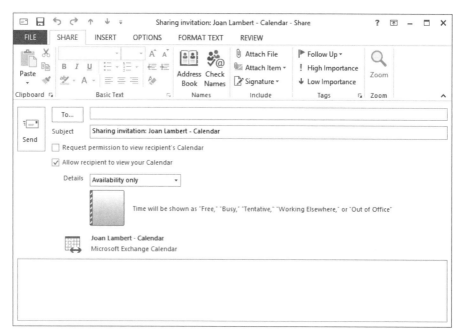

If you're sharing an Exchange calendar, the message is an invitation to share the calendar. If you're sharing an imported calendar, the message includes the calendar as an attachment.

3   Address the message to the person with whom you'd like to share your calendar. If you'd like to request that the person reciprocate by sharing his or her calendar with you, select the **Request permission to view recipient's Calendar** check box.

4   In the **Details** list, click the level of detail you want to share: **Availability only**, **Limited details**, or **Full details**.

5   Add any notes you want to in the content pane, send the message, and then click **Yes** in the **Microsoft Outlook** dialog box that asks you to confirm that you want to share the calendar with the specified permissions.

After you share a calendar, you can specify the actions each person with whom you share the calendar can take. On the Permissions page of the Calendar Properties dialog box, which you display by clicking the Calendar Permissions button in the Share group on the Home tab, you can select a permission level, which includes specific Read, Write, Delete, and other settings, or you can select individual settings in each category.

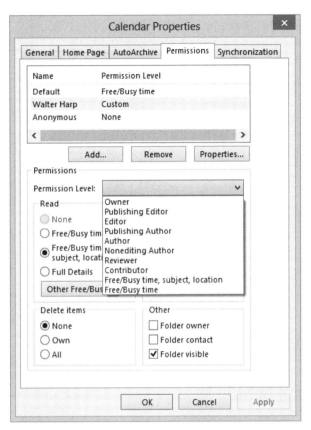

Write permissions include Create Items, Create Subfolders, Edit Own, and Edit All.

TIP From the Permissions page, you can change the default permission level to your calendar and permit co-workers to view more information than only your availability.

You can delegate control of your calendar so that a co-worker or assistant can create and respond to meeting requests on your behalf, and specify that meeting requests should be delivered to your delegate rather than to you. You receive copies of the meeting requests and copies of your delegate's responses, but you don't have to respond.

To delegate control of your calendar to another Outlook user, follow these steps:

1   On the **Info** page of the **Backstage** view, click **Account Settings**, and then click **Delegate Access**.

2   In the **Delegates** dialog box, click **Add** to open the **Add Users** dialog box.

3   In the **Add Users** dialog box, click the person you want to delegate control to, click **Add**, and then click **OK** to open the **Delegate Permissions** dialog box. Notice that you can delegate individual permission levels for each module.

The default permission level when delegating a calendar is Editor.

4   In the **Delegate Permissions** dialog box, set the permission level you want the delegate to have for each module.

5   Select the **Automatically send a message...** check box to ensure that your delegate is aware of the permissions you're delegating to him or her.

6   If you want to allow your delegate to view details of items that you mark as private, select the **Delegate can see my private items** check box.

7   In the **Delegate Permissions** dialog box, click **OK**. The delegate appears in the **Delegates** dialog box. You can modify the delegation permissions for an existing delegate, or rescind the delegation, at any time.

8

You can specify who receives meeting requests and responses for a delegated calendar.

8   In the **Delegates** dialog box, select the delivery option you want for meeting
    requests and responses, and then click **OK**.

Sharing calendar information outside of your organization

You can share calendar information with people who are not on your Exchange network by
sending it in an email message or posting it on the Internet. When you share a calendar by
using one of these methods, you can choose the period of time for which you want to share
information (Today, Tomorrow, Next 7 Days, Next 30 Days, or Whole Calendar, or you can
specify a custom date range) and the level of detail you want to share, as follows:

- **Availability only** Shows only whether time periods are marked as Free, Busy,
  Tentative, or Out Of Office during scheduled time periods

- **Limited details** Shows your availability and the subject of each appointment,
  meeting, or event scheduled on the calendar

- **Full details** Shows your availability and the full details (such as location and notes)
  of each appointment, meeting, or event scheduled on the calendar

The E-mail Calendar feature provides a simple method of sharing specific calendar information with people outside of your organization. For example, if a friend is arranging a

get-together and needs to know what days and times you're free this week, you can send her your free/busy information for the week.

If you need to distribute calendar information to many people outside of your organization, you can publish it to a website and then give specific people permission to view it.

The process for publishing calendar information externally is similar for both methods.

In this exercise, you'll embed information about your schedule in an email message.

SET UP You don't need any practice files to complete this exercise. Display your default calendar in any view, and then follow the steps.

1 On the **Home** tab, in the **Share** group, click the **E-mail Calendar** button to open a new message window and the **Send a Calendar via E-mail** dialog box.

2 In the **Advanced** area of the dialog box, click the **Show** button to display additional sharing options. These options are available only when you choose to share limited or full calendar details.

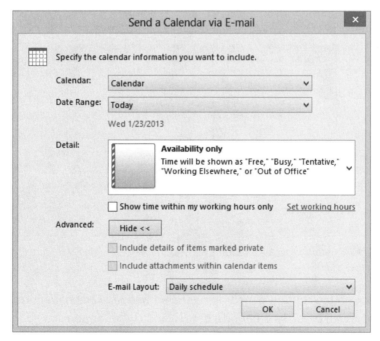

If you have multiple calendars in Outlook, you can choose the calendar from which you want to send information in the Calendar list.

3 In the **Date Range** list, click **Next 7 days**. Notice that the date range below the list changes to match your selection.

4   In the **Detail** list, click **Full details**.

> **TIP** In the Advanced area of the Send A Calendar Via E-mail dialog box, you can choose whether to include private appointment details and attachments, and whether to present schedule information as a simple list of events rather than in the default daily schedule format.

5   With **Daily schedule** selected in the **Email Layout** list, click **OK** to embed the selected calendar information in the email message window and also attach the same information as an .ics file. You can send the email message to any recipient. A recipient using Outlook or another email program that supports .ics files can view your calendar in that program.

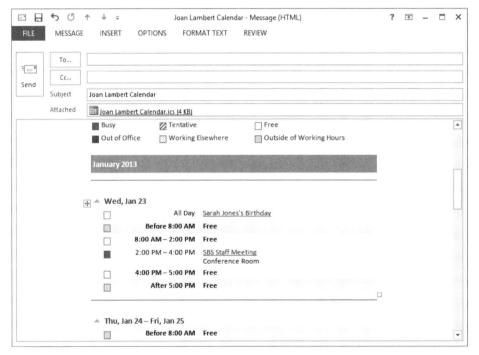

The Full Details option provides a monthly calendar overview, a daily summary, and details of each appointment.

6   Scroll through the content pane to view the embedded calendar information. Then experiment with other time periods, details, and layout options on your own.

✖ CLEAN UP Close or send the email message.

Printing a calendar

Sometimes, you might find it convenient to print a day, week, month, or other period of your calendar—for instance, if you're traveling without a laptop or want to have your weekly schedule quickly available in your briefcase. You can easily print any time period of your calendar. The amount of detail that appears depends on the period you print and the print style you choose.

Outlook offers several built-in print styles, and you can create others if you want. The available print styles vary based on what view you're in when you choose the Print command. The default print styles include the following:

- **Daily Style** Prints the selected date range with one day per page. Printed elements include the date, day, TaskPad, reference calendars for the current and upcoming months, a breakdown of working hours in 30-minute blocks, and an area for notes.

- **Weekly Agenda Style** Prints the selected date range with one calendar week per page, including reference calendars for the selected and following month.

- **Weekly Calendar Style** Prints the selected date range with one calendar week per page. Each page includes date range and time increments for working hours, and reference calendars for the selected and following month.

- **Monthly Style** Prints a page for each month in the selected date range. Each page includes the selected month with a few days showing from the previous and subsequent months, along with reference calendars for the selected and following month.

- **Tri-fold Style** Prints a page for each day in the selected date range. Each page includes the daily schedule, weekly schedule, and TaskPad.

- **Calendar Details Style** Lists your appointments for the selected date range, in addition to the accompanying appointment details.

You can select the date or range of dates to be printed and modify the page setup options to fit your needs.

8

In this exercise, you'll preview the available print styles, make changes to a standard print style, and print information from your calendar.

→ SET UP You don't need any practice files to complete this exercise. Display your calendar in Day view before beginning this exercise. For best results, display a day on which one or more appointments, meetings, or events appear on the calendar.

IMPORTANT To fully complete this exercise, you must have a printer installed. If you don't have a printer installed, you can perform all steps of the exercise other than printing.

1   Display the **Backstage** view. In the left pane, click **Print** to display the available printing options and a preview of the selected day's calendar as it would be printed in the **Daily Style** format.

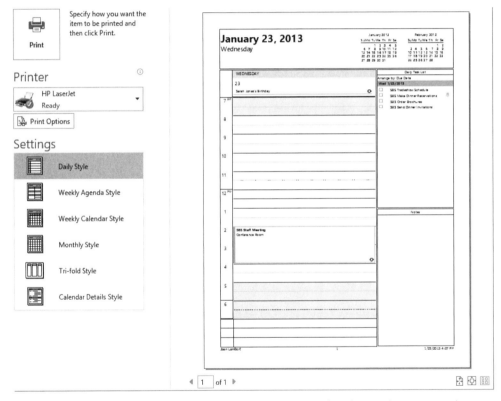

The Print page of the Backstage view displays print options and an interactive page preview.

2   In the lower-right corner of the page, click the **Actual Size** button. If necessary, scroll up or down the page to display appointment information. Notice that the calendar page entries are magnified to a legible size, with the **Actual Size** view selected. Scroll the page to the right to display the **Daily Task List** that prints to the right of the calendar.

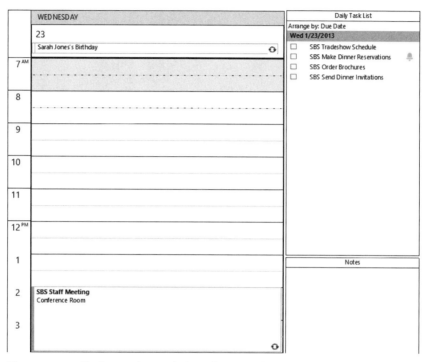

You can magnify the preview and view all pages of the calendar you're printing.

3   In the center pane of the **Print** page, click the **Print Options** button to open the **Print** dialog box, in which you can make many types of changes to the appearance of the printed content.

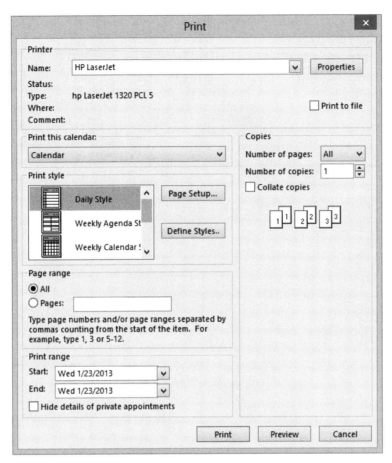

In the Print dialog box, you can change the calendar and date range being printed and the print style, in addition to the usual printer options.

4   In the **Print** dialog box, click **Preview** or **Cancel** to close the **Print** dialog box and return to the **Print** page of the **Backstage** view.

    TIP Clicking Print in the Print dialog box sends the calendar data to the active printer and then closes the Backstage view.

5   On the **Print** page, in the **Settings** list, click **Weekly Agenda Style**; and then in the lower-right corner of the page, click the **One Page** button to preview the print style in the right pane. Notice that the time period displayed in the printed calendar has been expanded to include the entire week (from Monday through Sunday) that contains the originally selected day.

Weekly Agenda Style displays a box for each day of the week, beginning on Monday. Saturday and Sunday share a space.

6   In the **Settings** list, click **Weekly Calendar Style** to preview the print style in the right pane. The time period displays the week from Sunday through Saturday. A vertical line precedes the day that is designated as the first day of the week.

SEE ALSO For information about setting the first day of the week, see "Defining your available time" earlier in this chapter.

Weekly Calendar Style displays a column for each day of the week.

7   Click the **Print Options** button and then, in the **Print** dialog box that opens, click **Page Setup** to open the **Page Setup** dialog box for the selected print style. For the **Weekly Calendar Style**, you can choose a vertical or horizontal layout, split the week across two pages, include a task list, add an area for handwritten notes, specify the range of hours to print, and print only your designated work week rather than a standard seven-day week.

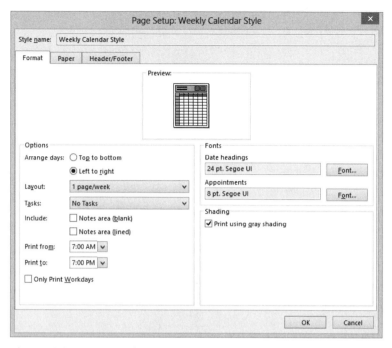

The available settings differ depending on the print style.

8   On the **Format** page of the **Page Setup** dialog box, do the following:

 ▪ In the **Tasks** list, click **To-Do List**.

 ▪ Select the **Notes area (blank)** check box.

 ▪ In the **Print from** list, click **8:00 AM**.

 ▪ In the **Print to** list, click **5:00 PM**.

 ▪ Select the **Only Print Workdays** check box.

9   Click the **Paper** and **Header/Footer** tabs to display the additional options, and then click **OK**.

10   In the **Print** dialog box, click **Preview** so that your changes are reflected in the page preview. Notice that when the calendar displays fewer hours, the timeslots become larger.

11   In the **Settings** list, click **Monthly Style** to preview the print style in the right pane, and then in the lower-right corner, click the **Actual Size** button. Notice that the calendar items will print at a size that is large enough to read. The time period displays the calendar month that contains the originally selected day.

January 2013				January 2013

January 2013

Su Mo Tu We Th
 1 2 3
 6 7 8 9 10
 13 14 15 16 17
 20 21 22 23 24
 27 28 29 30 31

SUNDAY	MONDAY	TUESDAY	WEDNESDAY	THURSDAY
Dec 30	31	Jan 1, 13 New Year's Day (United States)	2	3 12:30pm Lunch with Ben Miller (Fourth Coffee)
6	7 9:00am Sales team meeting (Conference room) - Sarah Jones	8	9	10
13	14 9:00am Sales team meeting (Conference room) - Sarah Jones	15 10:00am Spring product launch promotion (Tailspin Toys) - Joan Lambert	16 1:00pm SBS Lunch with Jane (Fourth Coffee) 2:00pm SBS Staff Meeting (Conference Room)	17 11:30am Executive Round Table 2:00pm Conference call with Tailspin Toys 3:00pm SBS Study

Printing a calendar in Monthly Style.

12   Change the preview area to display **One Page**. Then in the **Settings** list, click **Tri-fold Style** to preview the print style in the right pane. The left section displays the detailed schedule for the originally selected day, the middle section displays the **Daily Task List**, and the right section displays the seven-day week.

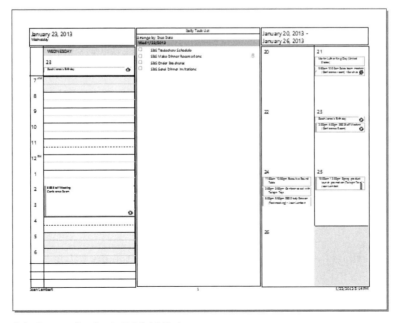

Printing a calendar in Tri-fold Style.

13   Click the **Print Options** button and then, in the **Print** dialog box that opens, click **Page Setup** to open the **Page Setup** dialog box for the selected print style.

14   In the **Options** area of the **Page Setup** dialog box, click the **Right section** arrow to display the elements you can place in the right section of the printed calendar.

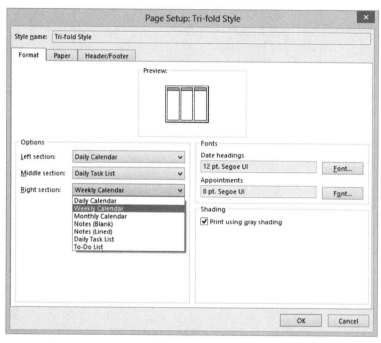

In Tri-fold Style, you can choose what calendar element appears in each section.

15   Experiment with various arrangements of information in the **Tri-fold Style** calendar, clicking **OK** in the **Page Setup** dialog box and **Preview** in the **Print** dialog box to preview the results.

16 On the **Print** page of the **Backstage** view, in the **Settings** list, click **Calendar Details Style** to preview the print style in the right pane, and display information for only the originally selected day.

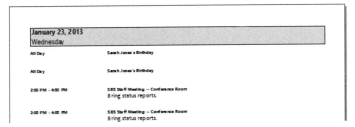

The appearance of a calendar printed in Calendar Details Style.

17 Experiment with different print styles and date ranges. If you want to print a calendar page, click the **Print** button on the **Print** page of the **Backstage** view.

✖ CLEAN UP If you don't print a calendar page, click the Home tab to close the Backstage view and return to your calendar.

Key points

- You can display a traditional calendar view of your schedule by the day, work week, full week, or month. You can also display multiple list views of calendar items.

- You can display multiple time zones, change your calendar as you travel between time zones, and schedule appointments or meetings that start and end in different time zones.

- You can import or subscribe to many types of calendars available from the Internet. Calendars that you subscribe to are automatically updated as new information is made available by the calendar publisher.

- You can view two or more calendars next to each other or as a composite. Outlook displays each calendar in a different color, so you can easily tell them apart.

- You can display multiple calendars in a horizontal view so that you can more easily compare schedules by scrolling through the calendars.

- You can share entire calendars or selected calendar information with people inside or outside of your organization.

- You can print selected schedule information in a number of different layout styles.

8

Chapter at a glance

Create

Create address books,
page 310

Import

Import and export contact records,
page 315

Group

Create contact groups,
page 325

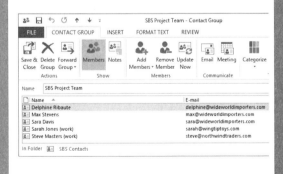

Personalize

Personalize electronic business cards,
page 337

Manage contact records   9

IN THIS CHAPTER, YOU WILL LEARN HOW TO

- Create address books.

- Import and export contact records.

- Create contact groups.

- Quickly locate contact information.

- Personalize electronic business cards.

If you regularly save contact information for business and personal contacts in Microsoft Outlook, you will quickly accumulate a large collection of contact records. Being able to organize and quickly locate specific contact information is important for efficient communications. The more people you deal with on a daily basis, the more important it is to keep your contact list organized. You can simplify communications with specific groups of people by creating contact groups to which you can address messages as you would an individual contact. You can also create purpose-specific address books and organize contact records within the address books to make it easier to locate specific contact records. You can add contact records to a custom address book either by moving contact records that are already stored in Outlook, or by importing contact records from another program or file.

The Search feature of Outlook 2013 makes it easy to find a specific contact record based on any text within the contact record or any attribute, such as a color category that you assign to it. Within each contact record, you can make preferred contact information easily discoverable by displaying it on the electronic business card version of the contact record. You can also display images, such as photographs or corporate logos on business cards, to provide additional information when you view contacts in the default Business Card view.

In this chapter, you'll first organize the contact records associated with this book into an individual address book. You'll import a fresh set of contact records into the custom address book, and then export a subset of the records. Then you'll create a contact group and send a message to a subset of the group. You'll locate specific contact records by using the Search feature and the commands available on the new Search tool tab. Finally, you'll personalize the content of an electronic business card.

Creating address books

Outlook displays your default address book when you click the People link or button on the Navigation Bar. The default address book content is stored in a folder named *Contacts*. If you connect to a Microsoft Exchange Server account, the default address book is part of that account, and the information you store in the address book is available on all devices from which you connect to your account. Exchange Server also provides a Global Address List (GAL), which is an address book maintained centrally by your Exchange administrator.

You can track all your contacts—business and personal—within the address book of your default email account. However, you might find it useful to create a separate address book that contains contact records for only a specific group of people. For example, you might want to have an address book that contains only clients, relatives, club members, neighborhood contacts, parents and teachers from your child's school, or sports teammates.

TIP When searching for a specific contact record, you can search a single address book or search all address books within your Outlook configuration, including your organization's GAL. For more information, see "Quickly locating contact information" later in this chapter.

You create an additional address book by creating a folder that has a designated purpose of containing contact items (a *contact folder*). You can move and copy contact records between address books in your Outlook configuration. As with other folders, you can share the contact folder with other Outlook users on your network, or you can export it for distribution to other people. Unlike the Calendar module, in which you can display multiple calendars, the People module can display only one address book at a time. When you have multiple address books, you can switch among them by choosing the address book you want to display from the list in the Folder Pane of the People module or from the Folder List in the Mail module.

TIP You can't display your organization's GAL from the Folder Pane. To display it, click the Address Book button in the Find group on the Home tab of the People module.

In this exercise, you'll create an address book and move existing contact records into it.

 **SET UP** You need the contact records you created in Chapter 4 to complete this exercise. If you didn't create those contact records, you may do so now or substitute any contact records of your own. Display the People module, and then follow the steps.

1   On the **Folder** tab, in the **New** group, click the **New Folder** button to open the **Create New Folder** dialog box.

Create New Folder

Name:

Folder contains:

Contact Items

Select where to place the folder:

- ⊿ joan@wingtiptoys.com
  - Inbox
  - Drafts
  - Sent Items
  - Deleted Items
  - ▷ Calendar
  - ▷ Contacts
  - Conversation History
  - Journal
  - Junk E-Mail
  - LinkedIn

OK   Cancel

Because you are creating this folder from within the People module, Contact Items is selected by default. However, you can create any type of folder from within any module.

2   In the **Name** box, enter SBS Contacts.

   TIP The name of this folder begins with *SBS* so that you can easily differentiate it from other folders in your mailbox.

3   In the **Select where to place the folder** list, click your account name (or **Mailbox**, depending on your account configuration) to place the new folder at the same level in the **Folder List** structure as your default module folders.

9

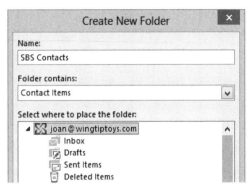

You can create a contact folder anywhere within the existing folder structure.

4   In the **Create New Folder** dialog box, click **OK** to create the **SBS Contacts** address book. The address book appears in the **My Contacts** list.

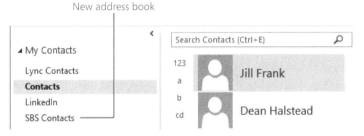

The Folder Pane of the People module lists all the available contact folders.

5   On the **Navigation Bar**, click the **Mail** button to display your **Inbox**. Notice that the **SBS Contacts** folder is not visible in the **Folder Pane**.

6   Click the **Folders** button to display the **Folder List**, which includes all the folders in your Outlook configuration rather than only those containing mail items. The **SBS Contacts** folder appears in alphabetic order in the list.

A contact card icon next to the folder name indicates that it is a contact folder, designed to hold contact items.

7   In the **Folder Pane**, click the **SBS Contacts** folder to display the currently empty address book. Although the **Folder List** still appears in the **Folder Pane**, the ribbon displays the groups appropriate to an address book.

8   On the **Navigation Bar**, click the **People** button to display the usual **People** module **Folder Pane**, which provides easy access to your address books.

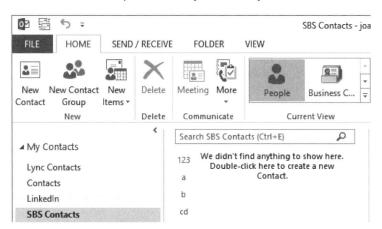

The same features available within your main address book, such as the contact index, are available within this custom address book.

9   In the **My Contacts** list, click **Contacts** to display your default address book, which currently contains the five contact records you created in Chapter 4.

10   In the contact list, click the **Jill Frank** contact record once to select it.

11   Drag the selected contact record from the contact list to the **SBS Contacts** address book in the **Folder Pane**. The record disappears from the contact list.

     TIP To copy rather than move a contact record, right-click and drag the contact record to the destination address book and then, when you release the mouse button, click Copy on the shortcut menu.

12   In the contact list, if the **Dean Halstead** contact record is not already selected, click it once to select it.

13   On the **Home** tab, in the **Actions** group, display the **Move** list.

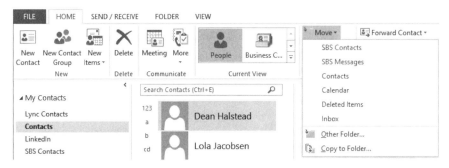

The Move list includes your custom and standard folders; you can browse to other folders.

14   In the **Move** list, click **SBS Contacts** to move the selected contact record.

       TIP If the SBS Contacts folder doesn't appear in your Move list, click Other Folder and then select SBS Contacts in the Move Items dialog box.

15   In the contact list, click the **Lola Jacobsen** contact record. Press and hold the **Ctrl** key, and then click the **Sarah Jones** and **Ben Miller** contact records in turn to select all the contact records you've created for this book that remain in your main address book.

16   Right-click any one of the selected contact records, click **Move**, and then click **SBS Contacts** to move the contact records.

17   In the **Folder Pane**, click **SBS Contacts** to display the custom address book, which now contains the five records you moved there.

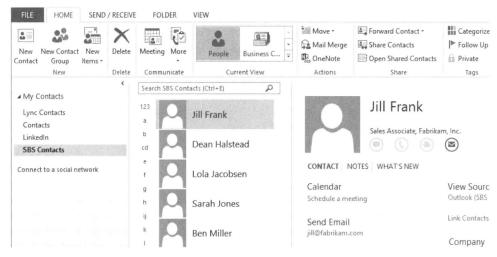

The contact records you've created for this book are now collected in the custom address book.

 CLEAN UP Retain the SBS Contacts folder and its contents for use in later exercises.

Importing and exporting contact records

In addition to copying and moving contact records between address books within your Outlook configuration, you can import contact records into an existing address book from external files and programs. Outlook accepts data imported from non–application specific files, files created in other Microsoft programs, and files created in third-party programs.

You can import data into Outlook from data files created in Outlook (.pst files) or from plain-text files that contain field values separated by commas (.csv files). Similarly, you can export contact records from Outlook for import into Outlook or another program.

TIP In previous versions of Outlook, you could directly import content from many other sources. To import content stored in another source program, export it from that program to a .csv file and then import the .csv file. To import a file that contains contact records into a separate address book, first create the address book, and then import the file.

In this exercise, you'll import contact records from a tab-separated (also referred to as *tab-delimited*) text file into an existing address book. Then you'll export a selection of records from the updated address book to a file that other Outlook users can import, and you'll test that you successfully exported only the records you wanted.

 SET UP You need the SBS Contacts address book you created in the previous exercise, and the SBSContacts file located in the Chapter09 practice file folder to complete this exercise. If you didn't create the address book, you may do so now or substitute any existing address book. Display the SBS Contacts address book, and then follow the steps.

1   Display the **Open & Export** page of the **Backstage** view.

Opening a file creates a link to the external file; importing adds the data to your Outlook folders.

9

2   On the **Open & Export** page, click **Import/Export** to start the **Import and Export** wizard.

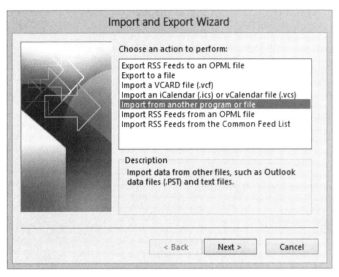

You can export and import specific items or entire RSS feeds.

3   With **Import from another program or file** selected in the **Choose an action to perform** list, click **Next** to display the list of file types from which you can import content.

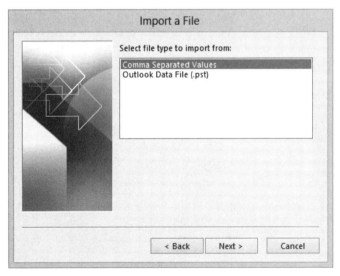

Outlook 2013 accepts data only from .csv and .pst files.

TIP Although the name shown in the title bar of the wizard changes to Import A File, this page is still part of the Import And Export wizard.

4 In the **Select file type to import from** list, click **Comma Separated Values**. Then click **Next**.

You can choose whether to allow, refuse, or replace duplicate files.

5 Click the **Browse** button to the right of the **File to import** box to open the **Browse** dialog box. In the **Browse** dialog box, navigate to the **Chapter09** practice file folder, click the **SBSContacts** file, and then click **OK**.

6 In the **Options** area, click **Replace duplicates with items imported**. Then click **Next**. Because you started the wizard from the **SBS Contacts** address book, that folder is already selected as the destination folder.

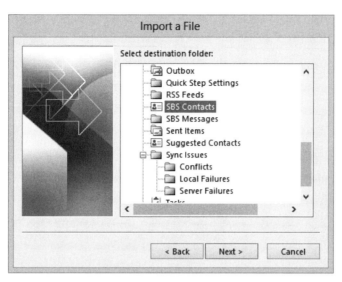

You can import content into any type of folder.

7 With **SBS Contacts** selected in the **Select destination folder** list, click **Next**. The wizard displays a description of the import operation and provides additional configuration options.

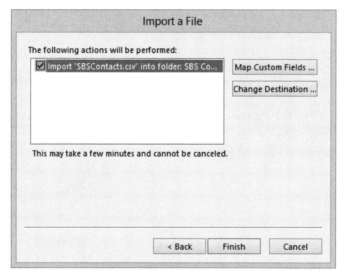

You can choose to map custom fields or change the destination of the imported content.

8 On the wizard's last page, click **Map Custom Fields** to open the **Map Custom Fields** dialog box. In this dialog box, you can match named fields from the import source

file to named fields in Outlook. You might need this functionality when you import content from a file that was not originally created in Outlook.

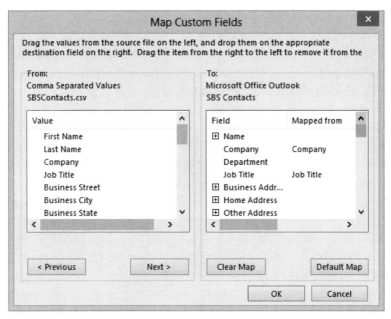

If the structure of the imported records is different from the Outlook contact record structure, you can match incoming data fields to Outlook data fields before you import the content.

9   Scroll down the **From** list and note the fields that are present in the source file. Then in the area below the **From** list, click **Next** to display in the **Map Custom Fields** dialog box the first record in the source file.

10 In the **To** list, click the **Expand** button to the left of **Name** to display all the name fields. The **Mapped From** column displays the value from the current source record that maps to each of the Outlook fields.

    TIP While testing this functionality, Outlook sometimes displayed the mapping results incorrectly, although the import process worked correctly. We hope that this issue will be resolved in a future software update.

11 Click **Next** a few times to view additional records, and scroll the **To** list to review the way the records map to the Outlook fields. Then click **OK** to close the **Map Custom Fields** dialog box.

12   On the last page of the **Import and Export** wizard, click **Finish** to import the contact records into the **SBS Contacts** address book. In a few seconds, the address book contains 11 contact records.

13   On the **Home** tab, in the **Current View** gallery, click **Card** to display information from multiple records. Notice that the five contact records you created earlier in this book now contain additional information. In fact, new versions of these contact records were imported from the **SBSContacts** file. Because in step 6 you selected the option to replace duplicate records, the new records, which contain additional information, replaced the records you created.

Imported and replaced contact records.

Now you'll export selected records from the updated address book for distribution to other Outlook users.

14   On the **Open & Export** page of the **Backstage** view, click **Import/Export** to start the **Import and Export** wizard.

15   In the **Choose an action to perform** list, click **Export to a file**, and then click **Next**. As with the import process, in Outlook 2013, you can export only to a .csv or .pst file.

16   In the **Create a file of type** list, click **Outlook Data File (.pst)**. Then click **Next**.

Now we'll select the records to export.

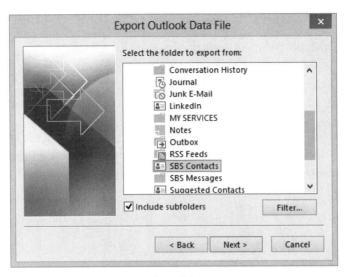

The SBS Contacts folder is selected for export.

17 With **SBS Contacts** selected in the **Select the folder to export from** list, click **Filter** to open the **Filter** dialog box. From this dialog box, you can filter the contents of the selected folder so that only items (in this case, contact records) that meet specific criteria are exported.

18 On the **Contacts** page of the **Filter** dialog box, enter Northwind in the **Search for the word(s)** box. Then click the **In** arrow to display the types of fields on which you can filter contact records.

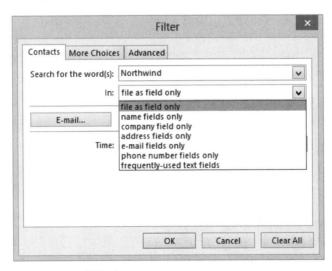

Contact record filtering options.

19 In the **In** list, click **company field only**. Then in the **Filter** dialog box, click **OK**.

20 In the **Export Outlook Data File** wizard, click **Next**.

The default settings for the export process save the exported file as *backup.pst* in a subfolder of your user profile named *Outlook Files*. Instead, we will save the file in the practice file folder.

21 To the right of the **Save exported file as** box, click the **Browse** button. In the **Open Outlook Data Files** dialog box, navigate to the **Chapter09** practice file folder. In the **File name** box, enter NorthwindContacts. Then click **OK**.

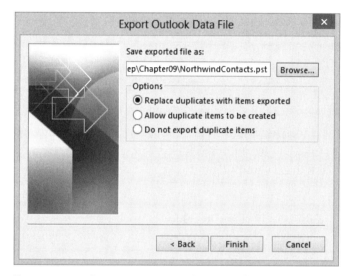

You can export items to a new or existing .pst file.

22 On the wizard's last page, click **Finish**. Before exporting the records, Outlook gives you the options to password-protect the file.

You can keep the contents of an Outlook data file confidential by assigning a password to the file.

23 In the **Create Outlook Data File** dialog box, click **OK** to create the file without assigning a password.

24 To test that you successfully exported the file, use the techniques you learned in this chapter to create a contact folder named SBS Northwind, as a subfolder of the **SBS Contacts** address book and import the **NorthwindContacts** data file into it. During the import process, the **Import Outlook Data File** wizard prompts you to select the folder you want to import and the import location.

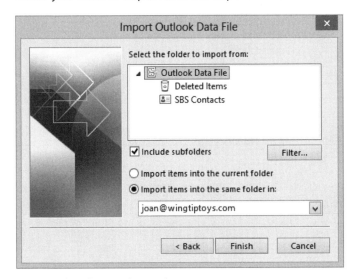

Contact record importing options.

25 In the **Select the folder to import from** list, click **SBS Contacts** (the folder from which you exported the data file). Click the **Import items into the current folder** option. Then click **Finish** to import the records from the **NorthwindContacts** data file into the **SBS Northwind** address book.

26 After you import the contact records, notice that the **People** cards for each contact display information from multiple sources.

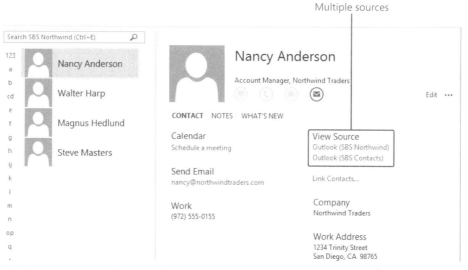

The People cards for Northwind Traders employees display information from both address books.

TIP Sources can include Outlook address books and external networks that you connect to, such as LinkedIn and Facebook. Contact records that contain matching information will link automatically; you can manually link or unlink contact records by clicking Link Contacts.

Now we'll delete the new address book to avoid confusion in later exercises.

27   In the **Folder Pane**, right-click the **SBS Northwind** address book, click **Delete Folder**, and then click **Yes** in the **Microsoft Outlook** dialog box that appears.

❌ CLEAN UP Retain the SBS Contacts address book and its contents for use in later exercises.

TIP In the preceding exercise, we imported and exported contact records, but you can use the same process to import and export other Outlook items.

Creating contact groups

If you frequently send messages to specific groups of people, such as members of a project team, club, or family, you can create a contact group that contains all the email addresses. Then you can send a message to all the group members by addressing it to the contact group.

Contact groups are like personal versions of distribution lists. A distribution list is available to everyone on your Exchange Server network; a contact group is available only from the local address book you store it in. You can, however, distribute a contact group to other people for their own use.

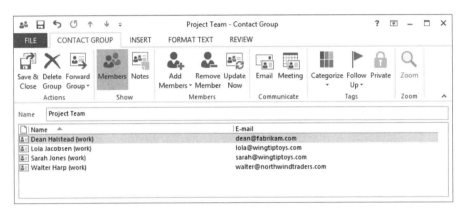

The ribbon provides a separate tab of commands for managing contact groups.

You add a member to a contact group either by selecting an existing contact record from an address book or by entering contact information in the Add New Member dialog box. When you add a member by using the latter method, you have the option to simultaneously create a contact record for him or her.

When you send a message to a contact group, each member of the contact group receives a copy of the message. If you want to send a message to most, but not all, members of a contact group, you can expand the contact group in the address field to a full list of its members, and remove individual people for the specific message at the time you send it.

In this exercise, you'll create a contact group and add new contacts to your address book. Then you'll send a message to all but one member of the contact group.

SET UP You need the contact records you imported into the SBS Contacts address book in the previous exercise. If you didn't import the contact records, you may do so now or substitute contact records of your own. Display the SBS Contacts address book in List view, and then follow the steps.

1   On the **Home** tab, in the **New** group, click the **New Contact Group** button to open the **Contact Group** window.

2   In the **Name** box, enter SBS Project Team. Then on the **Contact Group** tab, in the **Members** group, click the **Add Members** button to display the locations from which you can add contacts to the contact group.

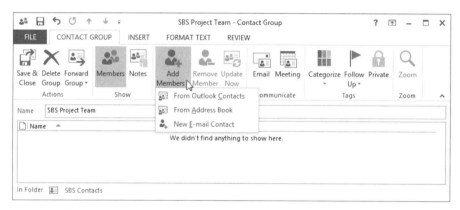

You can add members to a group from existing records or by entering email addresses.

3   In the **Add Members** list, click **From Outlook Contacts** to open the **Select Members** dialog box, which displays the contents of your default **Contacts** address book.

4   In the **Address Book** list, click **SBS Contacts** to display the contents of the **SBS Contacts** address book that you created and populated in previous exercises in this chapter.

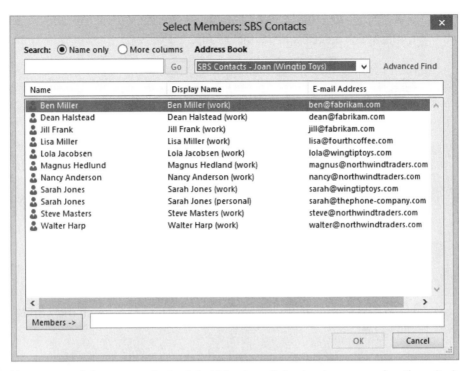

You can search for contacts in the Select Members dialog box by name or by other criteria.

5   In the **Name** list, click **Steve Masters**, and then in the lower-left corner of the dialog box, click the **Members** button to display **Steve Masters (work)** in the **Members** box. This is the display name stored in Steve's contact record.

6   In the **Name** list, double-click the first **Sarah Jones** entry to add **Sarah Jones (work)** to the **Members** box.

9

TIP You can add individual people, resources, distribution lists, public folders, mail-enabled Microsoft SharePoint site libraries, and other contact groups to a contact group. You can quickly add multiple entries to the Members box by double-clicking each name, or by holding down the Ctrl key while selecting multiple names, and then clicking the Members button.

7   In the **Select Members: SBS Contacts** dialog box, click **OK** to add the two contacts to the **SBS Project Team** contact group.

Contact group members added from an address book are listed by the Display As names saved in their contact records.

8   In the **Add Members** list, click **New E-mail Contact** to open the **Add New Member** dialog box.

9   In the **Add New Member** dialog box, enter Delphine Ribaute in the **Display name** box and delphine@wideworldimporters.com in the **E-mail address** box.

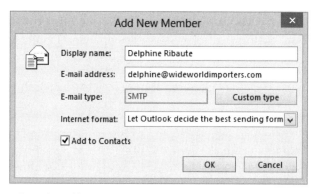

When the Add To Contacts check box is selected, the new contact group member will also be added to your default address book.

10   In the **Add New Member** dialog box, click **OK** to add Delphine to the **SBS Project Team** contact group and to your default address book.

> **TIP** We usually keep the contacts you create while working through the exercises in this book separate from your own contacts. For the purpose of the "Quickly locating contact information" exercise later in this chapter, we will create three contact records in your Contacts address book and clean them up in the later exercise.

11   Repeat steps 8 through 10 to add the following people to the contact group and to your **Contacts** address book:

Display name	Email address
Sara Davis	sara@wideworldimporters.com
Max Stevens	max@wideworldimporters.com

Each new contact group member appears in the contact group in alphabetical order.

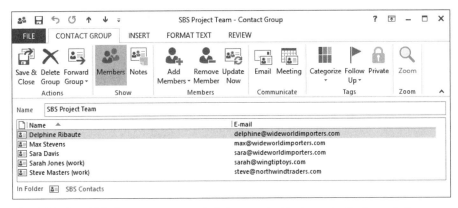

The folder in which the contact group is being created is shown in the lower-left corner of the dialog box.

12   On the **Contact Group** tab, in the **Actions** group, click the **Save & Close** button to create the contact group in the **SBS Contacts** address book.

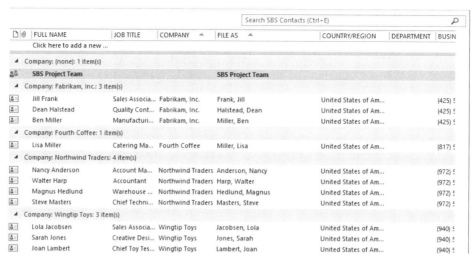

D	Ø	FULL NAME	JOB TITLE	COMPANY ▲	FILE AS ▲	COUNTRY/REGION	DEPARTMENT	BUSIN
		Click here to add a new ...						
▲ Company: (none): 1 item(s)								
▲		SBS Project Team			SBS Project Team			
▲ Company: Fabrikam, Inc.: 3 item(s)								
		Jill Frank	Sales Associa...	Fabrikam, Inc.	Frank, Jill	United States of Am...		(425) 5
		Dean Halstead	Quality Cont...	Fabrikam, Inc.	Halstead, Dean	United States of Am...		(425) 5
		Ben Miller	Manufacturi...	Fabrikam, Inc.	Miller, Ben	United States of Am...		(425) 5
▲ Company: Fourth Coffee: 1 item(s)								
		Lisa Miller	Catering Ma...	Fourth Coffee	Miller, Lisa	United States of Am...		(817) 5
▲ Company: Northwind Traders: 4 item(s)								
		Nancy Anderson	Account Ma...	Northwind Traders	Anderson, Nancy	United States of Am...		(972) 5
		Walter Harp	Accountant	Northwind Traders	Harp, Walter	United States of Am...		(972) 5
		Magnus Hedlund	Warehouse ...	Northwind Traders	Hedlund, Magnus	United States of Am...		(972) 5
		Steve Masters	Chief Techni...	Northwind Traders	Masters, Steve	United States of Am...		(972) 5
▲ Company: Wingtip Toys: 3 item(s)								
		Lola Jacobsen	Sales Associa...	Wingtip Toys	Jacobsen, Lola	United States of Am...		(940) 5
		Sarah Jones	Creative Desi...	Wingtip Toys	Jones, Sarah	United States of Am...		(940) 5
		Joan Lambert	Chief Toy Tes...	Wingtip Toys	Lambert, Joan	United States of Am...		(940) 5

Contact group names are displayed in bold font so that you can easily differentiate them from individual contact records.

TIP The three contact group members you added manually do not appear in this address book; Outlook created their contact records in your default Contacts address book.

13   In the contact list, click the **SBS Project Team** contact group. Then on the **Home** tab, in the **Communicate** group, click the **Email** button to open a message composition window. The message is addressed to the **SBS Project Team** contact group.

14   In the **To** box, click the **Expand** button to the left of **SBS Project Team**. Outlook displays a warning that you can't collapse the contact group after you expand it.

In a message header, the contact group name is bold and is preceded by an Expand button.

15   In the **Expand List** message box, click **OK** to replace the contact group name with the individual names or display names of its members. You can remove any group member from the address box before sending the message.

When you expand the contact group, the names of the group members replace the contact group name.

TIP If your organization uses a version of Exchange Server that supports MailTips, the individual message recipient names change to a green font, and a MailTip appears above the To box in the message header, notifying you that the message is addressed to recipients outside of your organization. MailTips are a feature of Exchange Server that displays information in email messages based on centrally stored information about the organization and its individual members.

16   Close the message window without saving or sending the message. (The message recipient addresses are fictitious.)

❌ CLEAN UP   Retain the SBS Project Team contact group and the Delphine Ribaute, Max Stevens, and Sara Davis contact records for use in later exercises.

Quickly locating contact information

You can use the Search feature in any Outlook module to immediately find a specific Outlook item within the current folder, an item of the same type in any folder, or an item of any type in any folder. Finding an item that contains, for example, a specific word is as simple as entering that word in the Search box at the top of the content area. When you position the cursor in the Search box, the Search tool tab appears on the ribbon. You can refine your search criteria or expand your search to include additional locations by using the commands available on the Search tab.

In this exercise, you'll locate specific contact records, and work with the contact records from the search results.

 **SET UP** You need the contact records you imported into the SBS Contacts address book earlier in this chapter, and the Delphine Ribaute, Max Stevens, and Sara Davis contact records you created in the previous exercise. If you didn't create those contact records, you may do so now or substitute contact records of your own. Display the SBS Contacts address book in Card view, and then follow the steps.

1   At the top of the contact list, click to position the cursor in the **Search** box, and activate the **Search** tool tab on the ribbon.

     KEYBOARD SHORTCUT Press Ctrl+E to position the cursor in the Search box of the current module.

Filters on the People module Search tool tab are specific to information stored in contact records.

2   In the **Search** box, enter sa. Notice that as you enter the letters, Outlook filters the list to display only those contact records that contain the letters you've entered, and highlights the matches in the contact records. This highlighting appears in any view other than **Business Card** view.

TROUBLESHOOTING If Outlook doesn't automatically filter the contact records, press Enter or click the Search button after you enter the search term.

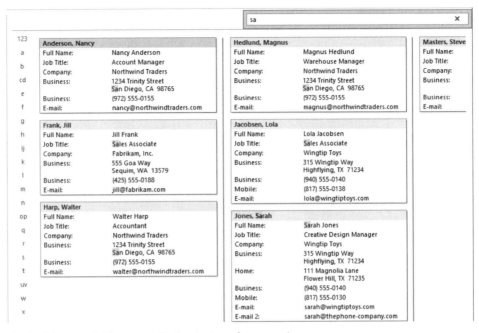

Outlook locates the letters at the beginning of any word.

3   In the **Search** box, replace **sa** with **steve**. As you type, Outlook filters the records in the **SBS Contacts** address book to locate **Steve Masters**.

     Let's focus our search on Mr. Stevens, who is a member of the SBS Project Team contact group.

4   On the **Search** tool tab, in the **Scope** group, click the **All Contact Items** button. The search results expand to display contact information for **Steve Masters** and **Max Stevens**, in addition to any other contacts that meet the criteria. Because we're no longer working specifically in the **SBS Contacts** address book, the view changes to the default **People** view.

5   In the contact list, click **Max Stevens** to preview his information.

     Next let's locate a co-worker of Mr. Stevens.

     TIP You can quickly repeat previous searches by clicking in the Search box to display the Search tool tab, clicking the Recent Searches button in the Options group of the Search tab, and then clicking the criteria of the previous search you want to repeat.

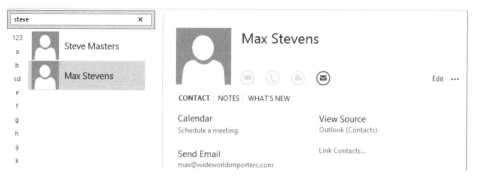

A refined search.

6   In the **Search** box at the top of the contact list, click the **Close Search** button (the X) to return to the **SBS Contacts** address book.

      TIP You can also cancel the current search by clicking the Close Search button on the Search tool tab.

7   Click in the **Search** box, and then on the **Search** tool tab, in the **Refine** group, click the **More** button. In the list, click **Company** to display a **Company** box in the **Search** pane.

8   In the **Company** box, enter Wide World Importers. As you enter the company name, Outlook populates the **Search** box with the correct criteria for the search.

We couldn't find what you were looking for.

When a single search criterion includes multiple words, Outlook encloses the words in parentheses.

The search returns no results because no contact records containing that phrase exist in this address book. You added the contacts from Wide World Importers to the address book when you created the SBS Project Team contact group, and the contact group entries included only the first name, last name, and email address for each person.

9   Click the **Remove** button to the right of the **Company** box to remove the corresponding criterion from the **Search** box.

10   In the **Refine** group, click the **More** button and then, in the list, click **E-mail** to display an **E-mail** box in the **Search** pane.

11   In the **E-mail** box, enter wideworldimporters to enter the corresponding search criterion in the **Search** box. Your search still yields no matching contact records because Outlook creates contact records in your default address book when adding people by email address to a contact group; you are currently searching the **SBS Contacts** address book.

12   On the **Search** tab, in the **Scope** group, click the **All Contact Items** button to locate the three contact records you created in the previous exercise. In the **Reading Pane**, the source is specified as your **Contacts** address book.

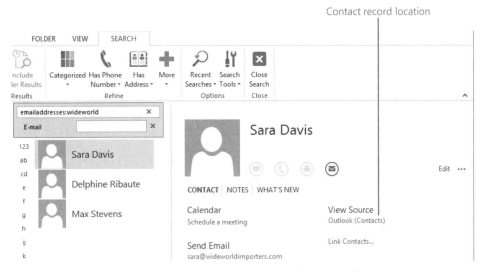

Email address is one of the criteria by which you can conduct a search.

13   In the contact list, click any one of the three contact records, and then press **Ctrl+A** to select all three. Drag the selected contact records from the contact list to the **SBS Contacts** address book in the **Folder Pane**.

14   In the **Folder Pane**, click the **Contacts** address book and verify that the three contact records are no longer there.

15   Click the **SBS Contacts** address book. On the **Home** tab, in the **Current View** gallery, click the **List** thumbnail. Confirm that the contact records for **Sara Davis**, **Delphine Ribaute**, and **Max Stevens** are now stored in this address book with the other contact records and the contact group that you have created while working through this book.

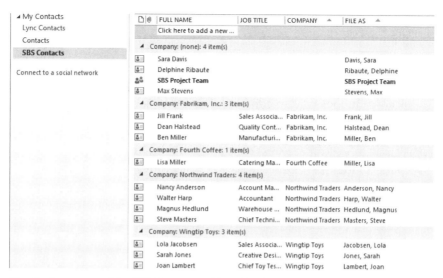

The final contents of the SBS Contacts address book.

CLEAN UP Click in the Search box to activate the Search pane, and then click the Remove button to the right of the Email box to remove this field from the pane.

Sending business cards

You can send entire contact records to other Outlook users to add to their address books or, if you prefer to share only the information shown on the associated business card, you can send the business card. To send an Outlook business card:

1 In any view of the address book, click the contact record whose business card you want to send.

2 On the **Home** tab, in the **Share** group, click the **Forward Contact** button, and then click **As a Business Card** to create a new message that has the business card attached as a file and displayed in the content area. The contact name is displayed in the **Subject** box in the message header.

3 Address and send the message.

TIP You can include a business card as part or all of your email signature by clicking the Business Card button while creating or editing a signature. For information about email signatures, see "Personalizing the appearance of message text" in Chapter 10, "Enhance message content."

Personalizing electronic business cards

Within each contact record window, information appears not only in the fields of the contact record but also in the form of a graphic that resembles a business card. When you enter a person's contact information in a contact record, basic information appears in the business card shown in the upper-right corner of the contact window. This data includes the person's name, company, and job title; work, mobile, and home phone numbers; and email, postal, webpage, and instant messaging addresses. (Only the first 10 lines of information fit on the card.) If an image is associated with the person through Exchange, SharePoint, or a social network to which you've connected Outlook, the contact record includes the image. You can change the types of information that appear, rearrange the information fields, format the text and background, and add, change, or remove images, such as a logo or photograph.

Creating a business card for yourself provides you with an attractive way of presenting your contact information to people you correspond with in email. You can attach your business card to an outgoing email message or include it as part (or all) of your email signature. The recipient of your business card can easily create a contact record for you by saving the business card to his or her Outlook address book.

SEE ALSO For information about email signatures, see "Personalizing the appearance of message text" in Chapter 10, "Enhance message content."

In this exercise, you'll modify the business card associated with a contact record.

 SET UP **You need the JoanLambert image located in the Chapter09 practice file folder and the SBS Contacts address book you created and populated in earlier exercises in this chapter to complete this exercise. Display the SBS Contacts address book in Business Card view, and then follow the steps.**

1   In the contact list, double-click the **Joan Lambert** contact record to open the contact record window. The business card in the upper-right corner displays information stored in the contact record fields. The grayscale graphic on the left side of the business card is a placeholder image.

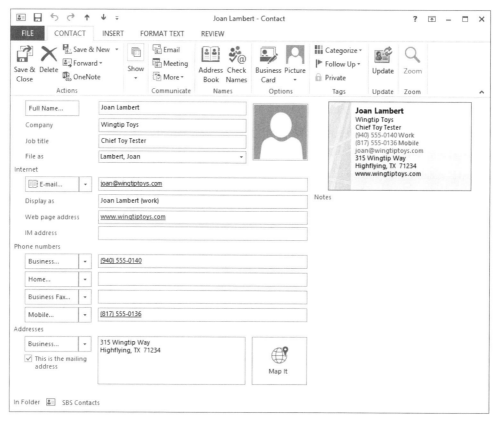

The default business card displays the information stored in the contact record.

2 On the **Contact** tab, in the **Options** group, click the **Picture** button, and then click **Add Picture**. The **Add Contact Picture** dialog box opens, displaying the contents of your **Pictures** library. You can add a business logo, your photograph, or any other image to a business card.

3 In the **Add Contact Picture** dialog box, navigate to the **Chapter09** practice file folder, click the **JoanLambert** image, and then click **OK** to replace the image placeholder in the contact record window and business card with the photo of Joan. Notice that the space allocated to the image changes and the content moves to the right.

4 In the **Options** group, click **Business Card** to open the **Edit Business Card** dialog box, in which you can modify the contents of the business card.

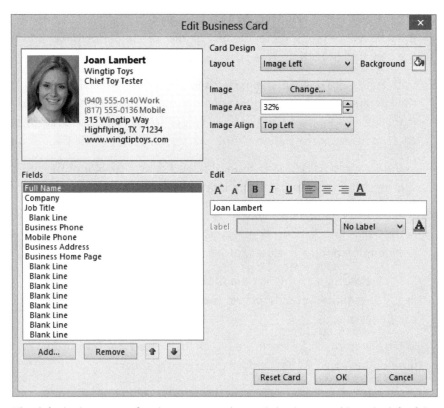

The default placement of an image on an electronic business card is to the left of the contact information.

5   In the **Card Design** area, in the **Layout** list, click **Image Right** to move the photo from the left side of the card to the right side.

6   In the **Image Area** box, enter or select (by clicking the arrows) **40%** to dedicate that horizontal portion of the card to the image.

7   In the **Image Align** list, click **Fit to Edge** to expand the photo to the full height of the business card.

8   In the **Card Design** area, click the **Background Color** button to open the **Color** dialog box. In the fifth row of the **Basic colors** palette, click the second swatch to select a brown color that coordinates with colors in the image.

9   In the **Color** dialog box, click **OK** to apply the new background color to the card preview. Notice that some of the text on the card might be difficult to read against the dark background.

10   With **Full Name** selected in the **Fields** list, click the **Font Color** button at the top of the **Edit** area (not the button associated with the **Label** field). In the **Color** dialog box, in the lower-right corner of the **Basic colors** palette, click the white swatch. Then click **OK**. The name on the business card now stands out from the background color.

11   In the **Fields** list, click **Company**, and then change the color of the company name shown on the business card from black to light yellow (the second swatch in the top row of the **Basic colors** palette).

12   In the **Fields** list, click **Job Title**. Then below the **Fields** list, click **Remove** to remove the job title from the business card (but not from the contact record).

13   In the **Fields** list, click the first **Blank Line** entry. Below the **Fields** list, click the **Move Field Up** button five times (pausing between clicks) to position a blank line after the company name.

14   In the **Fields** list, click **E-mail**. Then click the **Move Field Up** button two times to position the email address before the phone numbers.

15   Use the techniques you learned in this exercise to do the following:

   ▪ Remove the **Business Address** field from the business card.

   ▪ Insert a blank line between the **Mobile Phone** and **Business Home Page** fields.

   ▪ Change the color of the **E-mail**, **Business Phone**, and **Mobile Phone** information to light gray (the third swatch from the right in the last row) and the **Business Home Page** information to light yellow.

   After completing these changes, the business card looks very different from the original.

You can easily modify the layout and formatting of an electronic business card.

TIP You can modify field labels by clicking the field and then changing the label text, position, and color in the Label area to the right of the Fields list.

16   In the **Edit Business Card** dialog box, click **OK** to display the customized business card in the contact record window.

TIP You can undo all the changes you've made to a business card by clicking the Reset Card button at the bottom of the Edit Business Card dialog box.

17   On the **Contact** tab, in the **Actions** group, click the **Save & Close** button to display
the personalized business card among the default business cards in the address book.

A personalized business card stands out from other contact records.

CLEAN UP Retain the SBS Contacts address book and its contents for use in exercises
in later chapters.

Key points

- To more specifically organize contact records, you can create separate address books.

- You can import information into an Outlook address book from many external sources, and export information to share with other people who are using other programs.

- Creating and making use of contact groups saves time if you frequently send messages to a specific group of people.

- The Search feature makes short work of locating a specific contact or item of information in a contact record.

- You can customize the information shown in the electronic business card for each contact record, including your own.

9

Chapter at a glance

Personalize

Personalize the appearance of message text, page 346

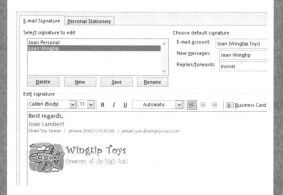

Insert

Insert and modify images, page 361

Create

Create and format business graphics, page 381

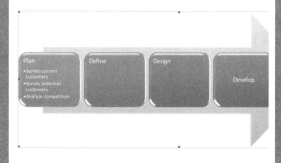

Change

Change message settings and delivery options, page 390

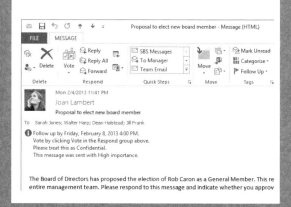

Enhance message content

IN THIS CHAPTER, YOU WILL LEARN HOW TO

- Personalize the appearance of message text.

- Insert and modify images.

- Create and format business graphics.

- Change message settings and delivery options.

Messages composed in and sent from Microsoft Outlook 2013 don't have to consist only of plain text. They can contain diagrams and graphics and can be visually enhanced by a judicious use of colors, fonts, and backgrounds. For more formal messages, you can attach a signature that includes your contact information, in addition to graphics such as a photograph or logo.

You can add visual information to a message, contact record, or other Outlook item to bring it to your attention or to the attention of the recipient. For example, you can indicate that a message is of high importance or contains confidential information. You can also set options that notify you when a recipient reads a message or prevents the recipient from forwarding or printing a message.

In this chapter, you'll first review formatting techniques, set default fonts for new messages and message responses, and create an email signature that's automatically included in all new messages. Then you'll insert and modify pictures, clip art, and shapes, and use the Screenshot and Screen Clipping tools to capture images of content displayed on your screen. You'll create and format graphical representations of business information and data. Finally, you'll learn about the message settings and delivery options you can set for outgoing messages.

PRACTICE FILES To complete the exercises in this chapter, you need the practice file contained in the Chapter10 practice file folder. For more information, see "Download the practice files" in this book's Introduction.

Personalizing the appearance of message text

By default, the text content of an Outlook message is shown in black, 11-point Calibri (a font chosen for its readability), arranged in left-aligned paragraphs on a white background. You can change the appearance of the text in a message by applying either local formatting (character or paragraph attributes and styles that you apply directly to text) or global formatting (a theme or style set that you apply to the entire document) in the same way that you would when working in a Microsoft Word document or Microsoft PowerPoint presentation. However, if you have a preferred font or theme for the messages you compose, you can save your preferences so that Outlook applies it to new messages you compose and to your message responses.

Configuring message text formatting preferences

You set your default font and theme preferences from the Signatures And Stationery dialog box, which you open by clicking Stationery And Fonts on the Mail page of the Outlook Options dialog box. The default settings use a black font for new messages and a blue font for message responses (replies and forwards).

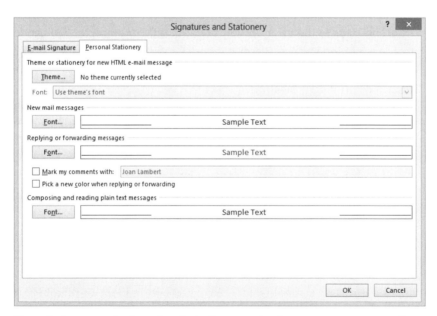

You select message fonts and control other aspects of message responses on the Personal Stationery page.

You can continue to use different colors to visually differentiate between original message content and your responses within a message trail. Or you might prefer to keep things clean and simple, and always use the same font regardless of whether a message is new—this simpler approach can help recipients to recognize message content from you.

Clicking the Theme button on the Personal Stationery page opens the Theme Or Stationery dialog box in which you can specify an email message theme (a preselected set of fonts, colors, and graphic elements) that Outlook will use when you create messages. Most themes include a colored or illustrated graphic background that you can include or exclude by selecting or clearing the Background Image check box.

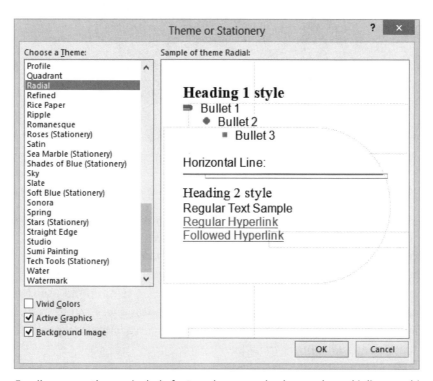

Email message themes include fonts, colors, page backgrounds, and inline graphic elements.

From the same dialog box, instead of choosing a complete email message theme, you can choose stationery (think of this as choosing a patterned paper on which to write letters). Some stationery options have quite pronounced graphic images (dozens of teddy bears parading across the page), whereas others are more subtle (green bubbles on a green background). Some stationery options have graphics across the entire page, whereas others confine the graphics to the left edge of the email "page" and leave a clear space for text and other email content.

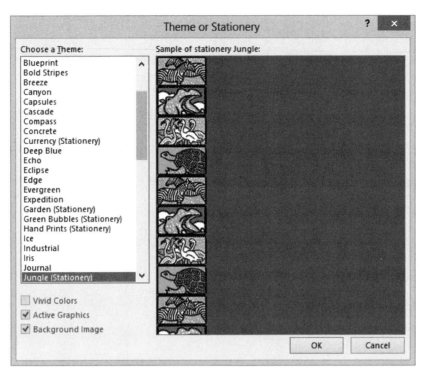

Stationery formats only the page background.

Your choice of stationery does not control your default message font; you must set that separately, as previously discussed in this topic. If you choose to use stationery (and I'd caution you to make this choice judiciously), take care to choose a font color that is visible against the stationery background and also visible to recipients who choose to block graphic elements of email messages. For example, it might be tempting to use clean white lettering against the brown background of the Jungle stationery, but for recipients who block graphics, the message will display white lettering on a white background—in other words, the message will appear to be blank.

If you prefer to apply thematic elements on an individual message basis, you can apply global formatting options—by using themes and style sets—with only a couple of clicks.

Nine of the standard Microsoft Office 2013 themes (which are not the same as the email message themes you can select in the Theme Or Stationery dialog box) are available from the Themes gallery on the Options tab in a message composition window. Each theme controls the colors, fonts, and graphic effects used in the message.

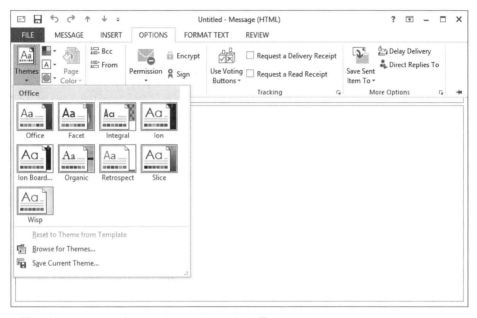

Office themes control fonts, colors, and graphic effects.

The default theme for all email messages, Word documents, PowerPoint presentations, Microsoft Excel workbooks, and other Office 2013 documents is the Office theme. If you don't apply another theme to your message, the colors, fonts, and effects in your message are controlled by the Office theme.

You can modify the currently applied theme by selecting a color set from the Theme Colors gallery, a font set from the Theme Fonts gallery, or an effect from the Theme Effects gallery, all of which are in the Theme group on the Options tab. The same colors and fonts are also available from the Change Styles menu in the Styles group on the Format Text tab.

TIP Office theme functionality is provided by Word 2013 and is available only when you have that program installed.

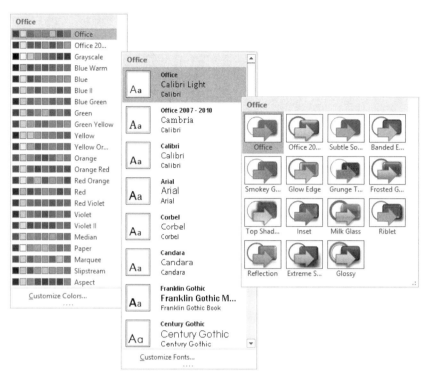

You can individually modify the colors, fonts, and effects used in the email message.

You can use *styles* to format text in email messages in the same way that you do in Word documents; however, most people won't compose email messages of the length and outline detail that would require those, so we'll discuss them only briefly in this book.

You can apply character and paragraph styles from the Styles gallery in the Styles group on the Format Text tab, or from the Styles pane that opens when you click the Styles dialog box launcher on the Format Text tab.

TIP If you create different types of Office documents (such as Word documents, PowerPoint presentations, and corporate email messages) for your organization, you can ensure the uniform appearance of all the documents by applying the same Office theme and style set to all the documents. For example, you might create a theme that incorporates your company's corporate fonts and logo colors.

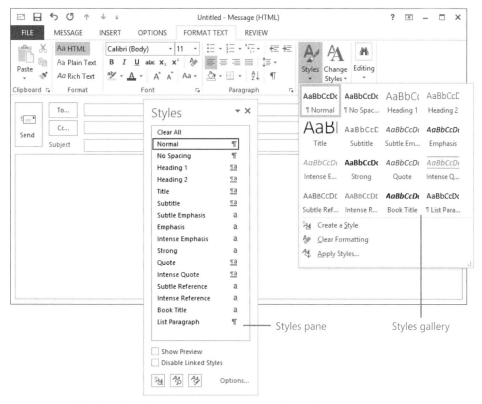

You can specify the styles that you want to appear in the Styles gallery and in the Styles pane.

TIP You can preview the effect of a style on the currently selected text by pointing to the style in the Styles gallery, but not in the Styles pane.

A *style set* changes the colors, fonts, and paragraph formatting of individual styles. You can change the appearance of all the styles in a message by selecting any of the 17 available style sets (or by creating your own). Selecting a style set changes the appearance of all the text in the current message, in addition to the appearance of the icons in the Styles gallery. You can preview or select a style set by clicking the Change Styles button in the Styles group on the Format Text tab, clicking Style Set, and then pointing to or clicking a specific style set.

10

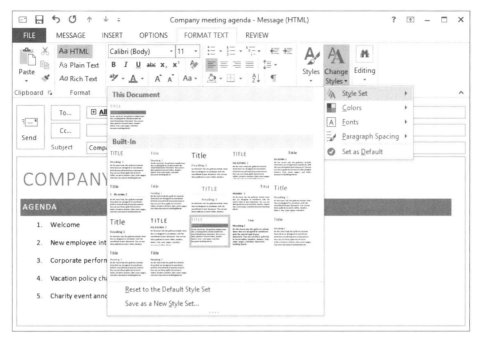

Choosing a style set.

SEE ALSO For more information about using themes, styles, and style sets to format content, refer to *Microsoft Word 2013 Step by Step* by Joan Lambert and Joyce Cox (Microsoft Press, 2013).

Manually formatting message text

You can manually format text in the content pane to differentiate it from your default font. The local formatting options available in Outlook 2013 are the same as those available in Word and other Office 2013 programs, and you might already be familiar with them from working with those programs.

Here's a quick review of the types of formatting changes you can make:

- **Font, size, and color** Hundreds of fonts in a range of sizes and in a virtually unlimited selection of colors

- **Font style** Regular, bold, italic, or bold italic

- **Underline style and color** Plain, multiple, dotted, dashed, wavy, and many combinations thereof, in all colors

- **Effects** Highlight, strikethrough, superscript, subscript, shadow, outline, emboss, engrave, small caps, all caps, or hidden

- **Character spacing** Scale, spacing, position, and kerning

- **Paragraph attributes** Alignment, indentation, and spacing

- **Character and paragraph styles** Titles, headings, and purpose-specific font formatting (such as for quotes and book titles)

TIP The available formatting and effects might vary based on the currently selected font.

In a message composition window, the local formatting commands are available both from the Message tab and from the Format Text tab. The formatting commands are available only when the cursor is in the content pane. When the cursor is in the message header (for example, in the To or Subject field), the formatting commands are grayed out.

Configuring message signature preferences

When you send an email message to someone, you will most likely "sign" the message by entering your name at the end of the message text. You can have Outlook insert your signature text in outgoing messages by creating an email signature and assigning it to your email account. Your email signature can include additional information that you want to consistently provide to message recipients.

10

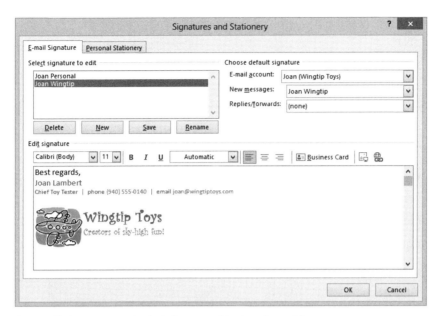

An email signature can include formatted text and graphics.

A typical email signature would commonly include your name and contact information, but depending on your situation, you might also include information such as your company name, job title, a legal disclaimer, a corporate or personal slogan, a photo, and so on. You can even include your electronic business card as part or all of your email signature.

SEE ALSO For more information about electronic business cards, see "Personalizing electronic business cards" in Chapter 9, "Manage contact records."

You can create different signatures for use in different types of messages or for use when you're sending messages from different email accounts. For example, you might create a formal business signature for client correspondence, a casual business signature for inter-office correspondence, and a personal signature for messages sent from another account. Or you might create a signature that contains more information to send with original email messages, and a signature that contains less information to send with message replies. You can format the text of your email signature in the same ways that you can format message text. If you want to apply formatting that's not available from the selections of buttons across the top of the signature content pane, you can create and format your signature, either in an email message composition window or in a Word document, copy the signature from its original location, and then paste it into the signature content pane. Using this technique, you can include artistic content such as WordArt objects and clip art images in your email signature.

TIP All Office programs share the Microsoft Office Clipboard, so you can easily copy and move content between programs. You don't need to work from the Clipboard to paste the most recently cut or copied text into another location; it's stored in the shared Clipboard, so all Office programs have access to it. For example, you can cut or copy text or an image in a Word document and then paste it into an Outlook email message without ever directly accessing the Clipboard.

If you have Outlook configured to connect to multiple email accounts, you can assign the same email signature to multiple accounts, or assign a unique email signature to each email account. The signature you assign to the specific account will appear automatically in new messages you send from that account. You can also manually insert any email signature you've created in any message. Outlook inserts the email signature at the end of the message, replacing any existing email signature.

To manually insert an existing email signature in a message:

1   On the **Message** tab, in the **Include** group, click the **Signature** button.
2   In the **Signature** list, click the name of the email signature you want to insert.

TIP If you have not previously set up a signature, clicking the Signature button displays a short list that includes a Signatures option; clicking this option opens the Signatures And Stationery dialog box in which you can create a signature.

To remove an email signature from a message, select and delete the signature content as you would any other text.

In this exercise, you'll first set the default fonts for new messages and for responses. Then you'll create an email signature and instruct Outlook to insert the signature in all new messages you create.

 SET UP You don't need any practice files to complete this exercise. Display your Inbox, and then follow the steps.

1   In the left pane of the **Backstage** view, click **Options**, and then in the left pane of the **Outlook Options** dialog box, click the **Mail** page tab.

2   In the **Compose messages** section, click the **Stationery and Fonts** button. On the **Personal Stationery** page of the **Signatures and Stationery** dialog box, notice the fonts that are currently specified for new messages and responses.

3   In the **New mail messages** area, click the **Font** button. In the **Font** dialog box, notice the many fonts you can choose from. Enter **g** to scroll the **Font** list to the fonts beginning with that letter, and then click **Garamond**. Notice that the sample text in the **Preview** pane changes to reflect your selection.

The options on the Font page provide many creative choices.

TIP Unlike the Font lists in other areas of Outlook, the Font list in this dialog box doesn't display font previews simply by pointing to one; you must select the font to display a sample in the Preview box. You can preview fonts in the font lists that are available in a message composition window, either from the Basic Text group on the Message tab or from the Font group on the Format Text tab.

4   Scroll down the **Font** list and click **Lucida Sans**. Notice that the options available in the **Font Style** list change. The available styles are specific to the fonts installed on your computer.

TIP Fonts are installed on your computer in the C:\Windows\Fonts folder. You can view all the installed fonts in that folder.

5   In the **Font style** box, click **Demibold Roman**, and in the **Size** box, click **9**.

6   Click the **Font color** arrow and then in the **Standard Colors** palette, click the third swatch from the right end (**Blue**). The **Preview** box reflects your changes.

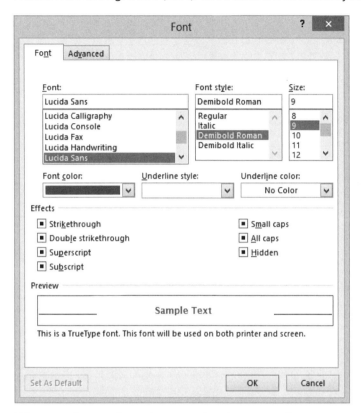

When you choose a font color, remember that some colors are more visible on the screen than others.

10

TIP If you intend to format individual messages by applying themes, you can select a color from the Theme Colors palette; the color will change to match the theme you choose in each message.

7   In the **Font** dialog box, click **OK**.

8   In the **Replying or forwarding messages** area of the **Signatures and Stationery** dialog box, click the **Font** button. Repeat steps 4 through 7 to set the same default font for message responses (Lucida Sans, Demibold Roman, 9-point, and Blue).

In this instance, you aren't differentiating between the color of the font in your new messages and message responses; you will differentiate between them by including an email signature only in new messages.

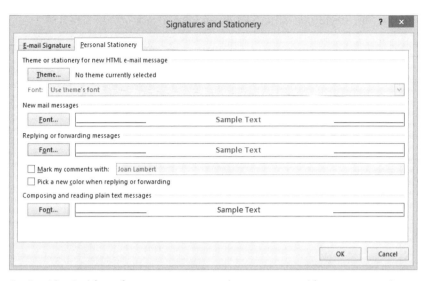

Setting identical fonts for new messages and responses provides a more consistent reading experience in an email trail.

9   In the **Signatures and Stationery** dialog box, click the **E-mail Signature** page tab.

10 Below the **Select signature to edit** box, click the **New** button. Outlook prompts you to supply a name for the new signature before you can work with the signature content.

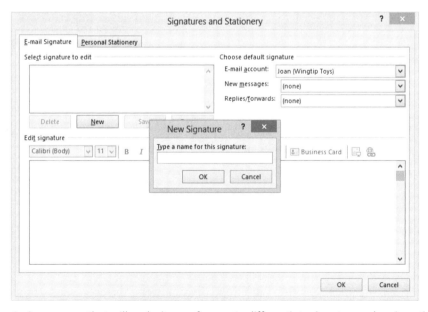

Assign a name that will make it easy for you to differentiate signatures when inserting them.

11   In the **Type a name for this signature** box, enter Casual. Then click **OK** to create the
      Casual signature, which is currently blank.

12   In the **Edit signature** box, enter Thanks!, press the **Enter** key, and then enter your
      first name.

13   Do not apply any formatting to the first line of the signature; leave this as the
      default font.

14   Select your name. In the **Font** list, click **Lucida Handwriting** (or any other font you
      like). In the **Font Size** list, click **14**.

15   Click the **Font Color** arrow and then, in the **Standard Colors** palette, click the **Blue**
      swatch. Then click away from your name to display the results of your changes.

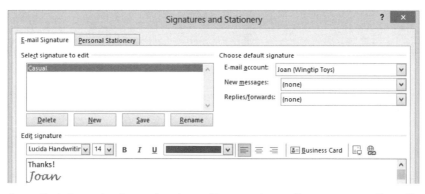

Formatted elements of your signature will appear in email messages exactly as they do here.

TIP If you want to include your electronic business card as part of your signature,
click the Business Card button. Then in the Insert Business Card dialog box, locate
and click your name, and click OK.

You can manually insert an email signature into a message, but you might find it
more convenient to instruct Outlook to insert the signature automatically. We'll do
that now.

16   In the **Choose default signature** area, ensure that your default email account is
      selected in the **E-mail account** box. Then in the **New messages** list, click **Casual** to
      instruct Outlook to insert your signature into all new email messages you send from
      this account. Do not select a signature in the **Replies/forwards** list.

17   Make any other changes you want, and then click **OK** in the **Signatures and
      Stationery** dialog box and in the **Outlook Options** dialog box.

18   On the **Home** tab, in the **New** group, click the **New Email** button to open a message composition window. Notice that your email signature is already present in the content pane, and the word **Thanks!** is formatted in the font you chose for new messages: blue, Demibold, 9-point, Lucida Sans.

19   Click to position the cursor in the blank line at the top of the content pane, and then enter I love using Outlook! Notice that the message text has the same formatting as the first line of the signature.

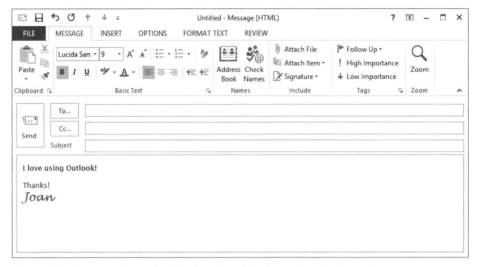

The default font you selected earlier is reflected in the settings in the Basic Text group.

❌ CLEAN UP Close the message window without saving your changes. Reset the New Messages signature to <none> if you don't want to use the Casual signature you created in this exercise, and set the default fonts for new messages and responses to the fonts you want to use.

TIP If you have more than one email account set up in Outlook, you can configure different signatures for each account. To do so, click the account in the E-mail Account list, click the signature you want to use with that account in the New Messages list and in the Replies/Forwards list, and then click OK.

Inserting and modifying images

Email is a means of communicating information to other people, and, as the old saying goes, a picture is worth a thousand words. Using Outlook 2013, you can communicate visual information in the following ways:

- Share photographs with other people by attaching the photos to messages or embedding them in messages.

- Share information from websites, documents, and other visual presentations by capturing images of your screen directly from Outlook and then inserting those images in your message.

- Explain complicated processes and other business information by creating SmartArt graphics within messages or by embedding SmartArt graphics that you create in other Office 2013 programs.

- Communicate statistical information by creating a chart within a message.

- Decorate message content by inserting clip art images.

You can insert all these types of images from the Illustrations group on the Insert tab into the content pane of an email message, calendar item, or task, or into the notes pane of a contact record. (One exception: you can't insert an image into a note.)

SEE ALSO For information about SmartArt graphics and charts, see "Creating and formatting business graphics" later in this chapter.

Inserting pictures

Pictures are created outside of Word—photographs from digital cameras, clip art images, or files created by using a computer graphics program. You can insert digital photographs or pictures created in almost any program into an Outlook email message. You specify the source of the picture you want to insert by clicking one of the following two buttons, which are located in the Illustrations group on the Insert tab:

- **Pictures** Click this button to insert a picture that is saved as a file on your computer, on a network drive, or on a device (such as a digital camera) that is connected to your computer.

- **Online Pictures** Click this button to insert a royalty-free clip art image from the Office.com website, a web search result from Bing, or an image stored on your Microsoft SkyDrive or another online source.

To insert a picture from a file into an email message or item, position the cursor in the content pane or notes pane in which you want the picture to appear, and then follow these steps:

1   On the **Insert** tab, in the **Illustrations** group, click the **Pictures** button to open the **Insert Picture** dialog box and display the contents of your **Pictures** library.

2   In the **Insert Picture** dialog box, browse to the folder that contains the picture you want to insert.

3   Click the picture to select it, and then click **Insert**.

> **TIP** To insert multiple pictures at one time, select the first picture you want to insert. Then either press Shift and click the last picture in a consecutive series, or press Ctrl and click each individual picture.

After inserting a picture from a file or from an online source, you can modify the picture and control the flow of text around it by using the commands on the Format tool tab that appears when the picture is selected.

Many interesting picture formatting options are available within an Outlook email message.

About online pictures

Clicking the Online Pictures button in the Illustration group on the Insert tab displays the Insert Pictures window. From this window you can search for a royalty-free clip art image on the Microsoft Office website, search for a published image on the Internet by using Bing Image Search, or browse your SkyDrive for an image.

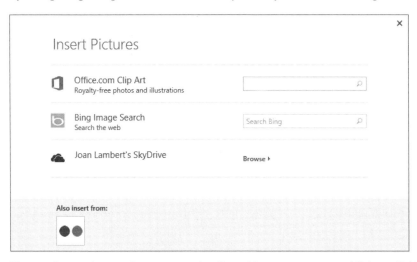

You can insert pictures that are stored online, either your own or publicly available images.

TIP If you aren't signed in to Outlook with a Microsoft account, the associated SkyDrive and other site options won't be displayed in the Insert Pictures window.

If you want to dress up an email message but don't have a suitable picture, you can use any of the clip art images available from the Office website without requesting permission from the image creator. Clip art available from Office.com includes illustrations and photographs that are free to use and don't have copyright restrictions.

Using Bing Image Search returns images that are published on the Internet but that might be otherwise copyrighted. If you want to use one of these images in any public way, you must check the copyright information associated with the image.

When you search any of these sources, the window displays results matching your search term. Point to an image and click the View Larger button to preview it.

Click an image to select it for insertion; to select multiple images, hold down the Ctrl or Shift key and select the other items you want. Then click the Insert button to insert the selected item or items in your document.

No matter what the origin of an image, you can change its size and its position in relation to other content directly in the item window. You can make additional changes to most types of images from within the message, such as cropping a picture or embellishing it by applying artistic effects. From the Format tool tab that appears when you select an image, you can do things like:

- Crop or remove background elements from an image.
- Sharpen or soften the image content.
- Colorize the image and control color saturation and tone.
- Apply artistic effects to make an image look as though it's rendered in pencil, chalk, marker, or paint, or has a pattern applied to it.
- Add shadows, reflections, and glowing or soft edges.
- Apply three-dimensional effects.

Certain effects can be applied to only specific types of files. For example, you can apply artistic effects to a photograph that's saved in .jpg format (a common format for digital photos) but not to an illustration that's saved in .wmf format (a common format for clip art illustrations).

Inserting shapes

You can insert many types of shapes into the content pane of an Outlook item and format them to create abstract drawings, banners, and other images. To insert a shape, follow these steps:

1　On the **Insert** tab, in the **Illustrations** group, click the **Shapes** button.
2　In the **Shapes** gallery, click the shape you want to insert.
3　In the content pane or notes pane, drag to draw the shape at the size you want.

Available shapes include lines and simple arrows, geometric shapes, common symbols, block arrows, mathematical operators, flowchart symbols, stars and banners, and more.

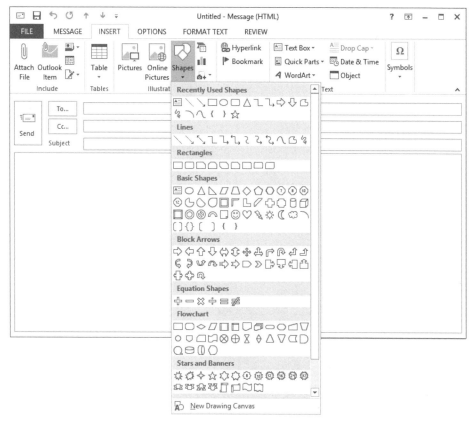

You can combine shapes on a drawing canvas within the message.

After inserting a shape, you can change its outline and fill colors and modify its appearance in many ways by using the commands available on the Format tool tab.

10

Inserting screen images

You can use the Screenshot and Screen Clipping tools to easily capture images of either an entire window that's open on your screen or a specific area of the screen that you select.

To capture and insert a screen image, follow these steps:

1 Ensure that the window you want to capture is not minimized or, if you plan to capture only a portion of a window, that it's visible on the screen. Ensure that nothing but the Outlook item window into which you want to insert the screen image is on top of the screen you want to capture.

2 In the Outlook item window, position the cursor in the content pane or notes pane where you want the image to appear.

3 On the **Insert** tab, in the **Illustrations** group, click the **Screenshot** button to display the **Available Windows** menu and a gallery of the currently open (non-minimized) windows.

You can capture an image of any open window by clicking it in the Available Windows gallery.

4 To insert an image of an entire open window into the Outlook item, click its icon in the **Available Windows** gallery.

5   To capture an image of a portion of a visible window, click **Screen Clipping**. Outlook minimizes the active Outlook item to the **Windows Taskbar** so that the content behind it is visible. White shading covers the screen, and the **Screen Clipping** tool (which at this point looks like a large plus sign) appears.

Screen Clipping tool

White shading indicates the portion of the desktop that's not being captured by the Screen Clipping tool.

6   Position the **Screen Clipping** tool in the upper-left corner of the area you want to capture. Press and hold the mouse button, and then drag to encompass the capture area to make a window in the shaded area that indicates the intended capture area. You can change the capture area until you release the mouse button.

TIP You don't have to be exact with the size of your outline because you can modify the screen clipping after you insert it into the Outlook item.

Screen capture area

The area that will be captured is unshaded and outlined.

7   When the entire area you want to capture is encompassed in the **Screen Clipping** box, release the mouse button to capture the image, restore the Outlook item from the taskbar, and insert the captured image in the content pane.

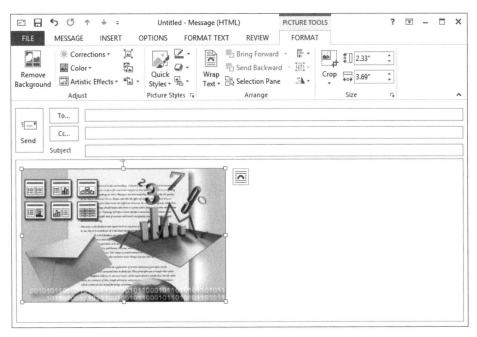

You can format and modify screen clippings in the same ways that you can pictures.

TIP Clicking the Layout Options button that appears when you insert an image displays options for aligning the image with the surrounding message content. For extensive information about configuring layout options, refer to *Microsoft Word 2013 Step by Step* by Joan Lambert and Joyce Cox (Microsoft Press, 2013).

In this exercise, you'll insert a photograph in an email message and then use several of the available picture-formatting tools to modify the photo before sending it.

SET UP You need the Lighthouse photograph located in the Chapter10 practice file folder to complete this exercise. Open a new message composition window, and then follow the steps.

1   Maximize the message window.

2   On the ribbon, click the **Insert** tab. Notice that while the cursor is in the **To** field, only the commands in the **Include** group are available.

3   Click to position the cursor in the content pane, and notice that the commands in the **Tables**, **Illustrations**, **Links**, **Text**, and **Symbols** groups become available. These commands are available only when the cursor is located in a content pane or notes pane into which you can insert content.

> **SEE ALSO** For information about inserting and formatting tables, see "Creating and sending messages" in Chapter 3, "Send and receive email messages."

4   On the **Insert** tab, in the **Illustrations** group, click the **Pictures** button to open the **Insert Picture** dialog box and display the contents of your **Pictures** library or the most recent location you browsed to when looking for pictures.

5   Navigate to the **Chapter10** practice file folder, click the **Lighthouse** photo, and then click **Insert** to display the photo in the email message content pane. The **Format** tool tab for pictures becomes active. Because the image is so large, only part of the photo is visible in the content pane.

External images are inserted at their original sizes; the dimensions of the selected image are shown in the Size group on the Format tool tab.

TROUBLESHOOTING The graphics in this exercise depict the message window at a width of 1024 pixels. If your screen width is set to higher than 1024 pixels, more of the photo will be displayed in the message window. Either change the size of your message window to match ours or simply follow along with the steps as written and be aware that your message window will appear different from those shown here.

First we'll resize the photo to fit within the content pane.

TIP The Format tool tab remains available only while the image is selected. If the tab disappears from the ribbon, simply click the image to redisplay it.

6   On the **Format** tool tab, in the **Size** group, notice that the current image height is **8"** and the width is **10.67"**. Click and hold the **Shape Height** down arrow until the height is set to **4"**, or select **8"**, enter **4** (you don't need to enter the inch mark), and then press **Enter**. The shape's width decreases proportionally with the shape's height so that the photo maintains its aspect ratio.

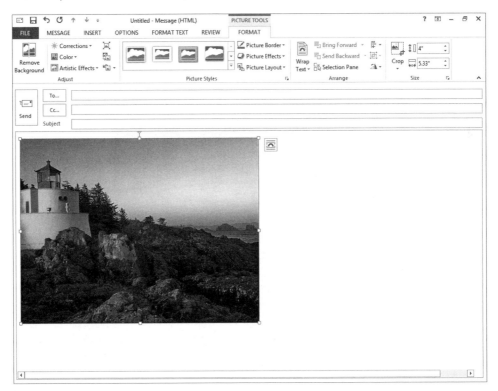

You can change the size of a graphic by setting specific dimensions or by dragging its resizing handles.

10

Now we'll use one of the fancier formatting tools available.

7 In the **Adjust** group, click **Remove Background** to activate the **Background Removal** tool, which obscures all but selected areas of the photo with purple shading. Resizing handles surround an area selector in the center of the photo, and the **Background Removal** tool tab appears on the ribbon.

The Background Removal tool makes its best attempt at identifying background areas in the photo; you can refine the selection to fit your needs.

The purple shading indicates the image content that the Background Removal tool will remove. Our goal in this exercise is to remove the sky and leave only the landscape.

8   Drag the upper-left resizing handle to the left edge of the photo, keeping it just
     above the top of the lighthouse. Then drag the lower-right resizing handle to the
     lower-right corner of the photo. (It's okay to drag beyond the edge of the photo.)
     Much of the sky is now obscured with purple shading.

Resizing the area selector is one way of controlling the area marked for removal.

9   On the **Background Removal** tab, in the **Refine** group, click the **Mark Areas to
     Remove** button. When you move the cursor back to the photo, it changes from an
     arrow to a pencil.

10   Click the area of sky that remains visible just below the purple shading. After a
     moment, a marker appears in the location you clicked, and the purple screen
     extends to cover the area defined by your clicks.

11   Click two more times (or as necessary) to shade the entire sky. (If a click results in an
     unintended effect, click the **Undo** button on the **Quick Access Toolbar** to remove the
     effect, and then try again.) Notice that each click affects the area that is similar to the
     marker location.

     KEYBOARD SHORTCUTS Press Ctrl+Z to undo the most recent action. Press Ctrl+Y to
     repeat the most recent action. For more information about keyboard shortcuts, see
     "Keyboard shortcuts" at the end of this book.

10

Removal Markers

Removal Markers are labeled with minus signs.

TIP You can indicate areas of a picture to keep by clicking the Mark Areas To Keep button in the Refine group on the Background Removal tab and then clicking the picture. Keep Markers are labeled with plus signs.

12   On the **Background Removal** tab, in the **Close** group, click the **Keep Changes** button to remove the purple-shaded area from the photo, leaving only a white background. The **Background Removal** tool tab disappears from the ribbon.

TIP You can redisplay the Background Removal tool tab at any time to modify or re-move your changes by clicking the Remove Background button in the Adjust group on the Format tool tab.

13   Click in the content pane, away from the photo, to reveal the full effect of removing the background from the photo. The lighthouse and landscape details are clearly outlined as though the photo had been carefully trimmed with scissors.

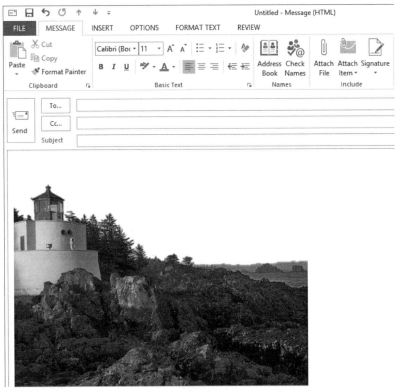

A three-dimensional effect can be achieved by removing the background from a picture.

Next, we'll crop and frame the image.

14   Click the photo to select it. On the **Format** tool tab, in the **Size** group, click the **Crop** arrow (not the button), and then click **Aspect Ratio** to display a menu of standard width-to-height ratios.

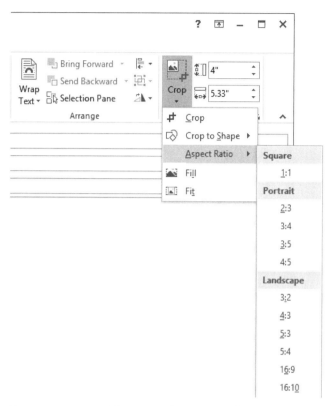

You can crop a graphic to a precise aspect ratio.

15   On the **Aspect Ratio** menu, click **1:1** to display a square selection area on the photo. The photo outside of the selection area is depicted in grayscale rather than in color.

16   Drag the photo to the right within the square selection area so that the left edge of the photo is aligned with the left edge of the square. (When the dashed and solid lines on the top, left, and bottom sides align, you've got it just right!)

17   Press and hold the **Shift** key, and then drag the lower-right crop handle of the selection area (not the photo) up and to the left until the square selection area encompasses the lighthouse and the trees and rocks closest to it. Release the mouse button first, and then the **Shift** key.

The resulting selection (as shown in the Size group on the Format tool tab) is just under three inches square.

TIP Holding down the Shift key maintains the aspect ratio while you crop or resize an image.

Crop handles

You can crop a picture to show only the portion you want.

18   In the **Size** group, click the **Crop** button (not the arrow) to crop the photo to the selected area.

TIP When you respond to a message that contains an embedded image, clicking the image in an open message window (but not in the draft response in the Reading Pane) activates a Format tool tab that contains a limited range of formatting options. (Fewer formatting options are available when you work with the modified image than were available in the original message window.)

10

19 In the lower-right corner of the **Picture Styles** gallery, click the **More** button to expand the gallery.

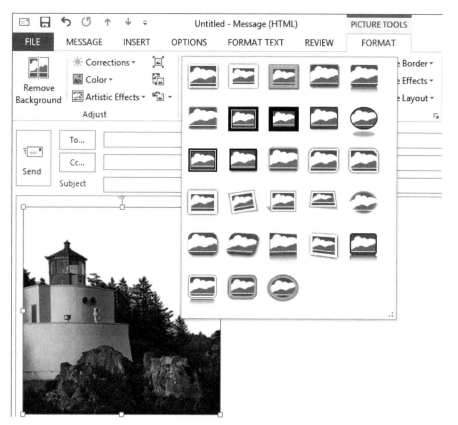

You can apply predefined sets of formatting to pictures to achieve a professional frame effect.

20 In the **Picture Styles** gallery, point to several of the icons to display their names and preview the effect of applying each of the styles to the selected photo. Then click the **Rounded Diagonal Corner, White** icon (the fourth icon in the third row) to apply a combination of shapes and shadows to the photo.

Finally, we'll modify the photo so that it looks like a painting.

21   With the photo still selected, click the **Artistic Effects** button in the **Adjust** group to display the **Artistic Effects** menu.

You can choose from a wide range of artistic effects.

22   In the **Artistic Effects** gallery, point to several of the icons to display their names and preview the effect of applying that style to the selected photo. Then click the **Watercolor Sponge** icon (the second icon in the third row).

23   Click in the content pane away from the photo to reveal the full effect. The artistic effect causes the photo to more closely resemble a painting than a photograph.

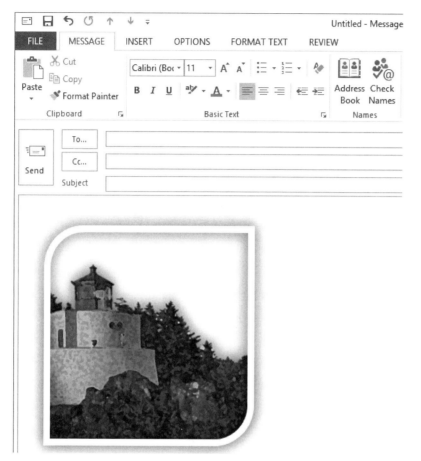

You can easily achieve an artistic effect by using the tools available in the message window.

24 In the message header, enter your email address in the **To** box and enter SBS Picture Tools in the **Subject** box. Then send the message to yourself so you can admire your creation.

25 When the message arrives in your **Inbox**, note that you can select and copy the embedded picture in the **Reading Pane** or in the open message window for use in other documents.

❌ CLEAN UP Close any open message windows. Move the SBS Picture Tools message to the SBS Messages folder and retain it for use in later exercises.

Creating and formatting business graphics

Images can be especially valuable in business communications, when you need to clearly explain facts or concepts, particularly to a global audience. In Outlook 2013 (and other Office 2013 programs), you can depict processes, cycles, hierarchies, and other relationships by using SmartArt graphics, and you can depict graphical representations of numeric data by using charts.

TIP SmartArt graphic and charting functionality is provided by Word 2013 and is available only when you have that program installed.

SmartArt graphics are graphical representations of lists of information. You can create a SmartArt graphic directly in an email message by selecting the type of graphic you want to create and then entering the information to populate it. You can modify the SmartArt graphic to fit the information you want to present, change the graphic type if your original selection doesn't best represent the final information, and format the graphic with professional themed color combinations and effects. When you send the message, Outlook converts the SmartArt graphic to a static graphic.

Charts are graphical representations of tables of data. Tables and charts are frequently created by using Excel. You can also create a chart directly in an Outlook email message. Charts you create in an email message look exactly like those you would create in an Excel workbook—because they are based on an Excel data source that is created from within Outlook.

To create a chart in a message or other Outlook item, follow these steps:

1   Position the cursor in the content pane or notes pane where you want the chart to appear.

2   On the **Insert** tab, in the **Illustrations** group, click the **Chart** button to open the **Insert Chart** dialog box.

10

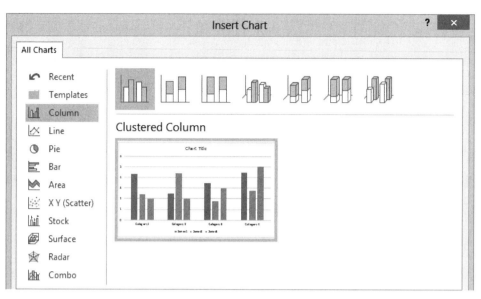

You can preview charts of the same type by clicking the icons at the top of the preview pane, and display other chart types by clicking a category in the left pane.

TIP Pointing to the chart in the preview area displays a larger version.

3   In the **Insert Chart** dialog box, click the icon of the chart type you want to create, and then click **OK** to display a basic chart in the Outlook item and a **Chart in Microsoft Word** window containing mock data from which the basic chart is built.

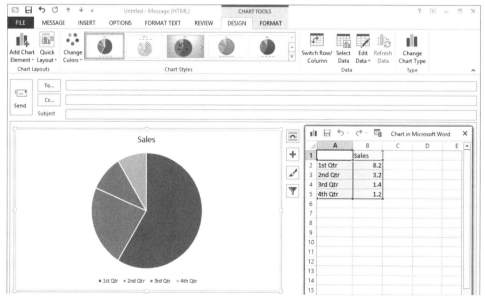

The chart immediately reflects changes you make to the data.

4   Update the mock data with your own. When you finish, close the **Chart in Microsoft Word** window. It's not necessary to save or name the worksheet that contains the data depicted by the chart; it is automatically saved with the chart.

In this exercise, you'll create a SmartArt flowchart in an email message.

SET UP You don't need any practice files to complete this exercise. Open a new message composition window, and then follow the steps.

1   Maximize the message window, and then click to insert the cursor in the content pane.

2   On the **Insert** tab, in the **Illustrations** group, click the **SmartArt** button to open the **Choose a SmartArt Graphic** dialog box.

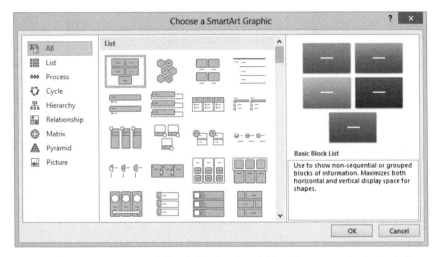

You can filter the contents of the dialog box by clicking the categories in the left pane.

10

3   With **All** selected in the category list in the left pane, scroll through the icons in the center pane to review the many available SmartArt graphics.

TIP You can display the name of a SmartArt graphic by pointing to it. You can't display a live preview of a SmartArt graphic before you create it, but you can do so when you change the graphic type.

4   In the left pane, click **Process**. Scroll to the top of the center pane, and then click the second icon in the second row (**Alternating Flow**) to display a color preview of the process diagram in the right pane.

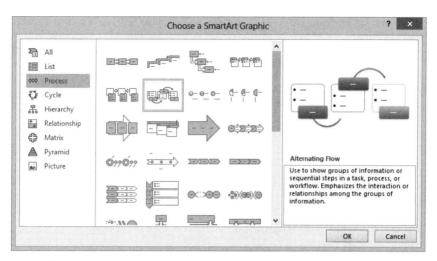

The default Alternating Flow process diagram depicts details of a three-step process.

5   In the **Choose a Smart Art Graphic** dialog box, click **OK** to insert a SmartArt graphic of the selected type into the content pane. It looks similar to the preview graphic, but without the colors and three-dimensional aspects. (You select formatting options later.)

The Text pane opens next to the graphic, and the Design and Format tool tabs appear on the ribbon. You can enter text in the Text pane or directly in the graphic—selecting a graphic element or positioning the cursor within the bulleted list also selects the corresponding element in the graphic or Text pane. The graphic name is shown at the bottom of the Text pane; pointing to it displays a ScreenTip that describes the purpose of the current type of graphic.

TIP You can display or hide the Text pane for any SmartArt graphic by clicking the graphic and then clicking either the Text Pane button in the Create Graphic group on the Design tool tab or the Text Pane tab on the left side of the drawing area.

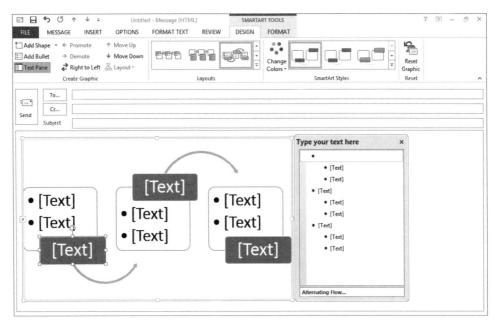

In the Text pane to the right of the graphic, you can build a hierarchical list that transfers content to the graphic.

6   With the first bullet in the **Text** pane active, enter Plan. (If the bullet isn't already active, click the **[Text]** placeholder to the right of it.) As you enter the text, it appears in the leftmost solid blue box in the diagram.

7   Click the **[Text]** placeholder to the right of the first second-level (indented) bullet, and enter Survey current customers. As you enter the text in the pane, the font size of the text in the diagram adjusts to fit the text into the available space.

8   Press the **Down Arrow** key to move to the next second-level bullet, and then enter Survey potential customers.

9   Press **Enter** to create a third second-level bullet in the **Text** pane and in the graphic, and then enter Analyze competition. In the diagram, the font size of all the second-level entries changes to fit the new bullet into the existing shape.

10   In the diagram, click the second solid blue box to select the placeholder, and then enter Define. As you enter the text in the diagram, it also appears in the second first-level bullet in the **Text** pane.

11   In the third solid blue box, enter Design.

12   On the **Design** tool tab, in the **Create Graphic** group, click the **Add Shape** arrow
(not the button) and then, in the list, click **Add Shape After** to display a fourth set of
shapes at the right end of the diagram and a fourth first-level bullet in the **Text** pane.
You can add shapes above, below, before, or after the selected shape, depending on
the diagram layout.

13   In the new solid blue box, enter Develop.

14   In the **Text** pane, click at the end of the word **Develop**, and then press **Enter** to add
a first-level bullet and set of shapes.

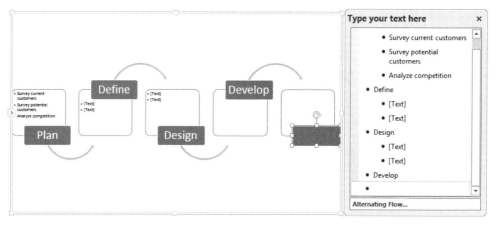

You can easily add to the structure of most SmartArt graphics.

15   In the new first-level bullet, enter Test and then, in the **Text** pane, click the **Close**
button. Notice that at its current size, the text within the diagram is very difficult
to read.

16   On the right side of the diagram, point to the sizing handle (the square). When the
pointer becomes a double-headed arrow, drag the handle to the right until the
diagram is wide enough to accommodate its contents.

   TIP If you prefer to set the width of your graphic to match ours exactly, click the
   Format tool tab and then in the Size group, set the Width to 8.6" without changing
   the Height.

17   On the **Design** tool tab, in the **Layouts** gallery, click the **More** button to display all
the available process diagram layouts.

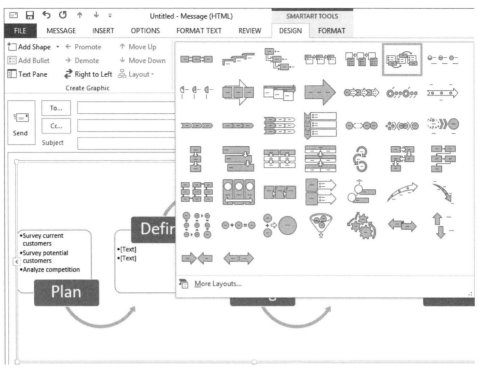

The Layouts gallery displays layouts of only the currently selected diagram type.

18 In the **Layouts** gallery, point to a few icons to preview the effect of the SmartArt layout on your content. Then click the second icon in the second row (**Continuous Block Process**) to change the layout of the existing process diagram.

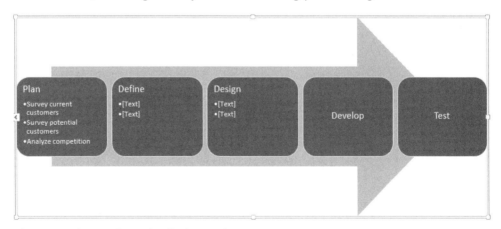

The content is reconfigured to fit the new layout.

19   In the **SmartArt Styles** gallery, click the **More** button to expand the **SmartArt Styles** gallery.

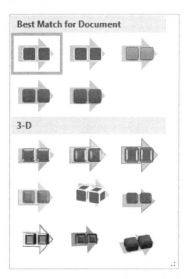

The SmartArt Styles gallery includes two-dimensional and three-dimensional styles.

20   In the **SmartArt Styles** gallery, point to a few of the icons to preview the effect of the style on your graphic. Then in the **3-D** section, click the first icon (**Polished**).

21   In the **SmartArt Styles** group, click the **Change Colors** button to display the **Change Colors** menu. The color schemes displayed in the **Change Colors** gallery are variations of the current theme colors, and they are organized in groups that reflect the six thematic accent colors (and a colorful mix of them). Changing the theme also changes the color schemes in the gallery.

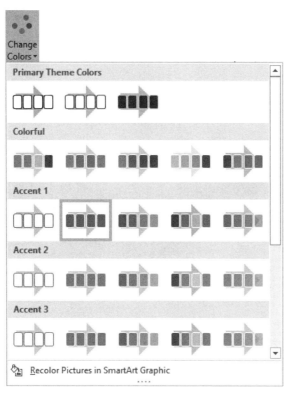

The colors shown in the gallery change to match the colors specified by the active theme.

22   In the **Change Colors** gallery, point to a few of the icons to preview the effect of the color scheme on your graphic. Then in the **Colorful** section, click the second icon (**Colorful Range – Accent Colors 2 to 3**) to format the process diagram with a subtle range of colors.

23   In the message header, enter your email address in the **To** box, and enter SBS Development Process in the **Subject** box. Then send the message to yourself.

24   When you receive the message, first display it in the **Reading Pane**. Notice that although you created a much larger graphic, the entire diagram is visible in the **Reading Pane**.

25   Open the message and then resize the message window. Notice that the SmartArt graphic resizes to fit the message window. Click the SmartArt graphic in the content pane and notice that it is now a static image (a picture). If you open the message from your **Sent Items** folder, you'll find that the same is true of the graphic in that message. You can copy and reuse the picture in other files, such as messages, documents, and presentations.

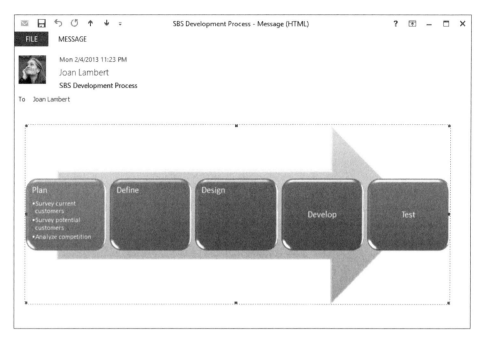

The selected static image in the received message window.

TIP When you forward or reply to the message, the diagram remains a static image, but if you resend the message it becomes an active SmartArt graphic in the outgoing message window.

❌ CLEAN UP Close the message window. Move the SBS Development Process message to the SBS Messages folder, and retain it for use in later exercises.

Changing message settings and delivery options

When you send a message, you can include visual indicators of the importance, sensitivity, or subject category of a message or other Outlook item, flag a message for follow-up, restrict other people from changing or forwarding message content, provide a simple feedback mechanism in the form of voting buttons, and specify message delivery options to fit your needs.

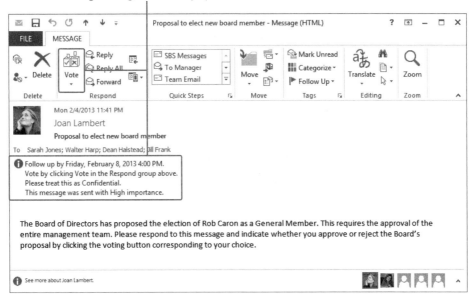

Message settings and delivery options

In the received message, tags are displayed as text on the InfoBar in the message header.

Common message settings and delivery options include the following:

- **Flags and reminders** You can place an outgoing message on your task list, add an informational reminder to it, or set a reminder to appear at a certain time and date, for yourself and for message recipients.

- **Importance** You can indicate the urgency of a message by setting its importance to High or Low. A corresponding banner appears in the message header and, if the Importance field is included in the view, an importance icon appears in the Inbox or other message folder.

- **Sensitivity** You can indicate that a message should be kept private by setting its sensitivity to Confidential, Personal, or Private. No indicator appears in the message folder, but a banner appears in the message header to indicate a sensitivity level other than Normal.

- **Security** If you have a digital ID, you can digitally sign the message; or you can encrypt the contents of the message.

- **Voting options** If you and your message recipients have Microsoft Exchange Server accounts, you can add voting buttons to your messages so that recipients can quickly select from multiple-choice response options.

10

- **Tracking options** You can track messages by requesting delivery receipts and read receipts. These receipts are messages automatically generated by the recipient's email server when it delivers the message to the recipient and when the recipient opens the message.

- **Delivery options** You can have reply messages delivered to an email address other than yours, specify a date and time for the message to be delivered and to expire, and set advanced attachment format and encoding options.

- **Categories** You can assign a message to a color category that will be visible to the recipient if he or she views the message in Outlook.

TIP You can easily sort and group messages by message settings by choosing the message setting in the Arrange By list.

The most commonly used options are available in the Tags group on the Message tab of the message window. You can access other options from the Properties dialog box, which you open by clicking the Tags dialog box launcher.

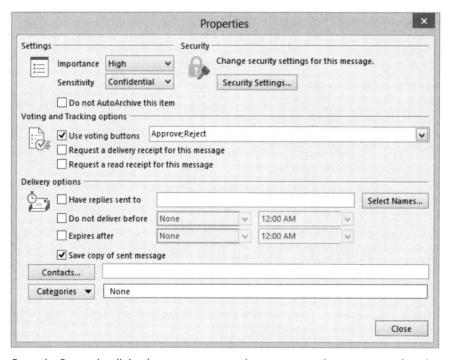

From the Properties dialog box, you can control message security, content, and settings.

You can limit the actions other people can take with messages they receive from you by restricting the message permissions. For example, you can prevent recipients from forwarding or printing the message, copying the message content, or changing the content when they forward or reply to the message. (Restrictions apply also to message attachments.) Within a message window, permission options are available both on the Info page of the Backstage view and in the Permission group on the Options tab.

SEE ALSO For information about digital signatures and for more information about restricting recipients from forwarding, copying, or printing messages you send, see "Increasing email security" in Chapter 12, "Manage email settings."

Key points

- You can format the text and background of your messages, either by choosing individual formatting options and styles or by applying a theme.

- You can automatically insert contact information in email messages by using an electronic signature. You can create different signatures for different purposes and instruct Outlook to insert a specific signature for each email account and message type.

- You can insert many types of images—including photos, screen clippings, and clip art—into an Outlook item and modify the appearance of the inserted image by using commands available from the tool tabs for pictures.

- You can create graphical representations of processes, hierarchies, and other organizational structures by using the SmartArt feature.

- You can create a chart directly in an Outlook item as a graphical representation of data stored in an associated Excel worksheet.

- You can make outgoing messages more useful by setting their properties to communicate information to the message recipient and by setting delivery options so you are informed when the message is received and read.

10

Program management

11 Customize Outlook 397

12 Manage email settings 445

13 Work remotely 479

Chapter at a glance

Personalize

Personalize the Outlook program window,
page 398

Configure

Configure Office and Outlook options,
page 403

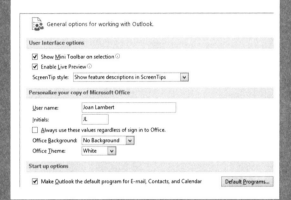

Customize

Customize the Quick Access Toolbar,
page 427

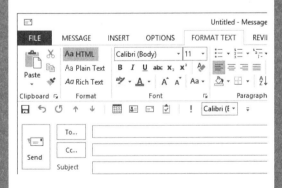

Manage

Manage add-ins,
page 440

Customize Outlook 11

IN THIS CHAPTER, YOU WILL LEARN HOW TO

- Personalize the Outlook program window.

- Configure Office and Outlook options.

- Customize the Quick Access Toolbar.

- Customize the ribbon.

- Manage add-ins.

Microsoft Outlook 2013 is a high-powered information management system. Microsoft has set up the program to function in the way that will be of the most use to the most people, but the fact is that each of us has a different working style and has different needs for our working environment. Fortunately, you can configure many aspects of the appearance and functionality of Outlook 2013 to make it the most efficient platform for the way you work.

To start with the obvious, you can change not only the appearance and arrangement of the elements in the program window, but also their functionality. You can specify the tabs that appear on the ribbon and the groups that appear on the ribbon tabs, and put frequently used commands at your fingertips by adding them to the Quick Access Toolbar.

After that, you can really get "under the hood" and modify many aspects of the way Outlook handles messages, calendar items, contact records, and general operations. You can tailor many aspects of the program to suit the way you work.

In this chapter, you'll first customize the primary program window panes. Next, you'll configure Office and Outlook settings to meet your needs. Then you'll change the commands that appear on the Quick Access Toolbar and on the ribbon. Finally, you'll learn how to work with add-ins.

PRACTICE FILES You don't need any practice files to complete the exercises in this chapter.

Personalizing the Outlook program window

In Chapter 2, "Explore Outlook 2013," we discussed the four primary areas of the Outlook 2013 program window in which you work with Outlook items: the Folder Pane, content area, Reading Pane, and To-Do Bar. Throughout this book you've worked with email messages, appointments, contact records, and tasks in each of these areas and experienced some of the ways in which you can modify the display of the window elements.

You might find that the default arrangement of these areas is ideal for the way you work. But if you're viewing the program window on a low-resolution screen, don't need all the available tools, or would like more space for the main work area, you can easily change the appearance and layout of the workspace of each of the program window elements.

- **Folder Pane** You can tailor this pane to suit your preferences in the following ways:

  - You can minimize or expand the Folder Pane by clicking the Minimize The Folder Pane or Expand The Folder Pane button (the left-facing or right-facing chevron, respectively) at the top of the pane.

  - You can change the width of the Folder Pane by dragging the vertical frame divider to the right or to the left.

- **Module content area** You can display and organize content in this area in many ways. These options are discussed in the chapters that cover individual modules.

- **Reading Pane** You can display this pane on the right side or bottom of the content area, or close it entirely. You can configure the Reading Pane presence for each individual module.

- **To-Do Bar** You can display information from the Calendar, People, or Tasks module on the To-Do Bar, arrange the module content in any order, and change the allocation of space to the module content by dragging the separators. You can increase the width of the To-Do Bar by dragging its left edge (but you can't minimize it). You can turn off the To-Do Bar but must then redisplay the content from each module—you can't turn the populated To-Do Bar on and off as you could in previous versions of Outlook. You can configure the To-Do Bar content and presence for each individual module.

- **People Pane** You can display this pane in its normal or minimized state in message windows and in the Reading Pane, or you can turn it off completely. You configure the People Pane presence for the entire program rather than for individual modules.

You can display or hide any of the workspace elements from the View tab of the ribbon. Your preferences are preserved from session to session. When you restart Outlook, the program window elements will appear the same way they did when you last exited the program.

In this exercise, you'll change the space allocated to the module content area, change the content displayed on the To-Do Bar, and learn how to move the menu bar and move or hide the toolbars.

 SET UP You don't need any practice files to complete this exercise. Display your Outlook Inbox, and then follow the steps.

1. On the **View** tab, in the **People Pane** group, click the **People Pane** button, and then click **Off**, if it's not already selected.

2. In the **Layout** group, click the **To-Do Bar** button, and then click **Off**, if it is not already selected.

3. Click the **Reading Pane** button, and then click **Right**, if it is not already selected.

4. Click the **Folder Pane** button, and ensure that **Normal** and **Favorites** are selected. Then click **Options**.

5. In the **Navigation Options** dialog box, change the **Maximum number of visible items** to **3**, clear the **Compact Navigation** check box, and then click **OK**.

The Navigation Bar changes to a separate element above the status bar and displays only the Mail, Calendar, and People module links.

6. In the upper-right corner of the program window, click the **Ribbon Display Options** button, and then click **Show Tabs** to hide the command area of the ribbon.

7. At the top of the **Folder Pane**, click the **Minimize the Folder Pane** button to contract the **Folder Pane** to display only a vertical bar on the left side of the program window.

11

Buttons on the minimized **Folder Pane** give you one-click access to the folders included in your **Favorites** list.

8   On the minimized **Folder Pane**, click the **All Folders** button to temporarily display the **Folder Pane** content.

You can maximize the content area by minimizing the ribbon and Folder Pane.

9   On the **Navigation Bar**, point to the **Calendar** link to peek at the **Date Navigator** and your upcoming appointments. In the upper-right corner of the **Calendar** peek, click the **Dock the peek** button to display the **To-Do Bar** with the **Calendar** peek pinned at the top.

> **TIP** In Outlook 2013, the Calendar peek displays the Date Navigator for the current month and your appointments for the current day. You can't modify these settings as you could for the Calendar area of the To-Do Bar in previous versions of Outlook.

10   On the **Navigation Bar**, point to the **People** link, and then click the **Dock the peek** button to pin the **People** peek to the **To-Do Bar**.

11   Click the **View** tab to temporarily expand the ribbon. In the **Layout** group, click the **To-Do Bar** button, and then click **Tasks** to pin the **Tasks** peek to the **To-Do Bar**. Notice that each of the module content areas occupies one-third of the **To-Do Bar**.

12   In the **People** area of the **To-Do Bar**, click the **Remove the peek** button (the X). Then drag the separator between the **Calendar** peek and **Tasks** peek to change the space allocated to each.

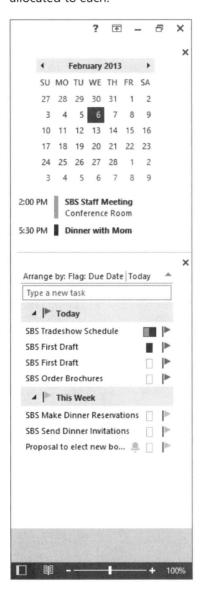

In Outlook 2013, the To-Do Bar can display the three module peeks.

13   Click the **View** tab. In the **Arrangement** group, click the **Message Preview** button, click **3 Lines**, and then in the **Microsoft Outlook** dialog box that appears, click **This folder**.

14   Click the **View** tab. In the **Layout** group, click the **Reading Pane** button, and then click **Bottom** to move the **Reading Pane** from the right side of the content area to the bottom.

15   On the **View** tab, in the **People Pane** group, click the **People Pane** button, and then click **Minimized**.

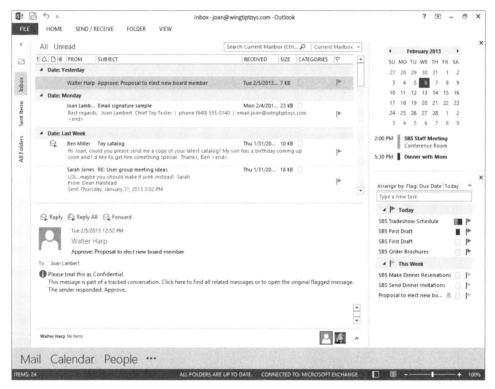

You can modify the layout of the program window to suit the way you work.

✖ CLEAN UP Using the techniques discussed in this topic, rearrange the Outlook window elements to your liking.

TIP Peeks are displayed on the To-Do Bar in the order that you add them. To change the order, remove all peeks other than the one you want on top, and then pin other peeks in the order you want them.

TROUBLESHOOTING Changes you implement might make your Outlook window appear different from those shown in this book. We depict the Outlook window with the Folder Pane open, the compact Navigation Bar, the Reading Pane displayed on the right side of the window, and the To-Do Bar off except when we're using it in an exercise.

Configuring Office and Outlook options

While you are still becoming familiar with Outlook 2013, you might be quite content to work with the default settings (and it's good to do so until you understand the reasons they are as they are). But as you become more experienced, you might want to adjust some of the settings to better suit the way you work.

You can change many of the default program settings from the Outlook Options dialog box, which you open by clicking Options in the left pane of the Backstage view. From this dialog box, you can control the settings and appearance of many Outlook features, including the following:

- Email accounts, functionality, and formatting

- Editorial and archive functions

- The Folder Pane and Reading Pane

- Your calendar, task list, and address books

- The indexing and search functions

- Message flagging

- The content of the Quick Access Toolbar and ribbon

The Outlook Options dialog box is divided into eight pages of function-specific settings, two pages of feature-specific settings (for the ribbon and for the Quick Access Toolbar), and two pages of security-related settings.

The default page of the Outlook Options dialog box is the General page.

11

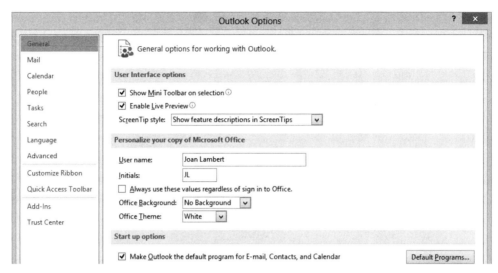

Click any blue information icon in the right pane to display information about the option.

The settings on the General page apply to all Outlook modules. These settings include showing the Mini Toolbar when you select text, enabling live previews of gallery options, and setting the ScreenTip style. In addition, you can specify your user information (name and initials) and preferred background and theme for all Office programs on this page.

TIP You can't set individual user information, backgrounds, or themes for individual Office programs running under the same user profile.

Configuring Mail module options

Many of the settings that users commonly modify are available on the Mail page of the Outlook Options dialog box. These include settings for composing original messages and responses; receiving and reading messages; cleaning up conversations; saving, sending, and tracking messages; and default message format options.

Outlook includes a selection of options so that you can manage your email most effectively. To avoid losing your work, you can choose to have Outlook save messages you have created but not yet sent. When new messages arrive, you can choose to have Outlook alert you by playing a sound, briefly changing the pointer to an envelope icon, showing an envelope icon in the notification area, or any combination of these effects. You can also set default options for sending a message. For example, if you are concerned about privacy, you might choose to set the sensitivity of all new messages to Private.

The options on the Mail page are divided into 11 sections. Because this is where you'll make most of your changes, we'll take a look at each of these sections.

Compose messages

The Compose Messages section of the Mail page includes options for changing the behavior of Outlook while you're creating a new message. These options control the way Outlook composes and proofs text; your email signatures; and your default fonts, stationery, and email themes.

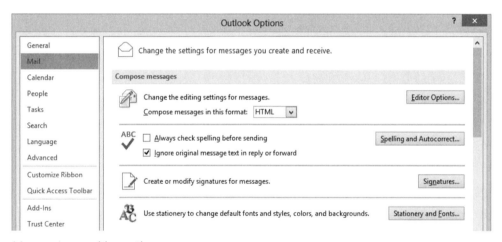

Message composition options.

Clicking either Editor Options or Spelling And Autocorrect in the Compose Messages section displays the Proofing page of the Editor Options dialog box. From the Proofing page, you can set AutoCorrect options to specify how Outlook will correct and format the content of your messages as you type them, and customize the spelling and grammar-checking settings.

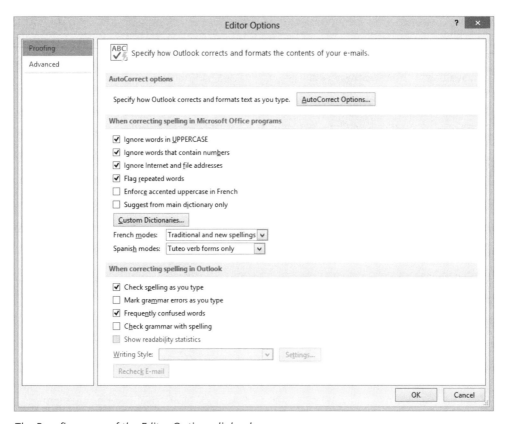

The Proofing page of the Editor Options dialog box.

On the Advanced page of the Editor Options dialog box, you can control the way Outlook works with text.

- In the Editing Options area of this page, you can turn on or off advanced editing features, such as how Outlook selects and moves text, whether to track formatting changes, and whether Overtype mode is available.

- In the Cut, Copy, and Paste area, you can specify whether Outlook will apply source or destination formatting to text copied within a message, between messages, and from other programs. You can also set options for smart cut and paste (whether to automatically add and remove spaces as needed) and the Paste Options button (whether it appears after a paste operation).

- In the Display area, you can set whether measurements are shown in inches, centimeters, millimeters, points, or picas; whether pixels are shown for HTML features; whether ScreenTips display keyboard shortcuts; and whether character positioning is optimized for layout rather than readability.

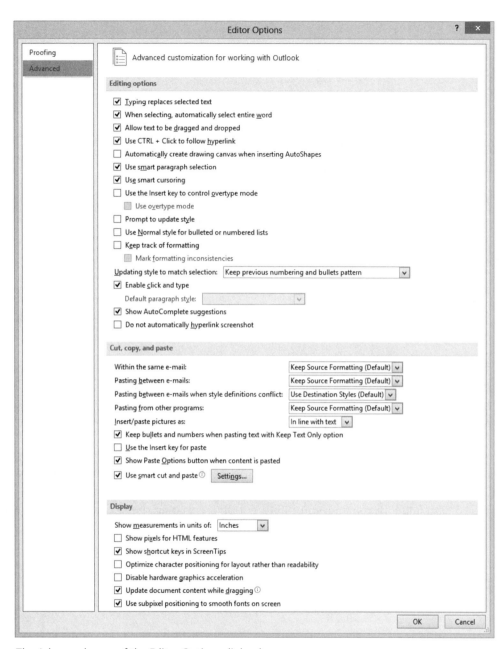

The Advanced page of the Editor Options dialog box.

SEE ALSO For information about email signatures, stationery, and fonts, see "Personalizing the appearance of message text" in Chapter 10, "Enhance message content."

Outlook panes

The Outlook Panes section of the Mail page includes only the Reading Pane button, which opens the Reading Pane dialog box.

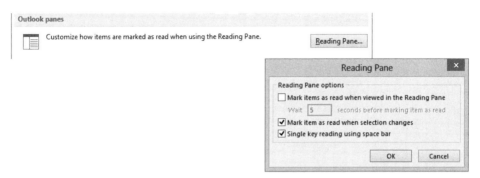

You can control the way you navigate through items in the Reading Pane and whether items displayed in the Reading Pane are marked as read.

You can display the Reading Pane in any Outlook module. It is most useful in the Mail module, of course, but can also come in handy in certain views of other modules.

By default, Outlook does not mark a message as read when you preview it in the Reading Pane, but does so when you select another message. You can change these default settings by selecting or clearing the Mark Items As Read When Viewed In The Reading Pane and Mark Item As Read When Selection Changes check boxes in the Reading Pane dialog box.

With the Single Key Reading feature, which is turned on by default, you can move up or down in the Reading Pane one page at a time by pressing the Spacebar. When you reach the end of a message, pressing the Spacebar again displays the first page of the next message. If you find it distracting, you can turn it off by clearing the Single Key Reading Using Space Bar check box in the Reading Pane dialog box.

SEE ALSO For information about working in the Reading Pane, see "Viewing messages and message attachments" in Chapter 3, "Send and receive email messages."

Message arrival

The Message Arrival section of the Mail page includes options for controlling the way Outlook notifies you of an incoming message.

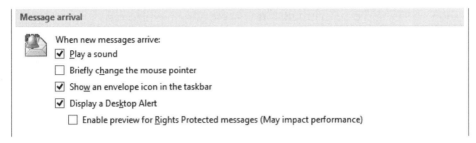

Message arrival options.

SEE ALSO For information about taskbar icons and desktop alerts, see the sidebar "Working with new mail notifications" in Chapter 3, "Send and receive email messages."

Conversation Clean Up

The Conversation Clean Up section of the Mail page includes options for the Clean Up command. If you don't want the command to delete redundant messages, you can specify a folder in which the command will place the redundant messages. (You could then review the contents of the folder and delete the redundant messages after verifying that they are, in fact, redundant.) You can also specify the types of messages that the Clean Up Conversation command moves and keeps.

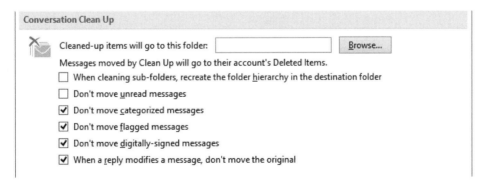

Conversation clean-up options.

SEE ALSO For information about managing conversations, see "Working with Conversation view" in Chapter 7, "Organize your Inbox."

11

Replies and forwards

The Replies And Forwards section of the Mail page includes options for managing the content of response messages. You can choose to close the original message window when you respond to a message, to insert your name or some other identifier before your response text, and whether and how to include original message text in a response.

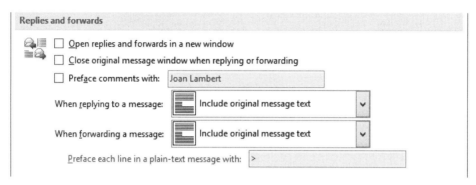

Options for replying to and forwarding messages.

When forwarding a message, you can attach the original message (as a separate message) or include the original message text in your response and optionally indent it or indent it and insert a vertical line to the left of the original message text block. When replying to a message, you have all the same options and additionally can choose to not include the original message text in your response.

SEE ALSO For information about replying to and forwarding messages, see "Responding to messages" in Chapter 3, "Send and receive email messages."

Save messages

The Save Messages section of the Mail page includes options for saving temporary copies of messages that have not yet been sent, message replies from a location other than the Inbox, the original versions of messages you have forwarded, and messages you have sent.

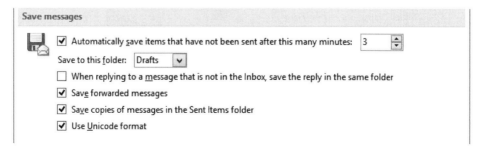

Options for saving messages.

By default, Outlook saves the first draft of a message three minutes after you begin composing the message, and resaves the message every three minutes thereafter. You can choose to save message drafts as frequently as once per minute or as infrequently as every 99 minutes, or choose to turn off the message draft saving feature.

The default location for saved message drafts is the Drafts folder, which is a top-level mailbox folder that appears in the Folder Pane at the same level as your Inbox. You can alternatively save message drafts in your Inbox, in the Sent Items folder, or in the Outbox.

SEE ALSO For information about message drafts, see "Creating and sending messages" in Chapter 3, "Send and receive email messages."

Send messages

The Send Messages section of the Mail page includes options for composing and sending messages, in addition to options for resolving names against known email addresses, handling meeting requests after you respond, and managing the Auto-Complete List.

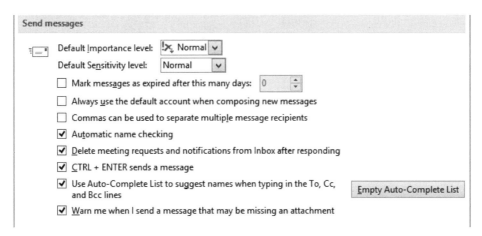

Message sending options.

An important option to note in this section is the Commas Can Be Used To Separate Multiple Message Recipients option. Until you select this check box, you must separate email addresses in the To, Cc, and Bcc boxes by using semicolons.

SEE ALSO For information about importance and sensitivity level settings, see "Changing message settings and delivery options" in Chapter 10, "Enhance message content."

11

MailTips

From the MailTips section of the Mail page, you can control the display of MailTips, which are server-generated messages that appear in the header of a message composition window to notify you of various conditions that apply to an outgoing message.

MailTips are an extremely useful feature of Microsoft Exchange Server. First introduced in Exchange Server 2010, MailTips are designed to help you when sending a message would result in a situation that you might want to avoid. For example, MailTips can warn you when you're composing a message to a sender who is currently out of the office, has a full mailbox, or is external to your organization. MailTips can also alert you when you're composing a message to a large distribution group, when a message is too large for you to send or for the recipient to receive, and when you reply to all recipients of a message that you were Bcc'd on.

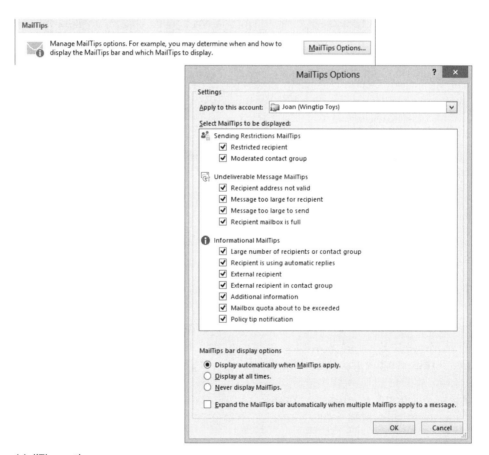

MailTips options.

Your Exchange administrator can turn specific MailTips on and off, and can also configure custom MailTips for your organization. MailTips are displayed for your information only; they don't stop you from sending an email message, but do let you know if the message might not reach the intended recipient (or might reach more recipients than you intend).

TIP Policy Tips are a feature of Exchange Server 2013 that can prevent you from sending messages that violate your company's security policies. For example, Policy Tips can prevent you from forwarding messages that contain bank account numbers, credit card numbers, driver's license numbers, or taxpayer identification numbers to external recipients. Your Exchange administrator can configure Policy Tips that notify you of potentially sensitive information in an outgoing message, require you to provide a business justification for sending the message, or prevent you from sending the message. Policy Tips are managed by your Exchange administrator and can't be configured from within Outlook.

MailTips settings are specific to each Exchange account you have configured Outlook to connect to. You set your MailTips preferences for each account by selecting that account in the Apply To This Account list at the top of the dialog box.

Tracking

The Tracking section of the Mail page includes options for requesting notifications when a message that you send is delivered to a recipient and when a message is marked by the recipient as read; and options for processing notification requests attached to messages that you receive. This section also includes options for processing responses you receive to meeting requests and voting requests that you send.

Tracking

Delivery and read receipts help provide confirmation that messages were successfully received. Not all e-mail servers and applications support sending receipts.

For all messages sent, request:

☐ Delivery receipt confirming the message was delivered to the recipient's e-mail server

☐ Read receipt confirming the recipient viewed the message

For any message received that includes a read receipt request:

○ Always send a read receipt

○ Never send a read receipt

◉ Ask each time whether to send a read receipt

☑ Automatically process meeting requests and responses to meeting requests and polls

☑ Automatically update original sent item with receipt information

☐ Update tracking information, and then delete responses that don't contain comments

☐ After updating tracking information, move receipt to: Deleted Items   Browse...

Message tracking options.

Delivery receipts can be a useful tool when you send an important message and need to know whether it's reached its intended recipient. (However, not all types of email accounts support all types of receipts.) When you receive a message that has a read receipt request attached, Outlook prompts you to confirm whether you want to send a read receipt. You can make this choice for each individual message or select the Never Send A Read Receipt option to refuse all read receipt requests.

TIP Be cautious when approving read receipt requests, because some mass-mailing companies use these to determine whether an email address is active.

Message format

The Message Format section of the Mail page includes options for specifying how Outlook displays your message content on the screen and the format in which Outlook sends messages outside of your organization.

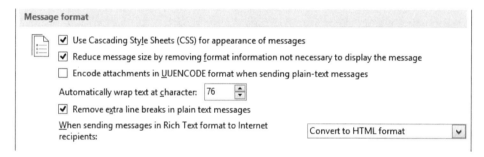

Message format options.

It's unlikely that you'll need to change any of these options, but they are available in the event that you want to.

Other

The Other section of the Mail page includes options for displaying the Paste Options button, allowing the use of Microsoft InfoPath forms, moving among open messages, and expanding conversations when navigating through the Inbox by using the keyboard. You can also specify what occurs when you move or delete an open item. Options include opening the previous or next item in the folder, or returning to the folder without opening another item.

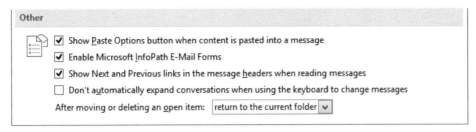

Other

☑ Show <u>P</u>aste Options button when content is pasted into a message
☑ Enable Microsoft <u>I</u>nfoPath E-Mail Forms
☑ Show Next and Previous links in the message <u>h</u>eaders when reading messages
☐ Don't a<u>u</u>tomatically expand conversations when using the keyboard to change messages
After moving or deleting an open item: return to the current folder ☑

Options in the Other section.

Configuring Calendar module options

Options on the Calendar page control settings for displaying and managing Outlook calendars, and for scheduling appointments and resources.

Many Outlook users will want to configure the days and times that constitute the work week. You do this in the Work Time section of the Calendar page. The times you specify as work hours (on the days you specify as work days) are available in Outlook for other users to schedule meetings with you. Specifying the first day of your work week controls the Work Week view of the calendar.

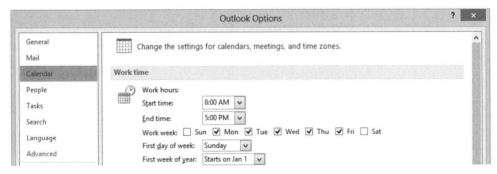

You can select all seven days as work days if necessary.

In the Calendar Options section, you can set the default reminder time for new appointments and meetings, control the Propose New Times settings, add the holidays of many countries and religions to your calendar, specify the level of detail that co-workers (as a group and individually) can see when viewing your availability, configure an additional calendar, control the format of external meeting requests, and control the display of the reminder icon for appointments and meetings.

SEE ALSO For information about managing holidays on the calendar, see the sidebar "Adding national and religious holidays to your calendar" in Chapter 5, "Manage scheduling."

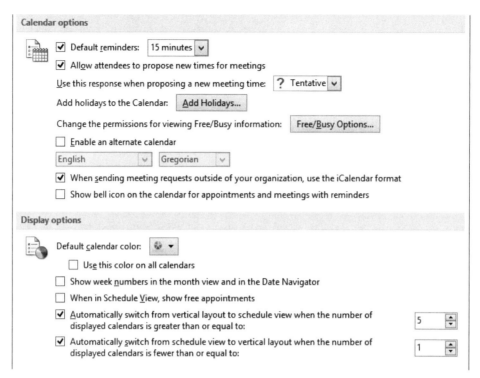

The Calendar Options section of the Calendar page includes a diverse array of options.

The Display Options section includes options for configuring the appearance and functionality of calendars. Of note in this section are the limits for the minimum and maximum number of calendars that can be displayed in Schedule view.

The Time Zone section includes options for displaying a label at the top of the time column in Day view, Work Week view, and Week view, and for managing a second time zone.

SEE ALSO For information about time zones, see "Configuring time zones" in Chapter 8, "Manage your calendar."

The Scheduling Assistant section of the Calendar page includes options for managing the display of information on the Scheduling Assistant page of a meeting window. (The Scheduling Assistant is available only for Exchange accounts.)

SEE ALSO For information about using the Scheduling Assistant, see "Scheduling meetings" in Chapter 5, "Manage scheduling."

In the Automatic Accept Or Decline section, you can click the Auto Accept/Decline button, which opens a dialog box in which you can configure Outlook to process meeting requests without your input.

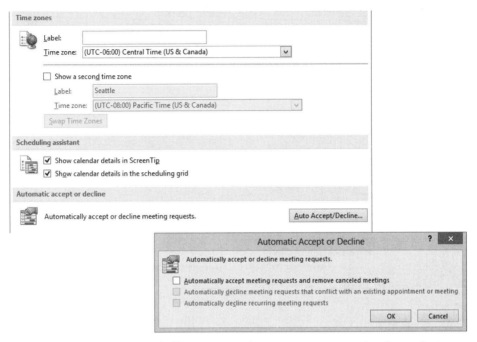

When you choose to automatically accept meeting requests, you can also choose the types of meeting requests to decline.

In the Weather section, you can control whether the Weather Bar (a new feature in Outlook 2013) is displayed in the calendar header, and whether it shows temperatures in Celsius or in Fahrenheit.

You configure the location for which the weather is displayed from the Calendar module.

11

Configuring People module options

Options on the People page control settings for creating and organizing contact records, displaying a second contact index (in Arabic, Cyrillic, Greek, Thai, or Vietnamese), and displaying pictures in Outlook items and in the People peek.

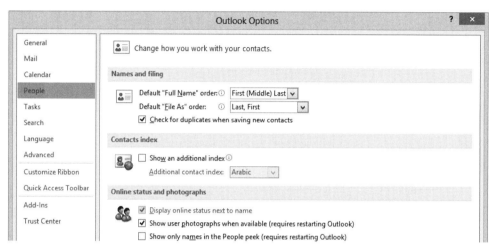

The People page of the Outlook Options dialog box.

SEE ALSO For information about working in the People module and with contact records, see Chapter 4, "Store and access contact information," and Chapter 9, "Manage contact records."

Configuring Tasks module options

Options on the Tasks page control settings for setting a task reminder time, managing assigned tasks, displaying overdue and completed tasks, and setting the default due date for flagged items. In addition, you can allocate a specific number of hours per day and per week that are available for working on tasks.

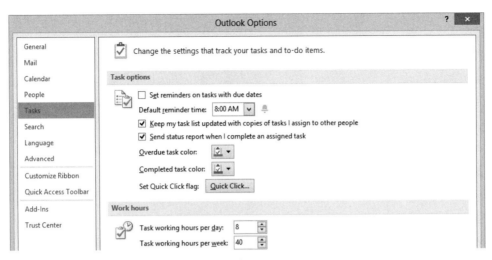

The Tasks page of the Outlook Options dialog box.

SEE ALSO For information about managing task items, see Chapter 6, "Track tasks."

Configuring search options

Options on the Search page control the scope of standard searches and the way Outlook displays search results.

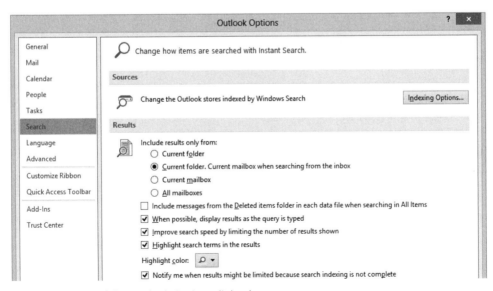

The Search page of the Outlook Options dialog box.

You can click the Indexing Options button in the Sources section of the Search page, to access options for controlling the indexing scope and advanced options.

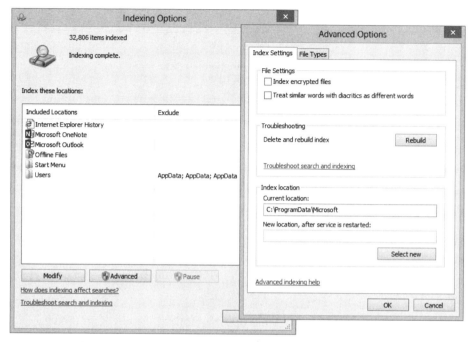

You can modify the scope of items being indexed to exclude specific folders and programs.

TROUBLESHOOTING If you experience significant trouble with the Outlook search feature, you might find that you need to rebuild the index. You can do so from the Advanced Options dialog box.

SEE ALSO For information about Outlook search, see "Quickly locating messages" in Chapter 7, "Organize your Inbox."

Configuring language options

Options on the Language page control the dictionaries used by Outlook when it checks the spelling and grammar of message content, in addition to controlling language options for button labels, tab names, Help content, and ScreenTips. To use a language other than the standard Windows language, you must install a language pack. Language packs are available for download from *office.microsoft.com* and might also be supplied to you through Windows Update.

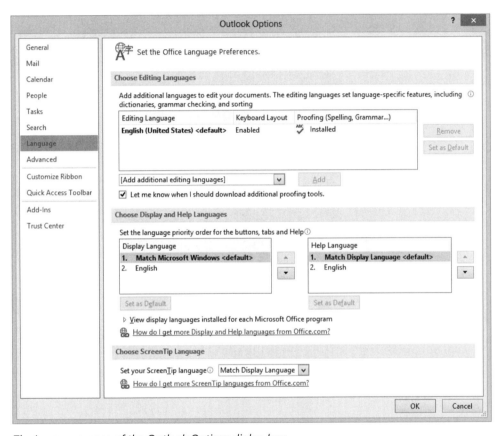

The Language page of the Outlook Options dialog box.

Configuring advanced options

Options on the Advanced page control settings for customizing a wide variety of standard Outlook actions and responses. All the settings that didn't fit into another category are available on this page, and that includes many of the settings that you will likely want to configure.

The Outlook Panes section of the Advanced page includes options for customizing the Navigation Bar and Reading Pane.

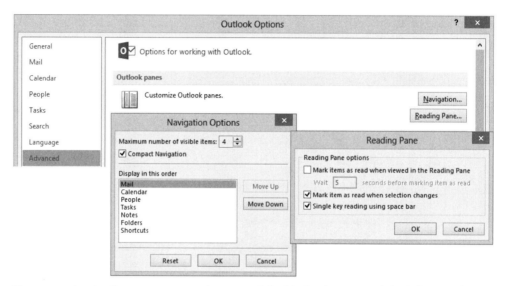

You can customize the appearance and content of the Navigation Bar and the behavior of the Reading Pane.

TIP In Outlook 2010, you could change the size of the font in the Folder Pane from that program's equivalent of the Navigation Options dialog box. That option is not available in Outlook 2013.

The Outlook Start And Exit section includes options for setting the default folder (the folder you first see when you start Outlook) and for emptying the Deleted Items folders (of all configured accounts) when you exit Outlook. Note that this option is not turned on by default. If you need to manage the size of your mailbox, selecting this option is a good starting point.

From the AutoArchive section, you can open the AutoArchive dialog box. In this dialog box, you can configure automatic archival operations separate from those that might be managed by your organization's Exchange administrator. The AutoArchive feature is turned off by default.

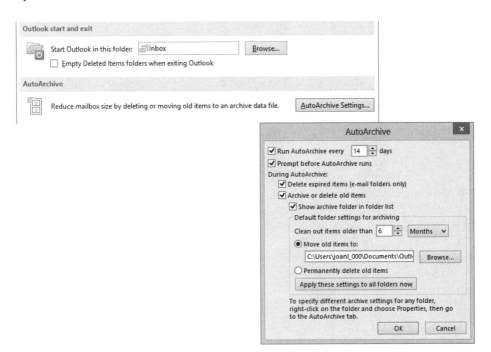

You can specify the frequency, actions, and locations for archiving Outlook items.

11

From the Reminders section, you can configure the display of task reminders and the accompanying audio signal.

From the Export section of the Advanced page, you can start the Import And Export wizard, with which you can move information between Outlook and other programs.

SEE ALSO For information about the Import And Export wizard, see "Importing and exporting contact records" in Chapter 9, "Manage contact records."

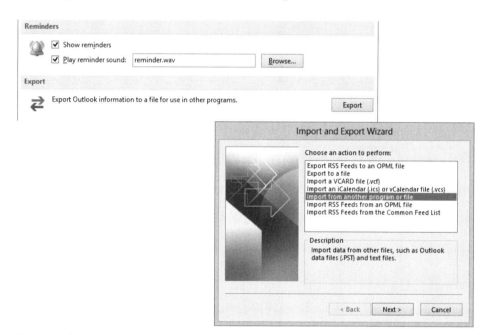

You can select an alternative sound to remind you of upcoming appointments.

You can use Outlook 2013 as an RSS feed reader; feeds that you subscribe to appear in the RSS Feeds folder. In the RSS Feeds section of the Advanced page, you can configure settings for the display and synchronization of RSS feeds.

From the Send And Receive section of the Advanced page, you can configure options for synchronizing Outlook with email servers when online and offline.

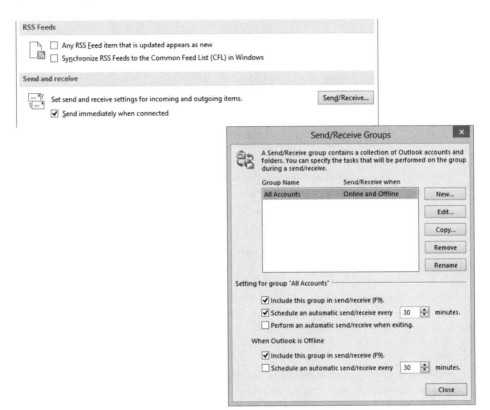

You can configure the way in which Outlook handles RSS feed content.

SEE ALSO For information about working in the Send/Receive Groups dialog box, see "Managing download options for slow connections" in Chapter 13, "Work remotely."

The Developers and Display sections of the Advanced page include options that will probably be used only by advanced Outlook users. The International Options section includes options for using English message flags and headers when working in another language, setting encoding for outgoing messages and business cards, managing international domain names in email addresses, and combining non-Latin and English characters in email messages and addresses.

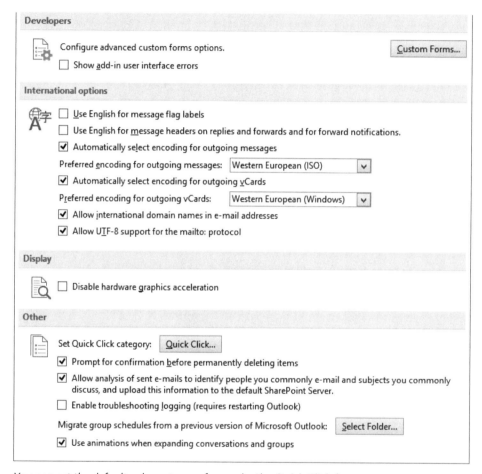

You can set the default color category for use by the Quick Click feature.

The Other section of the Advanced page includes useful options for setting the default color category and confirming the permanent deletion of items. From this section, you can also import group schedules that you created in a previous version of Outlook.

Customizing the Quick Access Toolbar

The commands you use to control Outlook are available from the ribbon, located at the top of the program window and in each Outlook item window. As you use Outlook, you will become familiar with the locations of the commands you use most frequently. To save time, you can place frequently used commands on the Quick Access Toolbar, which is located, by default, in the upper-left corner of the program window. To save even more time, you can move the Quick Access Toolbar from its default position above the ribbon to below the ribbon, so your pointer has less distance to travel from the content you're working with to the command you want to invoke.

TIP If you upgraded to Outlook 2013 from an earlier version of Outlook, as you use the program, you might identify a few commands that no longer seem to be available. Some of the lesser-used features have been removed from the user interface, but the code for the features is still part of the program. If you want to use one of these missing features, or any command that is not easy to get to, you can make it a part of your Outlook working environment by adding it to the ribbon or to the Quick Access Toolbar. You can find a list of all the commands that do not appear on the ribbon but are still available in Outlook by displaying the Customize Ribbon or Quick Access Toolbar page of the Outlook Options dialog box and then clicking Commands Not In The Ribbon in the Choose Commands From list.

In the program window, the Quick Access Toolbar displays the Send/Receive button and the Undo button. In the individual item windows, the Quick Access Toolbar displays the Save, Undo, Redo, Previous, and Next buttons.

You can add commands to the Quick Access Toolbar in three ways:

- From the Customize Quick Access Toolbar menu that appears when you click the button at the right end of the Quick Access Toolbar. Some of the most common commands, including the popular Quick Print command, are available from this list.

- By right-clicking a command on the ribbon and then clicking Add To Quick Access Toolbar. You can add any type of command this way; you can even add a drop-down list of options or gallery of thumbnails.

11

- From the Quick Access Toolbar page of the Outlook Options dialog box. On this page, you can customize the Quick Access Toolbar in the following ways:

  - You can define a custom Quick Access Toolbar for all documents, or you can define a custom Quick Access Toolbar for a specific document.

  - You can add any command from any group of any tab, including tool tabs, to the Quick Access Toolbar.

  - You can display a separator between different types of buttons.

  - You can move commands around on the Quick Access Toolbar until they are in the order you want.

  - You can reset the Quick Access Toolbar to its default configuration.

  TIP The settings on the Quick Access Toolbar page of the Outlook Options dialog box apply to the program or to the item window, depending on where you were working when you displayed the page.

If you never use more than a few buttons, you can add those buttons to the Quick Access Toolbar and then hide the ribbon by double-clicking the active tab or by clicking the Minimize The Ribbon button. Only the Quick Access Toolbar and ribbon tab names remain visible. You can temporarily redisplay the ribbon by clicking the tab you want to view. You can permanently redisplay the ribbon by double-clicking any tab or by clicking the Expand The Ribbon button.

As you add buttons to the Quick Access Toolbar, it expands to accommodate them. If you add many buttons, it might become difficult to view the text in the title bar, or all the buttons on the Quick Access Toolbar might not be visible, defeating the purpose of adding them. To resolve this problem, you can move the Quick Access Toolbar below the ribbon by clicking the Customize Quick Access Toolbar button and then clicking Show Below The Ribbon.

TIP Even though most commands are now available on the ribbon, you can still invoke many commands by using keyboard shortcuts. For more information, see "Keyboard shortcuts" at the end of this book.

In this exercise, you'll add and organize buttons on the Quick Access Toolbar that is shown in message composition windows.

SET UP You don't need any practice files to complete this exercise. Display your Outlook Inbox, and then follow the steps.

1   On the **Home** tab, in the **New** group, click the **New Email** button to open a message composition window. Notice the buttons that are displayed by default on the **Quick Access Toolbar**.

Only the Save button is active at this time.

2   At the right end of the **Quick Access Toolbar**, click the **Customize Quick Access Toolbar** button.

The Customize Quick Access Toolbar menu displays a list of frequently used commands that you can add to the toolbar.

11

3   On the **Customize Quick Access Toolbar** menu, click **High Importance** to add the command to the toolbar.

4   On the **Customize Quick Access Toolbar** menu, click **More Commands**.

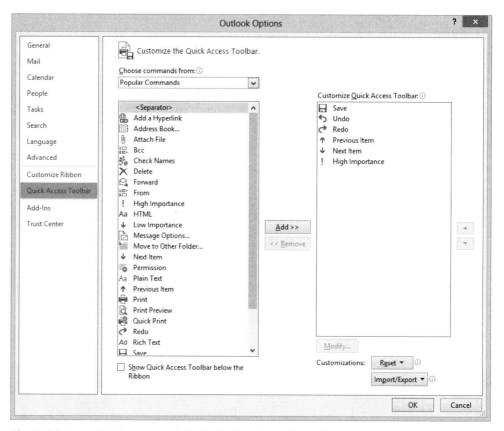

The Quick Access Toolbar page of the Outlook Options dialog box displays available commands on the left and current commands on the right.

5   In the **Choose commands from** list, click **All Commands**. All the available commands, including those not shown on the ribbon, appear in the available commands list.

TIP In some cases, multiple instances of a command appear in the All Commands list; these correspond to the locations in which the command appears within the program. Pointing to a command displays the command location in a ScreenTip. Commands that appear on tool tabs and commands that don't appear on any tab are also available from this list.

TIP You can display only those commands that aren't shown on the ribbon by clicking Commands Not In The Ribbon in the Choose Commands From list.

6   Scroll down the list of available commands to locate the **New Appointment** command. Click the command, and then click **Add**.

7   Double-click the **New Contact**, **New Email**, and **New Task** commands to add them to the **Quick Access Toolbar**.

8   In the **Customize Quick Access Toolbar** pane, click **Next Item**. Then scroll to the top of the **Choose commands from** pane, and double-click **<Separator>** to set off the original toolbar commands from those you've added.

9   In the **Customize Quick Access Toolbar** pane, click **High Importance**. Then to the right of the pane, click the **Move Down** button (the down arrow) four times to move the command to the end of the list.

10 Repeat step 8 to add a separator after the **New Task** command so that the commands related to creating new items are in their own group.

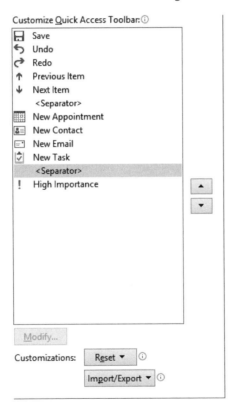

You can move and group commands on the Quick Access Toolbar.

11 In the **Outlook Options** dialog box, click **OK**.

12 Notice that the **Quick Access Toolbar** of the open message window now includes the default buttons and the **New Appointment**, **New Contact**, **New Email**, and **New Task** buttons, separated by a line.

You can now create a new Outlook item with a single click while composing a message, or mark the message as urgent when the ribbon is hidden.

13 Close the message composition window. (Don't save your changes if Outlook prompts you to do so.) Notice that there has been no change to the **Quick Access Toolbar** in the Outlook program window. It still displays only the **Send/Receive** and **Undo** buttons.

14 Open a new message composition window and notice that it has your modified **Quick Access Toolbar**.

15 Click the **Customize Quick Access Toolbar** button and then, at the bottom of the menu, click **Show Below the Ribbon**.

16 Click to position the cursor in the content pane. On the **Format Text** tab, in the **Font** group, right-click the **Font** arrow, and then click **Add to Quick Access Toolbar**.

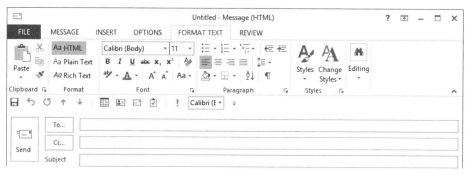

When positioned below the ribbon, the Quick Access Toolbar can host many commands without interfering with the title bar.

17   From the message composition window, display the **Quick Access Toolbar** page of the **Outlook Options** dialog box. In the **Customizations** area, click **Reset**, and then click **Reset only Quick Access Toolbar**.

18   In the **Reset Customizations** message box, click **Yes** to return the **Quick Access Toolbar** to its default contents. Then click **OK** to close the **Outlook Options** dialog box. The **Quick Access Toolbar** now displays only the default buttons for the message window, but is still located below the ribbon.

✖ CLEAN UP Reposition the Quick Access Toolbar if you want to, by clicking Show Above The Ribbon on the Customize The Quick Access Toolbar menu.

Customizing the ribbon

Even if Outlook 2013 is the first version of the program you've worked with, by now you'll be accustomed to working with commands represented as buttons on the ribbon. The ribbon was designed to make all the commonly used commands visible so that people could more easily discover the full potential of the program. But many people use Outlook to perform the same set of tasks all the time, and for them, seeing buttons (or even entire groups of buttons) that they never use is just another form of clutter.

SEE ALSO For information about minimizing and expanding the ribbon, see "Personalizing the Outlook program window" earlier in this chapter.

Would you prefer to display fewer commands, not more? Or would you prefer to display more specialized groups of commands? Well, you can customize the ribbon in both ways, from the Customize Ribbon page of the Outlook Options dialog box.

11

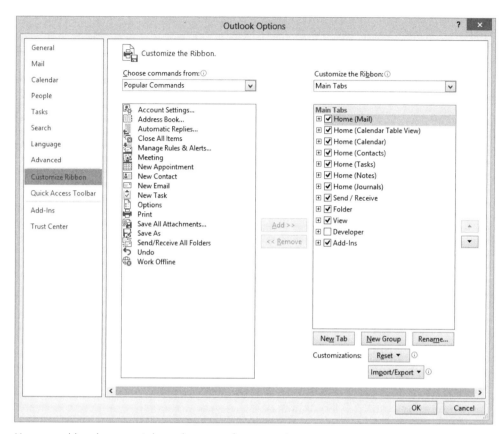

You can add and remove tabs and groups of commands.

On this page, you can customize the ribbon in the following ways:

- You can hide an entire tab.

- You can remove a group of commands from a tab. (The group is not removed from the program, only from the tab.)

- You can move or copy a group of commands to another tab.

- You can create a custom group on any tab and then add commands to it. (You cannot add commands to a predefined group.)

- You can create a custom tab. For example, you might want to do this if you use only a few commands from each tab and you find it inefficient to switch between them.

You can experiment with the ribbon to come up with the configuration that best suits the way you work. If at any point you find that your new ribbon is harder to work with rather than easier, you can easily reset everything back to the default configuration.

IMPORTANT Although customizing the default ribbon content might seem like a great way of making the program yours, we don't recommend doing so. A great deal of research has been done about the way that people use the commands in each program, and the ribbon has been organized to reflect the results of that research. If you modify the default ribbon settings, you might end up inadvertently hiding or moving commands that you need. Instead, consider the Quick Access Toolbar to be the command area that you customize and make your own. If you add all the commands you use frequently to the Quick Access Toolbar, you can hide the ribbon and have extra vertical space for document display (this is most convenient when working on a smaller device). Or if you really want to customize the ribbon, do so by gathering your most frequently used commands on a custom tab, and leave the others alone.

In this exercise, you'll turn off tabs, remove groups, create a custom group, and add a command to the new group. Then you'll create a tab and move predefined groups of buttons to it. Finally, you'll reset the ribbon to its default state.

 SET UP You don't need any practice files to complete this exercise. Display your Outlook Inbox, and then follow the steps.

1   Right-click a blank area of the **Home** tab, and then click **Customize the Ribbon** to display the **Customize Ribbon** page of the **Outlook Options** dialog box.

2   With **Home (Mail)** selected in the **Customize the Ribbon** pane on the right side of the dialog box, click the **New Tab** button to add a custom tab.

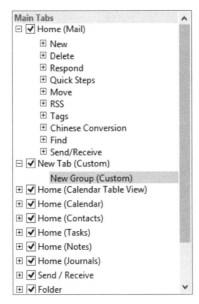

The new custom tab includes one custom group.

3 Click **New Tab (Custom)**, and then click the **Rename** button. In the **Rename** dialog box, replace **New Tab** with My Tab, and then click **OK**.

4 Click **New Group (Custom)**, and then click the **Rename** button to open a **Rename** dialog box that includes icons.

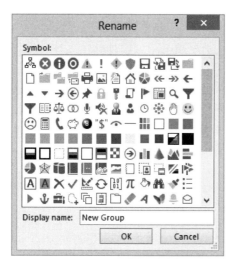

The icon you choose for your group is displayed on the group button when the ribbon is not wide enough to display the group.

5 In the **Rename** dialog box, click an icon that you like (we chose the happy face) and replace **New Group** with Housekeeping. Then click **OK**.

Now we'll add some commands to the custom group.

6 In the **Choose commands from** list, click **File Tab** to show only the commands that are available in the **Backstage** view, which you display by clicking the **File** tab.

7 In the list of available commands, click **Empty Deleted Items**. Then click the **Add** button.

8 Repeat step 7 to add the **Mailbox Cleanup** command to the custom group.

9   In the **Choose commands from** list, click **Main Tabs**, expand the **Folder** entry to display the groups of commands on that tab, and then expand the **Clean Up** entry to display the commands in that group.

You can add commands to a custom group but not to a predefined group.

10   In the **Clean Up** list of commands, click **Recover Deleted Items**. Then click the **Add** button to add the command to the custom group.

11   In the **Folder** list of groups, click the **New** group. Then click the **Add** button to add the entire group of commands to the custom tab.

12   In the **Customize the Ribbon** pane, in the **Home (Mail)** folder, click the **Move** group. Then click the **Remove** button.

11

13   Scroll to the end of the list, and clear the check boxes adjacent to the **Send/Receive** and **Folder** folders. Then in the **Outlook Options** dialog box, click **OK**.

14   Click the **My Tab** tab to display the groups of commands you added to it. Notice that the **New** group displays only the commands that apply to the **Mail** module.

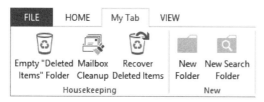

The customized ribbon displays only the File, Home, My Tab, and View tabs, and the Move group is missing from the Home tab.

15   Display the **Customize Ribbon** page of the **Outlook Options** dialog box. In the lower-right corner, click **Reset**, and then click **Reset all customizations**. Then in the message box asking you to confirm that you want to delete all ribbon and **Quick Access Toolbar** customizations, click **Yes**.

16   In the **Outlook Options** dialog box, click **OK** to restore the default ribbon configuration.

❌ CLEAN UP Make any modifications to the ribbon that you want before continuing.

Customizing the status bar

The status bar is a horizontal bar located at the bottom of the program window. It displays information about the contents of the currently displayed folder, overdue reminders, send/receive status, online status, and other information. At its right end, the status bar displays a set of zoom controls with which you can control the magnification of content in the Reading Pane and in item windows.

Almost all the available information is shown on the status bar by default; the only information not shown is quota information that helps you to track how much of your available mailbox storage space is currently being used.

To change the information displayed on the status bar:

1   Right-click an empty area of the status bar to display the **Customize Status Bar** menu.

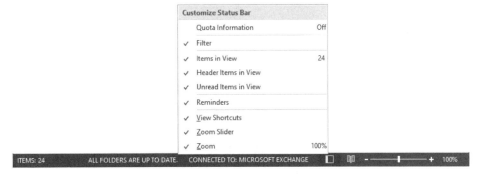

A check mark indicates information that is currently displayed on the status bar.

2   Click an item on the menu to add it to or remove it from the status bar.

Some of the status bar controls are active, meaning that you can click them to display additional information. For example, when the Reminders item appears on the status bar, it means that you have overdue reminders. Clicking the Reminders item opens the Reminders window in which you can see the current reminders.

11

Managing add-ins

Add-ins are utilities that add specialized functionality to a program (but aren't full-fledged programs themselves). Outlook uses COM add-ins, which use the Component Object Model. You can view and manage installed add-ins from the Add-Ins page of the Outlook Options dialog box.

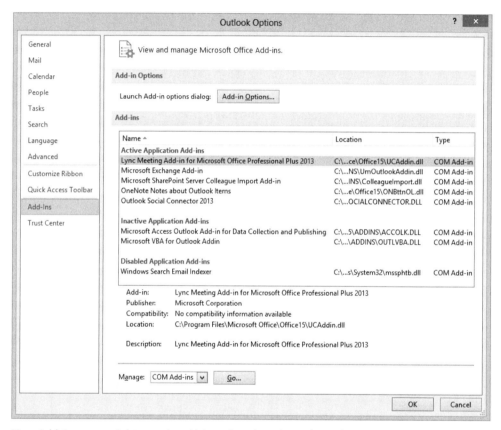

Your Add-Ins page might contain add-ins other than those shown here.

Outlook 2013 installs several add-ins based on the type of interaction you have with the program. Others might be installed by Office or other programs that you work with. In addition to the add-ins that are automatically installed by programs, you might download free add-ins from the Microsoft website or other websites, or purchase add-ins from third-party vendors.

To use some add-ins, you must first install them on your computer and then load them into your computer's memory, as follows:

1   At the bottom of the **Add-Ins** page of the **Outlook Options** dialog box, with **COM Add-ins** selected in the **Manage** list, click the **Go** button.

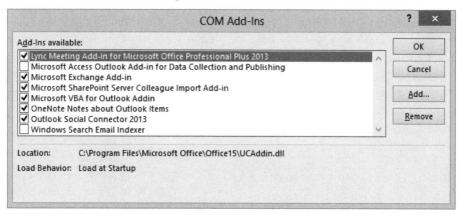

You can activate installed add-ins or add new add-ins from this dialog box.

2   In the **COM Add-Ins** dialog box, click **Add**.

3   In the **Add Add-In** dialog box, navigate to the folder in which the add-in you want to install is stored, and double-click its name to add it to the list of those that are available for use.

4   In the list, select the check box of the new add-in, and then click **OK**. The add-in is now loaded and available for use in Outlook.

    TIP In some cases, you will need to restart Outlook to complete the add-in installation.

11

Creating Outlook forms

Every Outlook item you create is based on a form; you create a message by entering information in a message form that is hosted in a message window; the appointment form consists of the Appointment page and the Scheduling or Scheduling Assistant page that you display in an appointment window; you store contact information in a four-page form (General, Details, Certificates, and All Fields) displayed in a contact window, and so on. The controls you use to interact with the form and its content are part of the item window.

The Outlook 2013 Standard Forms library includes 11 forms: Appointment, Contact, Distribution List, Journal Entry, Meeting Request, Message, Note, Post, Standard Default, Task, and Task Request. Additional forms might be installed by other programs that communicate with Outlook.

TIP To access the form libraries, click the New Items button in the New group on the Home tab of any module, click More Items, and then click Choose Form.

You can create your own form from scratch, or modify an existing form to fit your needs. For example, if you frequently send detailed messages that follow a standard format, want to limit or increase the fields available within a contact record, or want to control the actions a recipient can take with an email message, you can create a custom form that contains the specific fields or information you want to have available when you create an item based on that form. Forms can have multiple pages, and can include a variety of information, including static content, fields, scripts, and macros. You can specify form properties, including the icon that represents items based on the form; actions that item recipients can perform; and the prefix added to the item subject when they perform those actions.

You can save a custom form in your Personal Forms library so that it is available to you from any Outlook folder. Organizations that run Exchange Server can choose to create an Organizational Forms Library in which Outlook users can make forms available to anyone within the organization.

Key points

- You can rearrange the Outlook window to suit your working preferences. Any of the Outlook view panes—the Folder Pane, Reading Pane, and To-Do Bar—can be displayed in any Outlook module. Outlook preserves changes to the default arrangement from session to session.

- You can adjust many aspects of the Outlook environment to tailor its appearance and functionality to the way you work.

- Need one-click access to commands that are scattered in different places? Simply add those commands to the Quick Access Toolbar, or create a custom ribbon tab.

11

Chapter at a glance

Create

Create and manage Quick Steps,
page 446

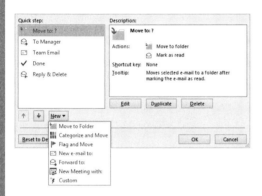

Process

Create rules to process messages,
page 451

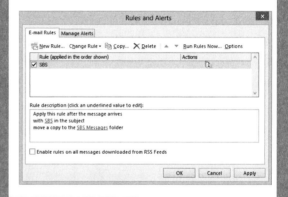

Block

Block unwanted messages,
page 459

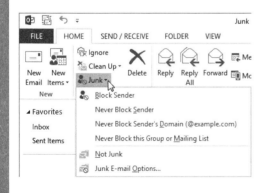

Secure

Increase email security,
page 467

Manage email settings 12

IN THIS CHAPTER, YOU WILL LEARN HOW TO

- Create and manage Quick Steps.

- Create rules to process messages.

- Block unwanted messages.

- Increase email security.

To more easily manage the information you receive through email, you can specify how Microsoft Outlook 2013 alerts you to and processes incoming messages. You can also take advantage of the many security features built into Outlook 2013 to keep your outgoing communications secure and to protect your computer system from spam, viruses, web beacons, and other modern electronic threats.

In this chapter, you'll create a custom Quick Step to manually process messages in your Inbox, automatically process incoming messages by using rules, and set up the Junk E-mail Filter to help manage unwanted messages. Then you'll learn about ways to help secure your email communications.

PRACTICE FILES The exercises in this chapter use Outlook items you created in exercises in previous chapters. If an exercise requires an item that you don't have, you can complete the exercise in which you create the item before beginning the current exercise, or you can substitute a similar item of your own.

Creating and managing Quick Steps

In a new installation of Outlook, the Quick Steps gallery includes five standard Quick Steps: Move To, To Manager, Team Email, Done, and Reply & Delete. You can modify the actions performed by existing Quick Steps, add other common tasks to the Quick Steps menu by choosing them from the New Quick Step list, or create a custom Quick Step from scratch.

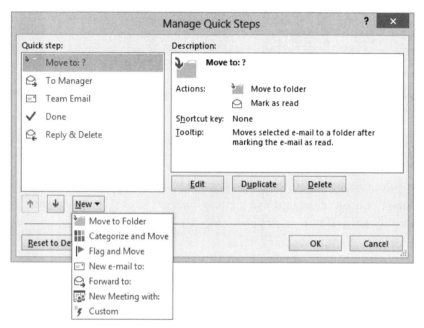

Choosing an action from the New menu provides a starting point for a new Quick Step.

SEE ALSO For information about using the built-in Quick Steps, see "Managing messages by using Quick Steps" in Chapter 7, "Organize your Inbox."

In this exercise, you'll create a custom Quick Step that sends an email message.

 SET UP You don't need any practice files to complete this exercise. Display your Inbox, and then follow the steps.

1   On the **Home** tab, in the **Quick Steps** gallery, click **Create New** to open the **Edit Quick Step** dialog box.

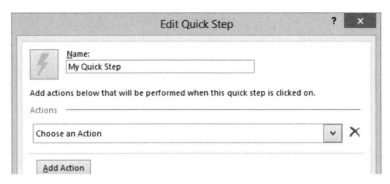

You can build a Quick Step from scratch or base it on a starter rule.

2 In the **Name** box, replace **My Quick Step** with SBS Messages. Then in the **Actions** area, click the **Choose an action** arrow to display the list.

You can choose from 25 actions in six categories: Filing; Change Status; Categories, Tasks and Flags; Respond; Appointment; and Conversations.

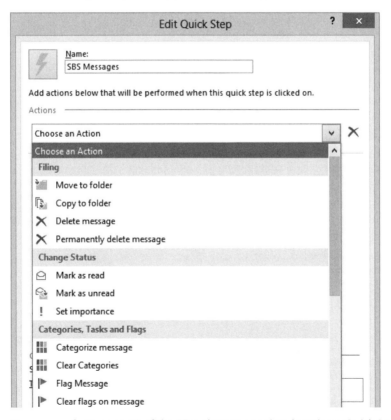

You can perform up to 12 of the 25 actions at one time by using a Quick Step.

3   Scroll down the list to view the available actions. Then, in the **Respond** category, click **New Message** to begin configuring the first action in the Quick Step.

4   Enter your email address in the **To** box. Then click the **Show Options** link to display optional settings for the new message the Quick Step will create.

In addition to the options shown, you can specify Cc and Bcc recipients for messages created by the Quick Step.

5   In the **Subject** box, enter SBS Quick Step Message.

6   In the **Flag** list, click **Flag for Recipients** to open the **Flag Message** dialog box.

You can flag an outgoing message for the recipient to follow up.

TIP Selecting any flagging option other than Flag For Recipients flags the message only for you, the sender. You can use this same option when you manually create or respond to a message.

7   In the **Flag** list, click **No Response Necessary**. In the **By** box, click the down arrow one time to set the flag time to **0** days. Then click **OK** to return to the **Edit Quick Step** dialog box.

8   In the **Text** box, enter This message was created by an Outlook 2013 Quick Step!

9   Select the **Automatically send after 1 minute delay** check box.

10   Below the existing **New Message** action, click the **Add Action** button to display a second list of actions.

      You can add more actions to the Quick Step by clicking an action in the list. However, the Quick Step you have created is one that doesn't take action on an existing message, so the other actions aren't appropriate.

11   To the right of the **Choose an Action** list, click the **Delete** button to remove the unconfigured action from the Quick Step.

12   In the **Shortcut key** list, click **Ctrl+Shift+1**.

13   In the **Tooltip text** box, enter Send myself a message to complete the configuration of your Quick Step.

12

The Edit Quick Step dialog box shows the actions that the new Quick Step will perform.

14 In the **Edit Quick Step** dialog box, click **Finish** to add the new Quick Step to the **Quick Steps** gallery.

15 On the **Home** tab, in the **Quick Steps** gallery, point to **SBS Messages** to display the Quick Step name, shortcut key, and tooltip you configured.

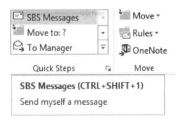

Adding a tooltip to a Quick Step helps you remember what actions it performs.

16   Click the **SBS Messages** Quick Step, and then in the **Folder Pane**, click your **Outbox**. Because you chose the **Automatically send after 1 minute delay** check box, the message sits in your **Outbox** for one minute, and then is sent.

17   Display your **Inbox** and open the **SBS Quick Step Message** message. Notice the InfoBar at the top of the message header.

The Quick Step message you configured is automatically created and sent.

❌ CLEAN UP Close the message window before continuing to the next exercise.

Creating rules to process messages

You can have Outlook evaluate your incoming or outgoing email messages and take various actions with them based on sets of instructions you set up, called *rules*. You can create rules based on different message criteria, such as the message sender, message recipients, message content, attachments, and importance. By using rules, you can have Outlook move, copy, delete, forward, redirect, reply to, or otherwise process messages based on the criteria you specify. You can choose from a collection of standard rules or create your own.

If you have a Microsoft Exchange Server account, you can set up rules that are applied to messages as they are received or processed by your Exchange server, and rules that go into effect only when you indicate that you are unavailable, by setting up an Automatic Reply. Whether or not you have an Exchange account, you can set up rules that are applied to messages stored on your computer.

SEE ALSO For information about setting up Outlook to respond to and process messages for you, see "Automatically replying to messages" in Chapter 13, "Work remotely."

12

In this exercise, you'll create a rule to process incoming messages that meet specific criteria.

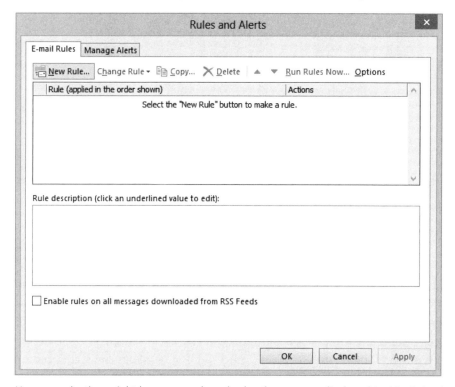 **SET UP** You need the SBS Quick Step Message message you created in the previous exercise and the contents of the SBS Messages folder you created in Chapter 7. If you have not already created and populated the folder, you can do so now, or you can substitute any messages in your Inbox and adjust the rule criteria accordingly. Display your Inbox, and then follow the steps.

1   On the **Info** page of the **Backstage** view, click the **Manage Rules & Alerts** button to display the **Email Rules** page of the **Rules and Alerts** dialog box.

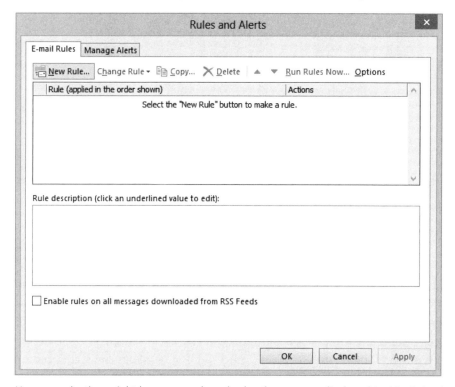

Your organization might have server-based rules that are not displayed in this dialog box.

TIP If you have Outlook configured to connect to multiple accounts, you can choose the account or accounts for which you want to manage rules from a list that appears in the upper-right corner of the Rules And Alerts dialog box. If multiple accounts are listed as a single selection, you can choose a specific account by specifying the Through The Specified Account condition when creating the rule.

2   On the **E-mail Rules** page, click **New Rule** to start the **Rules** wizard. You can base a rule on one of the nine rule templates provided by Outlook, or you can start from a blank rule for incoming or outgoing messages.

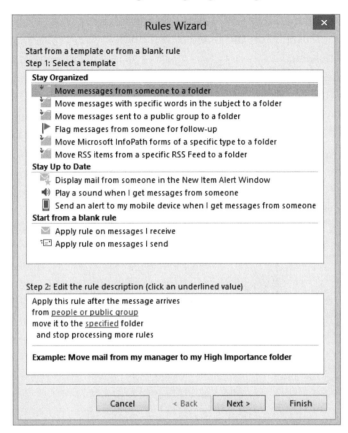

The wizard leads you through the steps of creating a standard or custom rule.

3   In the **Select a template** box, click each of the rule templates in the **Stay Organized** and **Stay Up to Date** lists. Notice that the criteria and actions associated with the selected rule appear in the **Edit the rule description** box.

TIP   The name of the box that lists the possible criteria begins with *Step 1*. This text remains at the beginning of the name as the wizard leads you through a series of steps. We therefore refer to the box by the descriptive name that follows.

4   In the **Start from a blank rule** list, click **Apply rule on messages I receive** to display the first criterion of the new rule in the **Edit the rule description** box.

5   In the **Rules** wizard, click **Next** to display a list of conditions that you can apply to incoming messages.

6   In the **Select condition(s)** box, scroll through the list to view the conditions you can apply. Then select the **with specific word(s) in the subject** check box to add the selected condition to the **Edit the rule description** box. You can specify as many conditions as you want.

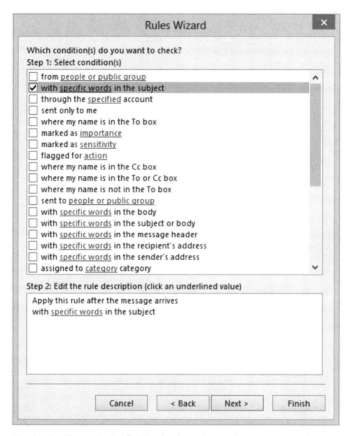

Outlook will apply the finished rule to incoming messages that meet the conditions you select.

7   In the **Edit the rule description** box, click the underlined term **specific words** to open the **Search Text** dialog box.

8   In the **Specify words or phrases to search for in the subject** box, enter SBS. Then click **Add** to move the specified term to the **Search list** box. Notice that the wizard encloses the term in quotation marks.

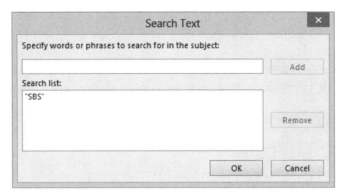

The rule will apply to messages with subjects that include the specified search term.

9   In the **Search Text** dialog box, click **OK**. Then in the **Rules** wizard, click **Next**.

10   Scroll through the **Select action(s)** list to review the actions Outlook can perform on incoming items that meet the criteria you specify. Then select the **move a copy to the specified folder** check box (not the Move It To The Specified Folder check box).

11   In the **Edit the rule description** box, click the underlined word **specified** to open the **Rules and Alerts** dialog box, which displays the folders in your mailbox.

You can choose an existing folder or create a new folder directly from the dialog box.

12

12 In the **Rules and Alerts** dialog box, scroll through the list of folders if necessary, click the **SBS Messages** folder, and then click **OK**.

TROUBLESHOOTING If you didn't create the SBS Messages folder in an earlier exercise, click your mailbox at the top of the Choose A Folder list, click New, enter *SBS Messages* as the folder name in the Create New Folder dialog box, and then click OK.

13 In the **Rules** wizard, click **Next** to display a list of conditions under which Outlook will not apply the rule to messages that meet the previously selected condition.

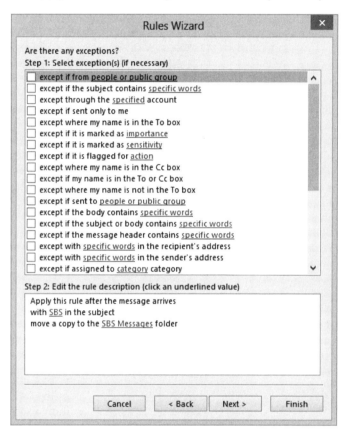

Exceptions you specify on this page overrule the conditions specified previously.

14 In the **Rules** wizard, without selecting an exception, click **Next** to summarize on the final page of the wizard the parameters of the SBS rule.

You can review the specified criteria and actions.

15 Select the **Run this rule now on messages already in Inbox** check box, and then click **Finish** to save the rule and run it on the contents of your **Inbox**. In the **Rules and Alerts** dialog box, the selected check box to the left of the rule name indicates that this rule is active and that Outlook will apply it to all incoming messages.

All the rules you've created appear in this list, whether or not they're turned on.

16   In the **Rules and Alerts** dialog box, click **OK**. Then return to the **Inbox** and locate the **SBS Quick Step Message** message you sent to yourself in the preceding exercise.

17   In the **Folder Pane**, click the **SBS Messages** folder. The folder contains practice messages you created in earlier chapters of this book, in addition to a copy of the **SBS Quick Step Message** message.

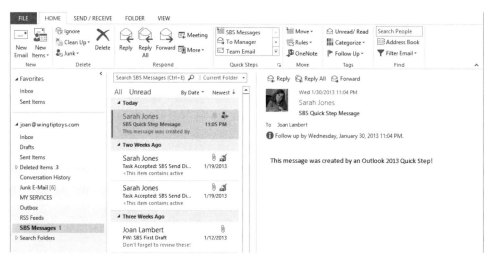

A copy of the SBS Quick Step Message message has been moved to the specified folder.

❌ CLEAN UP Retain the SBS Quick Step Message message, the SBS Messages folder, and the folder contents for use in later exercises.

Blocking unwanted messages

You can use Quick Steps to manually process messages, and rules to automatically process messages, but there are certain types of messages you don't want to deal with at all—junk email messages (also called junk mail, or spam) and phishing messages (which literally try to "hook" you into downloading viruses or other malicious code). Outlook offers levels of protection for managing junk email messages—the unsolicited advertisements, sometimes containing dangerous attachments, that can swamp your Inbox if your email address finds its way into the hands of unscrupulous mailing list vendors. When enabled, the Junk E-mail Filter either moves messages that appear to be junk email to a special folder or deletes them. You can specify a list of email addresses or domains whose messages should always be treated as junk; you can also specify a list of email addresses or domains from whom messages should never be treated as junk.

Outlook also helps protect you from phishing—a widespread identity theft scam. Phishing messages are email messages that contain links to phishing sites purporting to represent trusted, known entities, such as banks or e-commerce sites that would likely have your personal information on file. The messages request that you update your personal information through the link provided. If you do so, you inadvertently provide the requested information (which might include your Social Security number, bank account number, passwords, and other confidential information) to scam artists, who might then sell or otherwise use the information for their own financial gain. In the past, you were in danger only if you submitted your information through the phishing site, but these sites are becoming increasingly sophisticated, and many now host malicious keystroke-logging software. You can infect your computer just by visiting such sites, which makes it vital that you protect yourself from these threats.

Working with junk email messages

By default, when Outlook receives a message that it deems to be either junk mail or a phishing message, it delivers that message to the Junk E-mail folder associated with your account rather than to your Inbox. (Each account you configure Outlook to connect to has its own Junk E-mail folder.) You might not be aware that one or more messages has been redirected to your Junk E-mail folder; if someone tells you that he or she has sent you a message but you haven't received it, it's a good idea to check whether it's in your Junk E-mail folder.

12

You can display the contents of the Junk E-mail folder by clicking Junk E-mail in the Folder Pane. When the Junk E-mail folder contains one or more messages, the number of messages in the folder is shown in parentheses at the end of the folder name. If any of the messages in the folder have not been read, the folder name is bold.

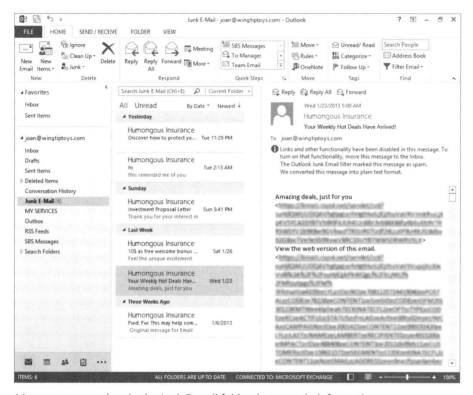

Messages may end up in the Junk E-mail folder that contain information you want.

Outlook converts message content in the Junk E-mail folder to plain text and disables any active links or content within the message. The InfoBar in the message header provides specific information about the message's status.

Any remote graphics (graphics that are displayed from Internet locations rather than embedded in the message—sometimes called *web beacons*) that were present in the message are converted to URLs, which reveals where the graphics originated.

SEE ALSO For more information about web beacons, see "Increasing email security" later in this chapter.

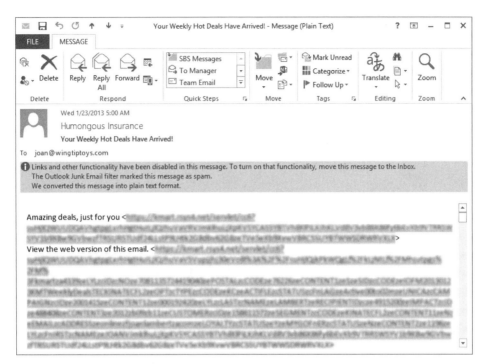

Outlook disables functionality in a message that it suspects to be spam.

Although the response options on the ribbon are active, you can't reply to a message from the Junk E-mail folder—you must first move it to the Inbox or another folder. You can forward a message from the Junk E-mail folder; you might want to forward a message to someone else who can verify for you whether the message is valid. The forwarded message will be in plain-text format rather than in the original message format.

You can delete messages from the Junk E-mail folder or indicate to Outlook how you would like the Junk E-mail filter to handle similar messages in the future.

To process a message from the Junk E-mail folder:

1 Select or open the message you want to process.

2 On the **Home** tab (if you selected the message) or the **Message** tab (if you opened the message), in the **Delete** group, click the **Junk** button to display the options for processing the message.

12

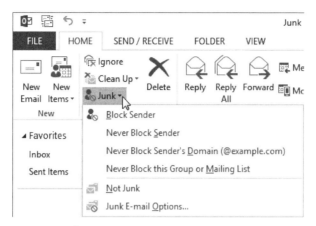

You can configure Outlook to block or allow specific senders.

3   Click one of the first four options in the **Junk** list to block the sender or to add the sender, the sender's domain, or the recipient group to your **Safe Senders** or **Safe Recipients** list. Clicking any of these options does not remove the message from the **Junk E-mail** folder.

4   To move the message to your **Inbox**, click **Not Junk**. If you want to add the sender to your **Safe Senders** list, select the **Always trust e-mail from** check box in the **Mark as Not Junk** message box. Then click **OK**.

The dialog box might look different, depending on your Outlook email account configuration.

TIP The Always Trust Email Sent To The Following Addresses box lists all message recipients. Selecting an email address in the list adds that message recipient to your Safe Recipients list. Think very carefully before taking this action, because it could expose you to spam or malicious content.

To process an open message, do the following:

■ Click the **Junk** button in the **Delete** group on the **Message** tab of the message reading window, and then click the option you want.

Configuring junk email options

You manage junk mail settings from the Junk E-mail Options dialog box, which you open by clicking Junk E-mail Options in the Junk list. You set specific junk email processing options for each email account to which Outlook is configured to connect. The account for which you're configuring options is shown in the title bar of the Junk E-mail Options dialog box.

The Junk E-mail Options dialog box has the following five pages:

■ On the Options page, you select a level of protection. If you don't have additional filters in place, such as those that might be supplied by your organization, you might prefer to click High. Otherwise, click Low.

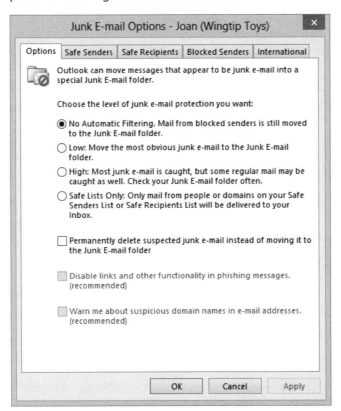

The Options page of the Junk E-mail Options dialog box is a great starting place for configuring Outlook to filter out junk mail.

12

If you want Outlook to automatically delete suspected junk email, select the Permanently Delete Suspected Junk E-mail Instead Of Moving It To The Junk E-mail Folder check box. Do not select this check box if you set the protection level to High or to Safe Lists Only. With these settings, it is likely that the Junk E-mail Filter will catch quite a few valid messages that you don't want deleted.

Note that the options to disable links and display warnings about suspicious domain names are unavailable to change. These settings are selected by default. Unless you are very confident that you have another protective system in place, leave these options selected.

■ On the Safe Senders page, you can add a specific person's email address to the Safe Senders list (for example, tom@contoso.com) or specify that email received from any sender at a particular domain is safe by adding only the domain (for example, @contoso.com).

To ensure that messages from your legitimate contacts aren't moved to the Junk E-mail folder, you can select the two check boxes at the bottom of the dialog box.

- On the Safe Recipients page, you can add distribution lists or mailing lists of which you are a member to your Safe Recipients list.

Adding contacts to the Safe Recipients list ensures that messages sent to you through the distribution list or mailing list will never be treated as junk email.

- On the Blocked Senders page, you can manually add email addresses and domain names to the Blocked Senders list, or Outlook will add them for you whenever you identify a received message as junk email.

You can add specific email addresses or entire domains to the Blocked Senders list.

TIP You can set junk mail settings for individual messages quickly by right-clicking the message in your Inbox or other mail folder, clicking Junk, and then clicking Block Sender, Never Block Sender, Never Block Sender's Domain, or Not Junk.

12

- On the International page, you have the option of blocking all messages from a top-level domain that is specific to a country or region (but not to domains such as .com, .gov, or .net), or all messages containing specific non-English text encoding.

If you frequently receive spam from an international domain and don't do business in that country or region, you might want to block all messages from the domain.

Click Blocked Top-Level Domain List to access the list of top-level domains you can block. Click Blocked Encodings List to access the list of languages you can block.

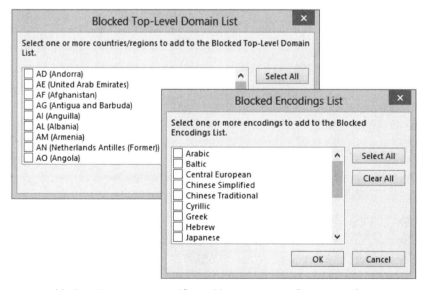

You can block entire country-specific and language-specific groups of messages.

Increasing email security

As your email messages travel from server to server en route to you or other message recipients, they are vulnerable to interception by hackers and others who are intent on viewing them. With Outlook 2013, you can safeguard your messages in several ways, including implementing digital signatures, encryption, plain text messages, and Information Rights Management (IRM). In certain corporate environments, particularly those such as legal firms and accounting firms that handle sensitive data, specific email security procedures might be mandated and enforced at a server level. In the absence of such guidance, only you can decide whether any of these additional security measures are appropriate for your situation.

Digital signatures

When sending messages, you can reassure message recipients that they are receiving valid messages from you by using a digital signature—a piece of code that validates the identity of a message sender (not the actual person, but the email account and computer from which the message originates).

Obtaining a digital ID

To send digitally signed or encrypted messages over the Internet, you must obtain a digital ID (a security certificate). The first time you try to digitally sign or encrypt a message without having a valid digital ID installed on your computer, Outlook prompts you to obtain one. If you prefer, you can obtain one before you need it. You can obtain a digital ID from an independent certification authority, from your organization's IT department, or you can create one for yourself. Each certification level connotes a different level of trust; the highest is that of an independent certification authority.

Obtaining some types of digital IDs, such as those used to certify the source of software programs, involves a stringent application process that can take weeks to complete. However, applying for a commercial security certificate to certify documents and email messages is a relatively simple process. Many US and international certification companies offer digital IDs to certify email. You'll probably be most comfortable purchasing a certificate in your native currency. Regardless of the location of the certification authority, the digital ID is valid worldwide.

12

To obtain a digital ID to sign or encrypt outgoing documents and messages:

1   On the **Trust Center** page of the **Outlook Options** dialog box, click **Trust Center Settings**, and then display the **E-mail Security** page of the **Trust Center** dialog box.

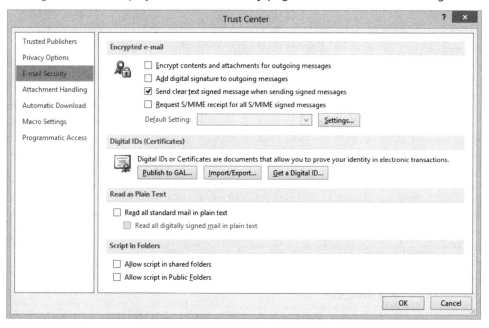

The Publish To GAL button is available only in a centrally administered Exchange environment.

2   In the **Digital IDs (Certificates)** area of the **Email Security** page, click **Get a Digital ID** to display the Digital ID page of the Microsoft Office website in your default web browser. This page lists providers from whom you can obtain a digital ID to certify documents and email messages.

TIP If you want to use a certification authority other than one of those listed on the Office website, search the web for *digital ID* or *certification authority*, and you'll find a number of options. You can apply for a digital ID from any certification authority through its website. Digital IDs from providers other than those recommended on the Microsoft website might have compatibility issues with Windows Internet Explorer.

3   Click the link at the end of a provider's description to display the provider's website.

4   Follow the instructions on the website to register for a digital ID. Some certifying authorities charge a small fee, but most offer free digital IDs or a free trial period. As part of the process, you'll likely be required to respond to an email message from your computer.

The commercial digital ID will be installed on the computer on which you complete the application process, but it is associated with your email address; if you need to use it on another computer, you can reinstall it from the provider's site, or you can export the digital ID files from the original computer and import them on the other computer.

To export or import a digital ID:

1   On the **E-mail Security** page of the **Trust Center** dialog box, in the **Digital IDs (Certificates)** area, click **Import/Export**.

2   In the **Import/Export Digital ID** dialog box, select whether you want to import or export your digital ID. Then provide the appropriate information, and click **OK**.

To obtain an S/MIME digital ID for use only on your computer, follow these steps:

1   On the **E-mail Security** page of the **Trust Center** dialog box, click the **Get a Digital ID** button.

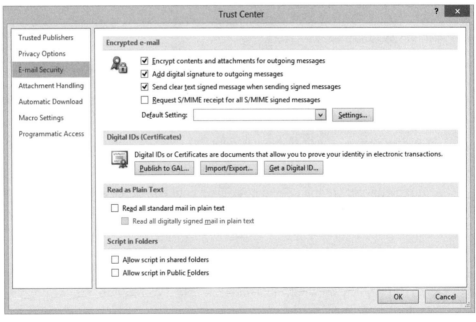

A digital ID permits you to authenticate items you create, only on your computer.

2   Follow the instructions on the resulting webpage to obtain the digital ID you want.

After creating the certificate, you can assign it a friendly name in the Certificate Manager.

To manage your certificates:

1   Press the **Windows** key, enter certificate, and then in the search results, click **Manage user certificates** to start the **Certificate Manager**.

2   In the **certmgr** console, expand the **Personal** node, and then click **Certificates**.

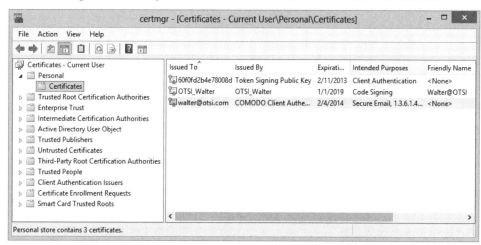

Your personal certificates are tracked in the Certificate Manager.

3   To give a friendly name to a certificate, right-click the certificate and click **Properties**. Enter the friendly name, and then click **OK**.

TIP Your organization's IT administrator or Exchange administrator might be able to issue you a digital ID.

You can have more than one digital ID on your computer, and you can select which one to use for each document or message. For example, you might have one digital ID for business use and one for personal use.

Digitally signing messages

You can digitally sign individual messages when you compose them, or you can instruct Outlook to digitally sign all outgoing messages.

The first time you digitally sign a message, you need to configure your security settings to use your digital certificate. You must do this from the Trust Center dialog box.

TROUBLESHOOTING You can follow a similar process to configure security settings from the message window, but at the time we prepared this book for publication, Outlook did not correctly complete the process from that location, so use the Trust Center process.

To configure digital certificate settings, follow these steps:

1   On the **E-mail Security** page of the **Trust Center** dialog box, in the **Encrypted e-mail** area, click the **Settings** button.

You need to specify digital signing and encryption certificates.

2   In the **Change Security Settings** dialog box, to the right of the **Signing Certificate** box, click the **Choose** button.

The dialog box displays the digital signing certificates available on your computer.

12

3   In the **Windows Security** dialog box displaying your valid certificates, click the digital certificate you want to use to digitally sign outgoing messages, and then click **OK** to display the selected certificate information in the **Change Security Settings** dialog box.

4   In the **Security Settings Name** box, enter a name by which you'll identify the signing certificate.

By default, Outlook also assigns the selected certificate for message encryption.

5   Click **OK** in the **Change Security Settings** dialog box, in the **Trust Center** dialog box, and in the **Outlook Options** dialog box.

After you complete this process, the Encrypt and Sign buttons appear in the Permission group on the Options tab of the message composition window.

After you install a digital ID, you can encrypt or digitally sign an outgoing message from the Options tab of the message window ribbon.

If the Encrypt and Sign buttons are not displayed in the Permissions group on the Options tab after you configure a digital certificate, or if you want to use a certificate other than the default to sign or encrypt the message, you can manage these features in the Security Properties dialog box.

You can choose from the configured security profiles.

To display the Security Properties dialog box, click the More Options dialog box launcher on the Options tab of the message window, and then in the Properties dialog box, click Security Settings.

To digitally sign an individual email message:

- On the **Options** tab, in the **Permission** group, click the **Sign** button.

A message with a valid digital signature has a red ribbon on its message icon and a digital signature icon (also a red ribbon) in its message header. When you receive a digitally signed message, you can click the digital signature icon to view information about the signature.

12

To digitally sign all outgoing messages:

1 On the **E-mail Security** page of the **Trust Center** dialog box, in the **Encrypted e-mail** area, select the **Add digital signature to outgoing messages** check box.

2 If your message recipients might not have S/MIME (Secure Multipurpose Internet Mail Extensions) security (for instance, if you're sending messages to people who you know aren't using Outlook), ensure that the **Send clear text signed message when sending signed messages** check box is selected (this is the default setting). Then click **OK** in all the open dialog boxes.

Encryption

You can secure the contents of outgoing messages by using encryption, which ensures that only the intended recipients can read the messages you send. A message recipient's email program must have corresponding decryption capabilities in order to read the message.

You can encrypt individual messages when you compose them, or you can instruct Outlook to encrypt all outgoing messages.

To encrypt an individual message:

■ On the **Options** tab, in the **Permission** group, click the **Encrypt** button.

To encrypt all outgoing messages:

1 Display the **Email Security** page of the **Trust Center** dialog box.

2 In the **Encrypted email** area of the **Email Security** page, select the **Encrypt contents and attachments for outgoing messages** check box.

3 To receive verification that a message recipient received an encrypted message in its encrypted format, select the **Request S/MIME receipt for all S/MIME signed messages** check box.

An encrypted message has a blue lock on its message icon and an encryption icon (also a blue lock) in its message header. When you receive an encrypted message, you can click the encryption icon to view the message security settings.

TIP If you try to send an encrypted message from Outlook to a recipient whose email configuration doesn't support encryption, Outlook notifies you and gives you the option of resending the message in an unencrypted format.

Plain text messages

These days, viruses and other harmful programs can easily be spread from computer to computer through active content embedded in or linked to from email messages. To ensure that you don't accidentally trigger active content in a received email message, you can display messages in plain text, rather than in Rich Text Format or HTML. Links, scripts, and other active content are disabled in plain text messages; unfortunately, so are formatting and graphics.

To receive all messages in plain text format:

- On the **E-mail Security** page of the **Trust Center** dialog box, in the **Read as Plain Text** area, select the **Read all standard mail in plain text** check box, and then click **OK**.

Information Rights Management

If you don't want a message recipient to forward, copy, or print your message, you can send it with restricted permissions. You use Information Rights Management (IRM) to set these permissions, which control who can read your messages and what they can do with them. If the restricted message includes an attachment, such as a Microsoft Word document, an Excel workbook, or a PowerPoint presentation, the recipient can't edit, copy, or print the attachment (unless you have set individual permissions to allow those actions within the document).

> **IMPORTANT** The use of IRM requires access to an IRM server.

To prevent message recipients from forwarding, printing, or copying a message:

- On the **Options** tab, in the **Permission** group, click the **Permission** arrow, and then in the list, click the restriction you want to apply.

Recipients can read a message sent with restricted permissions by using any version of Outlook since Outlook 2003. The InfoBar in the message header of the outgoing and received messages indicates what recipients can and can't do with the message.

12

Blocking external content

Email is increasingly used to deliver marketing information to current and potential customers. Many companies include pictures in their marketing messages to help explain their product or to make the message more attractive and noticeable, but these pictures can make email messages large. To avoid this problem, some companies include links to pictures that are hosted on their server. When you preview or open the message, the pictures are displayed, but they aren't actually part of the message.

Some junk email senders use this same method to include web beacons in their messages. *Web beacons* are small programs that notify the sender when you read or preview the email message. The notification confirms that your email address is valid, and as a result, you might receive more junk email.

To help protect your privacy, Outlook includes features that block external content such as pictures and sounds. In addition to helping ensure your privacy, this blocking technique can save bandwidth resources, because you choose whether to download images and sounds, instead of Outlook downloading them automatically when you open a message.

By default, Outlook 2013 blocks external content to and from all sources other than those defined in the Safe Senders list and Safe Recipients list. When you open or preview a message that contains blocked content, an InfoBar in the message header provides options for handling the blocked content.

To view the blocked content in an individual email message, click the InfoBar, and then click Download Pictures.

You can change the way Outlook handles external content from the **Automatic Download** page of the **Trust Center** dialog box. You can choose from among the following options, all of which are turned on by default:

- Don't download pictures automatically.

- Permit downloads in email messages from senders and to recipients defined in the Safe Senders and Safe Recipients lists.

- Permit downloads in RSS items, in SharePoint discussion boards, or from websites in the Trusted Zone security zone.

- Warn before downloading content when editing, forwarding, or replying to messages.

Under most circumstances, the security provided by the default settings far outweighs the slight inconvenience of manually downloading content. Many messages that contain blocked pictures are marketing messages that might not be of interest to you.

Key points

- You can create manual rules, called Quick Steps, to perform up to 12 actions on selected email messages in your Inbox.

- You can set up automatic rules so that Outlook will process messages for you based on specific criteria.

- Built-in filters block annoying or hazardous messages that conform to typical spam patterns or that contain active content. You can configure lists of safe and unsafe senders and modify the level of filtering performed by the Junk E-mail filter.

- You can digitally sign messages, encrypt them, and set permissions for them. You can also display messages in plain text to disable any active content.

12

Chapter at a glance

Work

Work with Outlook items while offline, page 480

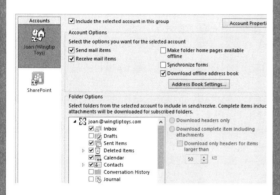

Connect

Manage download options for slow connections, page 489

Reply

Automatically reply to messages, page 491

Collaborate

Work with SharePoint site content, page 498

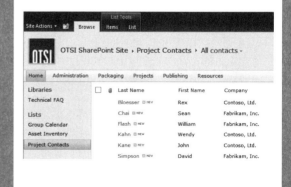

Work remotely

13

IN THIS CHAPTER, YOU WILL LEARN HOW TO

- Work with Outlook items while offline.

- Manage download options for slow connections.

- Automatically reply to messages.

- Work with SharePoint site content.

An active Internet connection is not required to access the information you have stored in Microsoft Outlook 2013; you can work with messages, appointments, and other Outlook items while your computer is offline, by using the Cached Exchange Mode feature. By using this feature, you can read messages and compose responses offline; for example, while you're on an airplane. When you're working online but have a slow Internet connection, you can configure Cached Exchange Mode settings to restrict the amount of information that is downloaded with each message so that you can dedicate the available bandwidth to the tasks you most urgently need to complete.

When you travel or will be unavailable to respond to incoming email messages for a period of time, you can use the Automatic Replies feature to inform message senders of your status and to set expectations for message response times.

It's increasingly common for people in geographically disparate locations to work together, with a collaboration site that provides a central location to store and distribute information and to manage team processes. Microsoft SharePoint products and technologies provide a simple and effective way for team members to share information and collaborate on projects. If your organization uses a SharePoint site to facilitate collaboration among team members, you can connect Outlook to SharePoint document libraries, lists, and calendars. Then you can work with the information stored on the SharePoint site from within Outlook, when you're online or offline.

In this chapter, you'll first configure Cached Exchange Mode so you can work offline in Outlook with a variety of items. You'll learn ways of working efficiently with Outlook items while you have a slow Internet connection. Then you'll set up automatic replies. Finally, you'll connect SharePoint document libraries, lists, and calendars to Outlook.

PRACTICE FILES You don't need any practice files to complete the exercises in this chapter.

Working with Outlook items while offline

Wireless Internet connections are now available at many coffee shops, restaurants, airports, and even on airplanes, either for free or for a small fee. It's easier than ever to connect to the Internet, but sometimes you will want to use your computer offline. You can use Outlook even when you don't have a connection to your mail server. You can read and create messages and other Outlook items while your computer is offline exactly as you do when it is online, by using the Cached Exchange Mode feature. This feature was introduced as an option with Outlook 2003 and, depending on your email service, might be stipulated as a requirement when you configure Outlook to connect to your account. It generally works in the background without any interaction from you.

Cached Exchange Mode creates a local copy (a copy that resides on your computer) of the contents of your Microsoft Exchange Server account mailbox. When you are working online (connected to Exchange), messages, appointments, meetings, tasks, and other Outlook items are synchronized between the server and the local cache. As a result, when you go offline (disconnect from Exchange, either voluntarily or involuntarily), you can still open and work with all your existing Outlook items—including attachments—as usual. You can't receive messages while you're offline, but you can send them—at least as far as your Outbox, where they are held until the next time Outlook connects to Exchange. Cached Exchange Mode has greatly streamlined the offline working process, making it simple, for example, to catch up on email on your laptop when you're in an airplane—of the old-fashioned sort, *without* onboard Internet.

Using Cached Exchange Mode in Outlook 2013, you can have offline access not only to the contents of your Exchange mailbox, but also to the contents of shared folders and public folders (if your organization uses them) that you have marked as your favorites.

Choosing to work offline

Even while you have an available Internet connection, you can still choose to have Outlook work offline; it might be useful, for example, when you don't want to be interrupted by incoming email messages but still want to have access to information stored in Outlook.

To switch between working online and working offline in Outlook:

- On the **Send/Receive** tab, in the **Preferences** group, click the **Work Offline** button.

When you're working offline, your offline status is indicated by the active (blue) Work Offline button on the Send/Receive tab of the ribbon in any module and by the connection status message on the program window's status bar.

Working offline is one way of minimizing distractions.

Choosing the Work Offline option in Outlook doesn't affect the online status of your Internet connection; you can still access the Internet through your web browser.

TIP At times, you might experience a service interruption that triggers Outlook to switch to offline mode. When the Working Offline indicator appears on the status bar, click the Work Offline button in the Preferences group on the Send/Receive tab to reconnect to the server.

Using public folders

Public folders are shared storage folders in an Exchange environment. Exchange doesn't create public folders automatically; your Exchange administrator must specifically enable this feature.

If your organization uses public folders, these folders are available from the Folder List, which you can display in the Folder Pane of the Mail module.

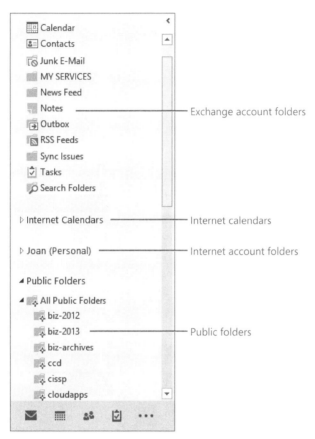

To display the Folder List and your organization's public folders, click the Folders link or button on the Navigation Bar.

You can store Outlook items in a public folder by manually copying or moving the items, or by creating a rule to automatically move or copy items that meet specific criteria.

If you have the necessary permissions, you can create public folders and make them available to the entire organization or to selected individuals or groups.

To create and configure a public folder, follow these steps:

1. On the **Folder** tab of any Outlook module, in the **New** group, click the **New Folder** button; or in the **Folder Pane**, right-click the **All Public Folders** folder and then click **New Folder**.

2. In the **Create New Folder** dialog box, enter a name for the public folder and select the type of items it will contain. In the **Select where to place the folder** list, expand **Public Folders**, and click **All Public Folders**. Then click **OK**.

3. In the **Folder Pane**, display the **Folder List** and expand the **All Public Folders** folder. Right-click the new folder, and then click **Properties**.

4. On the **Permissions** page of the **Properties** dialog box, specify the people and permissions you want to assign to the folder. (You can choose a predefined permission level or individually set read, write, delete, and other options.) Then click **OK**.

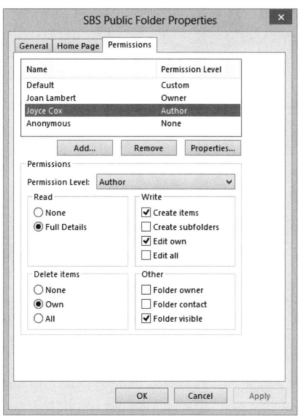

You can set the permissions of public folders for which you have administrative access.

13

By using Cached Exchange Mode, you can make the contents of specific public folders available to you when you're working offline.

To add a public folder to your Public Folder Favorites, follow these steps:

1 In the **Folder Pane**, display the **Folder List** and expand the **All Public Folders** folder.

2 Right-click the folder you want to make available offline, and then click **Add to Favorites** to open the **Add to Favorites** dialog box.

3 Click the **Options** button to display the subfolder and location options. If the public folder has (or might later have) subfolders, select the subfolder options you want.

*You can label a folder in the Favorites list
with a different name.*

4 In the **Add To Favorites** dialog box, specify the name and location of the public folder as you want it to appear in the **Favorites** folder. (Changing the **Favorites** folder display name does not change the name of the public folder, but might make it easier for you to identify the folder.) Then click **Add**.

Setting Cached Exchange Mode options

When configuring Outlook to connect to an account, or anytime thereafter, you can configure Cached Exchange Mode to keep shared folders and public folders, in addition to standard
Exchange account folders, in your local cache. Only the folders in your local cache are available to you when you're working offline.

To manage the Cached Exchange Mode settings for your Exchange account, follow these
steps:

1   On the **Info** page of the **Backstage** view, click the **Account Settings** button, and then
    click **Account Settings**.

2   In the **Account Settings** dialog box, select the account for which you want to config-
    ure offline folders, and click the **Change** button. Then in the **Change Account** dialog
    box that opens, click the **More Settings** button.

3   In the **Microsoft Exchange** dialog box that opens, click the **Advanced** tab. The
    check boxes available in the **Cached Exchange Mode Settings** area of the **Advanced**
    page depend on your organization's Exchange settings.

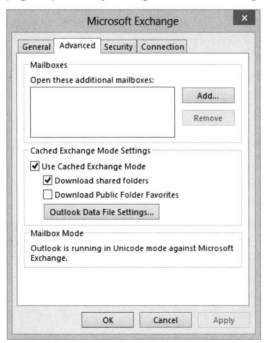

*If public folders aren't available in your Exchange environment, the Download
Public Folder Favorites check box doesn't appear in the dialog box.*

13

4   To turn off Cached Exchange Mode, clear the **Use Cached Exchange Mode** check box.

5   To turn on Cached Exchange Mode, select the **Use Cached Exchange Mode** check box. Then select the optional folders you want to cache:

   ▪ Select the **Download shared folders** check box to cache the contents of SharePoint document libraries and calendars and of shared Outlook calendars, contact folders, task folders, and note folders.

   ▪ Select the **Download Public Folder Favorites** check box to cache the contents of public folders that you add to your **Favorites** folder.

6   After turning Cached Exchange Mode on or off, exit and restart Outlook to effect the change.

Managing an offline address book

When Cached Exchange Mode is enabled, Outlook downloads a copy of the Global Address List (GAL) along with your mailbox. This local copy of the GAL provides access to your co-workers' contact information regardless of whether you are online. If your network connection is slow and the address book is large, this download might take a long time. If you prefer, you can disable the automatic download of the address book, and then manually update it at your convenience.

To exclude the offline address book from send/receive operations, follow these steps:

1   On the **Send/Receive** tab, in the **Send & Receive** group, click the **Send/Receive Groups** button and then, in the list, click **Define Send/Receive Groups**.

   KEYBOARD SHORTCUT Press Ctrl+Alt+S to open the Send/Receive Groups dialog box. For more information about keyboard shortcuts, see "Keyboard shortcuts" at the end of this book.

The All Accounts send/receive group is created automatically;
you can define other groups with different send/receive settings.

TIP By default, the Send/Receive Groups dialog box contains only one group, named All Accounts. You can create additional groups if you want to set different rules for each.

2 In the **Group Name** list, click the group you want to change. Then click **Edit** to open the **Send/Receive Settings** dialog box for the selected send/receive group.

13

Downloading an offline address book makes it easy to find contact information when you're not online.

TIP If the send/receive options are unavailable (dimmed) and the account icon is marked with a red X rather than blue circling arrows, the selected account isn't included in the scheduled send/receive operation for this group. To activate the send/receive options for the account, select the Include The Selected Account In This Group check box.

3   In the **Send/Receive Settings** dialog box, select the account for which you want to configure the address book download, and then clear the **Download offline address book** check box. Then click **OK** in the **Send/Receive Settings** dialog box, and click **Close** in the **Send/Receive Groups** dialog box.

TIP You can turn off the automatic address book update entirely by clearing the Download Offline Address Book check box in the Send/Receive Settings dialog box.

To manually update your offline address book, follow these steps:

1   On the **Send/Receive** tab, in the **Send & Receive** group, click the **Send/Receive Groups** button and then, in the list, click **Download Address Book** to display the relevant download options in the **Offline Address Book** dialog box.

2   In the **Offline Address Book** dialog box, with the **Download changes since last Send/Receive** check box selected, click **OK**.

TIP You can download an entirely new copy of the address book by clearing the Download Changes Since Last Send/Receive check box before clicking OK.

Managing download options for slow connections

When you have a high-speed Internet connection, you probably give very little thought to the size of the messages, and particularly the message attachments, that other people send to you. When your computer has a slow Internet connection, however, downloading large attachments can keep Outlook busy for a long time and cause it to perform slowly. To prevent such delays, you can select the Cached Exchange Mode download option that is most appropriate for your current Internet connection.

Outlook offers these Cached Exchange Mode download options:

■ **Download Full Items** This option downloads all your messages and their attachments one at a time. When your computer is online and you have a high-speed Internet connection, this is the best option because it uses the least bandwidth to download all your messages. If you have a slow connection or receive messages that have large attachments, messages might be slow to appear in your Inbox when you reconnect to your server.

■ **Download Headers and Then Full Items** This option downloads all the message headers quickly so that you can evaluate them while downloading the message bodies and attachments.

13

- **Download Headers** This option downloads only the message headers, and does not download the body of messages or their attachments until you preview or open the messages. This is the best option if your connection is very slow or if you are charged for the amount of bandwidth you actually use. You can evaluate a message based on its header information (such as sender, subject, or message size) and then choose whether to download the message and any attachments.

- **On Slow Connections Download Only Headers** You can select this option in addition to the Download Full Items option or the Download Headers and Then Full Items option. When Outlook detects that its connection to Exchange is slow, it downloads only the message header, but when the connection is not slow, it uses the original option. This option is not available when Download Headers is selected.

When you're connecting to the Internet through a local area network (LAN), broadband, or other fast connection, you probably won't notice much difference between the first two options. You'll notice obvious differences with the third option, and it might take some practice to determine whether to download a message based on only a few words in its header.

You can manage download options from the Send/Receive tab of the ribbon in any module.

General download options are in the Download Preferences list; download options for individual items are in the Server group.

To view or change general download options, click the Download Preferences button in the Preferences group on the Send/Receive tab, and then click to select Download Full Items, Download Headers And Then Full Items, or Download Headers. (A check mark indicates the selected option.) If you usually have a fast Internet connection but might also use your computer in locations with slow Internet connections, also select On Slow Connections Download Only Headers.

If you choose the Download Headers option or the On Slow Connections Download Only Headers option, you can control the download of full items by using the commands in the Server group. After your computer downloads message headers to your Inbox, you can mark specific item headers to indicate that you want to download the entire item; if you change your mind, you can unmark one or all the marked items. After marking the items you want to download, click the Process Marked Headers button to download the full items.

Automatically replying to messages

If your organization is running Exchange, you can use the Automatic Replies feature (previously called the Out Of Office Assistant) to inform people who send you email messages of your availability. When you turn on the Automatic Replies feature, Outlook replies automatically to messages received from other people (but only to the first message from each person). You provide whatever textual information you want within the body of the automatic reply message (commonly referred to as an *out-of-office message*, or *OOF message*).

The out-of-office functionality in Outlook is actually provided by Exchange Server, so the specific automatic reply features differ depending on what version of Exchange Server your organization is running. Regardless of which Exchange Server environment you're working in, this is a very useful feature. Your automatic reply message might also be displayed to co-workers in a MailTip at the top of messages they address to you, and displayed as part of your contact information in Microsoft Lync.

The purpose of the Automatic Replies feature is to provide standard information to message senders and co-workers. When you're away from your computer, an automatic reply can set expectations for when a correspondent can expect a personal response from you. You don't have to be physically out of the office to use this feature; some people use it to let other people know when responses will be delayed for other reasons, such as when they are working on a project that will prevent them from responding promptly to messages, or to inform customers who might be in different time zones of their standard working hours.

In addition to having Outlook send automatic replies, you can have it process messages that arrive while you are out of the office by using rules that are in effect only when the Automatic Replies feature is on.

SEE ALSO For information about using rules to automatically forward, reply to, delete, alert you to, or otherwise process incoming messages, see "Creating rules to process messages" in Chapter 12, "Manage email settings."

The Automatic Replies feature is off until you explicitly turn it on; it does not coordinate with your free/busy information in the Calendar module.

13

When you are using an Exchange account, Automatic Replies include the following features:

- You can create two auto-reply messages—one that Outlook sends only to people in your organization (on the same domain) and another sent either to everyone else or only to the people in your primary address book.

  When you have separate internal and external messages, you can distinguish the information made available to co-workers, to friends and business contacts, and to the general public (including senders of spam). For example, you might include your itinerary and mobile phone number only in an internal automatic reply, include your return date in a reply to your contacts, and not send any reply to other people.

- You can specify the font, size, and color of automatic reply message text and apply bold, italic, or underline formatting.

- You can format paragraphs as bulleted or numbered lists and control the indent level.

- You can specify start and end dates and times for your automatic reply message so that you don't have to remember to turn off Automatic Replies.

In this exercise, you'll configure Outlook to automatically reply to incoming messages and to send one automatic reply to co-workers and another to the general public.

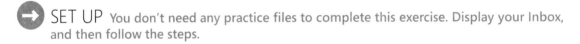 SET UP You don't need any practice files to complete this exercise. Display your Inbox, and then follow the steps.

1   Display the **Info** page of the **Backstage** view. In the account list at the top of the page, select the Exchange account for which you want to configure automatic replies. Then click the **Automatic Replies** button.

> **IMPORTANT** The functionality in this exercise is available only for Exchange accounts. If you select another account type, the Automatic Replies button is not available on the Info page.

The Automatic Replies dialog box for the current account opens. This dialog box includes two pages: Inside My Organization and Outside My Organization. The Outside My Organization page tab includes either *(Off)* or *(On)* to indicate either your organization's standard setting or, if you've previously used this feature, your most recent setting. The content pane is currently unavailable (dimmed).

2   Click the **Send automatic replies** option to make available the date and time range settings, content pane, and formatting commands.

3   Select the **Only send during this time range** check box. Then set the **Start time** to the current date and time (or as close as you can get), and the **End time** to the current date and one hour after the start time.

> **TIP** To set up automatic replies when you'll be out of the office for a week, set the start time to the end of the day on the last business day preceding the week you'll be out of the office, and the end time to the end of the day on the last business day before you return (for example, from 5:00 P.M. Friday until 5:00 P.M. the following Friday). By using this schedule, anyone sending mail that you won't be able to respond to within a normal business response time period will receive an automatic reply.

4   On the **Inside My Organization** page, in the content pane, enter I'm testing the Outlook automatic reply feature!

A more typical internal automatic reply might be *I'm on vacation! Call my mobile phone at (972) 555-0123 if you need to contact me.* For the purposes of this exercise, though, we'll take the safe route and not include a message that might be confusing to your co-workers.

5   Select the sentence you just entered. On the toolbar above the content pane, click the **Bold** button, click the **Italic** button, and then in the **Font Color** palette, click the **Purple** swatch. Click away from the sentence to reveal the results.

13

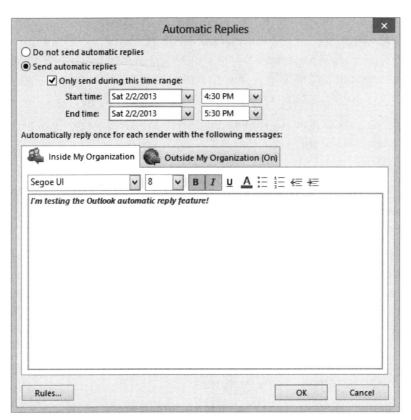

You can format the content of your automatic reply message by using the basic character and paragraph formatting commands available from the toolbar.

6   Click the **Outside My Organization** tab.

The Outside My Organization page includes options for sending automatic replies to all people outside of your organization, only to people with email addresses that are present in your primary Outlook address book, or not at all.

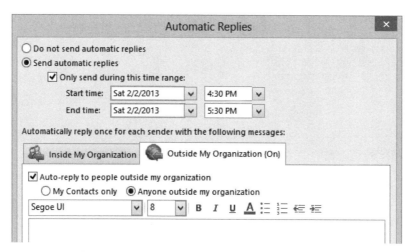

You can specify types of external message senders who will receive your automatic reply.

A typical external automatic reply might be something like this:

I am out of the office this week and will respond to your message as soon as possible. For more information about our products and services, please visit our website at www.wingtiptoys.com. Please direct urgent enquiries to sarah@wingtiptoys.com.

For the purposes of this exercise, you will not set up an external automatic reply message.

TIP If you make changes to either the internal or the external reply message, but not to both, when you close the Automatic Replies dialog box, Outlook displays a message box that asks whether you want to change the other reply message. This useful reminder helps ensure that you keep both versions up to date.

7 Clear the **Auto-reply to people outside my organization** check box, if it is currently selected.

8 In the lower-left corner of the **Automatic Replies** dialog box, click **Rules** to open the **Automatic Reply Rules** dialog box.

13

You can set up rules that Outlook applies specifically to messages that arrive when you are out of the office.

9   In the **Automatic Reply Rules** dialog box, click **Add Rule** to open the **Edit Rule** dialog box. Notice that the interface for creating automatic reply rules is much simpler than the interface for creating rules that apply to all messages.

You can create simple rules that Outlook applies only when automatic replies are turned on.

SEE ALSO For information about Outlook rules, see "Creating rules to process messages" in Chapter 12, "Manage email settings."

10 Click **Cancel** in the **Edit Rule** dialog box, and then click **Cancel** in the **Automatic Reply Rules** dialog box to close the dialog box without creating a rule.

11 In the **Automatic Replies** dialog box, click **OK**. On the **Info** page of the **Backstage** view, a yellow highlight alerts you to the fact that automatic replies are currently on.

You can turn off automatic replies manually from the Automatic Replies area of the Info page or from the information bar below the ribbon in the program window.

12 In the upper-left corner of the **Backstage** view, click the **Back** button to return to the **Inbox**. Notice that the **Automatic Replies** information bar appears below the ribbon, and the **Automatic Replies** menu appears on the status bar, because you specified that Outlook should begin sending automatic replies immediately.

13

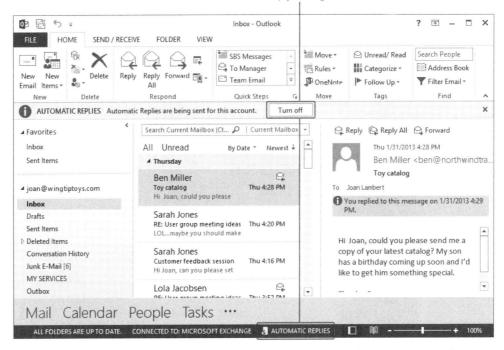

Automatic reply management tools

The Automatic Replies information bar and status bar item appear when automatic replies are on.

13   On the status bar, click **Automatic Replies**.

14   In the **Automatic Replies** dialog box, click the **Do not send automatic replies** option, and then click **OK** to turn off automatic replies.

✖ CLEAN UP If you have an out-of-office time coming up soon, you can set up the automatic replies for it now, before continuing to the next exercise.

Working with SharePoint site content

SharePoint products and technologies facilitate secure sharing of information within an organization. If your organization stores information on one or more SharePoint sites, you might work with data recorded in SharePoint lists, schedules tracked on SharePoint calendars, or Office documents stored in SharePoint document libraries. You can connect to SharePoint lists, calendars, and document libraries from Outlook, and you can work with data and documents stored on a SharePoint site from directly within Outlook.

Working offline with document library content

You can create a synchronized copy of a SharePoint document library as a folder in Outlook 2013. You can then preview in Outlook any document, workbook, or presentation that is stored in the document library, or you can work with a local copy of the document, workbook, or presentation on your computer. Changes that you make to a document from an Outlook folder synchronize with the file on the SharePoint site (and vice versa).

To connect a document library or folder therein to Outlook, follow these steps:

1   On your organization's SharePoint site, display the document library or subfolder you want to work with.

2   The next step varies based on the version of SharePoint your organization is running.

   ▪ In SharePoint 2013 or SharePoint 2010: on the **Library** tool tab, in the **Connect & Export** group, click the **Connect to Outlook** button.

   ▪ In SharePoint 2007 or SharePoint 2003: on the **Actions** menu at the top of the content area, click **Connect to Outlook**.

3   In the **Internet Explorer** dialog box and/or **Internet Explorer Security** dialog box that opens, click **Allow** to give explicit permission for SharePoint to access Outlook.

Outlook starts, if it isn't already running. A Microsoft Outlook dialog box opens, asking you to confirm that you want to connect the SharePoint document library to Outlook.

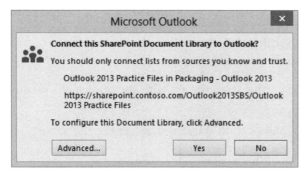

You will have more control if you configure advanced connection settings.

13

4   In the **Microsoft Outlook** dialog box, click **Advanced** to open the **SharePoint List Options** dialog box.

If you use Outlook on multiple computers, consider carefully whether you want to connect the document library to all of your computers.

5   Select or clear the **Display this list on other computers with the account** check box, as follows:

- To download a local copy of the document library to every computer on which Outlook is configured to connect to the specified account, select the check box.

- To download the document library only to the computer you're currently using, clear the check box.

6   Select or clear the **Update this subscription with the publisher's recommendation** check box, as follows:

- To have the site publisher control updates, select the check box.

- To manually control updates, clear the check box.

7   In the **SharePoint List Options** dialog box, click **OK**. Then in the **Microsoft Outlook** dialog box, click **Yes**. If a **Windows Security** or **Connect** dialog box appears, prompting you for your SharePoint site credentials, enter your SharePoint site user name and password, and then click **OK**.

Outlook creates and displays a folder, named for the site and document library, as a subfolder of the SharePoint Lists folder in your mailbox, and downloads a copy of each of the items stored in the document library as an Outlook item within the folder. The icon to the left of the item name indicates the file type (for example, document, workbook, presentation, or database).

TIP Outlook creates the SharePoint Lists folder the first time you connect a SharePoint list or library to Outlook.

If the document library or subfolder you connect to contains subfolders, the content of the subfolders is also downloaded. The presence of subfolders is indicated by a transparent triangle to the left of the document library name; click the triangle to expand the folder and display the subfolders. (A black triangle indicates an expanded folder.)

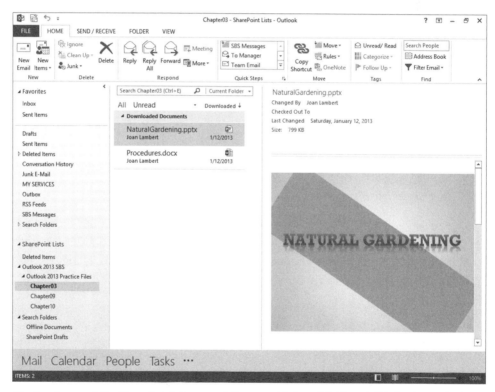

The local copy of the SharePoint document library, with its subfolders visible in the Outlook Folder List.

13

You now have a local copy of the document library or subfolder contents on your computer, and you can work with the files from within Outlook.

You can preview any item in the Reading Pane by clicking it, or you can open a read-only version of the item by double-clicking it. When you open an item, an InfoBar in the item header informs you that you're working in an Offline Server Document; if you want to make changes and later merge them with the document stored in the document library, click Edit Offline and enter your SharePoint credentials when prompted to do so.

TIP Opening an offline file does not check out the file to you in the document library.

While you work with an offline copy of a file, a local version is stored in your SharePoint Drafts folder (a subfolder of your Documents folder).

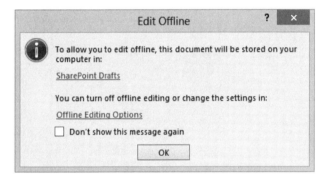

You can change the location from the Save page of the Outlook Options dialog box.

You can edit a document offline while another SharePoint user has it checked out, and then merge your changes into the online version later. After you edit a document offline and before you check in your changes, Outlook indicates in the SharePoint Lists folder that the local copy hasn't been synchronized with the SharePoint library.

Offline edit indicators

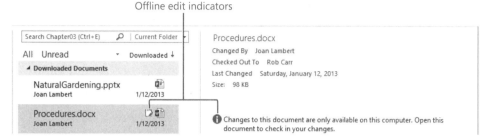

You can edit a document while another person has it checked out.

When you edit a file offline that is not checked out to another SharePoint user, you can synchronize your changes when you save and close the file.

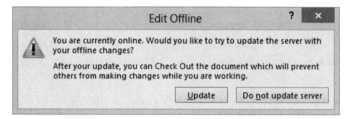

You can update the server version when you're ready to do so.

Importing SharePoint contact lists

Your organization's SharePoint site might include contact information for employees, project team members, or other groups of people. You can import the information stored in a SharePoint contact list into Outlook as an Outlook contact folder.

To connect a SharePoint contact list to Outlook, follow these steps:

1   On your organization's SharePoint site, display the contact list that you want to work with.

13

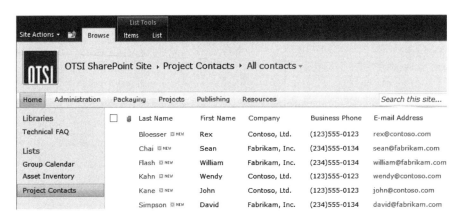

In its default view, a SharePoint contact list displays only selected information fields.

2 Follow steps 2 through 7 of the previous procedure for connecting a SharePoint document library to Outlook (except that in SharePoint 2013 or SharePoint 2010, the **Connect to Outlook** command for the contact list is on the **List** tab rather than on the **Library** tab).

Outlook creates an address book, named for the SharePoint site and contact list, that contains contact records created from the information stored in the SharePoint contact list. The new address book is available in the People module.

The imported SharePoint contact list in the Outlook Contacts module.

Changes that you make to the contact records in the Outlook address book are automatically synchronized with the SharePoint contact list, and vice versa.

Connecting to a SharePoint calendar

If your organization maintains team calendars on a collaboration site, you might find it convenient to view the calendar in Outlook rather than on the site. By connecting a SharePoint calendar to Outlook, you can display the SharePoint calendar in the Outlook Calendar module, either by itself, next to other calendars, or overlaid on other calendars. You can work with the SharePoint calendar as you would with any other calendar in Outlook. Any changes you make to the SharePoint calendar in Outlook are immediately reflected in the calendar on the collaboration site, and vice versa.

To connect a SharePoint calendar to Outlook, follow these steps:

1   On your organization's SharePoint site, display the calendar you want to work with.

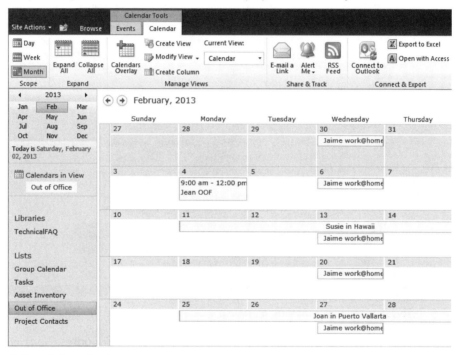

A SharePoint calendar.

13

2   Follow steps 2 through 7 of the procedure for connecting a SharePoint document library to Outlook (except that in SharePoint 2013 or SharePoint 2010, the **Connect to Outlook** command for the calendar is on the **Calendar** tab rather than the **Library** tab).

Outlook creates a calendar, named for the SharePoint site and calendar, that contains calendar items matching those recorded on the SharePoint calendar. The new calendar is available in the Calendar module.

The SharePoint calendar displayed in the Outlook Calendar module.

Changes that you make to the contact records in the Outlook address book are automatically synchronized with the SharePoint contact list, and vice versa.

Key points

- Working away from your network or without an Internet connection doesn't mean that you can't use Outlook. You have many options for accessing your email messages and other information you manage within Outlook.

- Cached Exchange Mode keeps a copy of your mailbox on your computer so you can keep working even when you are away from your network.

- Cached Exchange Mode handles connecting to and synchronizing your local mailbox for you. You can set it to cache all messages or just headers, to save bandwidth.

- When you'll be away from your computer for a while, Outlook can send an automatic reply once to each person from whom you receive a message. This is a convenient way of letting people know when to expect a personal response from you.

- You can maintain a local copy of document library contents in Outlook, work with files, and upload your changes to the SharePoint site.

- If your team keeps a calendar in SharePoint, you can work with that calendar from within Outlook.

13

Glossary

add-in A utility that adds specialized functionality to a program but does not operate as an independent program.

address book A storage folder within your mailbox that contains contact records and contact groups.

appointment A block of time you schedule on your calendar that has a defined start time and end time, and to which you do not invite other attendees.

appointment window The program window that displays the form in which you enter information about an appointment.

arrangement A predefined combination of grouped and sorted messages.

Cached Exchange Mode A feature that stores and synchronizes a copy of an Exchange Server account on a user's computer so that he or she can work offline, either by choice or due to a connection problem.

calendar A general reference to an appointment window, meeting window, or event window.

calendar item A general reference to an appointment, a meeting, or an event.

calendar item window A general reference to an appointment window, meeting window, or event window.

Calendar module The framework that provides the functionality to display and manage appointments, meetings, and events.

Calendar peek An interactive view of the current month's Date Navigator and the day's appointments associated with your default calendar, available from the Navigation Bar or the To-Do Bar.

client rule Or *client-side rule*. A rule that Outlook applies to messages after they arrive on your computer. See also *server rule*.

clip art Pre-made images that are distributed without copyright. Usually cartoons, sketches, illustrations, or photographs.

Clipboard A storage area shared by all Office programs where cut or copied items are stored.

color category A name and associated color by which you can categorize, locate, group, and filter Outlook items.

contact A person about whom you save information, such as street and email addresses, phone and fax numbers, and webpage URLs.

contact card An interactive informational box that appears when you point to a message participant's name or presence icon. The contact card contains contact information and options. The expanded contact card also contains information about the person's position within the organization and distribution list memberships.

contact group A personal distribution list that you create within an address book, which can include contacts, other contact groups, Exchange Server distribution lists, mail-enabled SharePoint libraries, and public folders.

contact index The alphabet bar located to the right of the contact list. Clicking a letter in this index scrolls the contact list to the first contact record that begins with that letter.

contact list The pane immediately to the right of the Folder Pane in the People module, which displays a list of contact records. Also, a SharePoint site list that stores contact information.

contact record A body of information you collect about a contact and store as an Outlook item.

contact record window The program window that displays the form in which you enter information about a contact to create a contact record.

content area The area to the right of the Folder Pane and below the ribbon, in which module content is displayed.

content pane The area of an email message in which you can enter and format message text, graphics, and other content.

contextual tab See *tool tab*.

conversation A means of organizing, viewing, and managing email messages that have the same subject line.

cursor A representation on the screen of the input device pointer location.

Date Navigator The small calendar displayed in the Folder Pane or in the Calendar peek that provides a quick and easy way of displaying specific dates or ranges of dates in the calendar.

delimited text file See *separated text file*.

desktop alert A notification that appears on your desktop when a new email message, meeting request, or task request is received in your Inbox.

dialog box launcher On the ribbon, a button in the lower-right corner of a group that opens a dialog box or pane containing features related to the group.

digital signature Data that binds a sender's identity to the information being sent. A digital signature may be bundled with any message, file, or other digitally encoded information, or transmitted separately. Digital signatures are used in public key environments and provide authentication and integrity services.

distribution list A group of recipients stored in Exchange Server that can be addressed as a single recipient. Administrators can create distribution lists that are available in the GAL. Users can create personal distribution lists called contact groups and add them to their personal address books.

document workspace A SharePoint site that is used for planning, posting, and working together on a document or a set of related documents.

domain On the Internet and other networks, the highest subdivision of a domain name in a network address, which identifies the type of entity that owns the address (such as .com for commercial users or .edu for educational institutions) or the geographical location of the address (such as .fr for France or .sg for Singapore).

draft A temporary copy of a message that has not yet been sent, located in the Drafts folder.

email Short for *electronic mail*. The exchange of electronic text messages and computer file attachments between computers over a communications network, such as a local area network or the Internet.

email message A message that is sent over a communications network such as a local area network or the Internet.

email server A computer that stores email messages for an organization.

email trail An email message and all responses to that message. When an individual message receives multiple responses, the email trail can branch into multiple trails. You can view all the branches of an email trail in Conversation view.

encryption The process of disguising a message or data in such a way as to hide its content.

event An activity that is not associated with a specific time, or an activity that occurs over a period of more than one day.

event window The program window that displays the form in which you enter information about an event.

filtering Displaying items that meet certain criteria; for example, filtering the Inbox to display only unread items. Filtering does not delete files, it simply changes the view so that you display only the files that meet your criteria.

Folder List A view that displays all mailbox folders, public folders, and connected SharePoint lists in the Folder Pane.

Folder Pane The pane that appears on the left side of the Outlook program window in every module. Its contents change depending on the module you're viewing. The Folder Pane can be minimized to display only folders that you designate as Favorites. Referred to in previous versions of Outlook as the *Navigation Pane*. See also *Navigation Bar*.

gallery A grouping of thumbnails that display options visually. Many galleries support the Live Preview feature.

Global Address List (GAL) The address book that contains all user, group, and distribution list email addresses in your organization. The administrator creates and maintains this address book. It may also contain public folder email addresses.

group An area of a ribbon tab that contains buttons related to a specific document element or function.

HTML In Outlook, an email message format that supports paragraph styles, character styles, and backgrounds. Most email programs support the HTML format.

HTTP A protocol used to access webpages from the Internet.

hyperlink A connection from a hyperlink anchor such as text or a graphic that you can follow to display a link target such as a file, a location in a file, or a website. Text hyperlinks are usually formatted as colored or underlined text, but sometimes the only indication is that when you point to them, the pointer changes to a hand.

InfoBar A banner near the top of an Outlook item window or the Reading Pane that displays information about the item.

information bar A banner across the top of the Outlook program window that displays information about the program and often contains commands related to changing the program status.

Information Rights Management (IRM) A policy tool that gives authors control over how recipients use the documents and email messages they send.

instant messaging (IM) The ability to see whether a person is connected to the Internet and to exchange messages. Most exchanges are text-only. However, some services allow attachments.

Internet Message Access Protocol (IMAP) A popular protocol for receiving email messages. It allows an email client to access and manipulate a remote email file without downloading it to the local computer. It is used mainly by corporate users who want to read their email from a remote location.

junk email Unsolicited commercial email (UCE). Also known as *spam*.

justifying Making all lines of text in a paragraph or column fit the width of the document or column, with even margins on each side.

keyboard shortcut Any combination of keystrokes that can be used to perform a task that would otherwise require a mouse or other pointing device.

Live Preview A feature that temporarily displays the effect of applying a specific format to the selected document element.

meeting request A message form linked to an Outlook calendar item. Meeting requests are generated by Outlook to manage meeting attendance.

meeting window The program window that displays the form in which you enter information to place a meeting on your calendar.

message header Summary information that you download to your computer to determine whether to download, copy, or delete the entire message from the server. The header includes the Subject, From, Received, Importance, Attachment, and Size fields.

message list The pane immediately to the right of the Folder Pane in the Mail module, in which messages and received items are displayed.

message window The program window that displays the form in which you create or respond to an email message.

Microsoft Office Clipboard See *Clipboard*.

Navigation Bar The bar located near the lower-left corner of the program window, above the status bar, that includes the navigation controls. It can be displayed as a compact vertical or horizontal bar that displays only module icons (compact view) or as a larger horizontal bar with text labels (standard view). See also *Folder Pane*.

offline address book A copy of an address book that has been downloaded so that an Outlook user can access the information it contains while disconnected from the server.

Outlook Help button The button located at the right end of the ribbon, labeled with a question mark (?), that provides access to the Outlook Help system.

Outlook Today A single-screen dashboard that displays the calendar events and scheduled tasks associated with your default email account for the current day, which you display by clicking your mailbox in the Folder Pane or by clicking Shortcuts on the Navigation Bar and then clicking Outlook Today.

palette A collection of color swatches that you can click to apply a color to selected text or an object.

People module The framework that provides the functionality to display and manage address books.

People peek An interactive view of favorite contacts and a search box associated with your default address book, which you display by pointing to People on the Navigation Bar or by pinning it to the To-Do Bar.

permissions Rules associated with a shared resource on a network, such as a file, directory, or printer. Permissions provide authorization to perform operations associated with these objects. Permissions can typically be assigned to groups, global groups, or individual users.

phishing message A technique used to trick computer users into revealing personal or financial information. A common online phishing scam starts with an email message that appears to come from a trusted source but actually directs recipients to provide information to a fraudulent website.

phishing site A website that prompts users to update personal information, such as bank accounts and passwords, which might be used for identity theft.

Plain Text An email message format that does not support character or paragraph formatting. All email programs support the Plain Text format.

plain text messages Messages that don't support character or paragraph formatting in the message content.

point to To pause the cursor over a button or other area of the display.

Post Office Protocol (POP) A standard method that computers use to send and receive email messages. POP messages are typically held on an email server until you download them to your computer, and then they are deleted from the server. With other email protocols, such as IMAP, email messages are held on the server until you delete them. You can configure Outlook to manage the retention of messages on the POP server.

presence icon A colored icon that indicates the online presence and status of a contact.

print style A combination of paper and page settings that determines the way items print. Outlook provides built-in print styles, and you can create your own.

Quick Access Toolbar A customizable toolbar that displays frequently used commands and can be located above or below the ribbon.

Quick Step A feature with which you can perform up to 12 actions with an email message in your Inbox by clicking one command.

recall To instruct Outlook to delete or replace any unread copies of a message that was already sent.

recurring item A calendar item or task that occurs repeatedly on a specific schedule. You can specify an appointment, meeting, or event as recurring, and specify the frequency of recurrence. Outlook then creates a series of items based on your specifications.

redundant message A message whose content is wholly contained within another message. Redundant messages are moved by the Clean Up tool.

reminder A message that appears at a specified interval before an appointment, meeting, or task that announces when the activity is set to occur. Reminders appear any time Outlook is running, even if it isn't your active program.

resend To create a new version of a sent or received message.

resolving The process of matching a user name to the information on a network server, resulting in the user name being replaced by a display name and the name underlined.

ribbon A user interface design that organizes commands into logical groups, which appear on separate tabs.

Rich Text Format (RTF) An email message format that supports paragraph styles, character styles, backgrounds, borders, and shading, but is compatible with only Outlook and Exchange Server. Outlook converts RTF messages to HTML when sending them outside of your Exchange network.

rules Sets of criteria defining specific actions that Outlook takes when the criteria are fulfilled.

screen clipping An image of all or part of the content displayed on a computer screen. Screen clippings can be captured by using a graphics capture tool such as the Screen Clipping tool included with Office 2013 programs.

ScreenTip A note that appears on the screen to provide information about the program interface or certain types of document content, such as hyperlinks within a message.

Secure Multipurpose Internet Mail Extensions (S/MIME) A protocol that supports secure mail features such as digital signatures and message encryption.

separated text file A file that contains unformatted text organized into fields and records. Records are separated by carriage returns; fields are separated by a specific character such as a comma, tab, colon, or semicolon. Separated text files might have the file name extension .txt or .csv.

server rule Or *server-side rule*. A rule that Exchange applies when receiving or processing a message, before delivering it. See also *client rule*.

shortcut menu A menu that shows a list of commands relevant to a particular item. Sometimes referred to as a *context menu*.

sizing handle A small circle, square, or set of dots that appears at the corner or on the side of a selected object. You drag these handles to change the size of the object horizontally, vertically, or proportionally.

SmartArt graphic A predefined set of shapes and text used as a basis for creating a diagram.

spam Unsolicited commercial email (UCE). Also known as *junk email*.

status bar A program window element, located at the bottom of the program window, that displays indicators and controls.

tab A tabbed page on the ribbon that contains buttons organized in groups.

task list The pane immediately to the right of the Folder Pane in the Tasks module, in which tasks or flagged items are displayed.

task originator The person who creates a task, specifically when assigning the task to someone else.

task owner The person to whom a task is currently assigned. After a task has been assigned, the task originator can no longer update the information in the task window.

task window The program window that displays the form in which you enter information to create or manage a task.

Tasks module The framework that provides the functionality to display and manage tasks and flagged items.

Tasks peek An interactive view of the tasks associated with your default email account, which you display by pointing to Tasks on the Navigation Bar or by pinning it to the To-Do Bar.

Tasks view An arrangement of the Tasks module, displaying a list of tasks associated with a specific email account in the content area. See also *To-Do List view*.

third-party add-in A software program created by one company (the "third party") that extends the capabilities of a larger program created by another company.

thread In email and Internet newsgroup conversations, a series of messages and replies that are all related to a specific topic.

thumbnail A small representation of an item, such as an image, a page of content, or a set of formatting, usually obtained by scaling a snapshot of it. Thumbnails are typically used to provide visual identifiers for related items.

title bar The horizontal bar at the top of a window that displays the window name and also contains the program icon; the Maximize, Minimize/Restore, and Close buttons; and the optional Help button.

To-Do Bar An optional pane that can be displayed on the right side of the program window, to which you can pin the Calendar peek, Contacts peek, and Tasks peek.

To-Do List view The default arrangement of the Tasks module, displaying a list of incomplete tasks and flagged items for your default email account in the content area. See also *Tasks view*.

tool tab A tab containing groups of commands that are pertinent only to a specific type of document element such as a picture, table, or text box. Tool tabs appear only when relevant content is selected.

Uniform Resource Locator (URL) An address that uniquely identifies a location on the Internet. A URL is usually preceded by http://, as in *http://www.microsoft.com*. A URL can contain more detail, such as the name of a page of hypertext, often with the file name extension .html or .htm.

unique message A message that contains content that is not present in other messages. Unique messages are not moved by the Clean Up tool.

view Different ways in which Outlook items can be arranged in the Outlook module window.

View Shortcuts toolbar A toolbar located near the right end of the status bar that displays buttons for switching between views of the current module.

web beacon A graphic that links to a webpage and is embedded in a message for use as a signaling device.

work week The days and times you define within Outlook as available for work-related activities.

Keyboard shortcuts

Throughout this book, we provide information about how to perform tasks quickly and efficiently by using keyboard shortcuts. This section presents information about keyboard shortcuts that are built in to Microsoft Outlook 2013 and Microsoft Office 2013.

TIP In the following lists, keys you press at the same time are separated by a plus sign (+), and keys you press sequentially are separated by a comma (,).

Outlook 2013 keyboard shortcuts

This section provides a comprehensive list of keyboard shortcuts built into Outlook 2013. The content has been excerpted from Outlook Help and formatted in tables for convenient lookup.

Create Outlook items or files

Action	Keyboard shortcut
Create an item of the current module type	Ctrl+N
Create a message	Ctrl+Shift+M
Create an appointment	Ctrl+Shift+A
Create a meeting request	Ctrl+Shift+Q
Create a contact	Ctrl+Shift+C
Create a distribution list	Ctrl+Shift+L
Create a task	Ctrl+Shift+K
Create a task request	Ctrl+Shift+Alt+U
Create a note	Ctrl+Shift+N
Create a folder	Ctrl+Shift+E
Create a Search Folder	Ctrl+Shift+P
Create a fax	Ctrl+Shift+X
Create a new Office document	Ctrl+Shift+H
Post to the current folder	Ctrl+Shift+S
Post a reply in the current folder	Ctrl+T

Navigate in Outlook

Action	Keyboard shortcut
Switch to the Mail module	Ctrl+1
Switch to the Calendar module	Ctrl+2
Switch to the Contacts module	Ctrl+3
Switch to the Tasks module	Ctrl+4
Switch to the Notes module	Ctrl+5
Display the Folder List in the Folder Pane	Ctrl+6
Switch to the Shortcuts module	Ctrl+7
Switch to the Journal module	Ctrl+8
Switch to the next message (with message open)	Ctrl+Period
Switch to the previous message (with message open)	Ctrl+Comma
Move between the Folder Pane, the content area, the Reading Pane, and the To-Do Bar	Ctrl+Shift+Tab or Shift+Tab
Move between the Outlook window, the smaller panes in the Folder Pane, the Reading Pane, and the sections in the To-Do Bar	Tab
Move between the Outlook window, the smaller panes in the Folder Pane, the Reading Pane, and the sections in the To-Do Bar, and show the KeyTips in the Outlook ribbon	F6
Move around message header lines in the Folder Pane or an open message	Ctrl+Tab
Move around within the Folder Pane	Arrow keys
Go to a different folder	Ctrl+Y
Go to the Search box	F3 or Ctrl+E
In the Reading Pane, go to the previous message	Alt+Up Arrow or Ctrl+Comma or Alt+Page Up
In the Reading Pane, page up/down through text	Shift+Spacebar/Spacebar
Expand/collapse a group in the email message list	Right Arrow/Left Arrow
Go back to the previous/forward to the next view in the main Outlook window	Alt+B or Alt+Left Arrow/Alt+Right Arrow
Select the InfoBar and, if available, show the menu of commands	Ctrl+Shift+W

Use the Outlook Backstage view

Action	Keyboard shortcut
Display the Info page of the Backstage view	Alt+F+I
Display the Save page of the Backstage view	Alt+F+S
Display the Save As page of the Backstage view	Alt+F+A
Display the Save Attachments page of the Backstage view	Alt+F+M
Display the Print page of the Backstage view	Alt+F+P
Display the Close page of the Backstage view	Alt+F+C
Display the Office Account page of the Backstage view	Alt+F+D
Display the Outlook Options dialog box	Alt+F+T
Close the Backstage view	Esc

TIP After displaying a page of the Backstage view, press the KeyTips displayed on that page to use features and commands.

Locate Outlook items

Action	Keyboard shortcut
Find a message or other item	Ctrl+E
Expand a search to include all items of the current type	Ctrl+Alt+A
Expand a search to include items from the current folder	Ctrl+Alt+K
Expand a search to include subfolders	Ctrl+Alt+Z
Use Advanced Find	Ctrl+Shift+F
Search for text within an open item	F4
Find and replace text, symbols, or some formatting commands in the Reading Pane on an open item	Ctrl+H
Clear the search results	Esc

Manage Outlook items

Action	Keyboard shortcut
Save (except in Tasks)	Ctrl+S or Shift+F12
Save and close (except in Mail)	Alt+S
Save as (only in Mail)	F12
Undo	Ctrl+Z or Alt+Backspace

Action	Keyboard shortcut
Delete an item	Ctrl+D
Print an item	Ctrl+P
Copy an item	Ctrl+Shift+Y
Move an item	Ctrl¦Shift+V
Forward an item	Ctrl+F
Forward an item as an attachment	Ctrl+Alt+F
Flag an item for follow-up	Ctrl+Shift+G
Send or post or invite all	Alt+S
Enable editing in a field (except in Mail or Icon view)	F2
Delete the selected category from the list in the Color Categories dialog box	Alt+D

Manage and format item content

TIP The cursor must be inside a text box when you use these shortcuts.

Action	Keyboard shortcut
Check spelling	F7
Cut	Ctrl+X or Shift+Delete
Copy	Ctrl+C or Ctrl+Insert Note: Ctrl+Insert is not available in the Reading Pane
Paste	Ctrl+V or Shift+Insert
Delete the next word	Ctrl+Shift+H
Display the Format menu	Alt+O
Display the Font dialog box	Ctrl+Shift+P
Switch case (with text selected)	Shift+F3
Format letters as small capitals	Ctrl+Shift+K
Make letters bold	Ctrl+B
Add bullets	Ctrl+Shift+L
Make letters italic	Ctrl+I
Increase indent or create a hanging indent	Ctrl+T
Decrease indent or reduce a hanging indent	Ctrl+Shift+T
Underline	Ctrl+U
Increase font size	Ctrl+] or Ctrl+Shift+>
Decrease font size	Ctrl+[or Ctrl+Shift+<
Clear character formatting	Ctrl+Shift+Z or Ctrl+Spacebar

Action	Keyboard shortcut
Left-align text	Ctrl+L
Center text	Ctrl+E
Right-align text	Ctrl+R
Justify text	Ctrl+Shift+J
Apply styles	Ctrl+Shift+S
Remove paragraph formatting	Ctrl+Q
Insert a hyperlink	Ctrl+K
Edit a URL in the body of an item	Hold down Ctrl and click the mouse button

Work with the Mail module and email messages

Action	Keyboard shortcut
Switch to the Inbox	Ctrl+Shift+I
Switch to the Outbox	Ctrl+Shift+O
Choose the account from which to send a message	Ctrl+Tab (with focus on the To box), and then Tab to the Accounts button
Check names	Ctrl+K
Send a message	Alt+S or Ctrl+Enter
Reply to a message	Ctrl+R
Reply All to a message	Ctrl+Shift+R
Reply with a meeting request	Ctrl+Alt+R
Mark a message as not junk	Ctrl+Alt+J
Display blocked external content (in a message)	Ctrl+Shift+I
Post to a folder	Ctrl+Shift+S
Apply Normal style	Ctrl+Shift+N
Check for new messages	Ctrl+M or F9
Go to the previous/next message	Up Arrow/Down Arrow
Open a received message	Ctrl+O
Delete and ignore a conversation	Ctrl+Shift+D
Open the Address Book	Ctrl+Shift+B
Add a Quick Flag to an unopened message	Insert
Display the Flag For Follow Up dialog box	Ctrl+Shift+G
Mark as read/unread	Ctrl+Q/Ctrl+U
Open the MailTip in the selected message	Ctrl+Shift+W
Find or replace	F4

Action	Keyboard shortcut
Find the next instance of the current search term	Shift+F4
Show the properties for the selected item	Alt+Enter
Create a multimedia message	Ctrl+Shift+U
Create a text message	Ctrl+Shift+T
Mark for download	Ctrl+Alt+M
Clear the mark for download	Ctrl+Alt+U
Display Send/Receive progress	Ctrl+B (when a Send/Receive is in progress)

Work with the Calendar module and calendar items

Action	Keyboard shortcut
Reply to a meeting request with a message	Ctrl+R
Reply All to a meeting request with a message	Ctrl+Shift+R
Move between Calendar, TaskPad, and the Folder List	Ctrl+Tab or F6
Go to a date	Ctrl+G
Switch to Month view	Alt+= or Ctrl+Alt+4
Switch to Week view	Alt+Minus Sign or Ctrl+Alt+3
Switch to Work Week view	Ctrl+Alt+2
View from 1 through 9 days	Alt+key for number of days
View 10 days	Alt+0
Select the previous appointment	Shift+Tab
Go to the previous/next day	Left Arrow/Right Arrow
Go to the same day in the previous/next week	Alt+Up Arrow/Alt+Down Arrow
Go to the previous/next week	Alt+Up Arrow/Alt+Down Arrow
Go to the previous/next month	Alt+Page Up/Alt+Page Down
Go to the beginning/end of the week	Alt+Home/Alt+End
Go to the previous/next appointment	Ctrl+Comma or Ctrl+Shift+Comma/ Ctrl+Period or Ctrl+Shift+Period
Set up a recurrence for an open appointment or meeting	Ctrl+G

Navigate in the Date Navigator

Action	Keyboard shortcut
Go to the first/last day of the current week	Alt+Home/Alt+End
Go to the same day in the previous/next week	Alt+Up Arrow/Alt+Down Arrow

Navigate in Day view

Action	Keyboard shortcut
Select the time that begins/ends your work day	Home/End
Select the previous/next block of time	Up Arrow/Down Arrow
Select the block of time at the top/bottom of the screen	Page Up/Page Down
Extend/reduce the selected time	Shift+Up Arrow/Shift+Down Arrow
Move an appointment up/down	With the cursor in the appointment, Alt+Up Arrow/Alt+Down Arrow
Change an appointment's start/end time	With the cursor in the appointment, Alt+Shift+Up Arrow/ Alt+Shift+Down Arrow
Move the selected item to the same day in the previous/ next week	Alt+Up Arrow/Alt+Down Arrow

Navigate in Week view

Action	Keyboard shortcut
Go to the start/end of work hours for the selected day	Home/End
Go up/down one page view in the selected day	Page Up/Page Down
Change the duration of the selected block of time	Shift+Left Arrow, Shift+Right Arrow, Shift+Up Arrow, or Shift+Down Arrow; or Shift+Home or Shift+End

Navigate in Month view

Action	Keyboard shortcut
Go to the first day of the week	Home
Go to the same day of the week in the previous/next page	Page Up/Page Down

Work with the People module and contact records

Action	Keyboard shortcut
Dial a new call	Ctrl+Shift+D
Find a contact or other item (Search)	F3 or Ctrl+E
Enter a name in the Search Address Books box	F11
In Table or List view of contacts, go to the first contact that starts with a specific letter	Shift+letter
Select all contacts	Ctrl+A

Action	Keyboard shortcut
Open a contact form for the selected contact	Ctrl+O
Update a list of distribution list members	F5
Open the Address Book	Ctrl+Shift+B
Use Advanced Find	Ctrl+Shift+F
Find a contact	F11
Close a contact	Esc
Send a fax to the selected contact	Ctrl+Shift+X
In a contact form, display the E-mail 1 information	Alt+Shift+1
In a contact form, display the E-mail 2 information	Alt+Shift+2
In a contact form, display the E-mail 3 information	Alt+Shift+3

Work in the Electronic Business Cards dialog box

Action	Keyboard shortcut
Open the Add list	Alt+A
Select text in the Label box when the field with a label assigned is selected	Alt+B
Open the Add Card Picture dialog box	Alt+C
Place the cursor at the beginning of the Edit box	Alt+E
Select the Fields box	Alt+F
Select the Image Align list	Alt+G
Select the color palette for background	Alt+K, then Enter
Select the Layout list	Alt+L
Remove a selected field from the Fields box	Alt+R

Work in Business Cards view or Address Cards view

Action	Keyboard shortcut
Select a specific card in the list	One or more letters of the name by which the card is filed or the field by which you are sorting
Select the previous/next card	Up Arrow/Down Arrow
Select the first/last card in the list	Home/End
Select the first card on the current page	Page Up
Select the first card on the next page	Page Down
Select the closest card in the previous/next column	Left Arrow/Right Arrow
Select or cancel selection of the active card	Ctrl+Spacebar

Action	Keyboard shortcut
Extend the selection to the previous/next card and cancel selection of cards after the starting point	Shift+Up Arrow/Shift+Down Arrow
Extend the selection to the previous/next card, regardless of the starting point	Ctrl+Shift+Up Arrow/ Ctrl+Shift+Down Arrow
Extend the selection to the first/last card in the list	Shift+Home/Shift+End
Extend the selection to the first/last card on the previous page	Shift+Page Up/Shift+Page Down

Move between fields in an open card and characters in a field

TIP To use the following keys, make sure a field in a card is selected. To select a field when a card is selected, click the field.

Action	Keyboard shortcut
Move to the previous/next field or control	Shift+Tab/Tab
Close the active card	Enter
Add a line in a multiline field	Enter
Move to the beginning/end of a line	Home/End
Move to the beginning/end of a multiline field	Page Up/Page Down
Move to the previous/next line in a multiline field	Up Arrow/Down Arrow
Move to the previous/next character in a field	Left Arrow/Right Arrow

Work with the Tasks module and tasks

Action	Keyboard shortcut
Accept/decline a task request	Alt+C/Alt+D
Find a task or other item	Ctrl+E
Open a selected item	Ctrl+O
Select all items	Ctrl+A
Delete the selected item	Ctrl+D
Switch between the Folder Pane, Tasks list, and To-Do Bar	Tab or Shift+Tab
Undo last action	Ctrl+Z
Flag an item or mark as complete	Insert

Work in the Timeline view when an item is selected

Action	Keyboard shortcut
Select the previous/next item	Left Arrow/Right Arrow
Select several adjacent items	Shift+Left Arrow or Shift+Right Arrow
Select several nonadjacent items	Ctrl+Left Arrow+Spacebar or Ctrl+Right Arrow+Spacebar
Open the selected items	Enter
Select the first/last item on the timeline (if items are not grouped) or in the group	Home/End
Display (without selecting) the first/last item on the timeline (if items are not grouped) or in the group	Ctrl+Home/Ctrl+End

Work in the Timeline view when a group is selected

Action	Keyboard shortcut
Expand/collapse the group tools	Enter or Right Arrow/Left Arrow
Select the previous/next group	Up Arrow/Down Arrow
Select the first/last group on the timeline	Home/End
Select the first item on the screen in an expanded group or the first item off the screen to the right	Right Arrow

Work in the Timeline view when a unit of time on the time scale for days is selected

Action	Keyboard shortcut
Move backward/forward in the increments of time shown on the time scale	Left Arrow/Right Arrow
Switch between active view, To-Do Bar, Search, and back to active view	Tab and Shift+Tab

Send and receive information

Action	Keyboard shortcut
Start a send/receive for all defined Send/Receive groups that include the F9 option	F9
Start a send/receive for the current folder	Shift+F9
Start a send/receive	Ctrl+M
Define Send/Receive groups	Ctrl+Alt+S

Use development tools

Action	Keyboard shortcut
Open the Visual Basic Editor	Alt+F11
Play a macro	Alt+F8
Create an InfoPath form	Click in an InfoPath folder, and then Ctrl+N
Choose an InfoPath form	Ctrl+Shift+Alt+T

Office 2013 keyboard shortcuts

This section provides a list of keyboard shortcuts available in all Office 2013 programs, including Outlook. Additional keyboard shortcuts are available in other Office programs.

Display and use windows

Action	Keyboard shortcut
Switch to the previous/next window	Alt+Shift+Tab/Alt+Tab
Move to a pane from another pane in the program window If pressing F6 does not display the pane that you want, press Alt to put the focus on the ribbon, and then press Ctrl+Tab to move to the pane	F6 or Shift+F6
Copy a picture of the screen to the Clipboard	Print Screen
Copy a picture of the active window to the Clipboard	Alt+Print Screen

Use dialog boxes

Action	Keyboard shortcut
Move to the previous/next option or option group	Shift+Tab/Tab
Switch to the previous/next tab in a dialog box	Ctrl+Shift+Tab/Ctrl+Tab
Move between options in an open list, or between options in a group of options	Arrow keys
Perform the action assigned to the selected button; select or clear the selected check box	Spacebar
Select an option; select or clear a check box	The underlined letter

Action	Keyboard shortcut
Open a selected list	Down Arrow or Alt+Down Arrow
Select an option from a list	The first letter of the list option
Close a selected list; cancel a command and close a dialog box	Esc
Run the selected command	Enter

Use edit boxes within dialog boxes

TIP An edit box is a blank box in which you enter or paste an entry.

Action	Keyboard shortcut
Move to the beginning/end of the entry	Home/End
Move one character to the left/right	Left Arrow/Right Arrow
Move one word to the left/right	Ctrl+Left Arrow/Ctrl+Right Arrow
Select or unselect one character to the left/right	Shift+Left Arrow/Shift+Right Arrow
Select or unselect one word to the left/right	Ctrl+Shift+Left Arrow/ Ctrl+Shift+Right Arrow
Select from the cursor to the beginning/end of the entry	Shift+Home/Shift+End

Use the Save As dialog box

Action	Keyboard shortcut
Open the Save As dialog box	F12
Open the selected folder or file	Enter
Open the folder one level above the selected folder	Backspace
Delete the selected folder or file	Delete
Move backward through options	Shift+Tab
Move forward through options	Tab
Open the Look In list	F4
Refresh the file list	F5

Undo and redo actions

Action	Keyboard shortcut
Cancel an action	Esc
Undo an action	Ctrl+Z
Redo or repeat an action	Ctrl+Y

Navigate the ribbon

Action	Keyboard shortcut
Activate or deactivate KeyTips	Alt or F10
Use a feature on the Quick Access Toolbar or ribbon	Press the KeyTip of the feature you want to use
Move to another tab of the ribbon	F10 to select the active tab, and then Left Arrow or Right Arrow
Expand or collapse the ribbon	Ctrl+F1
Move the focus to the next/previous command	Tab/Shift+Tab
Move among the items on the ribbon	Arrow keys
Activate the selected command or control on the ribbon	Spacebar or Enter
Display the selected menu or gallery on the ribbon	Spacebar or Enter
Activate a command or control on the ribbon so that you can modify a value	Enter
Finish modifying a value in a control on the ribbon, and move focus back to the document	Enter
Get help on the selected command or control on the ribbon	F1

Move around in text or cells

Action	Keyboard shortcut
Move one character to the left/right	Left Arrow/Right Arrow
Move one line up/down	Up Arrow/Down Arrow
Move one word to the left/right	Ctrl+Left Arrow/Ctrl+Right Arrow
Move to the beginning/end of a line	Home/End
Move up/down one paragraph	Ctrl+Up Arrow/Ctrl+Down Arrow
Move to the beginning/end of a text box	Ctrl+Home/Ctrl+End

Move around in and work in tables

Action	Keyboard shortcut
Move to the previous/next cell	Shift+Tab/Tab
Move to the previous/next row	Up Arrow/Down Arrow
Insert a tab in a cell	Ctrl+Tab
Start a new paragraph	Enter
Add a new row at the bottom of the table	Tab at the end of the last row

Access and use panes and galleries

Action	Keyboard shortcut
Move to a pane from another pane in the program window	F6
When a menu is active, move to a pane	Ctrl+Tab
When a pane is active, select the next or previous option in the pane	Tab or Shift+Tab
Display the full set of commands on the pane menu	Ctrl+Spacebar
Perform the action assigned to the selected button	Spacebar or Enter
Open a menu for the selected gallery item	Shift+F10
Select the first/last item in a gallery	Home/End
Scroll up/down in the selected gallery list	Page Up/Page Down
Close a pane	Ctrl+Spacebar, C
Open or close the Clipboard	Alt+H, F, O

Access and use available actions

Action	Keyboard shortcut
Move between options in a menu of available actions	Arrow keys
Perform the action for the selected item on a menu of available actions	Enter
Close the available actions menu or message	Esc

Find and replace content (when editing)

Action	Keyboard shortcut
Open the Find dialog box	Ctrl+F
Open the Replace dialog box	Ctrl+H
Repeat the last Find action	Shift+F4

Use the Help window

Action	Keyboard shortcut
Open the Help window	F1
Close the Help window	Alt+F4
Switch between the Help window and the active program	Alt+Tab
Return to the Help table of contents	Alt+Home
Select the previous/next item, hidden text, or hyperlink in the Help window	Shift+Tab/Tab
Perform the action for the selected item, hidden text, or hyperlink	Enter
Move back to the previous/forward to the next Help topic	Alt+Left Arrow or Backspace/ Alt+Right Arrow
Scroll a few lines up/down within the current Help topic	Up Arrow/Down Arrow
Scroll one page up/down within the current Help topic	Page Up/Page Down
Stop the last action (Stop button)	Esc
Print the current Help topic If the cursor is not in the current Help topic, press F6 and then press Ctrl+P	Ctrl+P
In a Table of Contents, select the previous/next item	Up Arrow/Down Arrow
In a Table of Contents, expand/collapse the selected item	Right Arrow/Left Arrow

Index

A

accepting meeting requests, 186, 417
accepting task requests, 214, 215, 216
Account Setup wizard, 10
accounts. *See* email accounts
Active view, 221
    for calendars, 189
    displaying, 224
actual size, previewing contacts in, 159
Add Holidays To Calendar dialog box, 174
add-ins
    defined, 509
    installing, 441
    managing, 440
Add New Category dialog box, 249
Add New Member dialog box, 328
Add To Favorites dialog box, 484
address books, 136. *See also* Contacts address book
    defined, 509
    adding contacts from email attachments, 111
    adding contacts to, 154
    creating, 137, 310, 311
    deleting, 324
    displaying, 74, 313
    displaying in People module, 310
    downloading for offline access, 486
    Global Address List (GAL), 138
    importing contact records into, 320
    importing from SharePoint contact lists, 503
    search order, changing, 92
    searching, 310
    selecting message recipients from, 148
    switching among, 310
    troubleshooting, 92
    views for, 149

addresses
    for contacts, setting, 139
    verifying, 147
Addressing dialog box, 92
addressing email messages, 88
    Auto-Complete List, cleaning up, 91
    checking names when, 90
    within Exchange network, 89
    to multiple recipients, 91
advanced Outlook options, 422
Advanced View Settings dialog box, 151
agendas, printing calendars as, 297, 300
alerts. *See* desktop alerts; notifications
aligning paragraphs, 353
Appointment Recurrence dialog box, 172, 178
appointment windows, 68
    defined, 509
    contents of, 168
appointments, 168
    defined, 509
    changing time of, 170
    changing to events, 72
    configuring options for, 415
    creating, 70, 168
    creating, from messages, 176
    emailing graphical representation of, 290
    Free/Busy time, setting, 171
    inviting attendees to, 70
    marking free/busy time, 168
    opening in own windows, 170
    private, setting as, 171
    recurring, 169, 172
    reminder messages for, 168, 171
    saving and closing, 173
    selecting, 170

appointments *(continued)*
    setting time zones for, 72
    time zones, specifying, 169, 281
archiving items, configuring, 423
arrangements
    defined, 509
    displaying gallery of, 222, 223
arranging
    calendars by day/week/month, 190, 195
    conversations, 237
    messages, 237
arrows, inserting, 364
artistic effects, adding to pictures, 379
aspect ratio, cropping pictures to, 375
assigning tasks, 214, 217, 218
    reclaiming declined, 216
attachments
    displaying, 115
    forwarding messages as, 124, 410
    grouping messages by, 239
    inserting in messages, 105
    opening, 110
    pictures, 107
    previewing, 115
    saving, 110
    viewing, 109
    working with, 103
Auto-Complete List
    cleaning up, 91
    configuring, 411
    modifying settings for, 91
AutoArchive, configuring, 423
AutoCorrect, configuring, 405
Automatic Replies dialog box, 493
Automatic Reply Rules dialog box, 495
automatically replying to email messages, 479, 491
    configuring settings for, 494
    formatting message text when, 493
    information bar for, 497
    managing automatic replies, 32
    outside your organization, 494
    rules for, 491, 495
    setting time range for, 493
    setting up, 492
    turning off, 498
    uses for, 491
availability. *See* free/busy time
availability icons. *See* presence icons

B

Background Removal tool, 372
backgrounds
    applying message backgrounds, 347
    removing picture backgrounds, 372
Backstage view
    of calendar item windows, 69
    of contact record windows, 76
    displaying, 32
    of message composition windows, 53
    of message reading windows, 56
    of task windows, 83
    working with, 32
banners, inserting, 364
Bcc field, copying recipients with, 89, 149
Bing Image Search, 363
birthdays, entering for contacts, 141
blind courtesy copies, 89
blocking
    external content, 476
    messages, 459, 466
book exercises, adapting for other display
    settings, 11
booklets, printing contacts as, 157
bulleted lists, 98
Business Card view, 150
business cards
    adding to address book, 111
    displaying, 150, 152, 337
    editing, 338
    fields, adding/removing, 340
    including in signatures, 336, 359
    layout, changing, 339
    personalizing, 337

pictures, adding, 338
   resetting, 341
   saving, 342
   sending by email, 336
   in signatures, 336, 359
business graphics, 381
button arrows, 28

C

Cached Exchange Mode, 479. *See also* offline mode
   defined, 509
   configuring, 485, 489
   download options, configuring, 489
   enabling, 123
   overview of, 480
   send/receive settings, configuring, 487
   turning on and off, 486
calendar item windows, 68
   defined, 509
   Backstage view of, 69
   opening, 70
calendar items
   defined, 509
   applying categories to, 247
   creating from messages, 176
Calendar module
   defined, 509
   calendar item windows, 68
   configuring, 415
   content in, 65
   Daily Task List, displaying, 220
   displaying, 65, 70
   months on display, changing, 192
   ribbon in, 66
   view options, 67
   views for, 189, 66
Calendar peek, *defined*, 509
Calendar Properties dialog box, 291
calendars
   defined, 509
   adding tasks to, 220

appointments, creating, 70
arranging by day/week/month, 190, 195
copying items between, 283
creating items on, 69
custom, 282
delegating control of, 292
display options, configuring, 416
displaying, 282, 283, 286
displaying current day, 194
dragging tasks onto, 168
emailing, 294
events, creating, 72
hiding, 282, 286
holidays, adding, 174
holidays, removing, 175
importing, 285
Internet, connecting to, 284
making default, 287
meetings, creating, 70
months on display, changing, 192
multiple, displaying, 282, 286
navigating, 191, 192, 196
Overlay Mode, viewing in, 286, 287
previewing, 196, 298, 300, 303
printing, 297
publishing to Internet, 290, 295
resetting views, 197
Schedule View, displaying, 288
selecting items in, 192
setting permissions for, 291
SharePoint, connecting to, 505
sharing, 282, 290, 294
Side-By-Side Mode, viewing in, 287
synchronizing with Exchange Server
   accounts, 177
time zones, configuring, 280
tri-fold, printing, 304
view, changing, 169, 288
views for, 189
weather, displaying in, 417
work week, defining, 276

calendars *(continued)*
>   work week, displaying, 190, 193
>   working with as folders, 67
>   zooming in and out, 288
calling contacts, 146
canceling meetings, 185
canceling search, 334
capturing screen images, 366
carbon copies. *See* courtesy copies
Card view, 150, 153
categories. *See* color categories
Cc field, copying recipients with, 89, 149
Certificate Manager, 470
certificates. *See* digital certificates
certification authorities, 468
Change Security Settings dialog box, 471, 472
character spacing, 60, 353
character styles, applying, 350, 353
charts, 381, 383
Check Address dialog box, 147
Check Full Name dialog box, 147
Check Names dialog box, 90
Choose A SmartArt Graphic dialog box, 383, 384
cleaning up conversations, 236, 409
clearing
>   categories, 248
>   formatting, 64
>   search results, 268
client application vs. Web App, 5
client rules, *defined*, 509
clip art, *defined*, 509. *See also* pictures
Clipboard, 58
>   *defined*, 509
>   sharing content between Office programs, 355
Close button, 26
closing
>   calendars, 282, 286
>   messages, after replying or forwarding, 125
collapsing
>   groups, 240, 242
>   ribbon, 28, 64

color categories, 244
>   *defined*, 509
>   applying, 247, 248
>   assigning, 226, 244, 250
>   assigning keyboard shortcuts for, 249
>   clearing from items, 248
>   colors, assigning, 249
>   creating, 245, 249
>   deleting, 250
>   grouping by, 239, 247, 250
>   for holidays, 175
>   modifying, 245, 249
>   naming, 249
>   Quick Click, designating, 246
>   setting default, 426
Color Categories dialog box, 248
coloring text, 61
colors. *See also* font colors
>   applying to business cards, 339
>   assigning to categories, 246, 249
>   for notes, 252
>   for SmartArt graphics, changing, 388
>   for themes, 349
columns
>   adding and removing, 240
>   removing from list view, 155
COM Add-Ins dialog box, 441
comma-separated values (CSV) files
>   exporting to, 320
>   importing from, 315, 317
commands
>   accessing on ribbon, 28
>   adding to Quick Access Toolbar, 30, 427, 430
>   configuring on ribbon, 434
commas, separating recipients with, 91
companies, searching by, 334
Completed view, 221
composing email messages. *See* creating email messages
conference rooms, scheduling meetings in, 180
configuring Outlook, 12

connecting SharePoint document libraries to Outlook, 499

connecting to Exchange Server, 18

connection
  problems, troubleshooting, 20
  status, viewing, 26

contact cards, 7, 119
  defined, 509
  opening, 141

contact folders. *See* address books; Contacts address book

contact groups. *See also* distribution lists
  defined, 509
  adding members to, 325, 326
  adding to contact groups, 327
  creating, 325
  expanding, 330
  saving, 329
  sending messages to, 325, 330

contact index, 73
  defined, 509

contact lists
  defined, 510
  importing from SharePoint, 503
  scrolling by alphabet, 73

contact record windows, 75
  defined, 510

contact records. *See also* People module
  defined, 510
  adding fields to, 79
  adding to address book, 111
  adding to groups, 325, 326
  business cards, personalizing, 337
  changing filing order of, 136
  closing and saving, 80
  communication types, displaying, 79
  copying, 313
  creating, 77, 134, 135, 138
  creating from existing records, 143
  creating from messages, 147
  creating tasks from, 202
  custom fields, creating, 156

customizing display of, 151

displaying details in, 78

editing, 141

fields, customizing, 154

filtering, 321

flagging for follow-up, 203

flags, removing, 213

formatting text in, 77

importing and exporting, 315

information in, 135

initiating communication from, 146

inserting items into, 76

mapping fields when importing, 318

mapping locations in, 147

moving, 313

opening, 337

opening in contact window, 141

opening messages and webpages from, 80

pictures, adding, 338

previewing, 159, 161

printing, 157

resolving email addresses with, 90

reviewing items in, 77

saving, 141

saving field information in, 75

scrolling with contact index, 152

searching, 332

searching and filtering, 151

searching for, 310

selecting, 162, 313

sending by email, 336

sorting, 153

verifying names and addresses, 147

viewing linked items, 141

views, changing, 152

views for, 149

websites, loading from, 146

working with, 75, 76

contacts
  defined, 509
  adding to address books, 154
  birthdays, entering, 141

contacts *(continued)*
    business cards, displaying, 152
    calling, 146
    email addresses, entering, 138
    mailing addresses, setting default, 139
    names, entering, 138
    photographs for, 121
    presence icons for, 119
Contacts address book, 136. *See also* address books
    contents of, 310
    displaying, 74
Contacts module. *See* People module
content area, 41
    defined, 510
    customizing appearance of, 48
content panes, *defined*, 510
context menus, *defined*, 514
contextual tabs. *See* tool tabs
Conversation view, 112
    customizing settings, 234
    enabling, 233
    troubleshooting, 237
    working with, 232
conversations
    defined, 510
    arranging, 237
    cleaning up, 236, 409
    deleting, 236
    displaying messages from specific folders, 234
    display options, 233
    expanding, 233, 235, 414
    finding messages in, 237
    ignoring, 236
    indenting, 235
    managing messages as a group, 236
    moving into and out of folders, 257
    searching, 237
    selecting all messages in, 236
    senders, displaying, 235
    splitting, 233
copying
    between Office programs, 355

    calendar items, 283
    configuring options for, 406
    contact records, 313
    messages, preventing, 475
    SmartArt graphics, 389
courtesy copies, 89
Create New Folder dialog box, 137, 255, 311, 312
Create Outlook Data File dialog box, 323
creating email messages, 51, 57, 88
    addressing, 88
    configuring options for, 405, 411
    entering content, 93
    opening message windows, 95
creating Outlook items, 95
cropping pictures, 373
    to aspect ratios, 375
.csv files. *See* comma-separated values (CSV) files
current view, customizing, 48
cursor, *defined*, 510
custom calendars, 282
Custom dialog box, 207
customer feedback program, 19
cutting and pasting, 406. *See also* copying

D

Daily Task List
    displaying, 220
    hiding, 277
data files, configuring, 17
Date Navigator, 191, 65
    defined, 510
Day view, 189
declining
    meeting requests, 186
    task requests, 214, 215, 216
default folder, setting, 423
Delegate Permissions dialog box, 293
delegating calendar control, 292
Deleted Items folder, 46
    emptying, 265, 423

deleting
- address books, 324
- categories, 250
- conversations, 236
- flags, 213
- holidays from calendar, 175
- junk email, 461, 464
- messages, 265, 414
- Quick Step actions, 449
- signatures, 355
- tasks, 202, 213

delivery receipts,
- configuring, 413
- requesting, 392

desktop alerts, 102, 106. *See also* notifications
- *defined*, 510
- configuring, 106, 404, 409
- managing, 32

Detailed view, 221
- displaying, 223

diagrams. *See* charts; SmartArt graphics

dial-up connections, discontinuation of, 8

dialog box launcher, 28
- *defined*, 510

dictionaries, configuring, 421

digital certificates
- displaying, 20, 78
- error messages, 20
- managing, 470
- renaming, 470

digital IDs
- importing and exporting, 469
- obtaining, 467
- S/MIME, obtaining, 469

digital signatures, 391
- *defined*, 510
- applying to messages, 470, 473
- configuring, 467

disconnecting Outlook from the Internet, 49

display options, configuring, 406

display settings, changing, 31

distribution lists, 120. *See also* contact groups
- *defined*, 510
- adding to contact groups, 327

docking, module peeks, 44, 400

document libraries
- connecting to other computers, 500
- connecting to Outlook, 499
- subfolders, indicators for, 501
- updating subscriptions to, 500
- working offline with, 499

document workspaces, 510
- *defined*, 510

domains
- *defined*, 510
- blocking messages from, 466

download options for Cached Exchange Mode, 489

drafts, 95
- *defined*, 510
- editing, 97
- saving, 95, 411

Drafts folder, 46, 94, 95, 411

drawings, inserting, 364

due dates
- grouping messages by, 239
- for tasks, assigning, 84, 418

E

Edit Business Card dialog box, 338

Edit Quick Step dialog box, 260, 446, 450

Edit Rule dialog box, 496

editing
- business cards, 338
- contact records, 141
- meeting requests, 185
- message drafts, 97
- Quick Steps, 260, 446
- rules, 453, 496
- signatures, 359
- tasks, 210

Editor Options dialog box, 405

electronic business cards. *See* business cards

electronic notes. *See* notes

email, *defined*, 510

email accounts
    adding, 12
    address books for, 136
    calendars, accessing, 282
    configuring, 10, 17
    connecting to, 10
    default folders for, 46
    encrypting, 22
    Exchange Server, 9, 15, 18, 177
    grouping messages by, 239
    Internet, 21
    managing multiple, 104
    manually configuring, 14
    multiple, adding, 10
    naming, 16
    problems connecting to, 14
    Quick Steps for, 258
    saved messages in, 95
    send/receive options, enabling, 488
    setting up, 8
    signatures for, 355, 359
    synchronizing with, 66, 177
    testing settings for, 23
    troubleshooting connection problems, 20

email addresses
    adding to messages, 53
    for contacts, entering, 138
    entering in messages, 89
    resolving, 89, 148, 411
    separating with commas, 411

email attachments. *See* attachments

email conversations. *See* conversations;
    Conversation view

email etiquette, 125

email messages
    defined, 510
    applying categories to, 247
    arranging, 237
    assigning categories to, 250

attachments, inserting, 105
backgrounds, applying, 347
blocking external content in, 476
calendars, sending as, 294
Cc field, copying recipients with, 89
Conversation view, 232, 233
creating calendar items from, 176
creating from contact records, 80, 146
creating tasks from, 202
deleting, 265, 414
delivery options, setting, 392
digitally signing, 391, 467, 470, 473
due dates, assigning, 203
editing drafts, 97
encrypting, 391, 468, 474
entering content, 93
filtering, 242
flagging for follow-up, 202, 204, 391, 449
flags, removing, 213
fonts, changing, 356
formats supported for, 93
formatting options, 414
formatting text, 54, 59
forwarding, 124, 128, 258
grouping, 239, 240, 241
headers and footers, adding, 272
icons for, 49
importance, setting, 53, 391
inserting items into, 54
junk email settings, configuring, 465
marking as read/unread, 244
marking for follow-up, 53
moving, 256, 258, 455
notifications for, 102, 106
opening in new windows, 118
organizing with folders, 253
participant information, viewing, 119
permissions, restricting, 393
permissions, setting, 475
personalizing, 93
pictures, inserting, 369
plain text, sending/receiving, 475

popping out into windows, 99
previewing, 108, 109, 114, 269, 402
printing, 268
Quick Steps for, 258, 446, 455
reading and opening, 109
recalling, 130
replying to, 123, 127, 258
resending, 130
restricting actions on, 475
saving, 94, 95, 410
in Search Folders, changing/deleting, 265
searching, 262, 266
selecting, 236
selecting account to send from, 104
sending, 102, 258
sensitivity, setting, 391
settings, changing, 390
sorting, 240, 241
stationery, applying, 347
status, changing, 244
styles, applying, 350
subject, including, 88
themes, applying, 347
tracking, 392
transferring to task lists, 202, 205
unread, displaying, 109, 243
viewing, 108, 112
viewing blocked content, 476
views for, 237
voting buttons, adding, 391
email servers, *defined*, 510
email signatures. *See* signatures
email trails, *defined*, 511
emptying Deleted Items folder, 265, 423
encoding, configuring, 426
encrypted connections
    problems with, 20
    setting up, 22
encrypting email messages, 391, 468, 474
encryption, *defined*, 511

event windows,
    defined, 511
    opening, 72
events
    defined, 511
    changing to appointments, 72
    creating, 72, 176
    recurring, 177
Exchange ActiveSync support, 7
Exchange Server accounts, 9
    Cached Exchange mode, configuring, 485
    configuring, 15
    connecting to, 18
    encrypted connection problems, 20
    MailTips, configuring, 412
    rules, creating, 451
    synchronizing calendars with, 177
    troubleshooting, 20
expanding
    contact groups, 330
    conversations, 233, 235, 414
    Folder Pane, 398
    groups, 240, 242
    ribbon, 428
Export Outlook Data File wizard, 322
exporting
    appointments, by email, 290
    contact records, 315, 320
    digital IDs, 469
    files, 32
extensions. *See* file types
external content, blocking, 476
external content, downloading, 108

F

Favorites list, adding folders to, 46
Favorites, Public Folder, 484
Field Chooser, 154

fields
    arrows for displaying related information, 78
    saving information in, 75
file attachments. *See* attachments
file types, displaying, 107
Filter dialog box, 322
filtering. *See also* rules
    defined, 511
    contact records, 151, 321
    messages, 242
finding. *See* searching
First Time Setup dialog box, 259
Flag Message dialog box, 449
flagging email messages for follow-up, 202, 204, 391
    Quick Steps for, 449
flags
    deleting items with, 213
    removing from items, 213
flowcharts
    creating, 383
    symbols, inserting, 364
Folder List
    defined, 511
    address books in, 137
    displaying, 47
Folder Pane, 6, 40
    defined, 511
    content of, 46
    customizing, 398, 399
    default folders in, 46
    Folder List view, displaying, 47
    minimizing/expanding, 398, 399
folders. *See also* public folders
    adding to Favorites list, 46
    creating, 254, 255, 311
    creating as address books, 137
    default, setting, 423
    importing contact records to, 317
    managing, 50
    moving messages into, 256
    organizing messages with, 253
    Search Folders, setting up, 264

searching, 262
selecting location for, 255
structuring, 253
font colors, 340, 346, 357, 359
Font dialog box, 59, 60, 356, 357
font size, in Reading Pane, 112
fonts
    changing, 59, 348, 356
    changing style, 353
    default, 346, 355
    location on computer, 356
    for message replies, setting, 357
    previewing, 356
    selecting for printing, 270
footers. *See* headers and footers
foreign languages. *See* languages
Format Text Effects dialog box, 61
formatting email messages, 414
formatting pictures, 362, 364, 371
    SmartArt graphics as, 384
formatting tables, 100, 101
formatting text, 59, 94
    in automatic replies, 493
    as bulleted lists, 98
    with character spacing, 60
    clearing all formatting, 64
    with colors, 61
    configuring preferences for, 346
    in contact records, 77
    with font effects, 60, 61
    manually, 352
    in messages, 54
    with shadows, 62
    in signatures, 359
    with styles and style sets, 350, 351
    with themes, 349
    undoing effects, 64
forms
    accessing form libraries, 442
    creating, 442
    saving, 442
    Standard Forms library, 442

forwarding email messages, 124, 128, 258
    as attachments, 410
    closing original messages, 125
    configuring options for, 410
    preventing, 393, 475
    setting signature for, 94
forwarding task requests, 217
free/busy time, 168, 171
    checking, 181, 187
    sharing, 294

G

galleries, *defined*, 511
geometric shapes, inserting, 364
Global Address List (GAL), 92, 138
    defined, 511
    Cached Exchange Mode downloading of, 486
    displaying, 310
graphics. *See* charts; pictures; SmartArt graphics
group schedules, importing, 426
grouping
    by category, 247, 250
    messages, 239, 240, 241
    tasks, 224
groups, contacts. *See* contact groups
groups, ribbon, 436
    defined, 511
    adding commands to, 436
    adding to tabs, 437
    removing, 437

H

headers. *See* message headers
headers and footers, printing messages with, 272
Help button, 33
    defined, 512
Help system, 33
    displaying Help window, 33, 34
    related information, displaying, 36
    searching, 35

hiding
    buttons on ribbon, 28
    calendar events from other users, 171
    calendars, 282, 286
    Daily Task List, 277
    Mini Toolbar, 99
    People Pane, 399
    ribbon, 428
    To-Do Bar, 399
holidays
    adding to calendar, 174, 415
    removing from calendar, 175
Hotmail accounts, connecting to, 7
HTML email messages, 93
    defined, 511
HTTP protocol, *defined*, 511
hyperlinks
    defined, 511
    in notes, adding, 252

I

iCalendar format (ICS) files, 284. *See also* calendars
ignoring conversations, 236
images. *See* charts; pictures; SmartArt graphics
IMAP accounts
    defined, 511
    configuring, 22
    troubleshooting, 21
Import And Export wizard, 316
    starting, 424
importance
    grouping messages by, 239
    marking, 53
    setting, 391
importing
    contact records, 315
    contact records, mapping fields when, 318
    digital IDs, 469
    external data, 315
    files, 32
    group schedules, 426

importing *(continued)*
>   Internet calendars, 285
>   SharePoint contact lists, 503

importing/exporting, discontinuation of, 8

Inbox
>   displaying, 312
>   organizing with folders, 253
>   viewing messages in, 108

Inbox folder, 46

indenting
>   conversations, 235
>   paragraphs, 353

Indexing Options dialog box, 420

indexing scope for search, configuring, 420

InfoBar, *defined*, 511

InfoPath forms, 414

information bar, *defined*, 511

Information Rights Management (IRM), 475
>   *defined*, 511

inline email message replies, 6

Insert Chart dialog box, 381

Insert Pictures window, 363

inserting items into email messages, 54

installing
>   add-ins, 441
>   digital certificates, 20
>   Outlook updates, 19

instant messages (IMs)
>   *defined*, 511
>   replying to email messages with, 125
>   sending from contact records, 146

international Outlook options, 426

Internet calendars
>   accessing, 282
>   connecting to, 284
>   displaying, 285
>   importing, 285
>   publishing, 290, 295

Internet Message Access Protocol (IMAP). *See* IMAP accounts

inviting attendees to appointments, 70

J

Junk E-Mail folder, 46

junk email messages
>   *defined*, 512
>   blocking, 459
>   blocking from specific countries, 466
>   blocking senders of, 465
>   checking status of, 460
>   deleting, 461
>   deleting automatically, 464
>   displaying in Junk E-mail folder, 459
>   graphic disabling for, 460
>   marking as not junk, 462
>   moving out of Junk E-mail folder, 461, 462
>   protection level, setting, 463
>   replying to, 461
>   settings for, managing, 463

Junk E-mail Options dialog box, 463

justifying text, *defined*, 512

K

keyboard shortcuts
>   *defined*, 512
>   for accessing send/receive groups, 486
>   for address resolution, 89
>   for categories, 245, 249
>   for clearing search results, 268
>   for collapsing ribbon, 64
>   for creating appointments, 70
>   for creating contact records, 77
>   for creating folders, 255
>   for creating messages, 57
>   for creating Search Folders, 264
>   for creating tasks, 84
>   for deleting categories, 250
>   for deleting messages, 265
>   for displaying calendar in Month arrangement, 196
>   for displaying Calendar module, 70
>   for displaying Contacts module, 77

for displaying Folder List view, 47
for expanding searches, 267
for ignoring conversations, 236
for marking messages as read/unread, 244
for moving to search box, 151
for redoing editing, 373
for saving draft messages, 94
for searching, 266, 332
for sending messages, 102
for switching calendars to Schedule View, 288
for switching calendars to Work Week
    arrangement, 193
for switching modules, 44
for undoing editing, 373

L

language packs, installing, 421
languages
    adding content indexes for, 73
    configuring options for, 421
List view, 151
list views
    for calendars, 189
    removing columns from, 155
Live Preview, 30
    defined, 512
    for tables, 99
logon credentials, requiring, 18
Lync Meeting group in Calendar module, 66

M

magnification
    adjusting, 27
    in Reading Pane, 112
Mail module
    calendars, displaying/hiding, 283
    configuring, 404
    Folder Pane, 46
    message windows, 50
    overview of, 45

ribbon in, 49
tabs in, 49
mailboxes, multiple, 17
mailing addresses for contacts, setting, 139
MailTips, 331
    configuring, 412
manually configuring email accounts, 14
Map Custom Fields dialog box, 318
mapping contact locations, 147
mapping fields when importing, 318
marketing information, blocking, 476
marking email messages
    for follow-up, 53
    as not junk, 462
    as read/unread, 244, 408
marking tasks as complete, 202, 205, 212
mathematical operators, inserting, 364
Maximize/Restore Down button, 26
maximizing the program window, 31
meeting attendees
    adding, 181, 183
    marking as optional, 180, 184
meeting requests
    defined, 512
    accepting automatically, 417
    checking availability for, 187
    configuring options for, 411
    creating, 70, 123
    creating, from contact records, 146
    editing, 185
    replying to, 126
    responding to, 186, 188
    schedules, checking, 71
    sending, 179
    tracking responses to, 182
meeting windows, 68, 179
    defined, 512
    Scheduling Assistant, 180
meetings
    attendees, adding, 181, 183
    attendees, marking as optional, 180, 184
    canceling, 185

meetings *(continued)*

    changing time and duration, 182, 184

    configuring options for, 415

    creating, 172, 182

    editing, 185

    Room Finder, 180

    scheduling, 178

    time zones, specifying, 281

    viewing, 184

memos

    printing contact records as, 157, 163

    printing emails as, 270

message body, 52, 56, 88

message composition windows, 51

    commands in, 53

message headers, 52, 56

    defined, 512

    downloading with Cached Exchange Mode, 489

    From button in, 104

    icons in, 108

message list, 6

    defined, 512

    columns, adding and removing, 240

    icons in, 49

    views for, 108

message participants

    contact cards, viewing, 119

    creating contact records for, 147

    presence icons for, 119

    recent interactions, viewing, 122

    viewing in People Pane, 121

message reading windows, 55

message recipients

    adding from address books, 148

    editing before replying, 124

message windows, 50

    defined, 512

    opening, 95

messages. *See* email messages; instant messages (IMs)

Microsoft Office Clipboard, 58

Microsoft OneNote 2013, creating entries from contact records, 147

Microsoft Outlook 2013. *See* Outlook 2013

Microsoft Outlook dialog box, 499

Microsoft Outlook Help button, 26, 33

Microsoft SharePoint. *See* SharePoint

Minimize button, 26

minimizing

    Folder Pane, 398, 399

    ribbon, 428

Mini Toolbar, 59

    displaying when selecting text, 404

    hiding, 99

module preview, 7

modules, 24

    displaying, 44

    keyboard shortcuts for switching between, 44

    peeking at, 44

months, changing display of, 192

mouse pointer, changing shape as notification, 106

moving

    contact records, 313

    conversations, 257

    messages, 256, 258, 455

    Quick Access Toolbar, 427, 428, 432

    text, between Office programs, 355

N

naming

    categories, 245, 249

    digital certificates, 470

    email accounts, 16

Navigation Bar, 6, 42

    defined, 512

    compact, 42

    configuring, 422

    customizing, 42, 43, 399

    resizing, 42

    standard, 42

Navigation Options dialog box, 43

Navigation Pane. *See* Folder Pane
New Column dialog box, 156
new features in Outlook 2013, 6
New Search Folder dialog box, 264
non-Latin/non-English characters, allowing, 426
Normal view, 40, 48
    of Calendar module, 65
    of People module, 73
    in Tasks module, 81
notes
    colors, changing, 252
    creating, 253
    creating tasks from, 202
    hyperlinks, adding to, 252
    recording information in, 252, 253
    searching, 252
Notes module, accessing, 252
notifications, 102, 106. *See also* desktop alerts
    configuring, 106, 409
    for message delivery, 413

◯

Office 365, 5
offline address books
    defined, 512
    configuring, 486
    manually updating, 489
offline help, 34
offline mode, 479. *See also* Cached Exchange Mode
    configuring, 425
    for SharePoint document libraries, 499
    for SharePoint documents, 502
    status indicator, viewing, 481
    switching out of, 481
    switching to, 49, 481
OneNote, creating entries from contact records, 147
online pictures, 363
Open & Export page of Backstage view, 315
opening
    appointments, 170

attachments, 110
contact cards, 141
contact records, 337
messages, 109, 118
task windows, 207
Tasks module, 206
optional meeting attendees, 180, 184
organizing tasks, 226
Outbox folder, 47
Outlook 2010, upgrading from, 6
Outlook 2013
    client application vs. Web App, 5
    configuring, 12
    in enterprise environment, 3
    features discontinued in, 7
    features, new, 6
    functions of, 4
    help with, 33
    starting, 12
Outlook Anywhere, 9
Outlook data files, 10
    exporting to, 320
    importing, 315
    password protecting, 322
Outlook forms. *See* forms
Outlook Help button, *defined*, 512
Outlook notes. *See* notes
Outlook Options dialog box, 278, 403
    Mail page, 106
Outlook Options window, 33
Outlook Today
    defined, 512
    displaying, 220
Outlook Web App (OWA), 5
Out of Office Assistant. *See* automatically replying to email messages
out-of-office messages, 491. *See also* automatically replying to email messages
Overlay Mode, viewing calendars in, 286, 287
Overtype mode, activating/deactivating, 406

P

page setup, changing, 160, 270
Page Setup dialog box, 160, 271, 302
paper options when printing, 271
paragraphs
    selecting, 58
    spacing, 353
    styles, applying, 350, 353
passwords
    entering, 13
    for Outlook data files, setting, 322
    setting up, 18
Paste Options button, 406, 414
peeking at modules, 44
peeks, docking, 44, 400
People module. *See also* contact records
    defined, 512
    address books, displaying, 310
    configuring, 418
    contact record windows, 75
    content of, 73
    displaying, 73, 77, 313
    ribbon in, 74
    view options for, 150
People Pane, 52, 56, 121
    customizing, 398
    detailed view, enabling, 123
    displaying/hiding, 399
People peek, *defined*, 512
People view, 150
permissions
    defined, 512
    for calendars, setting, 291
    for public folders, setting, 483
    restricting for messages, 393
    setting, 475
Personal Forms library, 442
Personal Store (PST) files, 8. *See also* Outlook
    data files
personalizing email messages, 93
phishing messages
    defined, 512
    avoiding, 459
    blocking, 459
phishing sites, *defined*, 513
phone directories, printing contacts as, 157
Phone view, 150
photographs. *See* pictures
Picture Styles gallery, 378
pictures
    adding to contact records, 338
    artistic effects, adding, 379
    aspect ratio, cropping to, 375
    backgrounds, removing, 372
    cropping, 373
    file formats for, 364
    formatting, 362, 364, 371
    inserting, 361, 362, 369
    online, inserting, 361, 363
    replying to messages with, 377
    resizing, 107, 371
    searching Internet for, 363
    selecting, 363
    sending, 107
    styles, applying, 378
    text flow, changing, 362
pinning peeks to To-Do Bar, 401
pinning the ribbon, 28
Plain Text format
    defined, 513
    messages, 93
    sending/receiving, 475
pointing, *defined*, 513
Policy Tips, 413
POP accounts
    configuring, 22
    connecting to, 9
    message retention with, 22
    problems on public networks, 23
    troubleshooting, 21
popping out email message replies, 99
Post Office Protocol (POP), *defined*, 513. *See also* POP
    accounts
PowerPoint presentations, previewing, 116

presence icons, 119
    defined, 513
Preview view for calendars, 189, 196
previewing
    attachments, 109, 115, 116
    calendars, 196, 298, 300, 303
    contact records, 159, 161
    document library contents, 502
    fonts, 356
    messages, 41, 108, 109, 114, 269, 402
    multiple pages before printing, 271
    SmartArt graphics, 383
    style sets, 351
    styles, 351
    tasks, 207
Print dialog box, 160, 163, 269, 299
Print page of Backstage view, 158, 269
print styles, *defined*, 513
printing
    calendars, 297
    changing page setup when, 160
    contact records, 157
    messages, 268, 272
    help information, 34
    options for, 33
    paper options, 271
    preventing, 393, 475
    previewing multiple pages before, 271
    from Quick Access Toolbar, 427
    task lists, 302
    work weeks, 302
process diagrams, creating, 383
profiles, creating, 10
program icon, 25
program window, 40
    elements of, 25, 40
    maximizing, 31
    personalizing, 398
    streamlining, 111
proofing options, 405
Properties dialog box, 392
Propose New Time dialog box, 188

proposing new meeting times, 186, 188
.pst files. *See* Outlook data files; Personal Store (PST) files
public folders
    accessing, 482
    adding to contact groups, 327
    creating, 483
    Favorites, 484
    permissions, assigning, 483
    searching, 263
public networks, POP email accounts and, 23
publishing calendars to Internet, 290, 295

Q

Quick Access Toolbar, 25
    defined, 513
    adding commands to, 30, 52, 427, 430
    configuring, 427
    customizing, 25, 26
    in message composition windows, 52
    in message reading windows, 56
    moving, 427, 428, 432
    moving commands on, 431
    printing from, 427
    resetting, 428, 433
    separators, adding, 431
    in task windows, 83
Quick Click category
    assigning, 247
    designating, 246
Quick Steps
    defined, 513
    actions, adding to, 447
    activating, 450
    built-in, 258
    creating, 446
    deleting actions from, 449
    editing, 260, 446
    for flagging messages for follow-up, 449
    keyboard shortcuts for, setting, 449
    managing, 446

Quick Steps *(continued)*
    managing messages with, 257, 455
    setting up, 259
    tooltips for, creating, 449

R

read receipt requests, 392, 413
reading email messages, 55
Reading Pane, 41, 51
    changing font size in, 112
    configuring, 408, 422
    customizing, 398, 399
    displaying/hiding, 49, 112, 221
    marking messages as read in, 408
    moving, 402
    Single Key Reading, configuring, 408
    viewing messages in, 115
    viewing tasks in, 207
Reading Pane dialog box, 408
Reading view, 40, 48, 111
    of Calendar module, 65
    of People module, 73
    in Tasks module, 81
rebuilding the search index, 420
recalling email messages, 130
    defined, 513
receiving email messages, notifications for, 102, 106
recipients
    adding to Safe Recipients list, 462, 465
    grouping messages by, 239
    multiple, addressing to, 91
    separating with commas, 411
reclaiming declined tasks, 216
recurring items
    defined, 513
    appointments, 169, 172
    events, 177
    tasks, 201, 213
redoing editing, 373

redundant email messages
    defined, 513
    deleting, 409
religious holidays
    adding to calendar, 174
    removing from calendar, 175
reminders
    defined, 513
    for calendar items, 168, 171
    configuring, 424
    displaying on status bar, 439
    for tasks, setting, 201, 208
renaming ribbon tabs, 436
repeating searches, 333
replying to email messages, 123, 127
    auto-filling recipient name, 89
    automatically, 479, 491
    closing original messages after, 125
    configuring options for, 410
    with embedded pictures, 377
    etiquette for, 125
    fonts, setting for, 357
    inline, 6
    with instant messages (IMs), 125
    from Junk E-mail folder, 461
    with meeting requests, 123
    with Quick Steps, 258
    in Reading Pane, 51
    sending to all recipients, 123
    setting signature for, 94
    signatures for, 354
resending email messages, 130
    defined, 513
resetting
    business cards, 341
    calendar view, 197
    Quick Access Toolbar, 428, 433
    ribbon, 438
    views, 155, 225, 243
resizing
    Folder Pane, 398

Navigation Bar, 42
pictures, 107, 371
SmartArt graphics, 386
To-Do Bar, 398
resolution. *See* screen resolution
resolving
defined, 513
email addresses, 15, 53, 89, 148, 411
resources
adding to contact groups, 327
inviting to meetings, 180, 184
searching, 334
responding to meeting requests, 186, 188
reviewing email message content, 55
ribbon, 26
defined, 513
in Calendar module, 66
collapsing, 28, 64
customizing, 433, 435
customizing display, 399
dynamic sizing of, 30
expanding, 401, 428
groups, adding, 436
hidden groups, displaying, 30
hiding, 428
in Mail module, 49
in message composition windows, 52
in message reading windows, 56
overview of, 27
in People module, 74
pinning, 28
resetting, 438
tabs, adding, 435
tabs on, 27, 29
in Tasks module, 82
tool tabs, 29
unpinning, 28
width of, 31
Ribbon Display Options button, 26
Rich Text Format (RTF)
defined, 513
messages, 93

Room Finder, 70, 180
RPC over HTTP. *See* Outlook Anywhere
RSS Feeds folder, 47, 425
RSS feeds, subscribing to, 425
RTF. *See* Rich Text Format (RTF)
rules
defined, 513
for automatic replies, 491, 495
creating, 451, 452
descriptions, editing, 454
editing, 453, 496
exceptions, adding, 456
managing, 32
running on existing messages, 457
selecting account to apply to, 452
setting up for Exchange Server accounts, 451
specifying actions for, 455
templates, creating from, 453
Rules And Alerts dialog box, 452, 455, 457
Rules wizard, 453
running rules on existing email messages, 457

S

Safe Senders list, adding to, 462, 464
saving
appointments, 173
attachments, 110
business cards, 342
contact groups, 329
contact records, 141
drafts, 411
forms, 442
messages, 94, 95, 410
tasks, 208, 211
Schedule View, displaying calendars in, 288
Scheduling Assistant
configuring, 416
meeting window page, 180
scheduling attendees for meetings, 71
scheduling windows, 68

screen clippings, 367
    defined, 514
    capturing and inserting, 366
screen magnification, changing, 31. *See also* zooming in and out
screen resolution, changing, 31
screenshots. *See* screen clippings
ScreenTips
    defined, 514
    configuring, 404
    displaying, 28, 33
    displaying keyboard shortcuts in, 406
Search Folders, 47, 264
    modifying, 265
Search Text dialog box, 455
Search tool tab, 262, 266
searching
    address books, 310
    canceling current search, 334
    clearing results of, 268
    configuring options for, 419
    contact records, 151, 332
    conversations, 237
    criteria, adding/removing, 334
    criteria, changing, 263, 267
    file properties, 263
    filtering when, 332
    folders, 262
    Help system, 35
    indexing scope, configuring, 420
    keyboard shortcut for, 332
    message content, 262, 266
    notes, 252
    overview of, 262
    public folders, 263
    repeating previous searches, 333
    scope of, expanding, 333
    for tasks, 226
securing email messages, 467
    by blocking external content, 476
    with digital signatures, 467

    with encryption, 474
    with Information Rights Management (IRM), 475
security
    add-ins, issues with, 441
    policies, avoiding violations, 413
Security Properties dialog box, 473
selecting
    appointments, 170
    calendar items, 192
    contact records, 162, 313
    messages, 236
    pictures, 363
selecting text, 58
    configuring options for, 406
    displaying Mini Toolbar when, 404
Select Members dialog box, 326
Select Name dialog box, 148, 149
semicolons, separating recipients with, 91
Send A Calendar Via E-Mail dialog box, 295
Send button, 95
send/receive groups, defining, 486
Send/Receive Groups dialog box, 425, 487
Send/Receive tab, 490
senders
    adding to Safe Senders list, 462, 464
    blocking, 465
    grouping messages by, 239, 241
sending email messages, 95, 102
    to address book contacts, 148
    configuring options for, 404, 411
    to contact groups, 330
    to multiple recipients, 91, 411
    using Quick Steps, 258, 446
    selecting account when, 104
sensitivity, setting, 391, 404
Sent Items folder, 46, 95
    displaying, 103, 234
separated text files, *defined*, 514
separators, adding to Quick Access Toolbar, 431
server certificates, error messages, 20

server ports, POP mail and, 23
server rules, *defined*, 514
shadows, applying to text, 62
shapes
    creating, 386
    inserting, 364
shared calendars, 282
shared folders, activating Cached Exchange Mode
    for, 486
SharePoint, 479, 498
    calendars, accessing, 282
    calendars, connecting to, 505
    contact lists, importing, 503
    document libraries, connecting to other
        computers, 500
    document libraries, connecting to Outlook, 499
    document libraries, updating subscriptions
        to, 500
    document libraries, working offline, 499
    document library subfolders, 501
    editing files offline, 502
    drafts, working with, 502
    granting permission to, 499
    libraries, adding to contact groups, 327
    opening files offline, 502
    previewing document library contents, 502
SharePoint List Options dialog box, 500
SharePoint Lists folder, 501
sharing
    calendars, 290, 294
    free/busy time, 294
sharing invitations, 290
shortcut menus, *defined*, 514
Show Columns dialog box, 240
Side-By-Side Mode, viewing calendars in, 287
signatures. *See also* digital signatures
    business cards, including in, 336, 359
    configuring, 353
    creating, 355, 358
    creating multiple, 354
    deleting, 355

editing, 359
for email accounts, 355
formatting, 359
inserting, 355
setting, for replies and forwards, 94
Signatures And Stationery dialog box, 346, 357, 358
Simple List view, 222
    displaying, 223
Single Key Reading, configuring, 408
Single view, switching to, 114
site mailboxes, accessing, 7
sizing handles, *defined*, 514
slow Internet connections, configuring Cached
    Exchange Mode for, 489
small caps, applying, 60
smart cut and paste, 406
SmartArt graphics
    defined, 514
    adding shapes to, 386
    colors, changing, 388
    copying and reusing, 389
    creating, 381, 383
    formatting, 384
    layouts, changing, 386
    previewing, 383
    sizing, 386
    styles, applying, 388
    Text pane, displaying/hiding, 384
S/MIME protocol
    defined, 514
    digital IDs, obtaining, 469
    receipts, requesting, 474
sorting
    contact records, 153
    messages, 240, 241
    tasks, 223
spam. *See* junk email messages
spelling and grammar checking settings, 405
splitting conversations, 233
Standard Forms library, 442
start dates, grouping messages by, 239

starting Outlook, 12
stationery
applying to messages, 347
fonts with, selecting, 348
status bar, 26
defined, 514
customizing, 439
indicators on, 26
status reports, on assigned tasks, 214, 217
sticky notes. *See* notes
style sets, 351
styles
applying, 350
for pictures, applying, 378
previewing, 351
for SmartArt graphics, applying, 388
subject line of email messages, 88
subjects
grouping messages by, 239, 242
rules, creating for, 455
subscribing to Internet calendars, 285
swapping time zones, 281
synchronizing Outlook, 66, 480
calendar reminders and, 168
configuring, 425

T

tab-separated text files, importing from, 315
tables
entering information in, 100
formatting, 100, 101
inserting, 99
previewing, 99
printing contact records as, 163
printing contacts as, 157
tabs, ribbon, 27, 29
defined, 514
adding, 435
adding groups to, 437
customizing, 434
renaming, 436

task folders, creating, 226
task lists
defined, 514
displaying, 189, 194
marking items as complete, 205
printing, 302
transferring messages to, 202, 205
task originators, *defined*, 514
task owners, *defined*, 514
task requests
accepting or declining, 216
forwarding, 217
sending, 214, 215, 218
task windows, 83
defined, 514
fields in, 84
opening, 207
tasks
arrangements for, 222
arranging, 223
assigning, 147, 214, 217, 218
categories, assigning, 201, 226
configuring options for, 418
creating, 84, 200, 201
creating, from Outlook items, 202
custom flags, setting, 207
deleting, 202, 213
displaying, 219
displaying details for, 84
displaying on To-Do Bar, 219
dragging to calendar, 220
due dates, assigning, 84, 206, 418
due dates, changing, 210
editing, 210
entering information for, 208
fields, modifying, 222
grouping, 224
marking as complete, 202, 212
marking as private, 201
opening, 207
organizing, 226
previewing, 207

priority, setting, 201
reclaiming declined, 216
recurring, 201
reminders, configuring, 424
reminders, setting, 201, 208
replying to, 126
saving and closing, 208, 211
scheduling, 168
searching for, 226
sorting, 223
status, changing, 210, 212
status reports on assigned, 217
status, tracking, 201
updating, 210
views, changing, 223
working with, 83
Tasks folder
displaying, 219
views for, 222
Tasks module
defined, 514
configuring, 418
content of, 81
displaying, 81, 84, 203
opening, 206
ribbon in, 82
task windows, 83
views for, 219
Tasks peek, *defined*, 514
Tasks view, *defined*, 514
Team Email Quick Step, 258
text. *See also* formatting text
effects, 61, 353
selecting, 58
text email messages. *See* Plain Text format
text files, importing from, 315
text flow around pictures, changing, 362
Theme Effects gallery, 349
Theme Or Stationery dialog box, 347
themes
applying, 347, 349

colors, applying, 357
configuring, 404
default Office theme, 349
modifying, 349
for Office documents, 350
third-party add-ins, *defined*, 514
threads, *defined*, 514. *See also* conversations
thumbnail galleries, 29
thumbnails, *defined*, 515
time zones
configuring, 280, 416
displaying multiple, 281
setting for calendar events, 72
specifying for appointments, 281
swapping, 281
title bar, 25
defined, 515
To-Do Bar, 42
defined, 515
arranging items on, 204
customizing, 398
hiding, 399
pinning module peeks to, 219, 401
resizing, 398
separators, moving, 401
To-Do List
displaying, 84, 219
displaying, 219
views for, 221
To-Do List view
defined, 515
displaying, 225
tool tabs, 29
defined, 515
tooltips, creating for Quick Steps, 449
touch-enabled devices, adapting exercises for, 11
tracking
assigned tasks, 214
changes, 406
configuring options for, 413
messages, 392

tri-fold calendars, printing, 297, 304
troubleshooting
    connection problems, 20
    Conversation view, 237
Trust Center dialog box, 468, 469
type, grouping messages by, 239

U

undoing editing, 64, 373
Uniform Resource Locators (URLs), *defined*, 515
unique email messages, *defined*, 515
unpinning the ribbon, 28
unread email messages
    displaying, 109, 243
    marking, 244
    viewing in Search Folder, 264
updates, installing, 19
updating
    offline address books, 489
    tasks, 210
URLs. *See* Uniform Resource Locators (URLs)
user information, specifying, 404
user interface, overview, 24
UTF-8 support, configuring, 426

V

validating email addresses. *See* resolving
verifying names and addresses, 147
View Shortcuts toolbar, 27
    defined, 515
viewing conversations, 112
views
    defined, 515
    accessing gallery of, 221
    in Calendar module, 189
    changing, 196, 223
    customizing, 40, 50
    personalizing, 151
    resetting, 155, 225, 243
    switching between, 40

VoIP calls, initiating, 125
voting buttons, 127
    adding to messages, 391

W

Weather Bar, 7, 417
weather, displaying in calendars, 417
Web App. *See* Outlook Web App (OWA)
web beacons, 460
    defined, 515
    blocking, 476
websites, opening from contact records, 80, 146
Windows Security dialog box, 472
Windows Taskbar, Outlook notification icon, 106
Word documents. *See also* attachments
    sending by email, 103
work week
    defined, 515
    appearance in calendar, 276
    defining, 276, 278, 415
    displaying, 190, 193, 277
    printing, 302
working offline. *See* offline mode
writing email messages. *See* creating email messages

Z

Zoom dialog box, 113
zooming in and out, 27
    of calendars, 288
    in Reading Pane, 112

About the authors

Joan Lambert

Joan has worked in the training and certification industry for 16 years. As President of Online Training Solutions, Inc. (OTSI), Joan is responsible for guiding the translation of technical information and requirements into useful, relevant, and measurable training and certification tools.

Joan is a Microsoft Office Certified Master, Microsoft Certified Application Specialist Instructor, Microsoft Certified Technology Specialist, Microsoft Technology Associate, Microsoft Certified Trainer, and the author of more than two dozen books about Windows and Office (for Windows and Mac). Joan enthusiastically shares her love of technology through her participation in the creation of books, learning materials, and certification exams. She greatly enjoys communicating the benefits of new technologies by delivering training and facilitating Microsoft Experience Center events.

Joan currently lives in a nearly perfect small town in Texas with her simply divine daughter, Trinity, slightly naughty dog, naturally superior cat, and the super-automatic espresso machine that runs the house.

Joyce Cox

Joyce has more than 30 years' experience in the development of training materials about technical subjects for non-technical audiences, and is the author of dozens of books about Office and Windows technologies. She is the Vice President of OTSI.

As President of and principal author for Online Press, she developed the Quick Course series of computer training books for beginning and intermediate adult learners. She was also the first managing editor of Microsoft Press, an editor for Sybex, and an editor for the University of California.

The team

This book would not exist without the support of these hard-working members of the OTSI publishing team:

- Jan Bednarczuk
- Rob Carr
- Susie Carr
- Jeanne Craver
- Elizabeth Hansford
- Kathy Krause
- Marlene Lambert
- Jaime Odell
- Jean Trenary

We are especially thankful to the support staff at home who make it possible for our team members to devote their time and attention to these projects.

Rosemary Caperton provided invaluable support on behalf of Microsoft Learning.

Online Training Solutions, Inc. (OTSI)

OTSI specializes in the design, creation, and production of Office and Windows training products for information workers and home computer users. For more information about OTSI, visit:

www.otsi.com

How To Download Your eBook

Thank you for purchasing this Microsoft Press® title. Your companion PDF eBook is ready to download from O'Reilly Media, official distributor of Microsoft Press titles.

To download your eBook, go to http://aka.ms/PressEbook and follow the instructions.

Please note: You will be asked to create a free online account and enter the access code below.

Your access code:

ZLPVZXW

Microsoft® Outlook® 2013 Step by Step

Your PDF eBook allows you to:

- Search the full text
- Print
- Copy and paste

Best yet, you will be notified about free updates to your eBook.

If you ever lose your eBook file, you can download it again just by logging in to your account.

Need help? Please contact:
mspbooksupport@oreilly.com
or call 800-889-8969.

What do you think of this book?

We want to hear from you!
To participate in a brief online survey, please visit:

microsoft.com/learning/booksurvey

Tell us how well this book meets your needs—what works effectively, and what we can do better. Your feedback will help us continually improve our books and learning resources for you.

Thank you in advance for your input!

31901051920926